CHINA'S GLOBAL ENGAGEMENT

CHINA'S GLOBAL ENGAGEMENT

Cooperation, Competition,
and Influence in
the Twenty-First Century

JACQUES DELISLE AND AVERY GOLDSTEIN
EDITORS

BROOKINGS INSTITUTION PRESS
Washington, D.C.

Library of Congress Cataloging-in-Publication data
Names: deLisle, Jacques, 1961– editor. | Goldstein, Avery, 1954– editor.
Title: China's global engagement : cooperation, competition, and influence in the 21st century / Jacques deLisle and Avery Goldstein, editors.
Description: Washington, D.C. : Brookings Institution Press, 2017.
Identifiers: LCCN 2017000420 (print) | LCCN 2017008162 (ebook) | ISBN 9780815729693 (paperback) | ISBN 9780815729709 (ebook)
Subjects: LCSH: China—Foreign relations—21st century. | China—Foreign economic relations—21st century. | China—Military policy. | BISAC: POLITICAL SCIENCE / Political Freedom & Security / International Security. | POLITICAL SCIENCE / International Relations / General.
Classification: LCC JZ1734 .C5488 2017 (print) | LCC JZ1734 (ebook) | DDC 327.51—dc23
LC record available at https://lccn.loc.gov/2017000420

9 8 7 6 5 4 3 2 1

Typeset in New Baskerville

Composition by Westchester Publishing Services

CONTENTS

Acknowledgments   vii

1 A Rising China's Growing Presence:
       The Challenges of Global Engagement   1
       AVERY GOLDSTEIN

2 True Revisionist: China and the Global Monetary System   35
       GREGORY T. CHIN

3 Rising Nationalism: China's Regulation of
       Investment Trade   67
       DANIEL C. K. CHOW

4 Teams of Rivals: China, the United States, and the
       Race to Develop Technologies for a Sustainable
       Energy Future   91
       EDWARD S. STEINFELD

5 Concentrated Interests: China's Involvement
       with Latin American Economies   123
       CYNTHIA A. WATSON

6   Competing Visions: China, America, and
the Asia-Pacific Security Order   155
JONATHAN D. POLLACK

7   Is There Something Beyond No? China and
Intervention in a New Era   183
ALLEN CARLSON

8   The Rise of the Chinese Navy: From Regional
Naval Power to Global Naval Power?   207
ROBERT S. ROSS

9   China's Territorial and Maritime Disputes
in the South and East China Seas: What Role
for International Law?   235
JACQUES DELISLE

10   China and the International Human Rights Legal
Regime: Orthodoxy, Resistance, and Legitimacy   291
PITMAN B. POTTER

11   Leaders, Bureaucrats, and Institutional Culture:
The Struggle to Bring Back China's
Top Overseas Talent   325
DAVID ZWEIG

12   The Chinese Dream in Popular Culture:
China as Producer and Consumer of Films
at Home and Abroad   359
STANLEY ROSEN

13   Chinese Culture in a Global Context:
The Confucius Institute as a Geo-Cultural Force   389
RANDY KLUVER

Contributors   417

Index   419

ACKNOWLEDGMENTS

The chapters in this book are based on papers initially presented at the third annual conference of the Center for the Study of Contemporary China at the University of Pennsylvania. We are grateful to a distinguished set of discussants at the conference whose comments and suggestions provided valuable guidance as the authors prepared their chapters. These individuals include Taylor Fravel, Tom Gold, Miles Kahler, Damien Ma, Phillip Saunders, Jeff Wasserstrom, Guobin Yang, and Minyuan Zhao.

We thank all of the conference participants for their helpful comments during lively discussions at our sessions, and thank the anonymous reviewer whose comments on our original manuscript helped improve the chapters. We are also very grateful to Bill Finan, Janet Walker, Elliott Beard at Brookings Institution Press, and Angela Piliouras at Westchester Publishing Services, who facilitated the preparation of this volume.

This book would not have been possible without the financial support of the Center for the Study of Contemporary China, whose funding is provided by the University of Pennsylvania's provost, as well as Penn's School of Arts and Sciences, Law School, Annenberg School for Communications, and Wharton School. We thank Yun Huang for assistance in running the conference. We are especially grateful to Dr. Yuanyuan Zeng, Associate Director of the Center for the Study of Contemporary China, whose distinctive combination of substantive expertise and administrative skills are vital to the success of the center's program of which this book is a part.

ONE

A Rising China's Growing Presence

The Challenges of Global Engagement

AVERY GOLDSTEIN

The second decade of the twenty-first century has been a period of transition within China and in China's international relations. At a moment in its history when China's leaders have been addressing domestic challenges that have emerged after three decades of dramatic reforms, they have also been refashioning their country's foreign policy to better fit what they see as China's place in a changing world order. The recalibration of China's foreign policy has been visible in an increasingly proactive approach to international economic affairs, a more vigorous approach to international security affairs, and a more focused approach to its engagement with international cultural and educational affairs. In each of these areas, the trajectory of China's international relations has reflected dramatic developments within China in the decades since the death of Mao Zedong and within the international system its leaders have faced. While the future of China's global role defies prediction, it is possible to take stock of national and international

1

factors that account for China's current posture. This chapter begins, however, by briefly looking backward, to put recent trends in historical perspective.

FROM A REGIONALIZED WORLD ORDER
TO THE MODERN ERA

China's rise to prominence in the twenty-first century actually marks the country's reemergence as a political entity with important relations extending beyond the realm over which its leaders formally rule. Beginning in 221 B.C., a series of imperial dynasties controlled territories in the area that is today's China. During these millennia, the empire's relations with the world beyond its boundaries were mostly regional rather than global in scope as interactions across often loosely defined borders and vast oceans were limited by prevailing transportation and communications technologies. In its part of the globe, however, China was typically the greatest economic and military power.

The Celestial Empire itself consisted of a political core (or heartland) that interacted with and typically dominated its periphery.[1] Connections between the core and periphery and the extent of the latter's subordination to the imperial throne varied over time but, in principle, their relations remained hierarchical; the latter paid deference to the throne's preeminent status within what John King Fairbank described as a distinctive "tribute system" that defined a Chinese world order.[2] The organizing principle of this order contrasted sharply with that of the modern international order of formally sovereign and equal states first established in the European regional system by the Treaty of Westphalia in 1648. But despite this distinctiveness, exchanges between the empire's core, its periphery, and even more distant reaches of the world resembled what we now think of as international relations. Goods and ideas (especially the religious beliefs of Buddhism and Islam) flowed into China across the mountains that marked the southern periphery and across the vast and desolate western periphery along what became known as the Silk Road. China's maritime reach, though generally limited, also led to interaction with the closest parts of the periphery in East Asia, including Japan, Taiwan, and Oceania.

China's prestige as the center of Confucian culture and the regional dominance of Sinitic civilization in East Asia proved resilient even during periods when the capacity of the ruling dynasty waned. On the two occasions when invaders from the northern periphery (Mongols in the thirteenth century and Manchus in the seventeenth century) used military victories to establish their own dynasties (the Yuan and the Qing) to rule the core, these "outsiders" embraced the essential practices of the political, economic, and cultural system already established by the Han Chinese "insiders" centuries earlier. Thus, for nearly two millennia imperial China's influence as the key player, if not always the omnipotent hegemon, within its regional system endured.

In the course of the nineteenth century, however, the regionalized era of international relations ended. Technology and industrial modernization provided Western countries (and, by the end of the century, Japan) with the ability and the motivation to challenge China's long-standing dominance in its neighborhood. Europeans and Americans grew increasingly frustrated by the unwillingness of the last of China's imperial rulers, the Qing, to accept diplomacy based on the principle of the formal equality of sovereign states that the West had embraced. International commerce, too, became an issue. Imperial China resisted efforts by the West, spearheaded by Great Britain, to promote commerce resting on the modern notion of mutually beneficial free trade rather than the traditional mercantilist notion of trade managed by and for the benefit of the state. As important, for the first time outsiders from well beyond the usual periphery were able to tap superior military force to impose their will on China's rulers. Their success required the Qing dynasty to agree to concessions that undermined China's erstwhile dominance of its regional subsystem. Defeat after military defeat at the hands of foreign powers not only cast doubt on the regime's claims about the superiority of China's Confucian civilization, the pillar of dynastic rule for centuries, but also compounded new internal military challenges arising within the empire's core that were testing the Qing court's grip on power. As imperial China's domestic control and international prestige were simultaneously being shattered, it began to lose political sway over its periphery; as it did, foreigners began establishing their own imperial influence in these surrounding areas. China had entered what later generations would retrospectively label a "century of national humiliation" that began in the 1840s. It was only after decades of civil strife triggered and then exacerbated by repeated foreign military attacks and interventions that the Chinese Communist Party (CCP) in 1949 finally succeeded in establishing a regime—the People's Republic of China (PRC)—that restored effective central rule over most of the territory once controlled by the Qing dynasty.

A CHANGING CHINA IN THE COLD WAR ORDER

The PRC emerged within an international order that was no longer regional. As it did, Beijing remained sensitive to the legacy of humiliation suffered by China at the hands of foreigners. While Chinese officials remained wary of international military and economic relations, under the leadership of Mao Zedong (1949–76) ties with the outside world were at times recognized as necessary, even if they might require unpleasant compromises of national autonomy.

Most notable among such compromises were those that facilitated the strategic cooperation needed to help ensure the regime's security. The PRC faced serious threats from much more powerful adversaries for most of the Cold War years—first from the United States, and then from the Soviet Union. Although the risk of a full-scale invasion and occupation was low, the superpowers' unprecedented power projection capabilities (including aircraft and missiles that could carry nuclear weapons) meant that they could use military force to coerce or attack China without first having to invade and occupy its territory. Until Beijing was able to develop its own military capabilities that could dissuade these adversaries by threatening to inflict punishing retaliation, Mao and his colleagues had little choice but to forge strategic links with one superpower as a way to check the other. China turned first to the Soviet Union to dissuade threats from the United States, and then later to the United States to dissuade threats from the Soviet Union.[3] Despite such collaborations, China's leaders resisted the closely integrated sorts of alliances that other countries formed (especially those allied with the United States) and instead limited their international strategic relations, even in the context of a formal Sino-Soviet treaty alliance, to what they deemed absolutely necessary.

China's international economic relations were also limited during the Cold War years. In the 1950s, while the United States encouraged its global partners to isolate China, Beijing's international economic engagement was mostly restricted to the Soviet-led socialist bloc. Although Soviet direct investment and technical assistance were helpful for China's initial industrialization, by the mid-1950s Mao and his associates were already chafing at what they saw as the unacceptable price of assistance—an unseemly need to defer to foreign (in this case, Soviet) leadership and advice. During the 1960s, ties with the Soviet Union unraveled entirely and China's modest international economic profile was further reduced. Perhaps making a virtue of necessity, Mao promoted an economic strategy that emphasized extreme self-reliance. Even when a serious military threat from the Soviet Union induced Beijing to pursue strategic ties with the United States in the 1970s, Mao continued to carefully circumscribe China's international economic engagement. It was only when the political succession to Mao Zedong yielded new leaders whose reform agenda included a redefinition of China's global role that Beijing's international economic policy shifted dramatically. Beginning with a landmark CCP Central Committee meeting in December 1978, Deng Xiaoping and like-minded colleagues decisively rejected Mao's one-sided emphasis on self-reliance and instead eagerly sought the benefits of increased international engagement. Over the last decade of the Cold War, this led to an unprecedented opening of China to the outside world that included trade with and investment by regional neighbors in Asia as well as Europe and the United States.

The new era of growing international involvement that dawned in the early 1980s was distinguished not only from the decades of Maoist isolation but also from the centuries-long traditions of imperial rule. Yet, the contrast with China's recent and more distant historical experiences should not be overstated. China's reformers, like national leaders in every country, were not interested in trading the extreme of Maoist autarky for dependence on others. They made clear that even as they pursued engagement and interdependence with the outside world, China's development would mainly rely on its own efforts. And, although they would not be resurrecting the deference that China enjoyed in the era of emperors, Beijing's leaders at times displayed a sensitivity to protocol that echoed rituals identified with their imperial predecessors. Of course, they no longer claimed cultural superiority. But they parlayed respect for China as the center of one of the world's great civilizations, as well as the foreign fascination with a country rendered exotic by its inaccessibility during much of the post-WWII era, into what might be termed modern diplomacy with traditional Chinese characteristics.[4]

A CHANGING CHINA AND THE END
OF THE COLD WAR WORLD

China's reform program under the leadership group headed by Deng Xiaoping was anchored in a dual mandate, "enliven the domestic economy and open to the outside" (*duinei gaohuo, duiwai kaifang*), that clearly linked China's own prospects to greater involvement with the outside world. Over the final two decades of the twentieth century, the new leaders crafted policies to integrate a lagging China with the global system. The PRC joined existing international economic institutions, most of which were established decades earlier under American leadership and from which the PRC previously had been excluded or that it previously had been uninterested in joining.

As part of the reforms, Beijing also adopted new policies that made it financially attractive for foreigners to invest in manufacturing and assembly of their products in China just as falling trade barriers and advances in communications and transportation were giving rise to the globalization of economic activity. When the end of the Cold War eliminated divisions reflecting Soviet-American rivalry and brought down most remaining barriers to the flow of goods and people, the process of globalization accelerated. Global production chains enabled China to leverage a large, relatively cheap, and disciplined labor pool, business-friendly government policies (including significant tax breaks), and a currency exchange rate that the government carefully managed to become a favored site for international corporations to establish manufacturing facilities. At first churning out mostly textiles and other low-end consumer goods, soon factories in China included those assembling imported components for electronics and appliances that would be re-exported for sale on global markets. By the end of the twentieth century, the economic significance of China for the world and of the world for China was dramatically increasing.

In contrast with China's transformation that reflected domestic economic reforms and globalization, the end of the Cold War did not result in comparably dramatic changes in the country's military-security situation. By 1983 Beijing had already become much less concerned about the threat that an internationally overextended and internally troubled Soviet Union could pose to China. As such, even before the Cold War ended, Beijing believed it faced a much less dangerous world, one that provided a more favorable environment in which China could focus its attention on economic modernization. The final decline of the Soviet Union that played out over the 1980s only reinforced that view.[5] To be sure, Beijing soon grew worried about the potential threat that an America unconstrained by concerns about its defunct superpower rival might pose to Chinese interests, especially after 1989 when the specter of internal instability was raised by massive demonstrations in Tiananmen Square and by the ouster of communist parties from power across Eastern Europe and eventually the Soviet Union itself. But the challenge was initially perceived as political rather than military in nature. The CCP responded by reasserting its grip on power—first by brutally crushing popular demonstrations in June 1989 that called for political reforms and then by standing firm in the face of the international condemnation of the crackdown that followed. Once it felt securely back in command, Beijing reengaged the global community. By the middle of the 1990s it was embracing a new, reinvigorated approach to foreign relations.

Under this approach, what some labeled the grand strategy of "peaceful rise," China placed top priority in its foreign policy on creating an international environment that was conducive to the country's economic development while minimizing what were seen as the low risks of military conflict. This strategy, banking heavily on creative diplomacy, reflected a recognition that China's continuing economic and technological shortcomings meant that Beijing could not rely mainly on its military capabilities to advance the country's national interests.[6] And despite misgivings about the possible implications of unchecked American military power, it also reflected a recognition that the United States and its Cold War legacy alliances in East Asia continued to supply the collective good of a peaceful environment that enabled the region's states, most notably China, to invest in economic development rather than military competition.

CHINA'S ECONOMIC ARRIVAL

By the opening years of the twenty-first century, China had reaped substantial and growing benefits from its engagement with an ever more globalized world economy and a peaceful East Asia. Indeed, China had benefited to the point that its choices were beginning to shape, as well as be shaped by, this international order.[7] As a surging China moved toward becoming the world's leading trading state and second largest economy, its demand for commodities and supply of low-priced goods on international markets meant that producers elsewhere were routinely faced with the challenge of adjusting to the "China price" in order to remain competitive. In the early twenty-first century, Beijing not only sought to maintain its role as the world's workshop, but also urged its businesses to "go out" and pioneer a wave of Chinese investment overseas. The result was another boom in China's international economic activity spreading well beyond its established export markets of Asia, Europe, and North America to Africa and Latin America. In what seemed like the blink of an eye by historical standards, China had gone from being an admirable success story in the developing world to a behemoth that all recognized as an essential player, and some began to view as a coming economic rival.

While foreign companies increasingly felt the pressure of Chinese competition, consumers in many countries benefited from China's economic expansion. Downward pressure on prices increased their purchasing power. In America, consumers also benefited from low interest rates partly driven by the Chinese government buying U.S. Treasury securities as Beijing invested the dollars from its foreign exchange reserves that swelled along with its trade surplus.[8] This benefit for Americans, however, soon became a double-edged sword when Washington's policies abetted risky home mortgages and generated a housing bubble that would burst in 2007 as the global financial crisis hit.

In short, during the first decade of the twenty-first century, China had clearly arrived as an economic great power whose decisions were having major effects around the world. As the international community began discussing how best to update the globe's major multilateral institutions for managing trade and finance to reflect a changing post–Cold War order, China's role loomed ever larger as a central consideration.[9] China's greater importance for the global economy was dramatically revealed again in 2015 as concerns about slowing growth in China, its volatile stock market, and its changing currency policy rattled trade partners and investors around the world whose prosperity was increasingly linked with the performance of a changing Chinese economy.[10]

Although China's new international economic role has become a global story, its significance has been most pronounced within the Asia-Pacific region, which has emerged as the world economy's center of gravity. The economic vibrancy of Asia created new opportunities for a rising China to undertake important initiatives on trade and investment within the region during the second decade of the new century. Two stand out.

In the fall of 2013 China's top leader, Xi Jinping, rolled out a Chinese government plan to develop infrastructure and promote trade along a wide swath stretching from maritime Southeast Asia through Central Asia all the way to Europe. Labeled the Silk Road Economic Belt and the Maritime Silk Road (popularly known as "One Belt, One Road"—OBOR—or *yidai yilu*), the initiative envisioned tapping China's domestic overcapacity for infrastructure development and industrial production to make investments in regions south and west of China, largely in countries where others (national governments and international financial institutions) have been reluctant to invest.

The risks that discouraged others from economic involvement in these countries may ultimately confound China's expectations for the success of this initiative. But success for Beijing may be measured in political as well as economic terms. OBOR offers China an opportunity to integrate more closely the economies of these countries with China and perhaps to cultivate in them a more Sinocentric set of policy preferences—a political-economic dynamic first analyzed in the mid-twentieth century by the economist Albert Hirschmann.[11] Moreover, in the westward-focused OBOR initiative, China is less likely to find itself competing with the economic clout of other advanced economies or triggering security concerns and a strong pushback from the United States and its allies, a challenge it faces in much of East Asia.[12] Instead, this initiative mostly focuses on a region where American interests have traditionally been weak and where China faces the comparatively easier task of allaying Russian and Indian concerns.[13]

Perhaps even more noteworthy than OBOR was Beijing's initiative a year later to set up and provide a founding financial stake for the Asian Infrastructure Investment Bank (AIIB). Remarkably quickly, a long list of countries from around the world, and not just Asia, decided to respond to Beijing's invitation to sign on as founding members. Their ranks included some, like Britain, that apparently bucked advice from Washington not to join what the United States saw as a potential rival to established international financial institutions. The United States reportedly warned that principles of responsible governance embodied in the Asia Development Bank, the International Monetary Fund, and the World Bank might not be honored in the rules of an AIIB dominated by China. Whether or not the American concerns about China's intentions were well founded (Chinese and many foreign analysts argued that they were not), in the end Beijing's surprising success in recruiting members to the AIIB effectively reduced China's ability to dictate decision-making standards (for example, on environmental or labor conditions in potential recipient countries), since voting shares were tied to each member's financial contribution to the bank. Moreover, the AIIB's charter set up rules that enable Beijing to exercise the kind of veto power the United States enjoys in the IMF on only a limited class of decisions that require a supermajority for approval.[14]

A changing regional order in the Asia-Pacific region and a changing China were providing unprecedented opportunities for Beijing to exercise leadership. But neither OBOR nor the AIIB represents a Chinese pivot to a narrow regional, rather than a global, economic focus. Beijing maintains a strong interest in playing a role commensurate with its growing economic power in global institutions—both those established during the era when the U.S.-led Western economies were preeminent, and new ones that reflect attempts at international coordination among the key emerging economies colloquially referred to as the BRICS (Brazil, Russia, India, China, and South Africa). Although a diverse group with sometimes divergent interests, the BRICS constitute an important subset of the biggest late-developing economies whose deliberations provide one more venue in which China may be able to play the kind of leading role that it cannot yet play in other global economic groupings—older ones, such as the Group of Seven or Eight, or G-7 / 8, of which it is not a member, or newer ones, such as the Group of Twenty, or G-20, in which the large membership dilutes China's influence.

These various changes in China's international economic role have reflected the growing significance of a more prosperous China as well as developments beyond China's borders. But as Evan Feigenbaum and Robert Manning have argued, in the Asia-Pacific region a second story line has emerged alongside these economic developments— the revival of serious military-security problems.[15]

CHINA'S MILITARY ARRIVAL

During the first decade of the twenty-first century, what had been China's steady, if at first slow, investment in military modernization since the early 1980s began to yield results. China was successfully exploiting the jump-start provided by the purchase of advanced aircraft and naval vessels from Russia, which was not party to the arms embargo imposed by the United States and Europeans after the June 1989 crackdown in Tiananmen Square. China was also more effectively ramping up its indigenous arms industries and improving its technological base. In part this was made possible by the economic and scientific benefits of the country's broader integration with the global economy. But in part this was a payoff finally resulting from the expanding resources the Chinese government had been investing in military modernization beginning in the early 1990s—annual double-digit percentage increases made possible by a booming economy.

As with its changing international economic profile, in the twenty-first century China's military profile was changing. The Chinese navy, in particular, while mainly focused on contingencies in the near seas, was beginning to undertake operations farther afield.[16] Most notably, China's role in antipiracy patrols off the Somali coast demonstrated the new competencies of the People's Liberation Army (PLA) Navy and permitted it to practice meeting the challenges of carrying out, sustaining, and resupplying long-range missions. Though still small in scale, other operations involving PLA air and naval forces, including the evacuation of Chinese nationals caught in Libya's domestic chaos, exploratory submarine patrols in the Indian Ocean, and port calls in the Mediterranean, while not signaling China's arrival as a force that would alter the global balance of power, hinted at a role for China that would no longer be limited to coping with the security challenges of American military deployments in East Asia.

In the near term, however, China's changing military profile was most dramatically altering the security landscape in East Asia. Previously viewed as a large but arguably second-rate military power, in the new century China was increasingly viewed as a country armed with an array of sophisticated capabilities that were making it an ever more dangerous potential adversary in the region. Moreover, the transformation in China's military profile coincided with a period in which U.S. military forces were dedicated to protracted, burdensome, and expensive military actions in Afghanistan and Iraq. Although these major American operations did not create a power vacuum in the Asia-Pacific, they did entail opportunity costs that observers criticized as a dangerous diversion of U.S. attention from an increasingly important Asian theater, a diversion that might be creating an opening for a stronger China to bolster its regional position. With the onset of the great global recession in 2007–08, during which

China seemed to be weathering the storm better than many others, concerns about the future of U.S. economic leadership compounded simmering concerns about a war-weary America's willingness to continue shouldering the burdens of military leadership in Asia as elsewhere.

The sense that both economic and military leadership in the Asia-Pacific might be shifting away from a beleaguered United States and toward a rising China began to take root, even if it was based on perceptions that were outracing reality. The concern that China's growing economic and military capabilities might presage a change in the regional order prompted responses from Beijing's East Asian neighbors and from the United States. Washington ramped up efforts to signal its continued engagement in the Asia-Pacific and to offset the impression that it had somehow been absent earlier in the century. Most notably perhaps, in 2011 the United States declared that it was undertaking a strategic rebalance in its foreign policy to focus on the Asia-Pacific region (a move that some labeled "the pivot"). Yet, the stubborn persistence of an arc of instability from Afghanistan through Syria and Iraq to Libya, Somalia, and Yemen continued to drain U.S. attention and resources. These challenges reduced confidence in the practical significance of the announced American strategic rebalance and preserved the perception that in East Asia a rising China would be less constrained than it might otherwise have been.

In this context, especially as Beijing embraced a more forceful approach to supporting its claims to East Asian maritime territories and their surrounding waters disputed by its neighbors, the implications of what some saw as an emerging China challenge to the status quo deepened apprehension in Tokyo, Manila, Hanoi, and Washington.[17] By 2015, after four years of increased regional tensions punctuated by incidents between China and Japan in the East China Sea, and in the South China Sea between China and the Philippines and China and Vietnam, the assessment of China's role in the region was changing. Growing concern fueled a debate about whether China's allegedly new assertiveness called for a more forceful response.[18] Even many previously optimistic observers, who had expected that inevitable frictions would accompany China's rise but that such problems would be manageable, became more pessimistic. The somber tone was captured well in David Lampton's uncharacteristically downbeat musing that China and the United States might well be at a "tipping point" with a much more difficult and confrontational relationship in the offing.[19] The transition to the Donald Trump administration after the 2016 U.S. presidential election reinforced such concerns.

In sum, by the second decade of the twenty-first century, potentially dangerous security problems in East Asia were attracting increased attention.[20] As they did, the United States repeatedly tried to allay China's fears of encirclement by stating that the United States did not seek to contain China, that it would not take sides in the sovereignty disputes in which Beijing was embroiled in the East and South China Seas, and that the rebalance was not mainly about military-strategic concerns but instead an adjustment reflecting the greater importance of the region, especially as its global economic significance had risen. Nevertheless, Beijing's view of such assurances was skeptical, if not dismissive. It instead focused on the need to better prepare for the possibility that it was witnessing the advent of a newly hostile U.S. strategic posture that would result in a security environment for China more dangerous than at any time since the early 1980s.

While Beijing's new security concerns may be exaggerated, there is little doubt that a rising China faces a growing array of foreign policy challenges in East Asia and that these challenges in part have resulted from its own improving military capabilities and the responses these improvements have triggered. China, its regional neighbors, and the United States all insist that their military preparations merely aim to defend the status quo. Yet they are unable to overcome disagreements about the definition of the status quo, harbor uncertainty about others' candor, and worry about the need to hedge against the durability of today's intentions in tomorrow's unpredictable circumstances. They confront what international relations scholars refer to as the security dilemma. As such, their interactions, not fully under any one state's control, continue to drive the evolution of this complicated regional dynamic while a changing China shapes and is shaped by a changing world.

CHINA'S CHANGING ROLE IN GLOBAL SOCIETY

When China's reform program was launched in 1979, its CCP archi-
tects sought to end the country's self-imposed isolation and to engage
with the outside world in ways that would advance China's modernization and ultimately provide the basis for becoming a stronger actor
on the world stage. But this opening was not just about trade and
investment or building a more powerful military. It was also about
lowering a broad array of barriers that had been interposed between
China and the world while Mao's self-reliant development strategy
prevailed. When Mao's successors opened China, they also exposed
it to the rich variety of modern life that was taken for granted in
much of the rest of global society. The improvement in the quality of
the Chinese people's daily lives that this opening would make possible
was a step that the reformers expected would help rebuild popular
support for the CCP that had frayed badly during the drab, barren
final decade of insular Maoist rule.

There were, however, limits to the Party's embrace of openness.
From the beginning of the reform era, it was determined to manage
the terms of China's engagement with global society. Initially, management mostly entailed filtering the foreign ideas and cultural products permitted to enter China, excluding those the CCP deemed unacceptable.[21] But as in the realms of economics and security, over time
a rising China's leaders shifted from their relatively passive posture of
selectively engaging the world the country encountered to playing a
more active role designed to reshape international society and China's
relation with it. And, as in the economic and military-security realms,
by the second decade of the twenty-first century the initially warm
welcome for a more active China's broader role in global culture and
society was giving way to concerns about its implications and sometimes a backlash.

Education, Information, and Soft Power

As post-Mao reforms ended China's self-imposed isolation, reen-
gagement with international society was most dramatically reflected
first in international education. After 1980, Chinese scholars and

students quickly became a highly visible presence on campuses around the world. Overseas education and research opportunities initially depended on financial support from the Chinese government or from foreign universities or foundations. Most of these pioneers headed abroad were either visiting senior scholars or graduate students. In the early twenty-first century, however, Chinese nationals were also becoming one of the largest contingents of foreign undergraduate students. China's growing prosperity was facilitating an expansion in the number as well as an increase in the diversity of those Chinese headed overseas for training. Some of China's increasing number of very prosperous families even began sending their children to private secondary schools overseas to improve their prospects for coveted admission to the best colleges and universities in the English-speaking world.

Although Beijing's reformers expected these expanded international educational opportunities to boost the contribution China's intellectuals could make to the country's modernization, at first a disappointingly small fraction were actually returning. Some remained overseas because they were not confident they could find employment in China that would allow them to put their hard-earned credentials to good use, worried that they were overqualified for the positions available in a Chinese economy that still lagged behind those in the advanced industrial world. Others worried that the importance of seniority and political connections for job placement and career advancement in China would pose challenges they could avoid by working overseas. And still others, especially in the immediate aftermath of the 1989 Tiananmen Square crackdown, hesitated to return to China because they worried about retribution for their open support of the pro-democracy demonstrators.

Yet, if the "yield" on the CCP reformers' investment in encouraging overseas education during the 1980s and 1990s may have fallen short of their hopes, the country's modernization clearly benefited from those who did return after acquiring the kind of academic training that was not yet readily available in China. And by the turn of the century, as the employment opportunities available in the PRC improved along with the economy's development, and as the perceived risks of previous political activities diminished, more of those trained abroad began to filter back to China, though some moved in that direction tentatively by first "parking on the doorstep" in Hong Kong.[22] Since 2000, the job market on the mainland has become sufficiently attractive to increase the fraction of those receiving education abroad who decide to pursue their careers in China, and the absolute number of returnees has risen as more have gone abroad to study. Nevertheless, Beijing still faces a tough challenge enticing the very best foreign-trained Chinese to return and settle in the PRC.[23] Despite advances in the economy, returnees (the "sea turtles," or *hai-gui*, in Chinese slang) continue to confront an array of professional complications (including political restrictions on the use of information technology, essential to a wide variety of modern careers, and an uncertain legal environment) and personal inconveniences (including worries about the health risks resulting from poor consumer product safety and environmental degradation) that they and their families would not face in many other countries where they could put their training to good use.

In addition to opening the door to Chinese seeking education abroad, the reforms launched in 1979 also made it possible for large numbers of foreigners to learn about China by studying in the PRC, a society that had been off-limits to all but a select group of politically acceptable foreign friends during the Maoist decades. And in 2004, as China's international presence expanded, the Chinese government launched an initiative to increase the availability overseas of a Chinese education about China. Echoing the "go out" policy aimed at China's business community, through the Ministry of Education's National Office for Teaching Chinese as a Foreign Language (the Hanban), Beijing subsidized, dispatched key staff members, and provided curricular materials for "Confucius Institutes" to promote familiarity with Chinese language, history, and culture around the world. These "CIs"—some affiliated with public schools, others with colleges and universities—vary in their role and mission, depending on the agreements struck with host institutions and local governments. To the consternation of their Chinese sponsors, however, their presence has at times provoked controversy. Some CIs have foundered because of local concerns about Beijing's control over the content of their curriculum. Some have triggered suspicion that in order to preserve funding for their CIs, administrators at host universities and colleges might defer to Chinese government sensitivities (especially about the issues of Tibet and Xinjiang) rather than uphold the principles of academic freedom of inquiry and expression in programs and events across their campuses.[24]

The unwelcome controversy that has accompanied China's CI education initiative notwithstanding, it remains part of Beijing's broader interest in enhancing China's soft power, international influence rooted in a country's appeal to others, a concept popularized by Harvard's Joseph Nye and that has attracted substantial attention in China.[25] Enthusiasts of soft power argue that countries that have it reduce, even if they do not eliminate, their need to rely on costly material incentives ("carrots and sticks") to shape the policy choices of international admirers. Confucius Institutes are one, but not the only, initiative aimed at enhancing China's soft power by managing the country's image in international society. Another has been the global spread of China's outlets for news and information in the twenty-first century. Including the state-run Xinhua News Agency and the CCTV network, this international expansion aims not simply to increase knowledge about or interest in China overseas, but also more reliably to convey a positive image of China around the world, offsetting what Beijing sees as overly negative coverage of the PRC in much foreign reporting.

Yet the payoff from these government-sponsored attempts to enhance China's soft power has thus far been disappointing. In part, this is because China's leaders have encountered the same problem as their counterparts in other countries who have undertaken such image-polishing initiatives.[26] Soft power, unlike hard power, is maddeningly difficult to manufacture. To the extent that it is rooted in the perceived virtues of a way of life, initiatives that are sponsored by a government are likely to be tainted from the outset because they so obviously reflect a political self-interest.[27] China's global public relations activities have often been viewed in this light, diminishing their usefulness for augmenting soft power. While China's engagement is welcomed by others, it is welcomed mostly because it provides tangible benefits (especially language training) at an acceptable cost. This is a straightforward transactional logic rather than one that reflects a deep-rooted attraction that might result in an inclination to identify with and defer to Chinese policy preferences, the sine qua non of soft power. Consequently, these efforts have not reduced the need for Beijing to rely mostly on hard power—tapping its growing material resources to influence others and to assuage their concerns about the price that comes with accepting China's larger international role.

Art Opening

During the 1980s and 1990s, the opening to the outside world also greatly expanded the availability within China of the creative arts from abroad. Music, painting, drama, television, and film that were part of contemporary culture around the world quickly became part of China's cultural scene as well. From the very start, however, a wary Communist Party set limits on the foreign influences permitted within China. And when a new generation of Chinese artists began to emerge in the more relaxed and cosmopolitan post-Mao Chinese society, the Party also tried to limit the role they could play internationally.

The revival of the film arts in the PRC after the regime eased the stultifying cultural blinders of the Maoist period typified the pattern. Party authorities permitted but selectively restricted the import of Western films, and censored their contents. They also closely monitored the growing number of Chinese films screened overseas as a new wave of work by Chinese directors attracted global attention and praise, including awards at major international film festivals.[28] As more Chinese films were made both for domestic and global audiences, those that touched on sensitive themes became the focus of controversy as Beijing occasionally resorted to heavy-handed censorship. Artists and their sponsors (including international film festivals that featured Chinese films in their awards competitions) confronted official and unofficial criticism, demands that films be edited to satisfy the politically tinged cultural tastes of China's censors, and the prospect of limits on distribution within the PRC.[29]

In the twenty-first century, two interacting trends in the movie industry have given rise to new frictions with the Chinese authorities. First, the market for foreign films on the mainland has surged along with the purchasing power of Chinese consumers. Second, more foreign directors have sought to shoot their films in China to take advantage of distinctive locations and lower production costs. As these trends furthered the integration of China into the international film community, foreigners bridled at accommodating the conditions that Beijing often imposed on work to be produced or consumed in China. Foreign concerns initially centered on simple censorship that entailed deleting sequences or altering scripts the Chinese authorities previewed. But more recently, as China's economic importance to Hollywood has grown at a time when the film market within the United States has sputtered, some in the international artistic community have expressed fears of self-censorship (similar to the concerns about deferential administrators at institutions hosting Confucius Institutes). To ensure access to China's lucrative distribution networks, some worry that foreign directors or producers might be altering content in anticipation of the need to account for the preferences of censors in Beijing. If so, the leverage of China's growing market power might shape the choices of foreign artists who covet the professionally and financially profitable distribution of their work on the mainland. Whether or not such fears are misplaced or exaggerated, the concern suggests that the film industry provides another example of the way China's changing international profile has affected its relations with a changing world, transiting the path from a country mainly coping with an international context it took as given, to a country that seeks to shape that context.

Human Rights

Over the past several decades, a growing transnational community of activists and nongovernmental organizations (NGOs), along with a wide variety of governments around the world, have endorsed and promoted what they view as universal human rights to which all members of international society are entitled. China's leaders, however, have long stood out in resisting this emerging consensus, rejecting the argument that all must conform with a single standard that fails to take into account the distinctiveness of each country's national historical experiences and current material conditions. Beijing's response to international criticism of its own record on human rights has emphasized the inviolability of the principle of state sovereignty that renders foreign interference in a country's internal affairs illegitimate. Beijing has coupled this argument with its advocacy of an expanded understanding of human rights that attends not only to civil and political rights but also to social and economic rights—areas where Beijing could credibly claim the conditions for China's people, and thus China's human rights record, had greatly improved. These positions remain the twinned pillars of the PRC's view articulated in international forums where human rights are discussed and invoked when others criticize China's human rights record.

In the twenty-first century, however, an ostensibly more self-confident Chinese leadership may be shifting to a posture that moves beyond this defensiveness and seeks instead to reshape the context of the international debate about civil and political rights in ways that would make China less of an outlier in global society. Under the leadership of Xi Jinping, China has moved on two fronts that reflect such efforts. One is its attempt to craft new international standards on the regulation of cyberspace that reflect the Chinese regime's strong preference for tighter restrictions on the right to circulate information. Beijing seeks safeguards against the spread of heterodox ideas that it believes could pose a threat to domestic political stability and ultimately the security of one-party rule by the CCP. The second is the drafting of China's new law regulating foreign NGOs operating in China, including those emphasizing the protection of citizens' rights. In both of these initiatives, China is taking steps to mold new international norms and rules rather than simply pushing back against the Western consensus that had become dominant in the post–Cold War era. And in doing so, China is not alone. It is joined by other authoritarian regimes, most notably Vladimir Putin's Russia, that share the CCP's concerns about the implications of international influence on domestic politics in their own countries, especially in the era of vibrant social media. Thus far, Beijing's challenge to the growing globalization of Western norms about civil and political rights that supersede national sovereignty has failed to gain widespread support. But in a world where a wide variety of regimes, including some in the West, worry about the blurred lines between innocent NGOs and transnational terrorist organizations and the trade-off between the desirability of an open Internet and its vulnerability to malicious exploitation by criminals, spies, and extremists, it is possible that China's position on these matters will not remain the outlier it once was.

The contributors to this volume explore some of the many issues raised by a changing China's interaction with the evolving global order in the twenty-first century. Gregory T. Chin, Daniel C. K. Chow, Edward S. Steinfeld, and Cynthia A. Watson focus on the dramatically increased importance of China's international economic role. Chin examines the PRC's influence in the global monetary system. He describes the growing significance of China as an international creditor (accelerated by the need for currency stability during the great recession of 2008 and then the sovereign debt crisis in Europe in 2011–2012) as well as China's concerns about American economic policies that led Beijing to push for the Chinese renminbi (or yuan) to play a larger role within a more diversified international monetary system. Chin's analysis suggests that Beijing's aim is not to fundamentally alter the system, but instead to revise and reform it in ways that are consistent with the original vision of the Bretton Woods order while better taking account of the changed economic realities of the current era in which the importance of other currencies (especially the euro and yuan) relative to the still dominant U.S. dollar has increased. Sounding a theme that reappears in other chapters, Chin portrays a China that is both interested in changing the world it is engaging and also better able than ever to press for such changes. He does not, however, see China mounting a direct challenge that threatens international stability or the interests of other states.

Daniel C. K. Chow's view is less sanguine. He sees China following a strategy that aims to advance its own economic interests at the expense of others. Focusing on Beijing's investment policies, Chow argues that these are designed to accelerate China's rise as a global economic power. He emphasizes two features of these policies. First, Beijing implements discriminatory rules that undermine the competitiveness of foreign-owned multinational companies operating within China. Second, Beijing gives its state-owned enterprises (SOEs) an advantage as they expand their overseas investments, especially in the developing world, by refraining from national regulations— especially those covering bribery of officials and codes of conduct covering labor conditions—that many of China's major foreign competitors impose on their businesses operating abroad. Chow notes that however unfair such practices may seem, they are technically not a violation of international legal obligations under the World Trade Organization (WTO). Consequently, objections to China's policies cannot be pursued within the international forum of the WTO's dispute settlement system. Instead, Chow indicates that the only recourse available is to pursue complaints through the Chinese legal system, an approach unlikely to provide a hearing that foreigners will deem fair or results that they will find satisfactory.

Edward S. Steinfeld, too, notes concerns and complaints about a rising China's economic policies and intentions, but argues that viewing these policies as the predatory approach of an aggressive economic rival is an unhelpful and inaccurate oversimplification. Examining the energy technology sector, Steinfeld sees elements of cooperation amid the inevitable commercial competition, and mutual benefit despite the self-interest underlying national policies. The rise of Chinese firms as suppliers of technologies and products has, Steinfeld indicates, boosted the availability of affordable clean energy alternatives around the world, thereby contributing to the broadly recognized need to address the problem of global warming. But Western critics have given this collective benefit short shrift, he notes, instead raising objections to Beijing's subsidies that preclude fair competition, its toleration of (and possibly support for) intellectual property theft that benefits Chinese companies, and its industry's failure to generate innovative technologies necessary to advance the struggle against global climate change. While acknowledging the merits in these concerns, Steinfeld views them as ahistorical (China's industrial policies are similar to those that were embraced by other rising economic powers in the past) and dangerously shortsighted (if others respond with their own self-interested industrial policies, rational pursuit of national interests may undermine the collective rationality of preventing global climate change—a classic "tragedy of the commons"). Yet Steinfeld hopefully adds that beyond the rhetoric of national competition, in practice, cooperation between Chinese and foreign firms continues to demonstrate tangible mutual benefits from the two-way sharing of technology and expertise in production. Thus, his depiction of a changing China's international role is one that realistically presents reasons for concern but also evidence that such concerns need not preclude cooperation.

Cynthia A. Watson traces the remarkably quick growth of China's engagement with Latin American economies in the twenty-first century. Much attention has been focused on China's newly significant economic role in Africa. Watson identifies a similar story playing out in another resource-rich part of the developing world. China's search for energy and minerals to sustain its breakneck pace of economic growth early in the century, and for suppliers of foodstuffs to complement domestic production, made Latin America a logical destination for Chinese overseas trade and investment once Beijing encouraged its businesses to "go out." As economic ties with the region expanded, Chinese investment in infrastructure to facilitate bilateral trade expanded as well. When these ties initially took off, many in the region anticipated that their economic relationship with China would be mutually beneficial and contrast sharply with what they saw as the exploitative nature of their earlier experience with Europeans and especially the United States. This apparent enthusiasm for China's arrival led some in Washington to express concern about a potential strategic rival making inroads in the Western hemisphere. Watson argues, however, that the region's hopes and Washington's fears were both exaggerated. China's distance from the region and foreign investment decisions that reflected its inexperience and narrow focus on self-interest greatly diminished the prospect that China would supplant American influence or fundamentally recast the role that international trade and investment plays in the development of Latin America's economies.

The next four chapters consider China's changing role in international security affairs. Jonathan D. Pollack, Allen Carlson, Robert S. Ross, and Jacques deLisle each examine the implications of a more powerful China in an evolving, uncertain, and potentially dangerous world.

Jonathan D. Pollack considers the prospects for adjustments in East Asia's security order which has continued, at least formally, to reflect arrangements dating to the early decades of the Cold War. Unlike Europe, where rivalry between two large alliances faced off for more than four decades until one of the alliances dissolved, in East Asia a hub-and-spokes network of bilateral arrangements between a dominant United States and its various regional allies and partners has persisted. Pollack assesses the implications as China and the United States figure out how to respond to China's rise and the resulting shifts in the balance of power. In so doing, he depicts the diversity of views and interests in Beijing and Washington that are shaping what remains a fluid, evolving regional order.

Allen Carlson looks at an aspect of security affairs, the role of intervention for military and humanitarian purposes, that is often undertreated in the international security literature and rarely the focus of attention in analyses of China's foreign policy. As Carlson notes, after the Cold War China has periodically debated the appropriateness of intervention in ways that depart from the PRC's once uniformly blunt rejection of all intervention as unjustifiable interference in the internal affairs of sovereign states. Examining a renewal of the debate among China's foreign policy elites, Carlson identifies two major positions. One amounts to a reassertion of the traditional view, suspicious of the rationale offered for intervention and worried that it is a pretext employed by the United States and its allies to ensure the preservation of an international order that serves their interests, while potentially constraining China or even jeopardizing its national interests. This view argues for a Chinese policy that responds to what is viewed as a worrisome increase in international intervention since the end of the Cold War and that more effectively resists departures from the traditional view of national sovereignty. This conservative position reflects China's own victimization at the hands of foreign powers during its "century of humiliation." By contrast, other analysts promote a more active role for China in molding new norms to set the terms for justifiable intervention. This progressive position has been most prominently advanced by those who see opportunities for the PRC to help shape an emerging international norm on a "responsibility to protect" that could serve as a carefully circumscribed basis for legitimate humanitarian intervention. Rather than reflecting China's past experience as a weak country, this position is consistent with a view of China as a newly emerging great power that has a right and a responsibility to play a key role in forging a new global order.

Robert S. Ross examines China's growing naval power, an aspect of China's military modernization that has increasingly drawn the attention of international security analysts. China's military modernization had previously given priority to land forces, air forces, and ballistic missiles. In the twenty-first century China began to elevate the role of, and to sharply increase the investment in, its navy. While agreeing with the conventional wisdom about the national interests driving China's naval modernization, Ross questions those who see China becoming a global maritime power, highlighting geopolitical circumstances that may prevent its navy from achieving this goal. He instead emphasizes the security challenges that face China in its immediate neighborhood, considerations that will constrain even a larger and more modern PLA navy to concentrate its deployments in East Asia. And, he adds, the rising economic and strategic significance of East Asia will also lead the United States to concentrate its naval power in the region to ensure its own interests as China's naval power expands. The result, Ross predicts, is likely to be a more fraught East Asian security landscape and growing insecurity elsewhere around the world as the U.S. Navy will no longer be readily available to play its longstanding role as a force for stability in other regions.

Jacques deLisle presents a fresh approach to thinking about the interaction of security and international law in the context of China's disputes with its neighbors in the East and South China Seas. Much of the literature that has addressed the renewed intensity of rivalry over these territorial sovereignty and maritime rights disputes has juxtaposed national actions aimed at consolidating, defending, or advancing claims to landforms at sea with an alternative that would rely on the application of international law to settle or manage disputes. DeLisle, however, argues that relevant international legal doctrines that are generally conducive to international peace and stability have, in the context of the South and East China Seas, in fact created incentives for states to act in ways that raise tensions and increase the possibility of military crisis or conflict. In particular, he identifies features of international law that encourage attempts to strengthen national claims to landforms because the law makes these the most reliable basis for establishing the important maritime rights to vast stretches of the economically valuable and strategically vital waters of the East and South China Seas that rival states seek. He also points to the ambiguity of legal doctrines, which encourage conflicting, self-serving interpretations and raise mutual distrust and suspicions that China is pursuing a revisionist agenda. DeLisle acknowledges the significance of considerations such as pride, honor, nationalistic fervor, and straightforward military competition also driving state behavior in Asia's waters. But he draws attention to the perverse incentives for assertive action that flow from relevant international maritime law as long as the states involved (especially China) are unwilling to submit to formal dispute resolution procedures such as the arbitration tribunal for which the UN Convention on the Law of the Sea provides. These disputes and their complex link with the relevance and usefulness of international law, then, suggest another issue area in which a rising China is both shaping and being shaped by the international order it faces.

The final group of chapters, by Pitman B. Potter, David Zweig, Stanley Rosen, and Randy Kluver, focus on changes in China's role in international society and culture. Though addressing substantively diverse topics, each indicates the growing significance of an increasingly capable and active China on the world stage on matters that extend beyond economics and security affairs.

Pitman B. Potter examines long-standing disagreements between China and the international community about human rights. Potter identifies major continuities in the position staked out by the CCP, which rejects foreign criticism of the limitations on civil and political rights enjoyed by the Chinese people and insists that such rights are subordinate to the stability and economic development that require strong Party leadership. But Potter also notes the growing challenges that leaders in Beijing face as they continue to defend this position against recurrent pulses of activism by citizens at home and growing support for these activists from the international community. Both press for expanding civil and political rights and focus on shortcomings in China's legal system, its treatment of national minorities, its limits on freedom of expression, and its tight constraints on religious freedom. Despite the regime's occasional concessions to address some of the most egregious abuses identified by domestic and foreign critics, Potter notes the limited effectiveness thus far of such pressure and concludes that there has been remarkably little improvement in these aspects of China's human rights record. Potter also suggests, however, that the persistence of such pressures that accompany China's engagement with the international community, essential to the regime's broader development agenda, may eventually have corrosive effects on the legitimacy of the CCP's human rights orthodoxy.

David Zweig explores the challenges Beijing faces in encouraging China's most talented scholars and businesspeople to return to the PRC after their education or employment abroad. He identifies several difficulties that shape the decisions of Chinese overseas as they ponder their future. These include concerns about the conservative organizational culture of many Chinese institutions, political uncertainties, and the jealousy felt by those who have not had similar international opportunities to advance their careers. The initial wave of Chinese scholars who took advantage of the educational opening at the advent of the reform era, Zweig notes, were motivated by a patriotic sense of responsibility to contribute to China's modernization. But since the mid-1980s those going abroad have increasingly given higher priority to career goals and family interests when they decide whether or not to return to live and work in the PRC. In light of these changing motivations, Zweig sees the extent to which China's leaders have succeeded in encouraging reverse migration as remarkable, and as a direct consequence of innovative policies they have adopted. Yet, although these policies mitigate the career and family concerns of China's overseas talent pool, the entrenched institutional interests and culture that have been the taproot of their concerns remain in place. Especially for the very best in the pool, the changes fall short of the fundamental reforms that are needed to convince them to forgo opportunities overseas in a global economy that offers attractive landing spots in a wide variety of advanced industrial countries.

Stanley Rosen examines changes in China's film industry and its growing international engagement. By 2015, China had become the world's second largest film market and was on a trajectory that could soon make it the world's largest. This box office boom has included many imported movies from Hollywood that have been spectacularly successful in China. Rosen notes the response to this success from the CCP regime, which includes attempts to filter the types and limit the number of Western movies shown in the PRC as well as attempts to foster a Chinese film industry whose movies will not only be warmly received at home but will also have global appeal. Rosen sees the regime's effort at promoting China's film industry as part of its broader push to increase China's soft power. As indicated in the preceding discussion of soft power, however, the results of this initiative have been disappointing. Rosen describes Beijing's quest for movies that market the "Chinese dream" at home and abroad as an alternative to the more familiar "American dream" so intimately interwoven with the films from Hollywood. But, Rosen explains, because the Chinese dream is a particularistic vision rooted in a single nation's culture and politics, it is predictably a hard sell in key overseas markets. Perhaps more surprisingly, and surely disappointingly for China's CCP leaders, it has also been a hard sell among Chinese youth who drive the domestic box office. They continue to find the culture and ideals reflected in American films more appealing, even if they remain hostile to American foreign policy. In short, Rosen's assessment of China's film industry suggests the complexities of the connection between cultural appeal and political appeal, and casts doubt on the feasibility of a rising China's state-sponsored attempts to boost its soft power.

The book concludes with Randy Kluver's chapter focusing on another element of a rising China's attempt to increase the international visibility and appeal of its culture—the Confucius Institutes (CI) established overseas beginning in 2004. Kluver disputes the frequent association of the CI initiative with Beijing's geopolitical strategy to advance the country's national interest in achieving greater international economic and military influence. Instead, Kluver argues that the initiative is mainly about a geocultural agenda that aims to reshape "global cultural flows" with little expectation of an immediate political payoff for China. He rejects the view that CIs are most importantly vehicles for political propaganda. In part because Kluver sees that mistaken impression resulting from a narrow focus on the reaction to CIs in the West, he offers a broader global view. It suggests that CIs have become a prominent feature of cultural globalization not simply because of Beijing's promotion but also because interest in China around the world has grown apace with the dramatic increase in its international economic and political role.

The chapters included in this volume chronicle key aspects of China's reemergence during the second decade of the new century as a more capable actor whose global engagement continues to reshape the international order. Changes within China have made it a more consequential player in world affairs than at any time in modern history. And changes in the international economic, security, and social-cultural order—some that China has sought and others that reflect the reaction to China's more salient role—are in turn altering the context within which the country's future role will be determined.

NOTES

1. John W. Garver, *Foreign Relations of the People's Republic of China* (Englewood Cliffs, N.J.: Prentice Hall, 1993), pp. 2–30; Michael D. Swaine and Ashley J. Tellis, *Interpreting China's Grand Strategy: Past, Present, and Future* (Santa Monica, Calif.: RAND, 2000), pp. 21–95.

2. John King Fairbank and Ta-tuan Ch'en, *The Chinese World Order: Traditional China's Foreign Relations.* Harvard East Asian Series (Harvard University Press, 1968).

3. See Avery Goldstein, *Deterrence and Security in the 21st Century: China, Britain, France and the Enduring Legacy of the Nuclear Revolution* (Stanford University Press, 2000); and *Rising to the Challenge: China's Grand Strategy and International Security* (Stanford University Press, 2005).

4. See David L. Shambaugh, *China Goes Global: The Partial Power* (Oxford University Press, 2013), pp. 56–57.

5. See Carol Lee Hamrin, "China Reassesses the Superpowers," *Pacific Affairs* 56, no. 2 (Summer 1983), pp. 209–31; also Goldstein, *Rising to the Challenge,* pp. 25, 119.

6. Goldstein, *Rising to the Challenge.*

7. Thomas J. Christensen, *The China Challenge: Shaping the Choices of a Rising Power* (New York: W. W. Norton, 2015).

8. These purchases also helped Beijing prevent the appreciation of the renminbi. China's trade surplus with the United States grew rapidly and dollars flowed into China. Determined to prevent the value of its currency from rising since that could hurt China's export sector, the authorities in Beijing bought up the billions of dollars to which the renminbi was pegged. The result was China's rapid accumulation of massive foreign exchange reserves, mostly dollars. Beijing's decision to invest a large fraction of those reserves in safe U.S. Treasury securities helped keep U.S. interest rates low, enabling Americans to borrow money cheaply.

9. One of the most visible signs was the leading role that China played alongside the United States as they sought to cope with the effects of the global recession at the Pittsburgh summit meeting of the G-20 in 2009.

10. See "China and the World Economy: Taking a Tumble," *The Economist,* August 29, 2015.

11. Albert O. Hirschman, *National Power and the Structure of Foreign Trade,* Publications of the Bureau of Business and Economic Research, University of California (University of California Press, 1945).

12. This logic is reflected in an interview with Peking University's Wang Jisi, one of the top Chinese experts on international relations and especially U.S.-China relations. Wang Jisi, "'Xijin,' Zhongguo diyuan zhanlüe de zaipingheng" ["Go West," China's geostrategic rebalance], *Huanqiuwang* [Global Network], October 17, 2012 (http://opinion.huanqiu.com/opinion_world/2012-10/3193760.html). See also Yun Sun, "March West: China's Response to the U.S. Rebalancing," *Brookings Blog,* January 31, 2013 (http://www.brookings.edu/blogs/up-front/posts/2013/01/31-china-us-sun).

13. See Evan A. Feigenbaum, "Central Asia Contingencies," in *Managing Instability on China's Periphery,* edited by Paul B. Stares and others (New York: Council on Foreign Relations, 2011), pp. 60–70.

14. See "A Look at the China-Led Asian Infrastructure Investment Bank," *Deutsche Welle,* July 9, 2015 (http://www.dw.com/en/a-look-at-the-china-led-asian-infrastructure-investment-bank/a-18541209). See also Article 28 of the Articles of Agreement founding the AIIB (http://www.aiib.org/uploadfile/2015/0814/20150814022158430.pdf available from The Multilateral Interim Secretariat of the Asian Infrastructure Investment Bank, http://www.aiibank.org/html/aboutus/Basic_Documents/).

15. See Evan A. Feigenbaum and Robert A. Manning, "A Tale of Two Asias: In the Battle for Asia's Soul, Which Side Will Win—Security or Economics?" *Foreign Policy,* October 31, 2012.

16. See Andrew S. Erickson, "China's Military Modernization: Many Improvements, Three Challenges, and One Opportunity," in *China's Challenges: The Road Ahead*, edited by Jacques deLisle and Avery Goldstein (University of Pennsylvania Press, 2014), pp. 178–203.

17. Not all saw China's approach as new or more assertive. See Michael D. Swaine, "China's Assertive Behavior—Part One: On 'Core Interests,'" *China Leadership Monitor*, no. 34 (Winter 2011), pp. 1–25; Michael D. Swaine and M. Taylor Fravel, "China's Assertive Behavior, Part Two: The Maritime Periphery," *China Leadership Monitor*, no. 35 (Summer 2011), pp. 1–34; Alastair Iain Johnston, "How New and Assertive Is China's New Assertiveness?" *International Security* 37, no. 4 (April 2013), pp. 7–48.

18. See Avery Goldstein, "U.S.-China Interactions in Asia," in *Tangled Titans: The United States and China*, edited by David L. Shambaugh (Lanham, Md.: Rowman & Littlefield, 2013), pp. 263–91.

19. See David M. Lampton, "A Tipping Point in U.S.-China Relations Is Upon Us," *U.S.-China Perception Monitor*, May 11, 2015 (http://www.uscnpm.org/blog/2015/05/11/a-tipping-point-in-u-s-china-relations-is-upon-us-part-i/.) The growing pessimism also drew attention to the views of those who had long proffered more alarmist views about China's rise and had called for a firm response. See Robert D. Blackwill and Ashley J. Tellis, "A New U.S. Grand Strategy Towards China," *National Interest*, April 13, 2015; Matthew Harries, "Survival Interview: Aaron L. Friedberg on the Debate over US China Strategy," *Politics and Strategy: The Survival Editors' Blog*, May 29, 2015 (http://www.iiss.org/en/politics%20and%20strategy/blogsections/2015-932e/may-7114/debate-over-us-china-strategy-f18a).

20. Although less pressing than events to the south in East Asia, deepening concerns about the implications of a nuclear-armed North Korea also posed challenges for China's foreign policy. The improvement in U.S. theater and national missile defenses to cope with North Korea's potentially dangerous unpredictability energized China's pursuit of more advanced technologies to ensure the continued reliability of its own nuclear deterrent despite a changing strategic environment. These include China's advances in anti-satellite, electronic-, and cyber-warfare capabilities, and most importantly increases in the number of its intercontinental ballistic missiles, some with multiple warheads.

21. Carl Minzner recalled Deng's expectation that the Party would need to deal with this concern: "When other party leaders criticized such policies for allowing dangerous foreign influences to circulate, Deng famously responded, 'If you open the window for fresh air, you have to expect some flies to blow in.'" In "China Is Again Slowly Turning in on Itself," *Los Angeles Times*, August 14, 2015.

22. David Zweig, "Parking on the Doorstep," Working Paper 3 (Hong Kong: Center on China's Transnational Relations, 2002) (http://www.cctr .ust.hk/materials/working_papers/WorkingPaper3.pdf).

23. See David Zweig, "Luring Back the Chinese Who Study Abroad," *New York Times,* January 21, 2013.

24. For a highly critical view, see Marshall Sahlins, *Confucius Institutes: Academic Malware* (Chicago: Prickly Paradigm Press, 2014). On the decision of the Toronto School District to close its Confucius Institute, see Karen Howlett and Caroline Alphonso, "TDSB Votes to Officially Cut Ties with Confucius Institute," *Globe and Mail,* October 29, 2014. For a range of academic opinion, see "The Debate Over Confucius Institutes: A China File Conversation," *China File,* June 23, 2014 (http://www.chinafile.com/conver sation/debate-over-confucius-institutes); "The Debate Over Confucius Institutes Part II," *China File,* July 1, 2014 (http://www.chinafile.com/conversation /debate-over-confucius-institutes-part-ii).

25. See Shambaugh, *China Goes Global,* 207–68; Mingjiang Li, ed., *Soft Power: China's Emerging Strategy in International Politics* (Lanham, Md.: Lexington Books, 2011).

26. American initiatives since the early 2000s to offset the perception that the United States is hostile to Islam, rather than just Islamic extremists, have also fallen flat.

27. See David Shambaugh, "China's Soft-Power Push," *Foreign Affairs* 94, no. 4 (2015), pp. 99–107.

28. In 1979, China began to submit movies to the Academy Awards for nomination for the Best Foreign Film Oscar. Only two have been nominated, and neither won. Still, by the early twenty-first century, Chinese directors such as Zhang Yimou and Chen Kaige had become globally renowned. Perhaps emblematic of the growing visibility of Chinese cinema was *Crouching Tiger, Hidden Dragon,* winner of Best Foreign Film for 2000. Although it was directed by Taiwan's Ang Lee, it was filmed on the mainland and entailed cooperation between film companies there and those on Taiwan and in Hong Kong.

29. In addition to facing political constraints, some Chinese filmmakers face challenges in finding a market for less conventional work at home. See Edward Wong, "Chinese Independent Filmmakers Look to Locarno Festival," *New York Times,* August 14, 2015.

TWO

True Revisionist

China and the Global Monetary System

GREGORY T. CHIN

This chapter examines China's growing role and influence in the global monetary system. Both elements are expanding faster than experts expected.[1] China has been playing an increasingly prominent role as an international creditor, having helped to maintain the stability of the two leading international currencies in the world, the U.S. dollar and the euro, during the great financial crisis of 2008–09, and the sovereign debt crises in Europe from 2011 to 2012. At the same time, China, motivated by its evolving global interests, and at times frustrated by U.S. economic policy, is trying to encourage a transition to a more diversified global monetary scenario, and reduce the dominance of the dollar. It is doing so by promoting the international use of its national currency, the renminbi (RMB), and by encouraging broader use of Special Drawing Rights (SDR), the multilateral reserve accounting tool that is issued by the International Monetary Fund and used by central banks. China cannot, however, achieve these more transformational goals without the participation and support of others. Therefore, the decisions of overseas partners in regard to whether they support the RMB's international use, or to what degree, also deserve attention.

How should scholars and policymakers characterize China's foreign policy in the global monetary realm? What concept or definition most accurately depicts China's interventions in the global monetary system? The terminology, and its accuracy, matter as it can strongly affect the foreign policy response of other states. The central empirical and conceptual argument here is that China is exhibiting a complex mix of behaviors in the global monetary system, a combination of conservatism and transformational aspiration, and that we need a concept that reflects the "pluralism" of China's behavior.[2] At one level, the People's Republic of China (PRC) has intervened to stabilize and preserve core elements of the existing global monetary system, such as the status of the U.S. dollar and the euro as leading international currencies; while at another level, it has advanced reforms that aim to change the global monetary system. It is suggested, here, that these two dimensions, together, add up to what can be called *true revisionism*.[3]

"Revisionism" has often been conceived in International Relations to mean a revolutionary or radically revisionist power, with "unlimited aims," willing to use any means necessary, whose appetite for risk in pursuing system change is high, and where the goal is a change *of* the system and the order.[4] In contrast, the understanding here is that the PRC is seeking change *in* the system, as the immediate and medium-term goal, aiming to preserve a leading role for U.S. dollar, though not 'the' leading role. At the same time, the Chinese authorities do also want to *gradually* reduce the overwhelming dominance of the dollar, over the medium term, thus explaining their interventions to stabilize the euro, and to increase the use of the RMB (and potentially the SDR) globally. Achieving the latter would mean a transition to an *actual* multi-centered and diverse global monetary system and order, with China's RMB (and perhaps some role for the SDR) alongside the dollar and the euro at the top of the currency pyramid. Notwithstanding these systemic changes, the PRC is led by a political elite whose preferred approach to global monetary change is likely to remain wedded to measured pragmatism and gradual evolution—true revisionism, not radical change—unless they are provoked in their relationship with the United States in ways that would be unprecedented during the last four decades. We will return to this new possibility in the Concluding section.

This chapter's analysis examines the specifics of China's calls for global systemic reform, namely diversification of the international monetary and reserve system, as distinguished from, but related to, the Chinese Communist Party's desire for multipolarity in the world economy. I then examine how the PRC has sought to stabilize and preserve core elements of the existing global monetary system, by shoring up the stability of the U.S. dollar, and then the euro. Despite their concerns about what they see as inherent deficiencies in the existing global monetary system, the *first-order response* of China's leadership and central bankers was to work together with their key counterparts around the world to stabilize the current global monetary (and financial) system. There was, however, a *second-order response*. I thus turn next to examining how China has also taken measures to influence change in the monetary system. Finally, I examine the decisions and evolving interests of key partner states and corporates in what is suggested here, as the *critical cases* of the Eurozone and the United Kingdom, for the RMB to become a global currency. The analysis details how and why European and British policymakers and corporations have responded proactively to the policy signaling from the PRC, and the potential global significance of their decisions.

At the outset, it is important to stipulate that, heretofore, the U.S. dollar remains, by far, the single most dominant international currency, going no lower than nearly 45 percent of global payments, while the RMB as its peak in November 2015 was 2.79 percent (according to the data of the Society for Worldwide Interbank Financial Telecommunications, or SWIFT, which supplies information messaging services and interface software to financial institutions worldwide), and the euro registered 27.2 percent, and the British pound was 8.45 percent. As Cohen and Benney put it, the situation remains far from what should be classified as "multi-polarity."[5] Nonetheless, as I have discussed elsewhere, since the early 2000s, China's monetary policy elite have been urging the international community to move toward a more "diversified" global monetary and reserve system, and multi-polarity in the world economy.[6] Depending on how far the Chinese are able to advance these systemic reforms—and the evolving domestic scenario in China gives one reason to pause—such changes could have consequences not only for the monetary system, but also for the global monetary *order*. We return to these points in the conclusion.

Below, we begin with China's intentions, at least as stated, for the global monetary and reserve system.

WHAT DOES CHINA WANT?

Analysts inside China, and outside, have assumed that the calls from China's leaders and central bankers during the great financial crisis (GFC) of 2008–09 and afterward, for a more diverse (*duoyuan hua*) international monetary system, signals a policy preference for a multipolar (*duoji hua*) currency system. While the assumption could turn out to be true, it would be useful to look more precisely at the actual statements of Chinese leaders and officials with regard to the global monetary system.

A review of the relevant policy statements reveals that China's Party and government leaders have not officially called for a multi-polar currency system, and their normative and policy preferences have been left somewhat ambiguous. Chinese leaders have avoided overt geostrategic power-balancing language when discussing the international monetary system, even though they have seemingly gauged the geo-economics, coolly, to assess the trends, and work out China's positioning according to its evolving national interests. What they have called for is a more "diversified" global monetary system, and system "reform." At the first Group of Twenty (G-20) Leaders' summit in Washington, D.C., on November 15, 2008, then Party General Secretary and State President Hu Jintao called on the leaders of the G-20 nations to give top priority to "improving the international currency system and steadily promote the diversity of the international monetary system."[7] Hu repeated the message again at the G-20 London summit in April 2009, amid the nervous gathering, urging the G-20 nations to "promote a diverse and reasonable international currency system."[8] At each of the so-called BRICS (Brazil, Russia, India, China, South Africa) leaders' summits starting in Russia in June 2009, Chinese leaders supported the BRICS consensus on the "strong need" for a "stable, predictable and more diversified international monetary system." When China hosted the BRICS summit in Sanya, Hainan, in April 2011, the BRICS nations issued their strongest call for global monetary reform, stating that "we support the reform and improvement of the existing international monetary system, with a broad-based international reserve currency system providing stability and certainty" and "we welcome the current discussion about the role of the SDR in the existing international monetary system including the composition of SDR's basket of currencies."[9]

The technical details were left to China's central bankers to work out. In February 2009, in a speech at the Bank Negara Malaysia, in Kuala Lumpur, People's Bank of China (PBOC) governor Zhou Xiaochuan highlighted the official Chinese view of the global systemic risks from over-relying on the U.S. dollar for "pricing and settling" the "bulk of international trade and financial transactions"; how the "over-concentration of foreign assets in one particular currency" can "end up in undesirable scenarios" when other countries experience massive inflows and outflows of that currency;[10] and the need to reform the international monetary system toward "more rational allocation of savings flow" and "diversification over the long run," including "enhancing the status of the SDR."[11] Zhou's proposals drew international attention when the PBOC posted his essay "Reflections on Reforming the International Monetary System" on its website on March 23, 2009.[12] In the piece, Zhou wrote that the financial crisis of 2008–09 had focused attention onto the problems of excess reliance on "credit-based national currencies" as major international reserve currencies. He argued that the global community was confronting a long unanswered question: "What kind of international reserve currency do we need to secure global financial stability and facilitate world economic growth?"[13] According to Zhou, reserve diversification

is needed to avoid the "Triffin Dilemma," where there is inherent conflict of interest between the domestic policy goals of the reserve issuing (national) government and the international liquidity needs of
the other countries in the system, especially for a stable international
currency. The "grand vision" he proposed was to "create an international reserve currency that is disconnected from individual nations
and that is able to remain stable in the long run."[14] Zhou reaffirmed
Special Drawing Rights as a "stable benchmark," "issued according to
a clear set of rules" to ensure orderly supply; suggested that its "supply
could be made flexible enough to allow timely adjustment according
to changing demand"; and said that such adjustments should be disconnected from the economic conditions and national interests of
any single nation.

China's finance minister at the time, Xie Xuren issued complementary statements (March 25, 2009) about the need to "accelerate
the diversification of the international monetary system," for better
monetary policy coordination between the key countries, in order to
ensure stability in the exchange rates of the major currencies, and
the need to pursue "full scale reform of the global financial system."[15]
He added that, "in the meantime," China would "accelerate the use
of the RMB beyond its borders." At the Autumn 2010 Annual Meeting of the IMF and World Bank Group (October 8, 2010), Governor
Zhou spelled out the Chinese position on exchange rate coordination, and placed the onus on the IMF: "We hope that the IMF and
the World Bank could sum up the experiences and lessons of this
global crisis . . . and rebuild the global economic and financial architecture accommodating new developments. . . . The IMF shall adjust
its focus of surveillance, paying more attention to the macroeconomic
policies of major reserve currency-issuing economies . . . it shall re-
fine the international monetary system, keeping the exchange rates
of the major reserve currencies relatively stable, while diversifying and
rationalizing the system."[16] A survey of the Chinese scholarly and
policy literature shows that many Chinese scholars quote the statements by Xie in 2009 and Zhou in 2010 as the definitive policy statements.[17] Elsewhere, I have chronicled how senior officials of the PBOC
and Chinese finance ministry had made similar calls for systemic
reform for nearly a decade, prior to the 2008–09 crisis, but they were

largely ignored by the Group of Seven (G-7) finance grouping of nations.[18]

The ambiguity regarding what exactly China's leaders want, and the assumption of many commentators that it is a multipolar monetary system, may be due to the fact that the Party leadership has made the aspirational statement that the "pattern of the world is moving in the direction of multi-polarization," at each of its major meetings since the Fifteenth Party Congress in November 1997. Moreover, as far back as April 2002, then PBOC governor Dai Xianglong did say (at the Spring Joint Meeting of the IMF and World Bank Group) that the "irrationality inherent in the international monetary system has [already] contributed to the uneven allocation of global resources and large fluctuations among major currencies," and "We support 'multi-polarization' of the world economy."[19] Dai added that "this will help promote harmonized and balanced development of the global economy, and the establishment of a new international political and economic order that is fair and rational." Also in a first for China's central bank leadership, Dai then added that "it is obviously beneficial to expand the use of SDRs as an international reserve currency." Recently, in his November 2014 speech to the Central Conference on Foreign Affairs Work of the CCP, General Secretary Xi Jinping reaffirmed once again, "We should be fully mindful of the complexity of the evolving international architecture, and we should also recognize that the growing trend toward a multi-polar world will not change."[20]

Chinese policy insiders have added to ambiguity about the PRC's intentions by offering assessments that tie the two systemic reform objectives together. For example, after Governor Zhou issued his essay, the editor of *Securities Times* (a Chinese newspaper that reports on securities markets and Chinese-listed companies), Huang Xiaopeng, suggested that "China should work together with other emerging economies and neighbouring countries in Asia to use their own currencies for international trade, to balance against the U.S. dollar," and Professor Yu Zhonghua at Liaoning University, agreed with the regional action in order to "cultivate multi-polar balance," and to "hasten the arrival of a multi-polar currency order."[21] Similarly, Professor Li Daokui, the "non-bank member" (that is, academic) of the PBOC's Monetary Policy Committee, is quoted in the official

Chinese media (September 2010) saying, "A multi-polar international monetary system is inevitable. The stimulus policies adopted by the U.S. and Europe would lead to excess liquidity in the global market, which in the long run, would weaken their status as international currencies."[22] Despite the geopolitics that feature in the arguments of the Chinese policy commentators, state officials have been careful to avoid the rhetoric of power-balancing, or to suggest or confirm a direct challenge to the dollar order. They have kept to more measured and technocratic language such as "reserve diversification" and "rationalizing the system."

For those who are skeptical about the significance of the self-stated objectives of Chinese policymakers or technocrats, let us turn next to what China is actually doing, how it has actually intervened, and the evolving national interests it has pursued in the global monetary system.

SYSTEM STABILIZER

Chinese leaders did not dump their dollar holdings during the free-fall of the U.S. and UK financial systems in 2008–09, despite their growing worries about the stability of their already large dollar holdings,[23] and despite their calls for a more diversified monetary system. They actually added to their dollar holdings. Nor did China undermine the euro when the Eurozone's stability was in question. Rather, the Europeans found they had an influential "new potential ally."[24] The PRC's *first-order* response in both cases was to intervene to restore stability in the global monetary system.

Supporting the Dollar

Why did China add to its dollar holdings despite the growing concerns about the value of the dollar? The most direct answer is that the bulk of China's own massive foreign reserve holdings are denominated in U.S. dollar assets. China's foreign exchange reserve had risen to a world leading U.S.$1.7 trillion by mid-2008, just prior to the freefall of the U.S. financial system, and it was estimated that about 70 to 80 percent of its official reserve was in U.S. dollar-denominated assets (the composition of China's official reserves was classified as "state secret").[25] In order to protect the value of its existing dollar assets, Chinese authorities need to defend the international standing of the U.S. dollar with further dollar purchases, when that currency is facing downward market pressure. Lawrence Summers famously called it, the "balance of financial terror."[26] Kirshner has described the dynamic as a kind of "dollar dependency," a form of monetary "entrapment" where China remains a central actor in the dollar bloc regardless of its frustrations with "dollar hegemony."[27]

It was therefore not surprising that China helped to shore up the value, and the global status, of the U.S. dollar during the great financial crisis. At the height of the crisis, in mid-September 2008, China's senior leadership reassured U.S. officials that they would prevent their own officials and financial institutions from selling U.S. dollar assets.[28] China's overall reserves increased from U.S.$1.5 trillion in 2008 to U.S.$2.4 trillion by the end of 2009, and a leak in *China Securities Journal* (an official Chinese newspaper) in September 2010 revealed that 65 percent (almost U.S.$1.6 trillion) of its U.S.$2.45 trillion reserves were in dollars.[29] According to U.S. Treasury Department data, China remains the largest foreign holder of U.S. Treasury securities at 7.2 percent (U.S.$1. 253 trillion, October 2014), while Japan is second at 7 percent (about one-third of U.S. debt, 34.4 percent, is owned by foreign countries). China's role was particularly important in calming global currency markets due to the size of its reserves. The combination of these reserve management decisions (on the part of the Chinese, the Japanese, and other large official holders of U.S. assets), and the decisions of private investors[30] who, as in previous crises, flowed into U.S. Treasury bills as a kind of safe haven amid the storm (rather than dumping dollars),[31] bolstered the dominance of the dollar and reaffirmed its unique status—at least, for the immediate term.[32]

Aiding the Euro

Beijing's support for the euro traces back to its launch in 1999, and it is rooted in the PRC's ongoing frustrations with so-called dollar hegemony.[33] At the time of the euro's launch, Chinese foreign minister

Tang Jiaxuan suggested (1999) that the euro would help "establish a more balanced international financial and monetary system."[34] In November 2006, when China's reserve holdings surpassed the U.S.$1 trillion mark, central bank governor Zhou Xiaochuan told an audience at the European Central Bank, in Frankfurt, that China had started to consider "lots of instruments" to diversify its foreign exchange reserves.[35] The Chinese returned to the diversification agenda in 2010, frustrated by U.S. monetary policy, specifically the second round of "Quantitative Easing" (QE2, the decision of the U.S. Federal Reserve to purchase another U.S.$600 billion of Treasuries) in November 2010, and then QE3 in September 2012. The Chinese saw these decisions as confirmation of the Triffin Dilemma, as the U.S. authorities predictably putting national interests ahead of systemic considerations, willingly debasing the value of their currency, despite the potential "shock" to emerging markets, "flooding them with capital, and destabilizing their financial systems."[36] Beijing has thus been looking for ways to reduce its holdings of dollar assets, as a percentage of its overall holdings, for a while. Buying euros has been one the few alternative reserve options, though the shift from dollar assets has been incremental.[37]

After the Eurozone debt crisis broke in early 2010, Chinese leaders tried to help boost international confidence in the euro by making public statements of support, and declaring to the foreign business media that Beijing would maintain its euro holdings. Behind closed doors, Chinese officials and state money managers debated intensely over how far China should intervene. The underlying consensus was that Germany and the ECB had to play the key role in stabilizing the Eurozone, and then "China would do what it can, to help."[38] Beginning in early 2011, China started purchasing considerable amounts of government bonds of troubled Eurozone countries, and the debt instruments that were issued from the European Financial Stability Facility, the temporary crisis resolution mechanism that was created by the euro area member states in June 2010 (which provided assistance to Ireland, Portugal, and Greece), and from the European Stability Mechanism, the permanent rescue mechanism, which started operations in October 2012. It has provided loans to Spain and Cyprus.[39]

There are no official figures on exactly how much European sovereign or regional debt China has taken on, as neither the European authorities nor the Chinese have disclosed the figures.[40] A conservative estimate, according to Otero-Iglesias, is that China has over U.S.$1 trillion in euros.[41] Much-quoted reports in the financial press have suggested that China decreased its dollar holdings from 65 percent to 54 percent between 2010 and 2011, to the benefit of the euro, and some observers estimate that China has increased its euro holdings to about 35 percent of its total foreign reserve holdings.[42] Chinese researchers at the Chinese Academy of Social Sciences (CASS) and the Development Research Center of the State Council and Otero-Iglesias estimate that from 2010 to mid-2013 China's euro holdings have gone from 26 percent to 30 percent—which correlates to China intervening dramatically in the foreign exchange markets to help stabilize the European single currency.[43] Chinese purchases of Eurozone government bonds were large enough that foreign journalists reported in the *Financial Times* (February 2011) that "the Chinese are buying European sovereign debt in a big—and for China—a very public way. . . . That means it is no longer just the ECB standing behind the euro. The Chinese are backstopping it, too."[44]

European analysts have suggested that China's backing of the euro reflected its own concrete national interests, in the sense that it needed to defend the value of its euro reserves, and because the EU is China's largest trading partner.[45] Moreover, since 2010, China has surged into Europe as a direct investor. According to figures compiled by Deutsche Bank, the total stock of Chinese direct investment in the EU quadrupled from an estimated Euro 6.1 billion in 2010 (less than India, Iceland or Nigeria), to Euro 27 billion by the end of 2012.[46] Since the onset of the sovereign debt crisis, Italy has been China's biggest investment target in Europe, and half of the U.S.$ 7 billion in Chinese investment in Italy came in 2014; Spain has seen steady increases of Chinese investment; Portugal saw jumps in 2011 and 2014; and the United Kingdom saw two years of soaring Chinese investment from 2012 to 2014.[47]

SYSTEM REFORMER

Although China's first-order response during the crises of 2008–09 and 2011–12 was to intervene to help restore stability to the U.S. dollar and the euro, the PRC did also initiate a system-reform agenda—its second-order response—to reduce the dominance of the dollar. This agenda has two main elements, or two tracks, to achieve gradual de-dollarization: a medium-term goal of promoting the international use of the RMB, and a longer-term goal of promoting the SDR as global multilateral reserve asset. By early 2011, however, it had become obvious to the Chinese that their SDR push was once again falling on deaf ears from the G-7 nations, and it was even resisted by Britain, Canada, and Japan (after the G-7 had supported a new SDR allocation in April 2009, the first since the early 1980s, and in response to pressure from China, Brazil, and Russia).[48]

PRC officials shifted their strategy from advocating *directly* on behalf of an expanded role for the SDR to pushing for the inclusion of China's currency in the SDR basket. At the same time, they focused more on promoting the international use of the RMB. As then-chairman of China Development Bank and former PBOC vice governor Chen Yuan put it, considering that "more and more trade and investment partners, in various countries, are willing to accept the RMB as a settlement currency," then a "more realistic" diversification option is to allow the RMB to "move toward becoming an international currency that can be used for trade settlement, exchangeable, and investable, as a store of value." Chen predicted that the RMB becoming a widely used international currency, "will exert corresponding influence in promoting the establishment of a scientific, rational, and stable and orderly international currency system."[49]

China launched the RMB Trade Settlement program as a pilot in July 2009, and expanded the programs from 2010 to 2012. As China's leading banks and tens of thousands of enterprises, both Chinese and their overseas trading partners, have participated in the programs to use the RMB for settlement of international trade and direct investment, and more recently for cross-border financial investment, the RMB has climbed steadily up the global rankings.[50] According to SWIFT data, the RMB rose from twenty-fourth ranking as an international payments currency in 2012, to thirteenth in 2013, to fifth in December 2014, surpassing the Canadian and Australian dollars, and it plateaued in fourth place in August 2015, surpassing the Japanese yen (by June 2016, the RMB had declined back to sixth). At its recent peak, the RMB constituted 2.79 percent of SWIFT payments (August 2015), slightly ahead of the Japanese yen at 2.76 percent, though still a ways behind the British pound at 8.45 percent, the euro at 27.20 percent, and the U.S. dollar at 44.82 percent. SWIFT Asia-Pacific suggested that, in 2015, the RMB had seen a "big shift" in becoming a "business as usual" payment currency.[51] SWIFT data shows that 1,800 financial institutions worldwide were using RMB for payments as of June 2016, a 12 percent increase from June 2015.[52] The addition of more offshore RMB clearing hubs beyond Hong Kong, especially Singapore, London, Taipei, Seoul, and Luxembourg, and the increasing RMB flows between these offshore hubs helped to drive growth in RMB use even as appreciation expectations ebbed in 2014 and 2015. In January 2015, China's central bank reported that the RMB was used for nearly a quarter of all payments across the country's borders. By 2015, the offshore pool of RMB totaled over RMB 2 trillion, and the RMB's cross-border use was supported by a global network of fourteen offshore RMB clearing banks, thirty-one local currency swap agreements (valued RMB 500 billion in total), R-QFII quotas with ten countries (totaling more than RMB 300 billion) as the channel for offshore RMB to flow back onshore, the R-QDII program as the outlet for onshore RMB to flow into offshore RMB markets (both programs, together, facilitate two-way flow).

China has recently driven the launch of three new regional and extra-regional multilateral arrangements, namely the BRICS New Development Bank (NDB[53]), Asian Infrastructure Investment Bank (AIIB[54]), and the "One Belt, One Road" initiative (New Silk Road),[55] in which member states are discussing RMB use for projects (and other local currencies). China's central bank reported (2014) that more than fifty nations had already included the RMB in their foreign exchange holdings; in other words, the RMB was already de facto a reserve currency even if, de jure, states did not report their RMB holdings in the official reserve statistics to the IMF. It was nonetheless another diplomatic win for China in November 2015 when the IMF announced that the RMB would to be included in the currency basket of the SDR, and at the third-highest weight ahead of the yen and the pound (effective October 2016, and including a two-year phase-in period for the PRC to follow through on regulatory reforms to meet the requirements). Although some analysts have dismissed the IMF's SDR decision as mere symbolism, it is suggested here that the symbolism is important as the decision confers official reserve status on the RMB, which adds another layer of international legitimacy to the RMB. The IMF's decision adds support to RMB internationalization, making it legitimate for central bankers to hold. However, the decision arguably also gives greater legitimacy to the SDR itself, in that the modified weighting in the SDR basket (to include the RMB) is a more accurate reflection of the relative balance of capabilities in the world economy today.[56]

Prior to the recent backsliding in the RMB's international rankings, some central bankers in leading economies (for example, Joachim Nagel of Germany's Bundesbank) suggested that the RMB's role as a trade settlement currency was "already established," and that the RMB was in the process of "solidifying its status" as an investment currency.[57] It is useful to note, however, that even at its peak, 2.79 percent is still a relatively low share of total global payments. Moreover, even if more than 50 nations have included the RMB in their foreign exchange holdings, as of the end of 2015, U.S. dollar assets still made up 64.07 percent of the allocated global currency reserves ($4.37 trillion of the $6.8 trillion in allocated foreign exchange holdings of the world's central banks), according to IMF statistics.[58] Skeptics would further point out that third-party use of the RMB for trade and investment transactions (where Chinese business partners are not directly involved) is still limited, and that the secondary market for RMB financial products is still small, even in Hong Kong, home to the largest offshore markets for RMB denominated equities and securities. In contrast, the U.S. dollar remains supreme in third-party use, with dollar payments registering nearly 41 percent of the global total in June 2016, according to SWIFT payments data.[59] There are deep and open secondary markets for dollar asset trading. The most recent Bank for International Settlements (BIS) data on daily foreign exchange trading (2013) showed that

U.S. dollar trading averaged $4.65 trillion a day in 2013, whereas the RMB traded per day was the equivalent of $120 billion a day, amounting then to only 2.2 percent of the global foreign exchange trading volumes. RMB optimists would highlight that the amount of RMB traded per day had more than tripled in three years. However, the reality is that there is a way to go before the RMB joins the dollar and the euro atop the global currency pyramid. In May 2016, the head of BIS Monetary and Economic Department reaffirmed the overwhelming dominance of the U.S. dollar in the global monetary and financial system, and was quoted in Reuters saying the U.S. dollar is involved in 87 percent of all foreign-exchange transactions around the world, is the currency of choice in nearly 60 percent of all international trade, and accounts for nearly 60 percent of official currency reserves as well as debts and assets outside of the United States.[60]

Skepticism about the RMB is thus the conventional wisdom among the expert community, with commentators emphasizing that, despite the growth in RMB use, China's remaining capital controls, its assumed unwillingness to run trade deficits, and the lack of an independent central bank (or transparent monetary policymaking) are fundamental barriers to the RMB becoming a major international currency.[61] Kawai and Takagi highlight other factors that are said to further constrain the international use of the RMB, such as globally competitive banks and other financial institutions operating freely within China that can offer a variety of products and services, and a judicial system that is open and gives confidence to foreigners in terms of protecting creditor and property rights (that is, rule of law).[62] These factors affect international confidence in the currency. Prasad, an economist, argues, similarly, that China's lack of a "broader and more credible set of public institutions," means that the RMB lacks the "world's trust," and therefore, the RMB cannot become *the* dominant reserve currency.[63] Skeptics argue that growth in RMB use has plateaued, and some suggest that the RMB may simply follow the pattern of the Deutsche mark, the yen, and even the euro, where international use rose rapidly, initially, for each, but then leveled off well before they managed to pose any real threat to the dominance of the dollar.[64]

Much of the conventional analysis on the constraints on the RMB tends to emphasize the changes that China must make to its *domestic* policy and governance arrangements in order for the RMB to gain wider acceptance and broader and deeper use among overseas traders and investors. I concur that domestic political economy and domestic politics will play a defining role in determining the global future of the RMB. However, grasping the types of governance reforms that are needed to support greater international use for the RMB, and that take the realities of the PRC seriously, requires thinking beyond the political arrangements that support the U.S. dollar, and grappling with the particularities of the Chinese case, as well as general theory of international money.[65] Moreover, it is also useful to note that Takagi Shinji, in a paper written for the BIS on the factors that constrained yen internationalization, showed that the domestic public policy changes that Japan undertook to liberalize and open its financial sector ("Big Bang") were not enough to push yen internationalization to a higher level. Takagi found that the relative economic might of Japan, and whether Japan's (Asian regional) partner countries were willing to undertake "major cooperation efforts" to "promote the role of the yen," were key missing ingredients.[66] The experience of the yen suggests therefore that domestic supply side changes *alone* are not enough, and that demand for the RMB's international use will *also* depend on whether China can maintain relatively robust national growth for the next decade (even if it is at a lower rate than the previous two decades of high-speed growth), and on what the foreign partners decide. Exogenous factors, the decisions of the partners or "followers"—to use the language of International Relations—will *also* play a crucial role in determining future acceptance of, and demand for, the RMB. In the next section, we examine how some of the leading states and corporate entities in Europe have shown a willingness, early on, to support the international use of the RMB, and why this matters.

KEY PARTNERS

The available data shows that international use of the RMB has seen the most growth inside the Asian region, where it was already acting as a secondary anchor currency (for the exchange-rate management of other central banks in the region) for the past decade, having surpassed the yen, and behind the U.S. dollar. The RMB is now Asia's most used payment currency with China and Hong Kong according to SWIFT (May 2015), averaging 31 percent of the region's payments.[67] China's trade and investment ties are dense with the economies in the region, and trading partners inside the region expect the pattern to continue. Banks and companies in Hong Kong, Taiwan, and neighboring states, including Singapore, Malaysia, Thailand, Indonesia, South Korea, and more recently, Japan, are active participants in internationalizing the RMB.[68] Governments and corporations in key economies in Africa and Latin America, including South Africa, Nigeria, Brazil, Argentina, and Chile, have also recently enrolled in using RMB to settle trade and investment. It is suggested here, however, that a key game changer, in terms of fostering a global role for the RMB may turn out not to be Asia, where RMB use has grown steadily but arguably is expected,[69] but rather Europe, where RMB growth took off after 2012.

This extra-regional dimension of RMB internationalization could turn out to be a key difference from Japan's experience in yen internationalization, where the results have been limited after three decades. In a presentation in Beijing at China's central bank Kawai Masahiro, an expert on yen internationalization, and the former dean of the Asian Development Bank Institute, observed interestingly that having an "international financial center where English is the medium of communication" may be one of the conditions for RMB internationalization to achieve success.[70] Dr. Kawai's reference to an English-speaking center to support offshore use of a currency can be read in different ways. It may be understood metaphorically to mean that Anglo-American regulatory systems would be more conducive to supporting the internationalization of a currency, or it could mean implicitly that a previous unwillingness of London and key European financial centers, and their respective national governments, to support greater use of the yen impaired its chances. In any case, London, Luxembourg, Frankfurt, Paris, and Zurich have all moved early to become "Western hubs" for RMB use. They have been motivated by a combination of five factors including high levels of trade between China and the EU and the surge of Chinese investment in Europe, but also by China's financial diplomacy in support of the euro and on behalf of the RMB, by intra-European rivalry between London and the European financial centers, and, perhaps most intriguing, by the strategic projections of key European capitals that China may emerge, over the medium term, as the main driver of the next phase of financial globalization.[71]

Under the leadership of the former Chancellor of the Exchequer George Osborne, then–Prime Minister David Cameron, and the City of London Corporation, the UK authorities became proactive supporters of the RMB's international use. In terms of national interests, the footprint of UK banks in China are bigger than any other nation in absolute terms and relative to capital (including the United States). HSBC and Standard & Chartered hold the lion's share of the claims. UK banks account for 23 percent of the foreign banking market in China, and British insurers are among the leading foreign players. The United Kingdom's FDI and portfolio linkages with China have also grown rapidly in recent years.[72] HSBC and Standard & Chartered have been two of the most visible foreign participants in cross-border RMB banking services. Starting in November 2010, Mr. Osborne worked closely with his Chinese counterpart, then–Vice Premier Wang Qishan, to strengthen financial cooperation between China and the United Kingdom, emphasizing that China's "contribution to prosperity in the United Kingdom is becoming increasingly important."[73] The former chancellor strongly backed the "City of London RMB Initiative," which advocated on behalf of the City's participation in offshore RMB business. He declared that the growth of RMB business is a "natural development" for London, citing the City's "long history of global financial inventiveness," running back "hundreds of years ago, to the development of the Eurodollar markets" in the 1960s, '70s and '80s, to global foreign equities more recently"—and where "RMB trading is the next step" in the long road.[74] With an eye to the growing competition from European financial centers (particularly Luxembourg), the chancellor emphasized, "We are not prepared to let anyone steal a march on us in terms of new products and new markets. We are the natural home in the West for those who want to invest in the Chinese economic success story. The increasing international use of RMB is an important development for China

and for the World Economy."[75] He declared, "It is the a..
the British government to make London a hub for the sector—wi..
all the benefits that this will bring our own economy. . . . By acting as
a bridge between East and West, we can secure London's position as
the leading financial center in the years to come—securing the
growth and prosperity for Britain."[76]

After some to-ing and fro-ing between the central banks of the two
nations, in June 2013, the Bank of England became the first among
the G-7 nations to sign a reciprocal three-year sterling / RMB swap
agreement with the People's Bank, with a maximum value of RMB
200 billion (£21.2 billion), to ensure that the BoE has the capacity to
facilitate RMB liquidity to eligible institutions in the United Kingdom
in the "unlikely event that a generalized shortage of offshore RMB
liquidity emerges."[77] In October 2013, the two sides signed the R-QFII
deal to allow UK fund managers to invest directly in China's restricted
domestic stock and bond markets. In June 2014, China's central bank
appointed China Construction Bank (London) as the offshore RMB
clearing bank for the United Kingdom, which meant that UK-based
businesses no longer needed to clear their RMB transactions via
Hong Kong, Singapore, or Taiwan.[78] They could do so directly via London. Mr. Osborne welcomed the appointment of CCB as London's
RMB clearing bank as "another step forward for the United Kingdom as *the* western hub of Chinese finance."[79] The longer-term impact of these official arrangements on London's role as an offshore
RMB platform is still to be seen, especially whether CCB can develop
its competitive niche in the global RMB market, and make full use of
the City's potential as the world's leading foreign-exchange trading
market.

German corporates have also enrolled early in using RMB internationally. There are ample opportunities for German companies to
earn RMB as China is Germany's largest non-EU export market after
the U.S. German companies are heavily invested in China. Volkswagen, Bosch, and Siemens were first movers in issuing "dim sum"
(offshore RMB) bonds in Hong Kong in 2012. Volkswagen was reportedly (September 2013) already settling over 30 percent of its
exports to China in RMB.[80] A European-wide survey (March 2013)
by Deutsche Bank noted that the number of companies that were

willing to consider RMB for invoicing had increased to 80 percent, marking a dramatic change from 2011.[81] Commerzbank reported (August 2013) that out of 158 large German companies surveyed, 73 percent thought they would be using RMB in the future, and around 40 percent believed that the appointment of an offshore RMB clearing bank in Frankfurt would help with overcoming hurdles.[82] In 2013, a group of leading German-based companies across the financial, manufacturing, and consulting sectors, including Deutsche Bank, Commerzbank, DZ bank, Volkswagen, Messer Gas, HSBC, Citibank, and the main Chinese banks, formed a RMB Center Initiative Group to advocate on behalf of Frankfurt as an offshore RMB hub. They were supported by the Ministry of the Economic Affairs of the German State of Hess, and Germany's federal finance ministry and the central bank.[83]

In July 2013, the Bundesbank added its authority when Dr. Joachim Nagel, member of the executive board of the Deutsche Bundesbank said, "Although international use of the RMB does not reflect China's economic prowess at present, with its increasing convertibility, the currency has the potential to become one of the future global reserve currencies. . . . Given China's growing economic importance, the internationalization of the RMB seems long overdue. . . . The high level of interaction between China's and Germany's real economies highlights the necessity for a more active RMB trade, perhaps even using Germany as a hub."[84] In October 2013, the European Central Bank (ECB) provided another layer of support for RMB use—regional multilateral—when it signed a currency swap agreement with the People's Bank of China, which gives the ECB access to RMB 350 billion, and the PBOC access to euro 45 billion in "backstop liquidity facility." The swap aims to "reassure euro area banks of the continuous access to Chinese RMB,"[85] given the existing Chinese currency controls that constrict the offshore supply of RMB. Two months before Frankfurt was officially appointed as the RMB clearing hub for Germany (in January 2014), finance minister Wolfgang Schauble stated that "the German government would very much welcome the establishment of a RMB center in Frankfurt and supports Frankfurt's initiative."[86] As Mr. Schauble put it, "Germany is China's most important trading partner in Europe, and China is Germany's most important trading partner in Asia. Frankfurt is the financial center, and the center of financial supervision for Germany and the Eurozone. Thanks to its strategic location, Frankfurt would make a good choice to complement offshore RMB centers in other parts of the world." The culmination came in March 2014, at the ceremony announcing the Sino-German agreement to create a payments and clearing arrangement for RMB in Frankfurt, when German chancellor Angela Merkel, standing beside Chinese president Xi Jinping, said, "We're very thankful that China made efforts during the euro crisis to consider the euro as a stable currency. China never questioned its trust in the euro, and I find that very important, and we will continue to see through the cooperation in Frankfurt with the RMB."[87]

CONCLUDING REMARKS

This analysis shows that China's role and influence in the global monetary system have been growing over the past decade, and at rates faster than anticipated by the experts. The preceding discussion highlights three main points for scholars and policymakers. First, China is acting like a *true revisionist* in the global monetary system. When facing the crisis of the U.S. dollar, and then of the euro, the first-order response of the PRC was to re-stabilize key elements of the existing global monetary system by intervening directly as a creditor to bolster the U.S. dollar, and then the euro. However, as a second-order response, the PRC has also worked with government and corporate partners in Asia, Europe, Africa, and Latin America to influence global monetary change, by promoting the international use of the RMB over the medium term, and an increased role for the SDR over the longer term. These two tracks appear to be two alternative routes to achieve the same goal, that is, to reduce the dominance of the dollar, and that Beijing sees the former track as the more direct route, and the latter as supportive.[88] The RMB has seen a steady climb in its international use since the launch of the RMB Trade Settlement Program in 2009, rising as noted to the fourth most used currency, globally, for payments in August 2015 (before receding to sixth ranking by June 2016). Beijing also achieved a diplomatic

victory when the IMF decided to include the RMB in the SDR basket. China is thus exhibiting pluralist behavior in the global monetary system that combines the maintenance of certain core elements
of the system, while also pushing for changes that *could* eventually
bring about more far-reaching changes in the system of international currencies.

Second, Europe appears to be stepping forward as a key partner in
helping the RMB to develop beyond a "neighborhood currency."
Moved by their respective local and shared interests, European financial centers and London have acted early to join as "Western hubs" for
RMB use. Policymakers in Europe and the United Kingdom have
also been moved by their expectations of China's future growth trajectory, and their assessments of the potential role that Chinese finance
may play in the next phase of financial globalization. However, this
perception in European capitals appears to be a directional prediction, and European strategists do not have an exact timeline on when
China will open and globalize its financial system. As such, the durability of the European and UK support is unclear—and especially if
there is a sustained slowdown in the Chinese economy. The latest
SWIFT data shows that growth in RMB use as a payment currency
declined in Europe and the United Kingdom in late 2015 to early
2016. However, if the RMB's international use can be sustained in Asia
over the medium term, if it can also gain traction in Africa and the
Americas, and growth in RMB payments returns in Europe, then the
RMB could emerge as more than a "neighborhood currency." RMB
internationalization would then escape the fate of yen internationalization, of being confined mainly to Asia, and then fading.

Third, and related to the points above, comparison between the
contemporary process of RMB internationalization and the past experience of Japan and yen internationalization is illuminating for
thinking about the potential for the RMB as an international currency.
Grimes has recently reminded us that the limited development of
Japan's capital markets in the earlier period inhibited yen internationalization.[89] In addition, Kawai and Takagi emphasize that China
is currently much further behind than Japan was in the early 1980s
with regards to capital account convertibility; that the amount of yen
traded in the 1980s was much higher than that of RMB today, when

the yen was the third-highest ranked, behind the dollar and the euro. However, Takagi highlights that the experience of yen international-ization also shows that the decisions of overseas partners and economic fundamentals (namely a nation's relative global economic weight) also matter. Japan's experience, as such, tells us that the push by the Japanese government to promote the international use of the yen likely came a decade or two "too late," after Japan had already peaked economically, and had already entered a long period of recession.[90] The PRC, in contrast, has moved earlier, more quickly, consistently, and in a more unified way, to promote international use of the RMB.

It is to be seen whether the growth in RMB use has plateaued. Kirshner, as well as Eichengreen and Kawai, suggest that the RMB is likely to be a regional currency in East Asia, due to the anticipated size of China in the world economy in the future, China's already domi-nant role as a trading nation, and the increasing role of the RMB as an anchor currency.[91] This chapter suggests that the RMB could have an even broader geographical reach than just the Asian region. How-ever, much depends on whether China's economy will remain strong, as well as on greater flexibility in China's exchange rate regime, further capital account liberalization, continued modernization and growth of China's financial markets, greater ease for RMB trading, easier access to RMB-denominated financial products, increased cross-border flow, greater depth and breadth in the range of product mar-kets, and ultimately, greater international demand for RMB assets and financial products.

Ultimately, much depends on how the situation evolves inside China, and with China's global integration. A continuing slowdown of the Chinese economy, or intense volatility in China's domestic finan-cial markets would create uncertainty for China's RMB agenda. Even if conditions remain relatively optimal, it is to be seen whether China is *really* ready to move ahead with the financial and currency re-forms that are needed for the RMB to be used, substantially, as an international currency. For now, the leading PRC banks and enter-prises, and their overseas partners, continue to use the RMB for inter-national trade and investment, even if some of the smaller and more speculative players have abandoned the field with the shift to RMB depreciation. Central banks in many nations continue to introduce new measures to use the RMB. We can say that, since 2009, international use of the RMB has grown more rapidly than the experts expected, and cross-border use of the RMB continues to broaden, globally.

It is still to be seen which side of China's pluralist behavior in the global monetary system will prevail, that is, its more conservative status quo–oriented side or more transformational side. The observable trends and patterns, examined here, suggest that the current CCP leadership leans normatively toward wanting change, however, given its low tolerance for destabilization, it will want the transition to be gradual and evolutionary. However, the discussion heretofore about China's global monetary strategy relates to how the PRC has been shaped by the last four decades. The last decade-and-a-half, the period of the George W. Bush and Barack Obama administrations, was when the Executive Offices of the United States government and their Chinese counterparts made significant diplomatic efforts to foster a higher level of bilateral strategic dialogue, including on the trade and currency fronts.

Looking ahead, there is one major wildcard. The incoming Trump presidency is bringing great uncertainty to the U.S.-China relationship. Interested observers will watch to see whether or to what degree the new administration will apply punitive trade measures against goods or investment from China, as Donald Trump threatened during the presidential campaign. If this happens, Beijing would almost certainly respond with countermeasures. Bilateral tensions would escalate, and it is quite possible that the PRC would reconsider its global monetary strategy. To retaliate, China's leaders would likely implement a raft of countermeasures, including moves to de-dollarize in more dramatic fashion than it is already doing. For example, the PRC could reduce its holdings of U.S. Treasuries or buy fewer American bonds in the future. Related, Beijing could also make a stronger push to use its own currency internationally. These actions could make it harder for the Trump administration to finance its plans to rebuild domestic infrastructure. They would also add to the transition to a less centralized, and less liberal global monetary order, over the medium-term.

To the extent that China achieves its agenda in both the domestic and global spheres, these changes will have consequences. Given this consideration, it is noteworthy that European financial centers and

London, and their respective governments, have decided to enroll in RMB internationalization, and early in the process. Kirshner reminds us that the stakes in such currency contestation are great, as the relative role of major currencies in the system has implications for the balance of power between states, and for the prospects for global monetary and financial comity and stability.[92] If China succeeds with its reforms, there would likely be implications not only for the monetary *system*, but also for the global monetary *order*. For now, though, we are still a long way from achieving such a multi-centered global monetary scenario.

NOTES

I thank officials at the Bank of England, Bank for International Settlements, City of London Corporation, Federal Ministry of Finance Germany, European Central Bank, Hong Kong Monetary Authority, Monetary Authority of Singapore, People's Bank of China, UK Treasury, and the International Monetary Fund, and staff of the Bank of China, Hong Kong and Shanghai Bank of China, Industrial and Commercial Bank of China, Standard Chartered Bank, and the State Export-Import Bank of China for the interviews. I thank Paul Bowles, Hongyi Chen, Benjamin J. Cohen, Andrew Filardo, Carla Freeman, Kevin Gallagher, William Grimes, Kurt Hanson, Dong He, Sandra Heep, Sebastian Heilmann, Eric Helleiner, Patrick Hess, John M. Hobson, Mikko Huotari, Alastair Iain Johnston, Jonathan Kirshner, Daniel Koldyk, Miguel Otero-Iglesias, Louis Pauly, Margaret Pearson, Simon Rabinovitch, Changyong Rhee, Robert Ross, Phillip Saunders, Edward Steinfeld, Wang Xin, Wang Yong, and Jeffrey Wasserstrom for their comments, and especially Miles Kahler, Damien Ma, and Minyuan Zhao, the discussants for this chapter at the conference. Special thanks to Avery Goldstein and Jacques deLisle for their editorial suggestions and project leadership. I thank the publisher's anonymous reviewers for their suggestions. My thanks to Dr. Christopher Swarat and Karl Shu Yan for their research assistance, and to the Social Sciences and Humanities Research Council of Canada for supporting the work. Responsibility for any errors of interpretation rests with the author alone.

1. For examples of the long list of early literature that suggested that the RMB internationalization would have negligible significance, see Paul

Krugman, "I Will Not See RMB Internationalization in My Lifetime," 2009; Wendy Dobson and Paul Masson, "Will the Renminbi Become a World Currency?," *China Economic Review* 20, no. 1 (2009), pp. 124–35; Gao Haihong and Yu Yongding, "Definition and Conditions of the Internationalization of the Renminbi," *International Economic Review* (Chinese) 1 (2011); Barry Eichengreen, *Exorbitant Privilege: The Rise and Fall of the Dollar and the Future of the International Monetary System* (Oxford University Press, 2011); Arthur R. Kroeber, *The Renminbi: The Political Economy of a Currency* (Brookings, 2011); Jeffrey Frankel, "The Rise of the Renminbi as an International Currency: Historical Precedents," VoxEU.org, October 11, 2011; Eswar Prasad and Lei Li, "Will the Renminbi Rule?," *Finance and Development*, 49, no. 1 (March 2012), pp. 26–29.

2. Chestnut and Johnston also refer to the "pluralism" in the China rising discourse. Sheena Chestnut and Alastair Iain Johnston, "Is China Rising?," in Eva Paus, Penelope Prime and Jon Western, eds., *Global Giant: Is China Changing the Rules of the Game* (New York: Palgrave, 2009), p. 237.

3. I thank Edward Steinfeld for highlighting the concept of "true revisionist."

4. For insightful discussions of the conventional understandings of revisionism in IR, see Randall Schweller, "Managing the Rise of Great Powers," in *Engaging China: The Management of an Emerging Power*, ed. Alastair Iain Johnston and Robert Ross (New York: Routledge, 1999), pp. 1–31; Alastair Iain Johnston, "Is China a Status Quo Power?," *International Security* 27, no. 4 (2003), pp. 5–56.

5. Benjamin Cohen and Tabitha Benney, "What Does the International Currency System Really Look Like," *Review of International Political Economy* 21, no. 5 (2014), pp. 1017–41.

6. Gregory T. Chin, "China's Rising Monetary Power," in *The Great Wall of Money: Power and Politics in China's International Monetary Relations*, edited by E. Helleiner and J. Kirshner (Cornell University Press, 2014), pp. 184–212.

7. Hu Jintao, "Hu Jintao Addresses the G20 Summit on Financial Markets and the World Economy," Ministry of Foreign Affairs of the People's Republic of China, November 16, 2008 (http://www.fmprc.gov.cn/mfa_eng/wjdt_665385/zyjh_665391/t522600.shtml).

8. Hu Jintao, "Cooperating Hand in Hand and Pulling Together at Times of Trouble," speech summarized in "The Second Financial Summit Takes Place in London," Ministry of Foreign Affairs of the People's Republic of China, April 3, 2009.

9. The State Council of the People's Republic of China, "Full Text of Sanya Declaration of the BRICS Leaders Meeting," *Gov.cn* (Xinhua News Agency), April 14, 2011 (www.gov.cn/misc/2011-04/14/content_1844551.htm).

10. Zhou Xiaochuan noted that IMF data showed that the share of foreign reserves denominated in U.S. dollars was 63.9 percent by the end of 2007.

11. Zhou Xiaochuan, "Some Observations and Analyses on Savings Ratio," keynote speech given at the High Level Conference hosted by Bank Negara Malaysia, Kuala Lumpur, Malaysia (February 10, 2009) (http://www.bnm .gov.my/files/publication/conf/hilec2009/01_keynote_zhou.pdf).

12. Zhou Xiaochuan, "Reform the International Monetary System," March 23, 2009 (originally posted on the website of the People's Bank of China) (http://www.bis.org/review/r090402c.pdf).

13. Ibid, p. 1.

14. Ibid, p. 2.

15. Han Jie, "Strengthening Cooperation for Development: Finance Minister Xie Xuren on the G20 Financial Summit" (Chinese), *www.News .cn* (Xinhua News Agency), March 25, 2009 (http://news.xinhuanet.com /fortune/2009-03/25/content_11073098.htm).

16. "Statement by the Hon. Zhou Xiaochuan, Governor of the Fund for the People's Republic of China," Annual Meetings of the International Monetary Fund and World Bank Group, Washington, D.C., Press Release No. 47, October 8, 2010 (http://www.imf.org/external/am/2010/speeches/pr47e .pdf).

17. The survey was carried out by the author and Karl Yan.

18. Chin, "China's Rising Monetary Power."

19. "Statement of Dai Xianglong, Governor of the People's Bank of China," International Monetary and Financial Committee (5th Meeting), Washington, D.C., April 20, 2002 (http://www.imf.org/external/spring/2002/imfc /stm/eng/chn.htm).

20. Xinhua News Agency, "Xi Eyes More Enabling International Environment for China's Peaceful Development," *China.org.cn*, November 30, 2014 (http://www.china.org.cn/china/Off_the_Wire/2014-11/30/content _34187877.htm).

21. Yu Zhonghua, "To Check the Hegemony of the U.S. Dollar by Cultivating a Multi-Polar Balance" (Chinese), *Guoji jinrong bao* [International Financial News], August 6, 2009; Huang Xiaopeng, "In Reforming the International Monetary and Financial System, China Should be Pragmatic" (Chinese), *Zhongquan shibao* [Securities Times], October 31, 2009.

22. Li Daokui is quoted in Li Xiang, "Multi-Polar Global Monetary System Bekons," *China Daily*, September 7, 2009 (http://www.chinadaily.com .cn/bizchina/2010-09/07/content_11267413.htm).

23. Mure Dickie, Krishna Guha, Peter Granham, and Michael Mackenzie, "China Voices Alarm at Dollar Weakness," *Financial Times*, November 20,

2007; Richard McGregor, "Beijing Lectures U.S. on Effect of Weak Dollar," *Financial Times,* December 13, 2007.

24. Eric Helleiner, "The Future of the Euro in a Global Monetary Context," in *The Future of the Euro,* edited by Matthias Matthijs and Mark Blyth (Oxford University Press, 2015), p. 244.

25. Gregory Chin and Eric Helleiner, "China as a Creditor: A Rising Financial Power?," in *Journal of International Affairs* 62, no. 1 (Fall–Winter 2008), pp. 88, 92.

26. Lawrence Summers, "The U.S. Current Account Deficit and the Global Economy," Per Jacobson Foundation Lecture, Washington D.C., 2004.

27. Jonathan Kirshner, *Currency and Coercion* (Princeton University Press, 1995).

28. Henry Paulson, *On the Brink* (New York: Business Plus, 2010), p. 242.

29. Zhou Xin and Simon Rabinovitch, "Heavy in Dollars, China Warns of Depreciation," *Reuters,* September 3, 2010.

30. Eric Helleiner, *Status Quo Crisis* (Oxford University Press, 2014).

31. Robert McCauley and Patrick McGuire, "Dollar Appreciation in 2008: Safe Haven, Carry Trades, Dollar Shortage and Overhedging," *BIS Quarterly Review,* December 2009; Marion Kohler, "Exchange Rates during Financial Crises," *BIS Quarterly Review,* March 2010, pp. 39–50.

32. Jonathan Kirshner, *American Power after the Financial Crisis* (Cornell University Press, 2014).

33. For the details of the Chinese frustrations with "dollar hegemony" that trace back to the late 1990s, see Chin, "China's Rising Monetary Power."

34. Tang Jiaxuan, "Asia and Europe Work Together to Create a Better Future," speech delivered to the Second ASEM Foreign Ministers' Meeting, Berlin, March 29, 1999.

35. Peter Garnham, "All Eyes on Dollar Reserves," *Financial Times,* November 16, 2006.

36. "China Says Fed Easing May Flood World Economy with 'Hot Money,'" *Bloomberg,* November 8, 2010 (http://www.bloomberg.com/news/articles/2010-11-08/fed-easing-may-flood-world-economy-with-hot-money-chinese-official-says); Wang Xiaotian, "U.S. Urged to Consider Effects of Policies," *China Daily,* April 4, 2012 (http://www.chinadaily.com.cn/cndy/2012-04/04/content_14975752.htm).

37. China only decreased its holdings of U.S. Treasuries by U.S.$65 billion from the end of 2013 to January 2015, which is a small percentage of China's total reserve holdings at around U.S.$4 trillion by the end of 2014 (http://www.treasury.gov/ticdata/Publish/mfh.txt).

38. Author's notes from a policy discussion hosted by the State Export-Import Bank of China, Beijing, October 2011.

39. The details are listed at "About EFSF," official website of the *European Financial Stability Fund* (http://www.efsf.europa.eu/about/index.htm).

40. Francois Godement et al., "The Scramble for Europe," Policy Brief No. 37, European Council on Foreign Relations, July 2011.

41. Miguel Otero-Iglesias, *The Euro, the Dollar and the Global Financial Crisis* (Abingdon and New York: Routledge, 2014).

42. N. Casarini, "For China, the Euro is Safer Bet than the Dollar," European Union Institute for Security Studies, Analytical Paper, Paris, June 2012; D. Freeman and Z. Wang, "The International Financial Crisis and China's Foreign Exchange Reserve Management," BICCS Asia Paper 7, no. 2 (March 29, 2013).

43. Otero-Iglesias 2014. A more conservative estimate is that, by 2012, Chinese officials placed as much as 25 percent of the government's reserves in euro and European assets, including German, French, Spanish, Hungarian, and Greek government debt. See Yang Jiang, "The Limits of China's Monetary Diplomacy," in *The Great Wall of Money*, edited by Helleiner and Kirshner, p. 166.

44. Senior bankers in Hong Kong speculated that Chinese buying took up as much as one-third of the Eurozone bond issuance, at that time. Henry Sender, "China Has Much to Gain from Euro Support," *Financial Times*, February 3, 2011 (www.ft.com/intl/cms/s/0/0489ad52-2fa2-11e0-834f-00144feabdc0.html#axzz3X2Uy6K1t).

45. Miguel Otero-Iglesias, "The Euro for China: Too Important to Fail, Too Difficult to Rescue," *Pacific Review* 27, no. 5 (2014), pp.703–8.

46. The Deutsche Bank figures are reported in Jamil Anderlini, "Chinese Investors Surged into EU at Height of the Debt Crisis," *Financial Times*, October 6, 2014 (www.ft.com/intl/cms/s/2/53b7a268-44a6-11e4-ab0c-00144feabdc0.html#axzz3Lw6z9fus).

47. Ibid.

48. Chin, "China's Rising Monetary Power," pp. 195–203.

49. Chen Yuan is quoted in Wang Yi, "Chen Yuan: Insist on International Reserve Currency Diversification" (Chinese), *Caijing*, November 10, 2011.

50. Gregory T. Chin, *The Political Economy of Renminbi Internationalization* (forthcoming).

51. SWIFT, "Chinese Yuan Demonstrates Strong Momentum to Reach Number 4 as an International Payments Currency," *SWIFT Special Edition of RMB Tracker for Sibos*, October 6, 2015 (file:///C:/Users/Owner/Downloads/rmb_sibos_special_edition_2015_final_pr 20(1).pdf).

52. SWIFT, "U.S. Dollar Remains Widely Used for Payments between China and US," *RMB Tracker,* June 28, 2016 (file:///C:/Users/Owner/Downloads/swift_bi_rmbtracker_june2016_en%20(1).pdf).

53. Gregory T. Chin, "The BRICS-led Development Bank," *Global Policy* 5, no. 3 (September 2014), pp. 366–73.

54. Gregory T. Chin, "Asian Infrastructure Investment Bank: Governance Innovation and Prospects," *Global Governance* 22, no. 1 (January–March 2016), pp. 11–25.

55. Gregory T. Chin, "China's Bold Economic Statecraft," *Current History* 114, no. 773 (September 2015), pp. 217–23.

56. Chin, *Political Economy of Renminbi Internationalization*.

57. Joachim Nagel is quoted in "Roundtable: Frankfurt Seeks to Reel in Offshore RMB Business," *Global Capital*, August 6, 2013, p. 2.

58. IMF Data, Currency Composition of Official Foreign Exchange Reserves (COFER), updated September 30, 2016. The IMF data includes partial reporting on reserve holdings from China (http://data.imf.org/?sk =E6A5F467-C14B-4AA8-9F6D-5A09EC4E62A4).

59. SWIFT, RMB Tracker Slides, July 2016 (file:///C:/Users/Owner /Downloads/swift_bi_rmbtracker_slides_july2016_en.pdf.pdf).

60. Claudio Borio, Head of the BIS Monetary and Economic Department, quoted in Jamie McGeever, "Global Financial Stability at Risk, with or without Pre-Eminent U.S. Dollars: BIS," *Reuters*, May 10, 2016 (http:// www.reuters.com/article/us-markets-dollar-bis-idUSKCN0Y10MC).

61. Barry Eichengreen and Masahiro Kawai, *Renminbi Internationalization: Achievements, Prospects, and Challenges* (Brookings Institution Press, 2015).

62. Masahiro Kawai and Shinji Takagi, "The Renminbi as a Key International Currency?: Lesson from the Japanese Experience," Notes prepared for the Asia-Europe Economic Forum, January 10–11, 2011, Paris.

63. Eswar Prasad, "The Dollar is Still King," *Project Syndicate*, May 14, 2014 (http://www.project-syndicate.org/commentary/eswar-prasad-on-why -china-s-renminbi-will-not-become-the-dominant-global-reserve-currency -anytime-soon).

64. For analysis of this line of inquiry, see Benjamin J. Cohen, *Currency Power: Understanding Monetary Rivalry* (Princeton University Press, 2015).

65. For a detailed discussion, see G. Chin, *Political Economy of Renminbi Internationalization*.

66. Shinji Takagi, "Internationalising the Yen, 1984–2003: Unfinished Agenda or Mission Impossible?," BIS Papers No.61, January 2012 (http:// www.bis.org/publ/bppdf/bispap61g.pdf).

67. SWIFT, "RMB Ranks #1 in Asia Pacific for Payments with Greater China," *RMB Tracker*, May 27, 2015 (http://www.swift.com/assets/swift_com /documents/products_services/RMB_May_2015_final.pdf).

68. Chin, *Political Economy of Renminbi Internationalization*.

69. Jonathan Kirshner, "Regional Hegemony and an Emerging RMB Zone," in *The Great Wall of Money*, edited by Helleiner and Kirshner, pp. 213–40.

70. Masahiro Kawai, "Renminbi (RMB) Internationalization: Japan and China," seminar at the People's Bank of China, Beijing, May 21, 2012 (http:// adbi.adb.org/files/2012.05.21.cpp.kawai.renminbi.internationalization .japan.prc.pdf).

71. See Bank of England analyst John Hooley (International Finance Division), and comments by Governor Mark Carney, and Ludger Schuknecht, Director General, Strategy and International Economy, Federal Ministry of Finance Germany. John Hooley, "Bringing Down the Chinese Wall," *Bank of England Quarterly Bulletin* (2013 Q4), pp.1–13; Mark Carney, "The UK at the Heart of Renewed Globalization," Speech by the Governor of the Bank of England, October 24, 2013; "Roundtable: Frankfurt Seeks to Reel in Offshore RMB Business," *Global Capital*, August 6, 2013, p. 2.

72. Hooley, "Bringing Down the Chinese Wall," p. 4.

73. HM Treasury, "China Economic and Financial Dialogue: Chancellor's Closing Press Statement," *UK Government—The National Archives*, November 9, 2010 (http://webarchive.nationalarchives.gov.uk/20130129110402 /http://www.hm-treasury.gov.uk/chx_asia_visit_efd_091110.htm).

74. "Speech by the Chancellor of the Exchequer, George Osborne, at the City of London RMB Launch Event," April 18, 2012 (https://www.gov.uk /government/speeches/speech-by-the-chancellor-of-the-exchequer-rt-hon -george-osborne-mp-at-the-city-of-london-rmb-launch-event).

75. Ibid.

76. Ibid.

77. Bank of England, "News Release: People's Bank of China Swap Line," June 22, 2013 (http://www.bankofengland.co.uk/publications/Pages/news /2013/082.aspx).

78. Bank of England, "News Release: Announcement of Renminbi Clearing Bank in London," June 18, 2014 (http://www.bankofengland.co.uk /publications/Pages/news/2014/091.aspx).

79. HM Treasury and The Right Hon George Osborne MP, "Chancellor Welcomes London Renminbi Clearing Bank," *Gov.UK*, June 18, 2014 (emphasis added) (https://www.gov.uk/government/news/chancellor-welcomes -london-renminbi-clearing-bank).

80. Interview with Bank of China Frankfurt staff, Germany, September 2013.

81. "Roundtable," p. 2.

82. Roman Schmidt, quoted in "Roundtable," p. 2.

83. The corporate and government members are listed at Renminbi Hub "Initiative Group," Frankfurt Main Finance website (http://www.frankfurt -main-finance.com/en/renminbi/financial-center-germany-rmb-center -frankfurt/initiative-group/).

84. Dr. Joachim Nagel, "The Internationalisation of the Renminbi," speech given at the Chamber of Industry and Commerce (IHK) conference, "Internationalisation of the Renminbi—Opportunities for Frankfurt," Frankfurt am Main, Deutsche Bundesbank, July 3, 2013 (http://www.bundesbank.de /Redaktion/EN/Reden/2013/2013_07_03_nagel.html).

85. The agreement is valid for three years. See "Press Release: ECB and the People's Bank of China Establish a Bilateral Currency Swap Line," European Central Bank, October 10, 2013 (https://www.ecb.europa.eu/press /pr/date/2013/html/pr131010.en.html).

86. Interview with Wolfgang Schauble, *Euroweek*, January 2014, p. 3.

87. Angela Merkel, quoted in Monica Houston-Waesch, "Bundesbank, PBOC Sign Deal to Settle Renminbi Payments in Frankfurt," *The Wall Street Journal*, March 28, 2014 (http://online.wsj.com/articles/SB10001424052702 3044184045794673720043680 80).

88. I thank Benjamin J. Cohen for suggesting that I clarify Beijing's preference.

89. William W. Grimes, "Japanese Financial Reform: Liberalization against the Clock," in *Power in a Changing World Economy: Lesson from East Asia*, edited by Benjamin J. Cohen and Eric Chiu (London and New York: Routledge, 2014), pp. 180–95.

90. I thank John Ravenhill for this point.

91. Kirshner, "Regional Hegemony and an Emerging RMB Zone" (2014); Eichengreen and Kawai, *Renminbi Internationalization*.

92. Jonathan Kirshner, "Same as It Ever Was? Continuity and Change in the International Monetary System," *Review of International Political Economy* 21, no 5 (2014).

THREE

Rising Nationalism

China's Regulation of Investment Trade

DANIEL C. K. CHOW

 The investment policies of the People's Republic of China (PRC) are part of China's overall strategy of using international trade to further its aggressive ascent as a global economic power in a rapidly changing world economy. These investment policies, often criticized as protectionist and nationalistic, are designed to promote China's massive state-owned enterprises (SOEs) sometimes at the expense of multinational companies (MNCs) with business operations in China and in other parts of the world. China seems to be pursuing a two-pronged strategy. First, at home, China seeks to weaken and compromise, at least in some cases, the ability of MNCs to compete in China and in countries abroad. This goal is accomplished by the use of various competition laws, such as the Anti-Monopoly Law[1] and the Anti-Unfair Competition Law.[2] Many MNCs argue that they are being singled out for discriminatory treatment under these laws. Second, in regulating investment abroad by its SOEs, China gives SOEs almost free rein in how to conduct their

business affairs, including the use of bribes by SOEs to foreign officials in host countries and the ability to set labor conditions. The lack of constraints on SOEs in their foreign investment activities abroad creates advantages over MNCs from countries such as the United States, which imposes a myriad of constraints on the conduct of U.S. companies. This two-pronged strategy allows SOEs to have advantages over MNCs both in China and in countries abroad, especially in the developing world. Each of these themes will be further developed below.

Although China has been criticized by MNCs and commentators for its investment practices, this study examines the PRC's investment policies and explains why China, in pursuing these aggressive positions, is not in violation of any international law obligations under the World Trade Organization. The most important consequence of this distinction is that China's actions are not subject to challenge under the WTO's dispute settlement system, which is widely regarded as the most effective international forum for the settlement of trade disputes. Since these policies relating to competition law are outside the scope of the WTO, any recourse must lie under Chinese domestic law, an avenue of redress that is probably illusory in this context.

CONTEXT

China's use of nationalistic policies has increasingly drawn the attention of multinational companies and foreign governments. Indeed, in some quarters, MNCs seem alarmed by some of the current trends. As China gains in stature as a global economic power, it appears to have become more aggressive in asserting its new-found power and status in the business, economic, and political arenas. China's use of investment law to further its overall objectives has created concern and some distress among multinational companies. The use of nationalistic policies has become so thinly disguised and apparent that MNCs believe that some actions must be taken now before the policies can be further extended. Whether such actions might receive support from the new Trump administration, which has expressed an aggressive anti-China stance, is a possibility worth monitoring.

By China's investment policies, this study refers to a web of policies and laws that govern foreign direct investment (FDI) in China and policies that govern China's FDI in other countries. FDI refers to the acquisition of a lasting ownership interest, usually accompanied by management control, of an entity located in one country by an entity located in another country. For example, suppose that a U.S. parent company established a wholly owned subsidiary in China or that the company establishes a joint venture in China with a Chinese domestic company, usually a state-owned enterprise. Or suppose that the U.S. parent company decides to acquire an existing Chinese company through a merger and acquisition (M&A) transaction. The business entity that is established or acquired in China is a Chinese legal entity formed under Chinese domestic law, but it is owned in part or in whole by the foreign parent, the foreign investor of the Chinese business entity. All of these transactions are examples of FDI. China's laws that govern inward FDI are contained in a complex set of statutes, regulations, and catalogs and require numerous government approvals. By investment policies, this study also refers to the policies supporting the expansion of state-owned enterprises both within China and abroad. Many SOEs have now established business entities in foreign nations, particularly in Africa. The PRC government policies toward this type of investment will also be discussed in the following. Further, by investment policies, this chapter also refers to China's national Industrial Policy goals, explicitly embedded in China's competition laws and in China's use of other laws, such as commercial bribery laws, that are applied to MNCs in China. Underlying these investment policies, according to some critics, are attitudes that are nationalistic, protectionist, and discriminatory.

ANALYSIS

It is important to emphasize that investment trade is not governed by the World Trade Organization (WTO), the world's most important international trade organization, which comprises the bulk of the world's trading nations, including China and the United States. The four major channels of trade in the world today are (1) trade in goods,

(2) trade in services, (3) trade in technology (intellectual property), and (4) trade in investment. The WTO regulates three of the four major channels of trade through major agreements that were part of the historic Uruguay Round negotiations leading to the establishment of the WTO in 1995. Trade in goods is governed by the General Agreement on Tariffs and Trade (GATT), trade in services by the General Agreement on Trade in Services (GATS), and trade in technology (or intellectual property) by the Agreement on Trade Related Intellectual Property Rights (TRIPS). For various historical reasons, member countries were unable to reach a similar general agreement on trade in investment, so FDI is not subject, with the exception of some minor limitations, to the discipline of the WTO. Moreover, there appears to be no political will among current WTO members to create a general agreement on investment, as priorities, especially among developing countries, have shifted elsewhere. The exclusion of investment from the WTO is significant because the other general agreements (the GATT, GATS, and TRIPS) inject substantial discipline into the channels of trade they govern. All WTO members, including China and the United States, have an obligation to abide by extensive WTO obligations with respect to the three channels of trade, including through the use of domestic implementing legislation, and these agreements have injected a greatly needed discipline and harmonization in these three channels in global trade. Also of great importance is that the WTO has an effective dispute settlement system, functioning essentially as a high court of international trade that resolves trade disputes among its members. Any member with a grievance against another member for a violation of its WTO obligations is able to bring a lawsuit within the WTO to resolve the dispute. Both the United States and China have been parties to several WTO disputes, and the creation of an effective dispute resolution mechanism is viewed as one of the greatest achievements of the WTO. The lack of a general agreement on investment within the WTO means that parties to an investment dispute are unable to use the dispute settlement mechanism of the WTO in the event a problem arises. This is an important point to emphasize because the exclusion of FDI from the WTO means that all disputes will need to be handled domestically, most likely in a Chinese domestic court or administrative entity of the Chinese government.

Not only is investment trade excluded from the WTO, but several other policies used by China against MNCs are also not covered by the WTO. A later section explains that China has used its Anti-Monopoly Law (AML) in ways that appear to be protectionist and discriminatory against MNCs in China. In addition, China has recently begun a widely publicized crackdown on commercial bribery by MNCs that resulted in a record fine of nearly $500 million imposed by a Chinese court on GlaxoSmithKline for giving bribes to hospitals and doctors for prescribing their drugs. This current crackdown is causing widespread concern among the international business community.

The exclusion of investment trade from the WTO means that China's investment policies are not currently subject to any international discipline but, in the absence of any bilateral treaty obligations (the United States and China currently do not have such a treaty), are purely a matter of domestic Chinese law, subject to redress under the Chinese legal system. Competition law, such as the AML, which also affects foreign direct investment, is also not covered by the WTO, nor are laws against commercial bribery as applied to MNCs. The exclusion of these areas from the WTO means that issues arising under Chinese investment, competition, and anti-bribery laws are subject to redress under China's legal and political system. China does provide in its written laws formal means of redress of all of these disputes from investment, competition, and anti-bribery laws through judicial and administrative review. In practice, however, these avenues of redress are probably illusory. Most MNCs are highly reluctant to use these legal avenues for fear of retribution by the Chinese government. Going forward, the lack of an effective means of relief from practices that discriminate in favor of SOEs has created a difficult conundrum for many MNCs.

STATE-OWNED ENTERPRISES AND MULTINATIONAL COMPANIES

As the main thesis of this chapter is that China uses its investment and trade policies to promote state-owned enterprises, often at the expense of MNCs, it is worth noting the role of SOEs and MNCs in

China today. The discussion in this chapter focuses on central-level SOEs (about 113 in number) under the supervision of the central-level State Assets Supervision Administration. State-owned enterprises are essentially business corporations that are administrative units of the state. SOEs are not owned by individuals or private business entities but by the state as a whole. SOEs are the main engines of China's state-controlled economy. At one time in its history, SOEs accounted for the vast bulk of China's industrial production. However, as SOEs were subsidized by the state and also served social welfare functions such as providing housing, education, and medical care for workers, SOEs were never concerned with profits and losses. Most SOEs were highly inefficient, and most suffered chronic losses. Beginning with the watershed economic reforms in 1978 that opened China up to trade with other nations, China's leaders have been engaged in reforming SOEs to avoid the chronic losses associated with this sector. One strategy that has emerged is to concentrate on developing fewer SOEs, but all in important economic sectors. Although as Nicholas Lardy has pointed out,[3] the share of industrial output of SOEs has shrunk considerably, China is still committed to strengthening certain SOEs as part of its industrial policy. SOEs continue to dominate all important strategic industries in China, such as oil and gas exploration; banking; transportation, including air and rail transport; telecommunications; and electricity supply. China has announced a policy of creating "national champions," SOEs large and powerful enough to compete with the most competitive MNCs in the world. These efforts are bearing results, with three SOEs already among the top ten largest companies in the world.[4] In November 2013, at the conclusion of the Third Plenum of the Communist Party, the Party pledged to "incessantly strengthen the vitality" of SOEs.[5] Critics, such as Lardy,[6] argue that these policies to strengthen SOEs are misguided, but the Party, misguided or not, is determined to promote SOEs. Note that the Party has not limited the development of SOEs to within China's borders. Developing SOEs must include promoting their power on a global basis, meaning that SOEs are directly investing in and establishing business entities and subsidiaries around the world, especially in developing countries. As of this writing in 2016, China is planning a reorganization of SOEs, including a wave of mergers and consolidation of SOEs that are designed to increase efficiency and competitiveness and that will result in fewer but larger and more powerful SOEs.

Understanding the importance of SOEs to China's national policy goals helps in understanding why China views MNCs as both creating important benefits for China and as posing threats to Chinese companies. On the one hand, MNCs are the most important source of FDI in China, as many of the world's largest MNCs have invested significant amounts of capital and have transferred advanced technology to China. When an MNC sets up an FDI project in China, the MNC must transfer capital (funds) to establish the business entity that will allow it to build a factory, purchase or lease equipment, buy raw materials and other inputs. Unlike other countries, such as the United States, in which no or minor minimum capital requirements are necessary to establish a business entity, the PRC government will require the MNC to invest sufficient capital to ensure that its China business entity will be successful. This can often be tens or even hundreds of millions of dollars. These funds, known as "registered capital," must be deposited in China as a condition for the establishment of a new China business entity. Moreover, not only must MNCs transfer significant capital inflows to China, they also transfer advanced technology to China as part of the FDI. The transfer of technology may be even more important than the capital inflows for China's economic development. For example, once an MNC establishes a business entity in China to manufacture its products, the MNC must then transfer the know-how, often embodied in some form of intellectual property rights, such as patents, trademarks, copyrights, and trade secrets, to its China subsidiary. If an MNC pharmaceutical company wishes to produce pharmaceuticals for sale in China, it is of little use to establish a manufacturing plant if the MNC does not also transfer the patents, trademarks, and know-how to the China business entity. Once the technology is transferred to China by the MNC, then China absorbs the technology. This is done because the MNC will hire local Chinese engineers, scientists, and managers to operate its China manufacturing facility. The MNC will train them in the use of the MNC's technology and this will lead to the absorption of the technology. In other cases, the technology transferred to China will be stolen or counterfeited without the consent of the MNC. (Of course, this does not occur with every technology transferred to China such as highly complex technology, which might be more difficult to absorb and replicate, but these cases are unusual.) For China, the major advantages of FDI by MNCs are that China benefits from capital inflow, and, equally or even more importantly, by the influx of advanced technology that China can then use to develop its own companies. As this process of MNCs establishing China business entities and technology transfer is repeated in different industrial sectors, China has been able to absorb advanced technology in sector after sector of its economy; this access to advanced technology has allowed China to quickly narrow the gap between itself and developed countries in the span of just two to three decades, a pace unprecedented in modern history, especially for a country that was mired in poverty and backwardness just half a century ago. In 2010, China surpassed Japan as the second largest economy in the world, and some project China to surpass the United States as the world's largest economy in the next decades of the twenty-first century. The role of FDI, mostly contributed by MNCs, plays a significant factor in China's rapid growth.

While MNCs are viewed as playing a significant role in China's economic development, MNCs have also come under increasing criticism in China. It is inevitable that as China develops its own domestic companies that these companies will one day view MNCs as competitors. China is not only developing SOEs, but has made it a national priority to make SOEs the "lifeline" of the economy and "national champions." These policies suggest that as SOEs and other domestic companies become more powerful, they will increasingly view MNCs as competitors. MNCs, once viewed as China's hope for advancement and industrial development, have come under increasing criticism as China's SOEs now see themselves as competitors with MNCs in the global economy. This criticism is reflected in views expressed by the Chinese authorities that MNCs possess "huge advantages in technology, scale, capital, etc. It is easy for them to gain a competitive edge, even monopoly positions in the market. . . . There is a need to impose countermeasures to regulate multinationals' anti-competitive conduct."[7] What was once viewed as an advantage that MNCs could offer China—technology, scale, and capital—is now the target of criticism as China has already largely reaped the benefits of that technology, scale, and capital in the past three decades. In the current environment, MNCs are being criticized for the very advantages that they brought to China in the first place; now MNCs are portrayed as using these advantages to exploit China by using their dominance to gain a competitive edge in China's market. The response of the Chinese authorities is that MNCs' behavior must be limited and controlled. As one commentator in China's state-controlled media proclaimed, "Multinationals in China must operate according to law."[8] This has led to the use of the AML, further discussed below, to limit what China views as anticompetitive conduct by MNCs, which are able to exploit their strengths to take unfair advantage of Chinese domestic companies and Chinese consumers.

Other state-controlled media outlets portray MNCs as greedy and unscrupulous, willing to use commercial bribery to obtain their business objectives. For example, one source notes "recent commercial bribery scandals have shown that those involving multinationals in China are on the rise—Certain foreign enterprises, it seems, are more emboldened to circumvent the law here."[9] Other media sources have noted, "Multinationals promoting business through bribery is nothing new; the concern is that they moved their corruption battlefront to developing countries, especially emerging economies like China."[10] These recent developments indicate while China was still early in its economic growth during the past three decades, China was eager to absorb capital and technology from MNCs; as China has already become a global economic power and continues to gain self-confidence, China seems to be taking a harsher attitude toward MNCs, indicating that China believes it must rein in the behavior of MNCs eager to exploit China.

REGULATION OF FOREIGN DIRECT INVESTMENT BY MNCS IN CHINA

As noted, MNCs contribute the bulk of the FDI inflows that China has enjoyed in the past several decades. All FDI in China is subject to government approval and regulation. Unlike many countries, such as the United States and the European Union, FDI in China is governed by a special legal regime with approval requirements that are far more extensive than laws governing the formation of business entities by domestic Chinese companies or persons. China requires that all FDI take the form of certain business vehicles prescribed by law.

China allows foreign investors (usually MNCs) to form joint ventures with Chinese domestic companies, usually state-owned enterprises, or to establish wholly foreign-owned enterprises (WFOEs). These entities are governed by the Equity Joint Venture Law (1979, revised 1990, 2001) and the Equity Joint Venture Implementing Regulations (1983, amended 1986, 1987, 2001, 2011) and by the Wholly Foreign-Owned Enterprise Law (1986, amended 2000), and the Wholly Foreign-Owned Enterprise Law Implementing Rules (1990, revised 2001). These laws apply in general to so-called Greenfield investments, which are newly established entities under Chinese law. Where the MNC seeks to acquire a domestic Chinese company in an M&A transaction, the acquisition may, depending on certain guidelines and thresholds set by PRC authorities, be subject to review under the Anti-Monopoly Law by the AML enforcement and approval authorities.

Most FDI in the world today occurs through M&A transactions, and while this is still not the case in China, FDI through M&A in China is on the rise. Many MNCs find that it is more efficient to acquire an existing Chinese company with an established reputation and goodwill than to set up a new business entity. If an MNC seeks to acquire an existing Chinese company, the transaction may be subject to review by Anti-Monopoly Law enforcement authorities, such as the Ministry of Commerce (MOFCOM). The AML was enacted to prevent monopolistic conduct, which would include undue concentrations of power created by mergers and acquisitions that could lead to monopolistic conduct. If the acquisition requires MOFCOM review, the ministry can approve the transaction, approve the transaction with conditions, or reject the transaction. In addition, the AML can apply to international investment even where the focus in not on an M&A in China itself. For example, if an MNC seeks to acquire the worldwide business operations of another MNC, it will be necessary to obtain approval by China's AML authorities if the M&A

transaction includes business entities owned by the MNCs in China. This review under the AML is necessary even if the MNCs have only minor business operations in China. Failure to obtain China's approval will mean that the worldwide merger may fail. It is in the area of M&A reviews under the AML and other provisions of the AML that China has shown tendencies that are deemed by many MNCs to be protectionist and nationalistic, serving to promote Chinese companies at the expense of MNCs.

The AML was enacted in 2008 to prevent monopolistic conduct. The overall goal of the AML, however, is not to promote fair, open, and market-based competition. Rather, the goal of the AML is to further the Industrial Policy goals established by the Party. These goals can result in the AML enforcement authorities enforcing the AML to benefit Chinese domestic companies, usually SOEs, at the expense of MNCs. References to the Industrial Policy goals are scattered throughout the AML. For example, Article 1 of the AML states,

> This Law is enacted for the purpose of preventing and restraining monopolistic conduct protecting fair market competition, enhancing economic efficiency, safeguarding the interests of consumers and interests of the society as a whole and *promoting the healthy development of the socialist market economy* (emphasis added).[11]

The phrase "socialist market economy" refers to public ownership and is a reference to SOEs. Other references to Industrial Policy goals include Article 7 (describing SOEs as the "lifeline of the national economy") and Article 8 (carving out a special role for "administrative monopolies"). These Industrial Policy goals have resulted in the enforcement of the Anti-Monopoly Law to strengthen SOEs at the expense of MNCs, to obtain technology transfers from MNCs at rates below those that MNC could be able to obtain from Chinese licensees without pressure from the state, and to protect famous Chinese brands from acquisition by MNCs. Examples illustrating each of these goals are set forth below.

In the Glencore / Xstrata[12] case, Genclore, a Swiss commodity and trading company, attempted to acquire Xstrata, also a Swiss company, for $41 billion. Although both companies had their major operations outside of China, the companies still needed the approval of the Ministry of Commerce because both companies owned minor, non-operating assets in China. MOFCOM approved the merger upon condition that Glencore sell a mine in Peru to a Chinese SOE to further China's ambitions of securing more natural resources from South America. The mine was not related to Glencore's operations in China, but did present an opportunity for MOFCOM to force an MNC to sell assets to an SOE to further China's own long-term global ambitions. Glencore / Xstrata can be viewed as an example of how China uses the AML to strengthen SOEs and to create "national champions."

The Microsoft/Nokia case[13] involved Microsoft's acquisition of Nokia in a worldwide merger that needed MOFCOM approval for the business entities of both companies in China. MOFCOM approved the acquisition upon the condition, among others, that Microsoft cap licensing fees of technology to domestic Chinese companies.[14] The Anti-Monopoly Law explicitly prohibits the "abuse of intellectual property rights to exclude or limit competition."[15] China's AML enforcement authorities have also pressured other MNCs, such as Interdigital and Qualcomm, to license their technologies to Chinese companies at rates lower than that MNCs believe they would otherwise be able to obtain from licensees. These cases can be seen as furthering China's Industrial Policy goals of acquiring advanced technology (intellectual property) from MNCs as a condition of doing business in China.

In the Coca-Cola / Huiyuan Juice case, Coca-Cola sought to acquire Huiyuan Juice Group Limited, a major, long-established Chinese juice maker, for $2.4 billion. MOFCOM refused to approve the acquisition. In a very short opinion, MOFCOM offered some reasons for its decision, but many have found the reasons to be deficient and believe that the purpose of the decision was to keep famous Chinese brands in Chinese hands. This decision reflects policies of earlier competition law calling for the protection of "well-known trademarks" of Chinese domestic companies and "Chinese historical brands."[16]

These cases are only a few examples of Anti-Monopoly Law cases decided by MOFCOM that have raised concerns among MNCs that

China is using the AML primarily to further its Industrial Policy goals as opposed to creating a free, open, and fair market. MOFCOM has decided numerous cases under the AML in recent years that reflect similar policies; there are too many to discuss in detail in this study but a catalog of these cases can be found in an exhaustive study by the American Chamber of Commerce.[17] The next section examines how recent fines under the AML have also caused ignited serious concerns among MNCs.

In addition to prohibiting M&A transactions that might result in monopolistic behavior, the AML also prevents existing monopolistic or anticompetitive conduct, such as monopoly agreements that can lead to price fixing or abuse of a dominant market position.[18] While MOFCOM reviews M&A transactions, China's National Development and Reform Commission (the NDRC) has authority to enforce the Anti-Monopoly Law provisions against existing anticompetitive conduct. What is disturbing to many MNCs is that the NDRC seems to have unlimited discretion in imposing fines for what it considers to be anticompetitive conduct under the AML. Moreover, the NDRC, unlike MOFCOM, has never issued a written opinion explaining the reasons for its fines. The NDRC has announced that it will focus on several key industries, including aviation, cosmetics, automobiles, telecommunications, pharmaceuticals, and household appliances. Several recent NDRC cases have caused serious concern among MNCs.

In February 2015, the NDRC imposed fines totaling $1 billion on Qualcomm's China business entities; in addition, Qualcomm agreed to lower licensing fees of its patents to Chinese firms by a third.[19] The fine imposed on Qualcomm was the largest ever imposed on a single company in China.[20] In 2014, the NDRC fined the China subsidiaries of Chrysler and Audi $45 million for price fixing.[21] In 2013, the NDRC fined MNC manufacturers of infant formula over $100 million and forced price reductions.[22] Tainted baby formula produced by Chinese manufacturers led consumers to purchase infant formula from more trusted MNCs and from sources abroad. In 2011, NDRC fined Unilever for threatening to implement price increases and forced other MNC consumer products companies, such as Procter & Gamble, to lower their prices.[23] These recent actions have led to claims that China is unfairly targeting foreign firms under its competition laws and that MNCs are feeling unwelcomed in China.[24]

This review of China's enforcement of its Industrial Policy goals through the AML contains examples of decisions that have been criticized by MNCs as protectionist, nationalistic, and discriminatory. Both the American Chamber of Commerce and the European Union has complained that China's selective and unfair enforcement of its competition laws may lead to a decline in future foreign direct investment by MNCs in China.[25] As I have noted, China seems to be seeking to weaken the positions of MNCS in China and abroad, which will only bolster the position of competing SOEs and other domestic Chinese companies. And with FDI and competition law not governed by the WTO, the only recourse for MNCs is to use the judicial and administrative remedies within China to challenge the decisions of AML authorities. Decisions to impose fines under the AML by the NDRC are not even accompanied by any written decisions, so it becomes difficult to see how an MNC could challenge such an action, even if it sought to pursue an appeal. As noted earlier, however, most MNCs will not challenge decisions by AML authorities for fear of retribution by the Chinese government.

CRACKDOWN ON COMMERCIAL BRIBERY BY MNCS

An issue that is related to competition law concerns is China's current crackdown on commercial bribery that also appears to be targeting MNCs. Commercial bribery, that is, the giving of bribes by MNCs to secure a business advantage, also compromises free competition and raises concerns similar to those underlying the AML. China is in the midst of a highly publicized crackdown on corruption and bribery. After he assumed China's top post in 2012, President Xi Jinping announced that China would engage in a major anticorruption campaign that would catch both "tigers and flies," or both top-level and lower-level officials. A major part of this crackdown targets corruption by government and Communist Party officials who misappropriate and misuse state funds or their positions to further their own economic interests or the interests of their families. These corrupt officials also accept bribes from businesses in an exchange of money for power. Since as early as 1989, China has announced periodic crackdowns on government corruption so this aspect of the current campaign is not novel. However, the current campaign is unusual as it also calls for a crackdown on commercial bribery, that is, the giving of bribes by MNCs to government, Party, or private individuals to obtain some business advantage. Note that there are two "choke" points in any bribery transaction, the supply side (the payment) of the bribe and the demand side (the receipt) of the bribe. In the past China has focused on the receipt of the bribe by corrupt government officials. In the current campaign, China has announced that it is also focused on the supply side or payer of the bribe, which often involves an MNC. These are two distinct, although related, parts of the current crackdown and there are reasons why a crackdown on commercial bribery, the supply side of the bribe, has political advantages for China. This section focuses on the crackdown on commercial bribery by MNCs and why this crackdown may also be part of China's goal of strengthening its own domestic companies at the expense of MNCs.

In the recent GlaxoSmithKline (GSK) case, a Chinese court imposed a record fine of nearly $500 million on GSK.[26] Several executives at GSK, including Mark Reilly, a UK national, were also given prison sentences. Imprisonment in China of a foreign national for a white-collar crime, such as commercial bribery, would create great fear among the upper-management ranks of MNCs, but Reilly, although sentenced, was later deported from China and never spent time in a Chinese prison. After a lengthy investigation, PRC authorities determined that GSK was involved in a massive bribery scheme that used travel agencies to give bribes and kickbacks with an estimated worth of $492 million to hospital administrators and doctors in exchange for purchasing and prescribing pharmaceuticals from GSK. The Chinese media has hailed this development as a triumph of the rule of law: According to Xinhua, China's official state news agency, the GSK case showed that "an open China is not a lawless one."[27] A state news agency has also proclaimed that a "crackdown on commercial bribery by multinationals is deeply significant to safeguarding the order of the market economy and protecting an environment of fair competition."[28]

Although China's state-controlled media has singled out MNCs as the main culprits behind the rise in commercial bribery, some observers have noted that while GSK was given a record fine, many Chinese state-owned pharmaceutical companies "are guilty of much more egregious conduct" but have escaped prosecution by PRC authorities.[29]

While it is true that China's crackdown on bribery also targets Chinese government and party officials, SOEs, and local Chinese companies, a common perception among MNCs is that they are being unfairly targeted by China's in its current anti-bribery crackdown.[30] Other observers believe that bribery prosecutions or the threat of such prosecutions being brought against MNCs are used by the Chinese government to force MNCs to reduce their prices for their products and services in China in the same way that threats of anti-trust investigations have been used to force MNCs to lower their prices. Moreover, China's SOEs are notorious for their culture of corruption, including the use of bribes, but, so far, China seems far more intent on pursuing commercial bribery by MNCs than bribery by its own domestic companies. This perceived selective and unfair enforcement of anti-bribery laws is causing some MNCs to reevaluate their long-term investment plans and warn that there is a risk that "China will permanently lose its luster as a desirable investment destination."[31] Just as FDI is outside the scope of the WTO, however, commercial bribery is also outside its scope so the only recourse for MNCs is to go through China's judicial and administrative system to challenge enforcement decisions. As noted earlier, MNCs are highly reluctant to challenge China's enforcement authorities, including in the area of commercial bribery, because of fear of retribution by the Chinese government.

CHINA'S REGULATION OF STATE-OWNED ENTERPRISES ABROAD

In the previous sections of this chapter, I have argued that China's investment policies have been perceived by MNCs as designed to weaken their position in China through selective and discriminatory enforcement. At the same time that the positions of MNCs are weakened in China, the positions of domestic Chinese companies, especially SOEs, are strengthened. This part of the chapter examines China's policies toward foreign investment by its own companies in foreign countries. As China has gained economic power and resources, it has begun to make foreign direct investments in many countries, especially developing countries. As further set forth below, FDIs by SOEs provide political, strategic, and business advantages that are not enjoyed by MNCs from many developed countries, such as the United States.

As noted, FDI is not governed by the WTO, but is subject to the domestic law of the host state. This situation in China applies to many MNCs, including MNCs from the United States: FDI is governed solely by domestic Chinese law. In order to inject some discipline into national FDI regulation and to promote FDI, many countries, including China and the United States, have entered into bilateral investment treaties (BITs) or Free Trade Agreements (FTAs) with other nations for the purpose of encouraging and protecting FDI between the two signatory countries, although note that there is currently no BIT or FTA in effect between the United States and China. The United States uses a 2012 model BIT approved by the U.S. State Department as the basis of all new BITs entered into between the United States and its trading partners. Among the features contained in the model BIT and all recent FTAs are explicit provisions related to workers' rights in the workplace, health and safety and standards at the workplace, and a direct prohibition of child labor. The recent approval of the U.S.-South Korea Free Trade Agreement was considered a breakthrough because South Korea agreed to adhere to the 1998 International Labor Organization Declaration on Fundamental Principles and Rights at work. This seems to set a precedent for all BITs and FTAs in the future. In addition, the 2012 model BIT and all recent FTAs contain provisions related to protection and conservation of the environment and increased transparency in governance. These provisions are designed to discipline U.S.-based MNCs that invest in trading partners that have a BIT with the United States. All recent U.S. BITs have been based on the 2012 model BIT and its predecessor versions issued by the U.S. State Department. In addition to provisions contained in its BITs with other countries, the United States has a complex of other laws that limit the conduct of its MNCs abroad, including regimes operated by the Office of Foreign Assets Control (OFAC), a part of the U.S. Treasury Department. OFAC sanctions prohibit or limit the ability of U.S. companies to deal with countries or persons on a restricted list due to national security and human rights concerns.

Like the United States, China has also entered into BITs and FTAs, mostly with developing countries. Unlike the United States, however, China does not have a standard model for its BITs. Moreover, China's investment treaties with other countries do not contain clauses related to workers' rights, labor conditions, or the environment. The lack of these restraints allows China's SOEs to incur fewer costs in compliance than MNCs from the United States and also the freedom to make their own decisions on labor conditions and conservation or pollution of the environment. In addition, unlike the United States, China lacks any type of legal regime similar to that administered by the OFAC that contains many economic sanctions imposed on foreign countries and nationals that restrict investment activities by U.S.-based MNCs. China's SOEs are subject to no such constraints.

A prominent example of the difference between how the United States and China regulates the behavior of its companies in investment activities in foreign countries is illustrated by a comparison of the U.S. Foreign Corrupt Practices Act[32] and China's equivalent contained in Article 164 of the PRC Criminal Law.[33] The FCPA prohibits MNCs from giving bribes to foreign officials for the purpose of obtaining or retaining business. For the past decade, the United States has been aggressively enforcing the FCPA against U.S. companies, with many of these cases involving illegal payments to foreign officials in China. In 2011, China amended its Criminal Law to add Article 164 to fulfill an obligation under the United Nations Convention Against Bribery. Article 164 was amended to prohibit the payment of bribes by PRC companies to foreign officials and is considered to be China's equivalent of the FCPA. Since its enactment in 2011, however, China has not brought a single prosecution under amended Article 164 against Chinese companies for paying bribes overseas. While

China has created much fanfare about its crackdown on commercial bribery by MNCs in China, China has allowed its SOEs almost free rein to engage in commercial bribery in countries abroad where SOEs are making their foreign investment. In fact, China's SOEs are notable for their use of bribes and other forms of corruption in their investment deals with its trading partners, notably developing countries in Africa.[34] In fact, China's investment policies in Africa have been characterized as supporting government corruption and China's involvement in Africa has been criticized as "non-democratic, non-transparent, and toxic."[35]

This review of China's laws regulating the investment activities of SOEs abroad suggests that SOEs are given nearly free rein to conduct their business affairs as they chose subject to the constraints of the domestic law of the host country of the investment. Since China's SOEs invest in many developing countries where government corruption, non-transparency, and neglect of the environment are common, China's SOEs are not subject to the kinds of constraints that MNCs from the United States and other Western developed countries have imposed on their MNCs. The lack of legal restraints or the failure to enforce restraints by China or the host country of the investment means that China's SOEs have greater freedom and lower costs in their foreign investment activities than do MNCs. China's regulation of foreign investment by its own companies creates advantages for China's SOEs that are not enjoyed by MNCs.

RECENT DEVELOPMENTS

On October 14, 2014, China led the establishment of the Asian Infrastructure Investment Bank (AIIB), with fifty-seven nations as charter members. These nations include some of the closest U.S. allies (such as Germany and the United Kingdom), which signed on despite pressure from the United States not to join. The United States is not a member of the AIIB and has no influence or power in the AIIB, which it sees as a competitor with the World Bank and International Monetary Fund (IMF), both of which lend money to developing countries. Dominated by the United States, the World Bank and the IMF make loans to developing countries that are conditional on those countries' accepting a set of economic policies that the recipient nation is expected to implement, including policies directed toward fiscal discipline; redirection of public expenditures toward fields that offer potential for economic return (such as primary health care, primary education, and infrastructure); tax reform; trade liberalization; privatization; and control of government corruption. By contrast, the AIIB is likely to provide loans without the package of conditions imposed by the World Bank and the IMF. For this reason alone, the AIIB is likely to become a competitor with the World Bank and IMF for the allegiance of developing countries around the world. In other words, while the World Bank and the IMF provide loans with strings attached—conditioning loans on accepting a package of reforms (called the "Washington Consensus")—the AIIB, created by China despite efforts by the United States to stymie its development, is expected to provide loans with no strings attached, which could provide attractive to many developing countries. While it is too early to determine how effective the AIIB will become, it is seen as a new salvo in the growing competition between China and the United States for global economic influence.

What will be the effect of the AIIB and other international efforts by China to project its economic power? The direction seems clear: China seems emboldened by its growing economic clout and is seeking to project its economic power around the world. In this light, China's nationalist policies toward its SOEs and discriminatory policies against MNCs are consistent with the overall aggressive trend of China's mercantilist approach to world trade.

CONCLUSIONS

China appears to be pursuing a two-tiered strategy in its regulation of FDI or investment trade at home and abroad. At home, China regulates the influx of FDI by MNCs through a legal regime that some MNCs perceive to be protectionist, nationalistic, and discriminatory. According to these MNCs, China is using its domestic laws in a manner that is designed to limit or weaken the MNCs' positions in China's market while at the same time strengthening the position of China's own domestic companies, most notably China's SOEs. China's approach to foreign investment abroad by its SOEs is to give them almost free rein, including the ability to make bribes to foreign officials, through the failure to enforce its own laws and through the use of investment treaties that place few restraints on the conduct of SOEs. By contrast, U.S.-based MNCs are subject to a myriad of export legal regimes that constrain their conduct in foreign countries. By giving its SOEs relatively free rein, China is able to give its SOEs advantages, such as lower costs because of the lack of the need for compliance, and greater freedom to conduct their business affairs to their own advantage. These advantages are not enjoyed by MNCs from countries such as the United States, which imposes a myriad of restrictions on the conduct of its MNCs abroad. Finally, as FDI, investment trade, competition law, and anti-bribery laws are outside the scope of the WTO, China's actions toward MNCs and SOEs, as set forth in this study, do not appear to be in violation of its international legal obligations under the WTO but is subject only to domestic Chinese law. The exclusion of these areas from WTO jurisdiction means that any disputes in these areas must be resolved outside of the WTO under domestic Chinese law. As noted earlier, such challenges to China's actions within China's own legal system, which is subject to control by the Communist Party, seems to be at present an illusory avenue of relief.

How the United States and its MNCs are able to influence and change China's Industrial Policy goals and behavior are issues that need further attention and study. It is beyond the scope of this study to make recommendations on how to deal with China's Industrial Policy goals, as this subject is linked to the much larger issue of how to curb China's mercantilist behavior in general, and no one seems to have found a good solution to that question. In any event, recommendations on how to deal with China's current aggressive behavior should be the subject of another study for another day. However, any recommendations should bear in mind that China is likely to become more aggressive, not less, in the future as China is determined to continue its ascent to the top tier of economic powers in the modern world.

NOTES

1. Anti-Monopoly Law of the People's Republic of China (AML) (adopted at the 29th Session of the Standing Committee of the Tenth National People's Congress and effective as of August 1, 2008).

2. Anti-Unfair Competition Law of the People's Republic of China (promulgated by the Standing Committee of the National People's Congress, September 2, 1993, effective December 1, 1993).

3. See Nicholas R. Lardy, *Markets Over Mao: The Rise of Private Business in China* (Washington, D.C.: Peterson Institute for International Economics, 2014).

4. See "Global 500, 2014," *Fortune* (http://fortune.com/global500/2014/).

5. See Bob Davis and Brian Spegele, "State Companies Emerge as Winners Following Top China Meeting," *Wall Street Journal*, November 13, 2013.

6. See Lardy, *Markets Over Mao.*

7. Daniel C.K. Chow, "China's Enforcement of Its Anti-Monopoly Law and Risks to Multinational Companies," *Santa Clara Journal of International Law* 14, no. 1 (2016), p. 103n25.

8. See Jin Shanming, "Multinationals in China Must Operate According to Law," *China Today*, September 22, 2013 (www.chinatoday.com.cn/english /economy/2013-09/25/content_569718.htm).

9. Ibid.

10. Ibid.

11. See AML, Art. 1.

12. See Ministry of Commerce Announcement No. 20 (April 16, 2013) on Conditional Approval of the Concentration of Business Operators by the Acquisition of Xstrata by Glencore International AG.

13. See Announcement No. 24 on April 8, 2014 of the Ministry of Commerce, Announcement on the Decision of Conditional Approval upon Anti-monopoly Review of the Concentration of Business Operators by the Acquisition of Nokia's Devices and Services Business by Microsoft.

14. Ibid.

15. See AML, Art. 55.

16. See Article 12, Regulations Regarding Mergers and Acquisitions of Domestic Enterprises by Foreign Investors (promulgated by the Ministry of Commerce on August 8, 2006 and effective September 8, 2006). Article 12 provides in relevant part: "When an acquisition of a domestic enterprise by a foreign investor results in . . . transfer of an actual control in a domestic enterprise which owns any well-known trademarks or Chinese historical

brands, the parties concerned shall report to and apply for approval from MOFCOM."

17. See U.S. Chamber of Commerce, *Competing Interests in China's Competition Law Enforcement* (U.S. Chamber of Commerce, 2014).

18. See AML, Art. 3.

19. Zach Warren, "Chinese Regulators to fine Qualcomm $1 billion in Antitrust Case," *Inside Counsel*, February 9, 2015 (www.insidecounsel.com /2015/02/09/chinese-regulators-to-fine-qualcomm-1-billion-in-a?slreturn =1476301853).

20. Ibid.

21. See Avaneesh Pandey, "China Fines Audi and Chrysler for Anti-Competitive Behavior," *International Business Times*, September 11, 2014 (www .ibtimes.com/china-fines-audi-chrysler-anti-competitive-behavior -1685494).

22. Fines were imposed by the NDRC on Biostime, Mead Johnson, Danone, Abbott Laboratories, Friesland, and Fonterra. See Charles Riley, "China Fines Six Companies for Baby Formula Price Fixing," CNN, August 7, 2013.

23. Stephen Shaver, "China to Fine Unilever for Telling Media it may Raise Prices," *Bloomberg Business*, April 6, 2011(www.bloomberg.com/news /articles/2011-05-06/china-to-fine-unilever-for-telling-media-it-may-raise -prices-1-).

24. See Anna Domanska, "China Targeting Foreign Firms Unfairly Says American Chamber," *Industry Leaders Magazine*," September 2, 2014 (www .industryleadersmagazine.com/china-targeting-foreign-companies -unfairly-says-american-chamber/).

25. See Victoria Ruan, "AmCham in China Echoes EU Gripes over Opaque Laws Unfairly Applied," *South China Morning Post*, March 27, 2015 (www .scmp.com/business/china-business/article/1583536/china-targeting -foreign-firms-amcham).

26. See Keith Bradsher and Chris Buckley, "China Fines GlaxoSmithKline Nearly $500 Million in Bribery Case," *New York Times*, September 19, 2014.

27. Ibid.

28. See "China Launches Crackdown on Pharmaceutical Sector," Reuters, July 17, 2013.

29. See Benjamin Shobert, "Three Ways to Understand GSK's China Scandal," *Forbes* (September 4, 2013).

30. See Simon Denyer, "U.S. Companies Feel Unwelcome in China, Complain of Unfair Treatment," *Washington Post*, September 2, 2014.

31. Ibid.

32. 15 U.S.C. § 78dd-1 et seq. (2012).

33. Criminal Law of the People's Republic of China (promulgated by the Standing Committee of the National People's Congress on March 14, 1997 and effective on October 1, 1997, last revised November 1, 2015).

34. See Yigadeesen Samy, "China Aid Policies in Africa: Opportunities and Challenges," *Round Table: Commonwealth Journal of International Affairs* 99 (2010), pp. 75–76.

35. Ibid.

FOUR

Teams of Rivals

China, the United States, and the Race to Develop Technologies for a Sustainable Energy Future

EDWARD S. STEINFELD

 On November 12, 2014, the leaders of China and the United States joined together in a bold statement of their collective commitment to addressing climate change. Both nations publicly dedicated themselves to the achievement of hard-target goals—in the case of the United States, to an economy-wide reduction of greenhouse gas emissions by the year 2025 to levels 26 to 28 percent below those recorded in 2005; and in the case of China, to the realization of peak CO_2 emissions by 2030 or sooner, and an increase in the share of non–fossil fuel sources of primary energy consumption to 20 percent of the nation's total by 2030.[1] Given the substantial economic, political, and technical hurdles that would have to be overcome by both nations to achieve these targets, the fact that public commitments were made at all signifies a departure from past behavior, and something arguably worth celebrating as a breakthrough.

Celebration, however, has hardly been the tenor of the times, regardless of whether we believe these commitments will be honored

92 EDWARD S. STEINFELD

during the Donald J. Trump presidency.[2] When public discourse in recent years has turned to U.S.-China or European Union–China interactions surrounding climate, energy, or natural resource issues, it has more often than not done so in the context of mutual accusations, mistrust, and rancor. In no small part that has been because the discourse has unfolded within the confines of overarching assumptions about commercial competition and rivalrous economic relations. Such assumptions have been underscored by the 2016 presidential election.

For many American and European observers, China today is not just the world's largest and fastest-growing emitter of greenhouse gases, but also a nation single-mindedly focused on becoming the world's dominant supplier of new energy technologies. Starting from a negligible production base just a decade ago, Chinese firms are now the world's largest suppliers of solar photovoltaic (PV) cells and modules.[3] Within China's domestic wind turbine market—the largest (by total installed capacity) and fastest-growing in the world—Chinese firms are now the largest suppliers, and are increasingly exporting.[4] In the domain of civilian nuclear power, China is now the world's largest market (accounting for twenty-eight of the sixty-seven nuclear plant builds under way globally as of 2014),[5] and Chinese firms are emerging as major suppliers of plant technology. In a number of renewable energy domains, particularly wind and solar, the sudden emergence of Chinese producers has come hand in hand with substantial declines in the cost of energy produced.[6]

Of course, conceptually, even if one believed such cost reductions stemmed solely from Chinese state subsidies, one could welcome them. After all, they could be seen as just another price inducement to increase the availability of clean energy for household and industrial consumers, an analogue on the technology supply side to the sorts of generous policy subsidies we have witnessed in recent years on the consumer demand side in Germany, the United States, Spain, and numerous other advanced industrial nations. Proponents would argue that price subsidies, whether on the technology production side or consumer demand side, encourage technology deployment at a massive scale in extremely short time frames. Rapid, high-volume deployment permits producers to realize scale economies, new markets to open up for technology improvements and follow-on innovations, and the environmental commons to improve given more prevalent use of low or zero-emissions power-generation systems.

That argument, however, has hardly carried the day in the West. Instead, three other points have dominated discourse, including in the 2016 presidential election. First, the rapid emergence of Chinese energy technology suppliers is understood to signify a violation on China's part of global trade norms and the rules of fair competition that it itself agreed to by joining the World Trade Organization. In late 2012, the U.S. Department of Commerce imposed punitive tariffs on China-based solar PV cell producers after concluding that such firms were capturing global export markets by "dumping" products and unfairly undercutting the viability of competitors from other nations. The specific accusation was that Chinese PV manufacturers were selling in U.S. markets at between 18 and 250 percent below their own production costs, behavior enabled, the Department of Commerce argued, by countervailing Chinese state subsidies of approximately 15 to 16 percent of these firms' production costs.[7] The tariffs were both broadened and further elevated (to an average level of approximately 52 percent) in December 2014.[8] The European Union (EU) imposed similar provisional antidumping duties in mid-2013. The bottom line is that the United States and the EU have officially taken the position, at least with respect to solar PV, that Chinese commercial competitiveness stems from unfair trade practices, and comes at the expense of American and European industry.

Second, there is widespread belief that Chinese "green tech" production, in addition to being heavily subsidized, is expanding on the basis of intellectual property theft, at least some of which is state-supported. In May 2014, the U.S. Department of Justice indicted five Chinese military officers for conspiring to hack into and steal proprietary commercial information from two U.S.-based firms: an Oregon-based production facility of the German Solar PV firm Solar-World, and Pennsylvania-based nuclear technology supplier Westinghouse (which is owned by Toshiba).[9] The indictment asserts that PLA hackers in the former case stole pricing information that enabled Chinese solar PV producers to outcompete SolarWorld, and in the latter case stole confidential design specifications (for pipes, pipe supports, and pipe routing) from Westinghouse that if transferred to competitors in China would allow those competitors to jump into global markets without having to develop their own in-house designs.

Of course, the situation is complex, in no small part because Westinghouse is currently building four of its state-of-the-art AP1000 reactors in China in explicit partnership with Chinese nuclear technology suppliers. A substantial element of each of those plant-build contracts involves agreed-upon technology transfers and shared design efforts between Westinghouse and its Chinese partners, most of which are state-owned.

Regardless of the details, though, FBI director James Comey captured prevailing sentiment in the United States when he declared in an October 5, 2014, *60 Minutes* television interview, "I liken them [Chinese hackers] a bit to a drunk burglar. They're kickin' in the front door, knocking over the vase, while they're walking out with your television set. . . . Their strategy seems to be: 'We'll just be everywhere all the time. And there's no way they can stop us.' "[10]

Third, stemming from the above, there is a widespread view that what the Chinese are doing does not constitute innovation. That is, they may be producing a lot of green tech products, and those products may ultimately prove useful for ameliorating environmental degradation and resource scarcity, but the production ramp-up itself is not based on new types of know-how, new forms of proprietary capabilities, or anything else that could seriously be considered "innovation." Instead, precisely because the Chinese are growing on the basis of subsidies and theft, their production activities—essentially duplicative of what advanced industrial incumbents mastered long ago—contribute neither new knowledge nor new product solutions to the global commons. The new Chinese upstarts simply grab what rightfully should have been the incumbents', be they American, German, Danish, or players from any other advanced industrial nation. Thus, in 2010 when then–Secretary of Energy Steven Chu characterized China's successes in clean energy technology as a "Sputnik moment" for the United States, the meaning—regardless of his intent—was fairly clear.[11] China represented a commercial and technological threat, one that had to be addressed and countered.

The point of this paper is not to thoroughly invalidate this perspective. After all, there is considerable empirical basis for believing that IP theft in China is rampant, that the Chinese government explicitly uses technology transfer as an instrument of national industrial development (after all, it publicly acknowledges the aspiration in its five-year plans), and Chinese firms routinely receive subsidization. And, there is equally valid evidence for arguing that IP theft has happened in every industrializing nation since Britain in the late eighteenth century,[12] that technology transfer has long been an instrument of industrial policy in the West,[13] and that firms worldwide, including in the United States, are today, and have long been, frequent recipients of state subsidies.[14] Why would we possibly think that China is an exception? Indeed, one could argue that the most powerful upholders of the current global economic order—nations like the United States, Japan, and Germany—all have engaged in, or even currently engage in, the very kinds of industrial promotion efforts that when observed in the contemporary Chinese case are taken as evidence of China's rejection of global norms. The point is that if historical comparisons to nations like the United States and Japan are at all indicative, nothing in China's current industrial posture—including its IP violations, its subsidization efforts, or even its industrial espionage—is inconsistent with China's emergence as a great power supporter, rather than disrupter, of the contemporary Bretton Woods economic order.

Even that relatively optimistic observation, however, leaves us in a seemingly intractable dilemma. Reasonable individuals today, no matter where they reside, can agree that climate change represents an existential challenge to humankind. They can similarly agree that technology, while not a "magic bullet" solution in itself, has been, and will continue to be, part of every conceivable solution for sustaining human existence on Earth. But so too can reasonable people assert that every nation has a rightful aspiration to be not just a consumer of these technologies, but also a producer. No forward-looking society can be expected to take a complete pass on trying to become a supplier of the key technologies that will likely drive future global economic growth.

Thus, whatever we think of the claims and counterclaims about who exactly is violating which international norms and global trading regimes, we are left with what appears to be a typical "tragedy of the commons"[15] problem. Everybody recognizes that we share a constrained ecological commons, one that cannot endure rising levels of greenhouse gas emissions, but at the same time, no major industrial nation is willing to back off its demand to be a technology seller as well as consumer. Hence, even though the biggest polluters like China and the United States may be willing to make broad commitments to limit emissions, far more attention—and far more actual policy making—gets directed toward self-serving industrial policies and "beggar thy neighbor" protectionism. In a fashion that can arguably be considered rational, short-term national interest ends up trumping long-term global interest. It is a straightforward prisoner's dilemma.

The argument of this chapter, however, is that this prisoner's dilemma—this typical common resource problem in which various claimant nations seem to be competing in ways that defy their long-term collective interests, and seem to be doing so in an international commercial arena seemingly devoid of trust—reflects but one part of reality. Indeed, what is so fascinating and puzzling is that this zero-sum, competitive pattern is unfolding simultaneously alongside at least three other phenomena that do not share such zero-sum characteristics. The phenomena are as follows:

1. The development within Chinese industry today of unique, world-leading innovative capacities surrounding certain types of technology production, including in the renewable energy domain. In short, Chinese industry today is doing something new. What Chinese firms are producing, and how they are producing, reflects more than just subsidization or basic factor cost advantages (that is, lower labor costs, cheaper capital, and the like). Subsidies exist, as do some factor cost advantages, but the point is that those advantages have been coupled with knowledge such that firms now possess proprietary capabilities.

2. Much of this innovative activity is happening in deep partnership with foreign firms, partnerships that involve far more than just one-way technology transfers followed by duplication and mimicry. Rather, the partnerships involve highly networked interactions, extensive coordination among the various players, joint development of knowledge, and multi-directional learning across

international borders. While the Chinese are learning from foreign partners through these interactions, foreign partners are now learning from the Chinese as well.

3. In the above-described networks, skill upgrading by Chinese firms is in some cases complementing and enabling skill upgrading by their foreign partners. Put somewhat differently, the innovative capacity possessed by some Chinese firms is proving both necessary and useful for unlocking other types of innovative capacity in their foreign partners. Hence, at least some advanced industrial firms, through their interactions with Chinese partners, and through the learning they glean as a result, get propelled forward into new areas of proprietary knowledge, new types of products, and new business domains. In this sense, we are arguably witnessing on the innovation front, including in the green tech domain, a sort of analogue to Kaname Akamatsu's traditional "flying geese" model of regional economic development.[16] Now, though, the firm-level networks are global rather than just regional, the interactions involve deep knowledge sharing and technology co-development instead of just arms-length trade, and the outcomes involve not just growth, but completely new industrial know-how and knowledge generation.

Simply describing these three phenomena is imperative, for their existence seems to be poorly understood and rarely acknowledged by observers more focused on interstate competition and rivalry. But just as important analytically, the simultaneous appearance of such divergent patterns of international interaction—intense geopolitical economic rivalry on the one hand, and equally intense commercial cooperation on the other—raises fundamental questions about the nature of international order. Interstate economic rivalry and its whole "tragedy of the commons" quality is purported to derive from the deficit of trust and absence of a sovereign rule maker that ostensibly characterizes the global arena. Yet, in some of the same industrial sectors over which rival states are currently battling, companies from those very rivals are cooperating with each other, apparently on the basis of trust. How could this be? How could it all be happening simultaneously? And, what does this say about the assumptions we bring to bear about the fixedness or mutability of the international order?

CHINESE COMMERCIAL INNOVATION

It has become a truism to assert that Chinese technology firms invent no new products and realize no major scientific breakthroughs. The position is empirically defendable (as it would generally have been for Japanese firms during Japan's period of rapid industrial catch-up, U.S. firms during America's period of rapid industrial catch-up, and so on). It says nothing, however, about whether the Chinese innovate commercially. Commercial innovation can be understood broadly to describe activities surrounding the introduction of new products at reasonable (commercially viable) cost, or the reintroduction of existing products at substantially lower cost. Innovation is not the same as invention. Indeed, innovation frequently describes the activities or know-how needed to translate inventions into commercially viable products. This translation often involves proprietary knowledge about how to redesign prototypes into objects that can be manufactured at scale, how to integrate new and old technologies into actual products, how to establish effective sourcing networks for componentry, how to manage large-scale production operations, and how to add new functionality to existing products, just to name a few. The fact that so many inventions worldwide get sold off or licensed at very low prices—meaning that inventors often fail to reap substantial commercial rewards when their inventions find their way into products— underscores how challenging (and potentially lucrative) many of these post-invention, translational activities really are. Whether manifested as new product development, new process development,[17] or new product architecture,[18] they constitute the bulk of what is typically understood as commercial innovation.

Within this general domain, Chinese firms of late have met particular success in what Loren Brandt and Eric Thun term the "fight for the middle,"[19] the transformation of existing high-tech products into much less expensive variants. Because of their low cost, these variants—whether in automobiles, construction equipment (i.e., front loaders, excavators, and so on), machine tools,[20] motorcycles,[21] smart-phones,[22] solar PV equipment, or wind turbines[23]—do more than just supply existing middle-tier customers. Rather, they create entirely new middle-tier markets, making available products to customers who had never previously imagined being able to afford them. In essence, the redefinition of the product creates new demand, and often does so on a massive scale. In a number of industrial and consumer product categories, middle-tier markets—often concentrated in emerging economies, including China—are among the fastest growing worldwide. Profit margins are often narrow, but the total volume of product demanded is high, thus creating opportunities too lucrative for high-tech producers to ignore.

My own research team[24]—in a manner consistent with Brandt and Thun, Breznitz and Murphee,[25] and Ge and Fujimoto—argues that the success of Chinese firms in capturing these opportunities involves more than just factor cost advantages or government protection. Such price advantages are certainly present in China, but so too are they in many other economies that have *not* realized the kind of industrial upgrading and commercial success that China has. My team has sought in particular to delve deeply into the operations of the firm to understand exactly what kinds of capabilities are being developed to translate favorable factor cost conditions into actual profit-making activities.[26]

The capabilities we have identified include the following:

First, there is the ability to manage teams of product development engineers operating at the intersection of upstream product definition and downstream manufacturing. These teams take existing high-tech products sold by advanced industrial incumbents, and find ways to redesign them so as to achieve "cost out" (cost reduction). Redesign efforts in some cases involve changes in the entire product architecture, thus allowing highly engineered components to be swapped out for much simpler, more standardized, and far less expensive variants that are available locally in China. In other cases, the redesigned (or reengineered) products are changed so as to make them much easier to manufacture. And in still other cases, expensive customer interfaces are dropped in lieu of much simpler options that do not involve things like computer displays and complex software.

In all such cases of engineering-intensive "cost out," the real challenge involves accomplishing redesigns without utterly compromising the performance, functionality, and reliability of the product. That a number of Chinese firms have been able to achieve this across diverse manufacturing sectors (that is, Sany in construction apparatus, Huawei in telecommunications equipment, Xiaomi in smartphones, Meyer in optical sorters, Goldwind in wind turbines, and so on) is remarkable. As respondents in the global wind turbine sector reported to our team, Chinese mid-size turbines by the end of the last decade may have been 10 percent less reliable than multinational variants, but they proved 30 percent less expensive to manufacture.[27] Many customers are willing to forgo a certain amount quality in exchange for economy, particularly if the product is "good enough."

Second, there is the ability to scale production. In highly technical analyses, scholars have noted that the cost advantages enjoyed by Chinese solar PV producers stem less from government subsidies (i.e., low-priced capital) than from scale economies realized in the fabrication and component sourcing process.[28] But realizing such scale economies requires expertise. The supplier network in many Chinese regional ecosystems is dense and highly competitive, thus permitting final assemblers significant cost advantages. Those assemblers, however, particularly when they are managing large-scale, high-volume production facilities, must navigate through that density to identify consistently reliable, high-quality suppliers. Moreover, once the componentry enters the plant, throughput must be maintained, production facilities must be kept online, and product quality (yields) must remain consistently high. These high-volume operations have very little fault tolerance, thus making them risky to enter, and challenging to master commercially. It is part of the reason why Chinese PV production is dominated by a relatively small number of firms. It is also the reason why in other sectors such as consumer electronics, single assembly firms like Foxconn are so critical for the production of brand-name smartphones and laptop computers.[29]

Third, there is the willingness and ability to meet unique preferences associated with middle-tier customers. Such customers, whether household or industrial in nature, and especially in China, are at once impatient, frugal, and sophisticated. For any given product, they demand new functionality, unprecedentedly low price, and rapid delivery. Unwilling to wait for the development of a fully mature, reliable product, they instead want it now (even if "now" means the product won't perform perfectly), they want it cheap, and they want immediate service when bugs or other problems are uncovered. And, meanwhile, they exhibit little brand loyalty, jumping at a moment's notice to competitors' products when new functionality, better reliability, or lower prices are offered. The pattern obtains in products ranging from mobile phone handsets (where the purchaser is a household consumer and the product life cycle may amount to only a few months) all the way to wind turbines (where the purchaser is a commercial power generator and the product life cycle is counted in decades).[30]

Fourth, overarching everything is the ability to deliver at an extremely rapid tempo. In other words, much of Chinese commercial innovation involves the ability to move quickly. Products are redesigned for cost-out with great rapidity. Component sourcing networks are set up quickly. Manufacturing gets scaled up (and sometimes scaled down) with rapidity and flexibility, the hallmark capability of Foxconn, the world's largest consumer electronics assembler. And, when the middle-tier customers in the world's fastest-growing markets make demands—for example, to have an optical sorter for rice be reengineered to sort corn—the producers are close enough to hear the request, they listen, they quickly translate the request into a directive to their R&D operation, and they just as quickly retool production to accommodate the new designs that the R&D staff churns out. The resulting new products are then put into the field, often with some bugs and stability problems, but the problems get immediately addressed by service personnel based in close proximity to the customer. Tempo is of vital importance in markets that open and close in short time frames, a quality that describes markets for products as varied as wind turbines and industrial-sized food processing equipment.

Of course, one could ask why advanced industrial incumbents do not jump at these opportunities. Why should the Chinese be any better at cost-out, scaling, customer accommodation, or high-tempo operations, particularly given that incumbents have far more experience in all of the given product areas? That none of this seems particularly challenging lends credence to the idea that Chinese firms embody no unique knowledge or know-how, but are just hiding behind subsidies and trade barriers.

Of course, similar accusations were leveled against the Japanese in the 1970s and 1980s. Subsequently, it came to be recognized that Japanese firms, whatever degree of protection they received, did develop a particular way of producing, what today is routinely termed the "Toyota Production System" or, more generally, the "lean revolution."[31] Describing what "lean" production entails in the abstract is a trivial exercise. One can talk simply about rearrangements of machines on the shop floor, steady attention to waste reduction, "Kaizen" management teams, and so on. Nothing of this seems like high-end science. Yet, actually achieving lean production on the shop floor to this day represents a major challenge to firms, a fact underscored by the myriad consultancies that now teach lean manufacturing to industrial customers worldwide.

It is reasonable to suggest that what Chinese firms are doing, while not the same as "lean," is analogous. It signifies a different way of doing things, a kind of commercial innovation—or a collection of innovative approaches—that permits both the creation and capture of new value.

That this value is "real" is in part suggested by the fact that some advanced industrial incumbents are trying to learn from the Chinese, and are finding the process challenging. My team has worked closely with several Western high-tech manufacturing firms that recognize what the Chinese are doing as innovative, but find it difficult to duplicate, even when these foreign firms have operations in China. In many cases, not unlike what happened when American automakers were confronted by Japanese lean production, Western multinationals are inhibited by problems of organizational culture. For example, with regard to redesign for cost-out, what Chinese engineers may see as opportunities for savings and simplification, the original Western designers just dismiss as "dumbing down" or a compromise of an already optimal design. Similarly, Western R&D staffs may acknowledge the need to respond to a low-end or middle-tier customers' request for new product functionality, but they are organizationally unwilling or incapable of moving quickly. They tend to emphasize the reliability and certainty of the new engineering solution rather than the speed at which they can get it out the door. Moreover, they often respond from the perspective of technology experts, telling the customer that what s / he wants is neither necessary nor possible. Meanwhile, by the time they actually get around to delivering, a Chinese competitor has already jumped in with a solution, one that may not be as refined as what the Westerner might deliver, but one that is "good enough." The sole point of these accounts is to emphasize that they are coming from foreign managers themselves—people who believe that Chinese innovation is real, and who are operating within China under many of the same factor cost conditions, but who find it organizationally difficult to duplicate their Chinese counterparts' performance. Many outsiders now see that there exists in the Chinese business ecosystem a complex opportunity for learning (one that extends across management, engineering, R&D, and services), but the learning curve is steep and dynamically changing.

SINO-FOREIGN JOINT INNOVATION

Learning for some American and European firms simply comes though a process of localization into the Chinese business environment. In other words, the foreign firm acquires a local Chinese company (or enters a joint venture) in order to get a foothold into the Chinese domestic market, while at the same time gleaning some of the operational techniques that seem to accord Chinese firms advantages in middle-tier markets.

Yet my research team's findings suggest that learning entails interactions more complex than just in-country observation or the purchase of an in-country business unit. Instead, we are now witnessing many cases of multi-firm, joint innovation, including in some of the most sophisticated high-tech sectors. While a full discussion is beyond the scope of this paper, several variants, all drawn from the new energy sector, will be discussed below.

First, there is the time-honored tradition of capital equipment suppliers seeking new customers in emerging markets. When textile mills began to arise in the early nineteenth century in places like Norway to challenge the monopoly held by Lancashire spinners, they did so not primarily by stealing secrets or otherwise mimicking the production techniques of their English brethren. Rather, their rise was directly enabled by English capital equipment producers—the manufacturers of spinning machines and entire textile production lines—who were eager to expand their machine sales into new markets, and train new customers in how to use those machines.[32] This is an important example, for it shows that while producers in one nation may be hostile to the emergence of competitors in another nation, the equipment suppliers to those producers may be more than happy to sell their machines in new markets, thus directly fostering and enabling new overseas competitors. Indeed, the equipment suppliers, once their home market gets saturated, aggressively seek such markets, and endeavor purposively to build up a new customer base—whether through consultancy services or training in equipment use—when such a base is lacking in previously untapped overseas locales. The machine sellers are perfectly situated to provide such training, for they have witnessed in detail how production operates in their home-country customers, ostensibly the world's leaders.

We witness something comparable today with the Chinese solar PV industry. China's largest, most sophisticated solar cell and module manufacturers acquire most of their production equipment from leading Western suppliers. For "best-in-class" production line vendors like Applied Materials—which provides equipment for solar PV manufacturing, flat-panel display production, and silicon chip fabrication—roughly 90 percent of their solar PV customer base in recent years has been in China. Companies like Applied Materials supply not just state-of-the-art production equipment, but also state-of-the-art automation software, maintenance services, and upgrades for installed base equipment. This author is in no position to judge whether Chinese solar PV producers have stolen proprietary business information from U.S. or European competitors. What is clear, though, is that that the knowledge and equipment needed to produce at a cutting-edge level is available for legal purchase in global markets.

The relationship between firms like Applied Materials and their China-based customers, as all the training and upgrading services suggest, goes beyond just arms-length transactions. On the shop floor of Chinese solar PV "fabs" (fabrication plants), engineers from equipment suppliers work hand in hand with the PV fab's own engineers, and the learning is often multi-directional. The equipment suppliers provide upgrades and training. At the same time, they can observe how their equipment is being used at scale, the faults that develop, and the new opportunities that might exist for upgrading. Interaction with major customers ends up being an important driver of the equipment supplier's own innovation process. Meanwhile, whether in flat-panel display, solar PV, or silicon chip fabrication, production engineers employed by the customer often use their own in-house knowledge to modify the equipment they purchase. By being present on the shop floor, the supplier can observe this, and learn from the modification.

As in many business relationships, though, supplier-buyer relationships here, deep as they are, involve combinations of trust and competition. Points are occasionally reached at which the buyer no longer lets the supplier see or service equipment on the shop floor that s / he had previously installed. In such cases, the buyer's modifications embody enough of the buyer's proprietary process knowledge to make the buyer reluctant to share that information with the supplier. There is always a concern that the supplier will carry the information over to the next customer (most likely in China), just as has been done since time immemorial. This is just a normal pattern of business, and more often than not, one conducted among people who have long known one another in tight networks. Indeed, the senior management teams of Chinese solar PV firms are larded with individuals who had previously worked for equipment suppliers like Applied Materials, Lam Research, or ASML.

In a second pattern, particularly when the sale of large-scale technology systems is involved—as is the case with civilian nuclear power plants—the ability and willingness of the technology vendor to transfer knowledge to the buyer, often a government entity, is central to the vendor's ability to win the deal.[33] And it is certainly not uncommon for former recipients of technology transfers to later become major global sellers and disseminators of technology themselves. French nuclear firm Framatome, for instance, received extensive guidance on equipment manufacturing from Westinghouse in the 1970s. Several years later, Framatome would deliver reactor pressure vessels and manufacturing know-how to the United Kingdom as a partner of Westinghouse.[34] Westinghouse, much like its French competitor Areva, made comparable technology transfer commitments when it sold four AP1000 nuclear power plants to China in 2007. This author has no basis on which to judge the U.S. Department of Justice's claim that Chinese hackers stole information from Westinghouse about plant piping. However, in the technology transfer agreements surrounding nuclear power plant sales, it is routine for technology vendors, in this case Westinghouse, to outsource the detailed design work for things like plant piping and wiring to their local partner, in this case the Shanghai Nuclear Engineering Research and Design Institute (SNERDI). Similarly, French technology vendor Areva's Chinese partner for such tasks has been the China Nuclear Power Technology Research Institute (CNPRI). It is conceivable that technology vendors are willing to outsource detailed design for relatively standard areas such as wiring and piping, because these areas do not involve the kind of overarching conceptual knowledge needed to design and optimize the entire plant or organize relations with major subsystem providers (many of whom are other multinational firms).

What is interesting today is that beyond these sorts of standard supplier-buyer technology transfers, foreign nuclear technology vendors and their Chinese partners have begun to team up to bid jointly on third-party overseas nuclear deals. In June 2012, Westinghouse teamed with its Chinese partner, the State Nuclear Power Technology Corporation, to bid for a plant-build project in the United Kingdom. Areva, in turn, teamed with its Chinese partner, China Guangdong Nuclear Power Holding Company, to bid on the same project. In each case, the foreign lead firm was utilizing its partner's ability to produce plant subsystems at low cost, as well as the partner's ability to provide financing, in order to offer a more attractive bid than the lead firm could generate on its own. Such collaborative bids between highly networked advanced industrial nuclear plant designers and emerging market subsystem suppliers are increasingly becoming the norm in the civilian nuclear power industry.

At a third level, the relationship between Chinese firm and foreign partner extends even deeper into the technology origination process. Here, a good example involves the relationship between Innovalight, a Silicon Valley start-up launched in 2002, and Shanghai-based JA Solar, one of the world's largest fabricators of solar cells and modules. JA Solar is a state-of-the-art producer, but it operates in an intensely competitive environment in China. Its competitors all use essentially the same state-of-the-art production lines (supplied by the same handful of overseas vendors), all produce high-quality products, and all must operate with very narrow profit margins. The name of the game in this industry is to simultaneously achieve extremely high production volumes and extremely high production efficiencies. Slight changes in the profit margin can have major implications for the firm's bottom line and its competitive position vis-à-vis counterparts in the industry. Such changes can be achieved through better management of scale on the fab floor (resulting in fewer faults and higher product yields), or through better management of scale with respect to suppliers (resulting in lower input prices). The profit margin can also be widened through performance enhancements to the product. That is, if new technologies can be added to the solar module to make it generate electricity more effectively, then a slightly higher price can be charged. While competitors will eventually learn to copy the technology, being a first-mover allows the firm a window of opportunity to capture higher-than-normal revenue. Put simply, firms like JA Solar have an incentive to absorb new technologies into their production process as quickly as possible, as long as the absorption can be done efficiently without undermining the plant's overall product yields.

Into that picture entered Innovalight, a U.S. firm that had invented a nanomaterial silicon ink with potential applications (as a component) in the solar PV, flat-panel display, and silicon chip industries. With funding from the U.S. Department of Energy and in cooperation with the U.S. National Renewable Energy Laboratory, Innovalight was able to demonstrate that its silicon ink could increase the efficiency of solar cells by 7 percent.[35] Yet, while Innovalight could confidently say how its material could affect the performance of a single cell, the firm lacked the knowledge needed to apply the material at scale in a commercial solar PV fab. Could the ink be applied at reasonable cost? Could product yields be maintained? How would the application impact other parts of the production process? Without answers to these questions, the silicon ink would remain an interesting invention, but not a commercially viable product. Further product development—innovation, essentially—would be required.

Innovalight eventually sought to partner with Chinese solar PV producers to commercialize the ink. Several of those partners were unwilling, for they knew that developing the ink would require having Innovalight engineers spend considerable time on the shop floor of their fabs. The concern was that if Innovalight engineers observed how they, the solar PV fabricator, were applying the ink, those engineers would then transfer the information to other China-based solar PV producers who would become Innovalights next customers. Ironically in this case, it was the Chinese, rather than the foreigners, who were most concerned with IP theft (theft of their process knowledge).

Ultimately, Innovalight in 2010 found a partner in JA Solar, with whom it signed a three-year contract for the supply of silicon ink, as well as a strategic agreement for the joint development of high-efficiency cells (involving the application of the ink).[36] Under this agreement, JA Solar and Innovalight engineers worked together on the shop floor to develop the ink application process, ensure its reliability, and optimize the tooling necessary to fully integrate the component into the cell fabrication process. In essence, they commercialized the product collaboratively.

JA Solar arguably benefited during this three-year period by having sole access to the newly commercialized silicon ink. Able during this period to sell a higher efficiency cell than its competitors, JA Solar presumably realized gains in its bottom line.

For Innovalight, the benefits were more tangible. By commercializing its ink with JA Solar, Innovalight established itself as a player in the global solar industry, and began licensing its technology to other solar manufacturers. Having demonstrated its value, Innovalight in 2011 was acquired by Dupont, which was already a supplier of metal pastes and solar cell backing films to solar PV fabricators. With silicon ink now added to its product portfolio, Dupont has subsequently emerged as one of the world's largest suppliers of high-end componentry to the global solar PV industry. As with Applied Materials, the vast bulk of Dupont's PV customers are based in China.

COMPLEMENTARY INDUSTRIAL UPGRADING INTO THE EXTENDED FUTURE

Whenever Chinese and foreign firms collaborate, and particularly when that collaboration extends into deep forms of knowledge sharing and joint innovation, the possibility always exists for zero-sum gains and losses. With IBM's announcement in 2015 of technology licensing agreements with Chinese partner Teamsun, concerns have been raised yet again about U.S. firms giving away the keys to the kingdom, caving into Chinese governmental demands, and compromising U.S. interests.[37]

But there is another possibility as well—that through these networked interactions, foreign and Chinese firms are all upgrading simultaneously, effectively moving up together, and moving up apace, along a common ladder of industrial development and growth. Again, the metaphor would be something akin to the "flying geese" model originally used to describe complementary growth through the interactions of East Asian economies arrayed along different points of the income spectrum. Here, though, the phenomenon would pertain to varying forms of value creation and innovative capacity across firms operating at different levels of technological sophistication and industrial development.

The possibility is particularly important today, since numerous observers believe that we are at present experiencing another industrial revolution, one in which the management of information and data—rather than the management of physical production—is becoming the key locus for commercial power and value creation. Of course, prominent voices of doubt can still be heard.[38] People like PayPal cofounder Peter Thiel and economists Tyler Cowan and Robert Gordon all argue that worldwide technology innovation has effectively plateaued and stagnated in recent decades, thus calling into question the likelihood of any soon-to-be-realized massive productivity payoff from the IT revolution.[39]

Many other observers, however, are fully on board with the idea that we are living through an era of dramatic and accelerating change. Eric Bynjolfsson and Andrew McAfree argue that the physical technologies of the IT revolution—computers, routers, fiber-optic networks—are really just now being coupled with the type of algorithmic advances that allow those technologies to be used to their full potential.[40] In other words, only now are we beginning to realize breakthroughs in data analytics, machine learning, artificial intelligence, and smart automation—the kinds of advances that give real meaning to terms like "big data," "the internet of things," "advanced manufacturing," "additive manufacturing," and "Industry 4.0."

To the extent this is true, Chinese innovation, which is leading to massive cost reductions in the manufacture of physical products, potentially does more than just challenge or otherwise disrupt Western incumbents. Rather, it provides them impetus—and a platform—to move up into higher-value, innovation-intensive data collection and management domains. Developing country innovation, in effect, becomes both a motivator and enabler for advanced industrial innovation. The Chinese move up, but so too do the Americans, Europeans, and Japanese.

My research team has identified some empirical evidence for this phenomenon. At a fairly straightforward level, one can point to the Apple-Foxconn relationship, in which the cost efficiencies of a China-based assembler permit tablet computers and smartphones to become available to a wide swath of the world's consumers. Apple, then, moves up into music streaming, cloud-based health monitoring services, and wearable devices. Google and Facebook, meanwhile, transform the customer into a product by gleaning data about the customer's buying habits, mobility patterns, and social preferences, and then developing commercial applications that respond to those data.

A similar pattern can be discerned in the civilian nuclear power sector. It is likely the case that Chinese firms—as their German, French, and Korean counterparts had done earlier—will become global suppliers of key nuclear power plant subsystems, and even entire plant architectures. At the same time, just as the cost of these subsystems has come down (in part because of Chinese participation), Western incumbents—and a number of Western tech start-ups—have moved rapidly into newly emerging information technology domains associated with, but not always exclusive to, the nuclear sector. Growth areas include the development of IT systems to perform overall project management during the plant-build phase, simulation software for modeling reactor performance under different technical conditions, and data-sensing systems for optimizing plant performance and managing preventive maintenance.

Along roughly similar lines, we now see Boeing moving from being a traditional fabricator of aluminum airplanes to being an IT systems provider for its newest "electric" jet, the 787. Given the complexity and scope of its electronic systems—including electronic flight controls, widespread data collection from aircraft subsystems, transmission of those data to ground-based centers, and subsequent analysis of those data for aircraft and total fleet optimization—the 787 has been jokingly described as a series of flying servers. Perhaps not surprisingly, then, Boeing, given its new IT capabilities, has moved into the smart grid business, including in collaboration with Chinese partners who are keen to deploy these energy-saving technologies in Chinese cities.

In the wind power sector, Danish firm Vestas now embeds sensors in virtually all of the turbines it sells globally. Those sensors collect data not just on individual turbine performance, but also on meteorological conditions, wind behavior, and a variety of other factors, including the impact of one turbine's performance on others in close proximity. These data become important not just for servicing and conducting preventive maintenance on individual turbines, but also on developing total solutions for power plant (wind farm) optimization. Vestas, like IMB in a sense, is increasingly becoming a solution provider rather than a traditional equipment manufacturer. It is not completely surprising that is happening as Chinese firms have increasingly squeezed cost—and, arguably, profit—out of the production of turbines. Nor is it surprising that Vestas, this once very traditional manufacturer of "windmills," is today running the largest supercomputing facilities in Denmark.

Broadly speaking, we can observe that across many industries, as Chinese innovation commodifies the physical machinery—that is, the wind turbines, the solar panel fabrication equipment, the nuclear reactor subsystems, and so on—new forms of value creation are being discovered (generally by foreign firms) surrounding the IT-intensive design tools needed to produce and deploy these technologies. Similarly, foreign equipment producers are increasingly embedding advanced sensing devices in their products, thus allowing the collection of data that can be used either to serve existing customers or create entirely new data-related products. Particularly in the energy technology domain, China is providing an opportunity to see whether what has been termed "Advanced Manufacturing" in the United States[41] or "Industry 4.0" in Germany is truly unfolding, and unfolding in a way that is driving new forms of industrial revolution for the twenty-first century.

CONCLUSION

It would be foolish to argue that economic competition between nations is thoroughly baseless, or that governments have no role to play in promoting national economic competitiveness. It would be equally foolish to argue that agreed-upon rules of global commerce—and violations of those rules—can and should be ignored, whether because such rules, as some argue, have often been violated historically, or because applying those rules to one's own nation is inconvenient.

However, this chapter has argued that we should be cognizant of the risks of overextending the paradigm of interstate economic rivalry. We should be equally careful about assuming that fixed conditions in the global system—namely, the absence of a sovereign, and the ongoing pursuit of national interest—make economic rivalry inevitable and omnipresent.

As this chapter has suggested, in the midst of interstate economic rivalry, we also witness several patterns involving intense commercial collaboration, joint knowledge development, and mutual learning between firms hailing from ostensibly rival nations. In ignoring these latter patterns, we risk falling into errors of analytical interpretation that can have real consequences for national policy. For example, to the extent we treat the emergence of the Chinese solar PV industry as exclusively an artifact of state industrial policy and commercial IP theft, we ignore the absolutely central, and completely legal role that Western suppliers of capital equipment and production solutions have played. In some ways, this is an old phenomenon, dating back to the first moments that new industries began arising in Europe to challenge British incumbents. Today, such patterns of above-board technology sales and exchanges of commercial information have only deepened. The entire phenomenon simply does not fit the traditional model of silo-like national industries competing against one another in the global arena.

As the solar PV case underscores (in a manner not so different from the case of textiles in early nineteenth-century Europe), some national producers clearly do appear silo-like, and they do compete head-to-head with foreign counterparts. Germany's SolarWorld clearly competes with, and is threatened by, comparable solar PV fabricators in China. At the same time, other national producers—production equipment suppliers, most notably—have every interest in developing new customers, essentially new silo-like manufacturing industries in emergent nations. For the production equipment suppliers, their survival is arguably imperiled if they do not create these new customers abroad. Without new customers, certainly the revenue to innovate, and possibly even the impetus to do so, evaporates.

What all of these cases suggest is that in advanced economies, economic stakeholders are not of one voice with regard to the rise of new competitors, whether in China or anywhere else. Some of those stakeholders clearly are threatened, and they seek redress. With respect to their industries, the dominant paradigm is clearly zero-sum interstate rivalry. Other stakeholders, however, welcome the rise, and even facilitate it. For their industries, the paradigm is one of cross-border collaboration, mutual learning, and complementary upgrading. Yet, all of these stakeholders can justifiably be understood to represent aspects of national interest economically.

How to navigate across these simultaneously existing, empirically defendable paradigms is a reasonable question for policy. Simply denying the existence of any one of these paradigms, however, is a recipe for trouble. Of course, as evidenced by the 2016 presidential campaign, particularly during times of economic downturn, the sensitive issue of jobs often overshadows other discussion. A series of questions now routinely come up, especially in high-tech domains. Doesn't the rise of Chinese technology firms, whether in the renewable energy sector or elsewhere, imperil jobs? Shouldn't the U.S. government do something about this? And, shouldn't U.S. firms that are enabling Chinese counterparts or otherwise offshoring some of their own production operations (often to China) be stopped? Isn't job protection a legitimate domain of national interest, not to mention a driver for rational interstate rivalry?

The job issue is complicated, to say the least. In domains like renewable energy technology production, Chinese firms have clearly expanded their position in global markets. One could, of course, argue that the Chinese have "taken" jobs from U.S. or European firms that failed to capture these new markets. But that position, by presuming that advanced industrial firms could have (or even should have) done this, discounts the possibility both that Chinese entrants had unique production capabilities, and that Western firms lacked them. The empirical evidence presented in this paper should make us skeptical about these sorts of assumptions.

The job issue is further complicated by the upside growth opportunities that have accrued to some Western firms that work in close collaboration with Chinese partners. As previously indicated, firms like Applied Materials and Dupont (and Dow Corning) have boomed by becoming technology or high-end component suppliers to the Chinese. For Westinghouse, as with any Western nuclear technology vendor, the Chinese market is a lifeline, all the more so since the shuttering of the civilian nuclear sector in Germany and the near shuttering in Japan. And for a tech start-up like Innovalight, its value as a company—and by extension, its ability to grow and expand an employee base—was realized only through its access to a Chinese partner's product development capabilities. And, finally, on an even simpler note, the fastest-growing segment of the U.S. renewable energy sector, at least in terms of job creation, is the solar panel installation business. While the sector has boomed in part due to U.S. government subsidies for solar PV consumers, it has also boomed because it is capturing additional margin from the availability of unprecedentedly inexpensive solar arrays coming from China. Again, to the extent one believes these low-priced arrays represent the fruits of Chinese innovation (as opposed to simply reflecting Chinese government subsidization), one could argue that the rise of Chinese producers has stimulated employment, particularly in technology-related service sectors (that is, solar PV installation) in a variety of global locales.

The job issue points to broader concerns about the role of manufacturing in advanced industrial systems. In recent years in the United States, numerous scholars, not to mention Donald Trump during his presidential campaign, have sought to demonstrate the outsize role manufacturing plays in stimulating innovation,[42] expanding high-quality employment,[43] and undergirding national economic competitiveness.[44] Much of this scholarship is responding to both the substantial decline in manufacturing-related employment in recent decades in the United States, and the rise of new competitors in places like China. These works often take on a normative bent, calling for some kind of societal response to the declines at home and emergent challenges from abroad. The response need not be protectionist, but at the very least, it is expected to involve some sort of effort to revive that which is ostensibly declining, and bring back that which had wandered off abroad.

This chapter's findings again raise a cautionary note about such perspectives. While there is nothing intrinsically wrong with seeking to stimulate manufacturing, there *are* risks in equating reshoring (the bringing back of manufacturing activities from abroad) with an enhancement of U.S. innovative capacity. As this chapter has argued, the Chinese business ecosystem is now a repository for unique, manufacturing-related innovative capacity. Rather than pulling away and trying to compete from afar, an equally or more plausible response would involve leaning in and drawing closer, if only to learn the techniques and practices that the Chinese have developed.

Again, the analogy to Japanese lean manufacturing is important. For years, U.S. business denied the possibility that there was anything to learn from rising Japanese competitors. The rise was attributed to anything but knowledge—copying, IP theft, government subsidies, and so on. Many U.S. firms, assuming that they themselves embodied global best practice, for years closed themselves off to learning from new competitors. The situation changed only when U.S. firms lapsed into dire economic straits. Today, many years later, of course, regardless of how the Japanese economy is performing, lean production is widely recognized as not just a fundamental example of innovation, but also as a core managerial and operational competency that firms worldwide must master. To the extent we believe that the Chinese, too, have developed something equivalent to "lean," a "pro manufacturing" position in the United States should ostensibly emphasize not so much the countering of China, but rather an aggressive effort to learn from them.

In a somewhat deeper sense, though, this chapter raises questions about whether manufacturing really will "make America great again." I have suggested numerous cases in which some of the world's most sophisticated technology vendors—firms like IBM, Westinghouse, Siemens, Vestas, and Applied Materials—are propelling themselves forward from the supply of physical equipment to the supply of data intensive IT solutions, whether in the form of production line control software, IT-based project management and construction scheduling systems, power plant optimization solutions, or smart grid solutions. Some of this movement has been closely coordinated with Chinese firms that are increasingly either supplying or using the equipment upon which these data-based solutions reside.

Who is to say really that the innovation surrounding physical equipment is somehow more important than, or primary to, that which is happening in the virtual domain? We already know in the security domain—with the "Stuxnet" case, among others—that a weaponized computer virus may be more effective than traditional kinetic weapons in destroying hardened military facilities. Similarly, in the commercial world, why should we believe that a physical device somehow has more value than an IT solution or software, particularly if the software resides in the cloud, and can be accessed through many different types of devices?

The point is that a number of leading technology companies seem to believe that in the future, their most innovative products, their most important forms of proprietary knowledge, and their best opportunities for long-term value creation are primarily going to exist in the virtual domain. For many of these companies, close partnership with Chinese customers is an important vector for testing these hypotheses and building related commercial capacities. Many of these capacities have applications in the energy and environmental domain. Some might prove to be environmental game changers. As such, they might also prove to be drivers of national innovative capacity and commercial specialization.

The risk is that by overemphasizing the interstate rivalry paradigm, we will interpret these commercial partnerships and their concomitant technology development efforts not as opportunities for environmental remediation and national industrial upgrading, but instead as misguided decisions by U.S. firms to give away technology, enable foreign competitors, and appease a foreign rival state. That could prove to be a costly mistake not just for the global commons, but also for core U.S. national interests.

NOTES

This chapter is based on fieldwork supported by the U.S. Army Research Office and the Minerva Research Initiative of the U.S. Department of Defense.

1. "U.S.-China Joint Announcement on Climate Change," Beijing, November 12, 2014 (www.whitehouse.gov/the-press-office/2014/11/11/us-china -joint-announcement-climate-change).

2. That said, some within the environmental policy domain recognized the importance of the announcement. See, for example, Tim Boersma, "US-China Joint Announcement on Climate Change Is a Big Deal," November 13, 2014, *Brookings PlanetPolicy Blog* (www.brookings.edu/blogs/planet policy/posts/2014/11/13-us-china-joint-announcement-on-climate-change -boersma).

3. Michaela D. Platzer, "U.S. Solar Photovoltaic Manufacturing: Industry Trends, Global Competition, Federal Support" Congressional Research Service, January 27, 2015, p. 14.

4. "China was world's largest wind market in 2012," *Bloomberg New Energy Finance*, February 4, 2013 (http://about.bnef.com/press-releases/china-was -worlds-largest-wind-market-in-2012/).

5. Mycle Schneider and Antony Froggatt, "The World Nuclear Energy Status Report 2014," *World Nuclear Report,* July 2014 (www.worldnuclearreport .org/-2014-.html).

6. Alan C. Goodrich and others, "Assessing the Drivers of Regional Trends in Solar Photovoltaic Manufacturing," *Energy and Environmental Science* 6 (2013), pp. 2811–21; Ryan Wiser and Mark Bolinger, *2013 Wind Technologies Market Report* (U.S. Department of Energy / Lawrence Berkeley National Laboratory, August 2014), pp. 41–46 (http://emp.lbl.gov/sites/all/files/2013 -wind-technologies-market-report-ppt.pdf).

7. U.S. Department of Commerce / International Trade Commission, "Commerce Finds Dumping and Subsidization of Crystalline Silicon Photovoltaic Cells, Whether or Not Assembled into Modules from the People's Republic of China," October 10, 2012 (www.seia.org/sites/default/files /Solar%20Cells%20AD%20and%20CVD%20Fact%20Sheets.pdf).

8. U.S. Department of Commerce / International Trade Administration, "Commerce Finds Dumping of Imports of Certain Crystalline Silicon Photovoltaic Products from China and Taiwan and Countervailable Subsidization of Imports of Certain Crystalline Silicon Photovoltaic Products from China," December 16, 2014 (www.finance.senate.gov/imo/media/doc /Certain%20Crystalline%20Silicon%20Photovoltaic%20Products%20 Factsheet1.pdf).

9. U.S. District Court Western District of Pennsylvania, "United States of America v. Wang Dong, Sun Kailiang, Wen Xinyu, Huang Zhenyu, Gu Chunhui," Indictment, Criminal No. 14-118, May 1, 2014 (www.justice.gov /iso/opa/resources/5122014519132358461949.pdf).

10. CBS News, "FBI Director on Threat of ISIS, Cybercrime," *60 Minutes,* October 5, 2014.

11. U.S. Department of Energy, "Secretary Chu: China's Clean Energy Successes Represent Sputnik Moment for America," November 29, 2010 (http://apps1.eere.energy.gov/news/daily.cfm/news_id=20827).

12. See Peter Andreas, *Smuggler Nation* (Oxford University Press, 2014); Fritz Machlup and Edith Penrose, "The Patent Controversy in the Nineteenth Century," *Journal of Economic History* 10, no. 1 (May 1950), pp. 1–29.

13. Kristine Bruland, *British Technology and European Industrialization* (Cambridge University Press, 1989).

14. Louise Story, "As Companies Seek Tax Deals, Governments Pay High Price," *New York Times,* December 1, 2012. The article estimates that $25.5 billion in incentives are extended to manufacturing firms annually in the United States. Some analysts have suggested that relative to U.S. or German subsidies, particularly with respect to upstream R&D, Chinese subsidies in the solar PV sector have been fairly modest. See: Thilo Grau et al., "Survey of Photovoltaic Industry in Germany and China," *CPI Report,* March 2011.

15. Garrett Hardin, "The Tragedy of the Commons," *Science* 162 (December 1968), pp. 1243–48.

16. Kaname Akamatsu, "A Historical Pattern of Economic Growth in Developing Countries," *Journal of Developing Economies*, 1, no. 1 (1962), pp. 3–25.

17. For a description of process innovation in the Korean context, see: Alice H. Amsden, *Asia's Next Giant: South Korea and Late Industrialization* (Oxford University Press, 1989); Linsu Kim, *Imitation to Innovation: The Dynamics of Korea's Technological Learning* (Boston: Harvard Business School Press, 1997).

18. Rebecca M. Henderson and Kim B. Clark, "Architectural Innovation: The Reconfiguration of Existing Product Technologies and the Failure of Established Firms." *Administrative Science Quarterly* 35, no. 1 (1990), pp. 9–30; Dongsheng Ge and Takahiro Fujimoto, "Quasi-open Product Architecture and Technological Lock-in: An Exploratory Study on the Chinese Motorcycle Industry," *Annals of Business Administrative Science* 3, no. 2 (2004), pp. 15–24.

19. Loren Brandt and Eric Thun, "The Fight for the Middle: Upgrading, Competition, and Industrial Development in China," *World Development* 38, no. 11 (2010), pp. 1555–74.

20. Brandt and Thun provide in-depth analysis of autos, construction equipment, and machine tools.

21. See especially: Dongsheng Ge and Takahiro Fujimoto, "Quasi-open Product Architecture and Technological Lock-in: An Exploratory Study on the Chinese Motorcycle Industry," *ABAS: Annals of Business Administrative Science* 3, no. 2 (2004), pp. 15–24.

22. See especially: Dieter Ernst and Barry Naughton, "Global Technology Sourcing and Chian's Integrated Circuit Design Industry: A Conceptual Framework and Preliminary Research Findings," *East-West Center Working Papers, Economics Series* (Honolulu, HI: East-West Center, 2012).

23. Jonas Nahm and Edward S. Steinfeld, "Scale-up Nation: China's Specialization in Innovative Manufacturing," *World Development* 54 (February 2014), pp. 288–300.

24. In addition to myself, the team includes Jonas Nahm (postdoctoral fellow, Brown University), Florian Metzler (Ph.D. candidate, MIT), and Troels Beltoft (independent business consultant).

25. Dan Breznitz and Michael Murphee, *Run of the Red Queen: Government, Innovation, Globalization and Economic Growth in China* (Yale University Press, 2011).

26. Since 2012, the team has conducted 107 interviews in China in the wind power and solar PV industries, and an additional 117 interviews with wind- and solar power–related firms in Europe and the United States. In the Chinese nuclear power sector, we have conducted sixty-seven interviews

spread across both Chinese indigenous and multinational firms. We have also engaged in extensive participant observation in a handful of firms in the wind power sector and in capital equipment production (including in the food processing and optical sorting domains).

27. Edward S. Steinfeld and Troels Beltoft, "Innovation Lessons from China," *MIT Sloan Management Review*, Summer 2014.

28. Goodrich and others, "Assessing the Drivers of Regional Trends in Solar Photovoltaic Manufacturing."

29. See: Charles Duhigg and Keith Bradsher, "How the U.S. Lost Out on iPhone Work," *New York Times,* January 21, 2012.

30. Steinfeld and Beltoft, "Innovation Lessons from China."

31. For a quintessential statement of this, see James P. Womack, Daniel T. Jones, and Daniel Roos, *The Machine that Changed the World* (New York: Free Press, 2007). See also Edward S. Steinfeld, "China, High Tech, and the 'High Tempo Cost Out' Revolution," *Brookings TechTank Blog,* May 12, 2015. https://www.brookings.edu/blog/techtank/2015/05/12/china-high-tech -and-the-high-tempo-cost-out-revolution/

32. Bruland, *British Technology and European Industrialization.*

33. Florian Metzler and Edward S. Steinfeld, "Sustaining Global Competitiveness in the Provision of Complex Products and Systems: The Case of Civilian Nuclear Power Technology," in Richard Locke and Rachel Wellhausen, eds., *Production in the Innovation Economy* (MIT Press, 2014).

34. B.V. George, "The Establishment of PWR Technology in the United Kingdom in Support of the Sizewell B Project," in *Transactions of the Third International Conference on Nuclear Technology Transfer: ICONTT-III* (Madrid, 1985).

35. Bill Scanlon, "Silicon Ink is Spot On, NREL Experiments Show," NREL press release, 2011. (www.nrel.gov/news/features/feature_detail.cfm /feature_id=1596).

36. JA Solar, "JA Solar Signs Strategic Agreements with Innovalight for Joint Development of High Efficiency Solar Cells," 2010 (http://investors .jasolar.com/phoenix.zhtml?c=208005&p=irol-newsArticle&ID=1446 259&highlight=).

37. See Paul Mozur, "IBM Venture with China Stirs Concerns," *New York Times*, April 20, 2015.

38. For an overview of the debate, see "Has the Ideas Machine Broken Down?," *The Economist,* January 12, 2013.

39. Peter Thiel, "The End of the Future," *National Review,* October 3, 2011; Tyler Cowan, *The Great Stagnation* (New York: Dutton, 2011); Robert J. Gordon, "Does the 'New Economy' Measure Up to the Great Inventions of the Past?" *Journal of Economic Perspectives* 14, no. 4 (Fall 2000), pp. 49–74.

40. Erik Brynjolfsson and Andrew McAfee, *The Second Machine Age* (New York: W. W. Norton, 2014).

41. President's Council of Advisors on Science and Technology, "Report to the President on Capturing Domestic Competitive Advantage in Advanced Manufacturing. Executive Office of the President," Washington, D.C., 2012.

42. Gregory Tassey, "Rationales and Mechanisms for Revitalizing US Manufacturing R&D Strategies." *Journal of Technology Transfer* 35, no. 3 (2010), pp. 283–333.

43. Susan Helper, Timothy Krueger, and Howard Wial, "Why Does Manufacturing Matter? Which Manufacturing Matters? A Policy Framework," *Metropolitan Policy Program* (Brookings, February 2012).

44. Gary P. Pisano and Willy C Shih, *Producing Prosperity: Why America Needs a Manufacturing Renaissance* (Boston: Harvard Business Review Press, 2012).

FIVE

Concentrated Interests

China's Involvement with Latin American Economies

CYNTHIA A. WATSON

 Prime Minister Li Keqiang's tour of major South American capitals in May 2015 elicited substantial press coverage, significant pockets of national pride within the region, and an array of promises about Chinese investment in the region. In short, the trip looked much like Communist Party General Secretary Hu Jintao's visit to capitals in November 2004 coincident with that year's Asia Pacific Economic Cooperation forum in Santiago, Chile. On the surface, Li's visit might seem to indicate substantial expansion of bilateral economic interdependence between Latin America and the Middle Kingdom. By the end of 2015, China's loans to regional governments reached $29 billion.[1] This followed on commitments by President Xi Jinping to spend U.S.$250 billion in the region over the next decade, most notably saying it will build and finance a U.S.$10 billion railroad from west to east across South America to give Pacific port access for products from Brazil, a stunning change to South America's geographic reality.[2]

123

At the same time, suspicions continue cropping up in Africa and Latin America, and even Russia, that China's engagement in those regions amounts to new colonialism, hardly different from that of Europeans or Americans.[3] While most of the concerns voiced come from the countries receiving Chinese attention, a chorus of growing doubters in the Middle Kingdom are wondering whether the expanding array of loans, investments, and trade pacts are in China's interest as well.[4] And then there was the proposed railway across Mexico that was canceled over questions of fraud, misrepresentation, and malfeasance, as occurs with Chinese proposed interventions globally.[5]

Digging below the surface, however, the nature of the Chinese investment is not nearly as startling a shift in economic engagement as it would appear. Instead, the nature of Chinese investment remains concentrated in the following areas, rather than in the priorities that a government in the region might have set for its infrastructure (including employment of domestic labor): (1) industries producing energy and minerals to fuel China's voracious appetite for economic growth; (2) the foodstuffs that Latin America so easily produces now at precisely the time China seeks to import food rather than produce it domestically; and (3) the infrastructure necessary to get goods to the major ports, which will allow their export to the Pacific. The result includes a rising doubt in some quarters of region as to how this economic development is any better for the region than have been similar investment booms over the past two hundred years that still left the region badly enmeshed in a trade and political system that favored the investors rather than the producers. A decade after the tremendous boom of the 2000s, Latin American populations wonder where the believed economic maturation, diversification, and increased political respect went.

All of this is transpiring as China assumes much greater visibility as a player in the international community, at times taking positions clearly aimed at altering the international systemic status quo while at other instances unsure of the weight it can throw around and seemingly unable to anticipate some of the costs of its behavior. While the most obvious example of this latter phenomenon is in the evolving Chinese position on the land features of the South China Sea, China's role in what was called the Third World may be similar as the partners seek to understand whether China truly represents a fresh view of international relations or is behaving as others have behaved in prior generations.

This chapter explores Latin American views of the emerging Chinese economic role in the region, arguing that this is not a fundamentally different experience for Latin America from many other economic relationships over the past three hundred years. Instead, China's relationship is not one likely to create boundless opportunities, as some originally hoped, nor one without significant drawbacks for Beijing in a region where it traditionally has had little role.

China's increasing economic prowess coincides with greater confidence in the international sphere as a raft of scholarly articles and policy analysts have noted.[6] While the overwhelming majority of the manifestations of this resulting engagement around the world focuses outside of Latin America, the role that China is playing in this traditional U.S. sphere of influence is indisputable. This chapter will not endeavor to catalog each and every Chinese entry into the region, as Dr. R. Evan Ellis of the Strategic Studies Institute at the Army War College does that well and regularly.[7] Instead, I focus on the strategic implications of China's increasing engagement with economies in the region, identifying the differences in types of interaction and analyzing the implications for China, Latin American nations, and the United States for the future. Additionally, China's awkwardness as an emerging power plays into this discussion, although Beijing's expanding ties do appear to indicate sustained interests in Latin America.

Washington, while aware of increasing "outsider" activities, does not focus on the transformation of the region in the clear manner that Latin America and China do because it has been absorbed with other regions' concerns for a full generation, if not two. For Latin America, however, the expectation that another state's commitment to long-term association has held the prospect of opening the door to a new role in global activities. China was a new interlocutor with whom this transformation appeared possible.

An expectation that many analysts on both sides of the Pacific might have anticipated—that Latin America and China would be able to share political and economic sympathies—is not borne out by the current relationship, which is proving fraught with the same difficulties that affect other economic ties around the world. Put otherwise, China is proving far more traditional as a state interested in purchasing Latin America's lower-end products—food, energy, and material—rather than as a dramatic engine for helping the region move up the value chain. Perhaps the answer is as simple as unrealistic expectations on both sides, but the future of the Chinese engagement in the region's economies does not appear easy or as threatening as alarmists fear. But, as Damien Ma notes, in its interaction with the economies of the region, Beijing has already exploited about as much complementarity as is possible.[8]

While not the focus of this chapter, China's recent experiences in Latin America and Africa are relatively comparable, primarily because the two regions have experienced similar resource provider roles in the global system over the past several generations. The desires Beijing seeks to satisfy—the sense of achieving energy and resource self-sufficiency resulting from bilateral arrangements with states in Africa and Latin America, establishing relationships which will sustain longer-term ties for decades to come, and providing opportunities for Chinese to operate as an investor of last resort, as some of the regimes have exhausted the trust, if not the patience, of traditional lenders—all represent the significantly enhanced role China is playing in the twenty-first-century context.

HISTORICAL OVERVIEW

Vast technological changes in the twentieth and twenty-first centuries cannot alter the geographic reality that Latin America—whether Tierra del Fuego or Baja California or Lake Maracaibo—remains thousands of miles from China. This distance has transcended any serious desire by any government on either side of the Pacific to aim for the close political ties or natural friendliness that geographic proximity may foster. Put another way, Latin America did not play into China's interests through most of history nor vice versa, with the Chinese tributary system focused on those areas closest to the Middle Kingdom or, in the majority of the modern era after 1800, where outside powers had the ability to force their way into the Chinese system. Similarly, Latin America had significant dominant empires, whether the Mayan, Toltec, or Aztec in the northern reaches of the region or the Chibcha or Incan empires farther south, which dominated regional trade prior to European arrival in 1492 but proved unable to better the colonial powers that ruled between the sixteenth and early nineteenth centuries or the economic might of Britain or the United States in the subsequent years. In both China and Latin America, political and military weaknesses led to the states feeling fundamental weakness in their relationships with other partners, including those with whom they had trade relationships.

For Latin America during the post-independence period, poor governance and difficulties in establishing genuinely participatory political systems beyond a small elite in most countries, and an abundance of natural resources at a time of European, followed by U.S., economic expansion left the states of the region vulnerable to the elasticities of the international marketplace. With little military might and virtually constant desire to garner outside investment for infrastructure development through much of the nineteenth and twentieth centuries, Latin American states became sensitive to the belief that their dependence upon exporting minerals, foodstuffs, and energy compromised their sovereignty. Similar to China's strong national desire to protect sovereignty seemingly above virtually any other national objective, Latin American states adopted policies, particularly in the mid-twentieth century, and pursued economic growth strategies that frequently adversely affected overall growth but seemingly sustained nationalist fervor. These policies included import substitution industrialization (particularly under strongly nationalist regimes such as Juan Domingo Perón's in 1940s and early 1950s Argentina or the multi-decade rule of the *Partido Revolucionaro Institionario* [PRI] in Mexico), raising high tariffs on imported goods, requiring domestic majority ownership of enterprises; and the 1960s and 1970s policies of promoting economic nationalism under the anticommunist guise of the "national security states" of Argentina, Brazil, Chile, and Uruguay, which were codes for technocratic growth without political debate. While the economic history of each Latin American state is obviously unique, the overall pattern was one of profound frustration, upheaval, and disappointment, with the region lagging seriously behind many other parts of the world.[9]

The end of the Cold War in 1989 led to a reconsideration of the policies that often put the region at odds with the United States, which advocated a more open economic system. The Latin Americans were not entirely convinced that the "Washington Consensus," as the changed policies often became known, were the most appropriate for the region, but the lack of any alternative to U.S. economic and political dominance in the international system signaled the decline of the socialist model and the end of the alternative Soviet-driven bloc that had embraced Fidel Castro's Cuba since the early 1960s.

With the end of the bipolar ideological struggle characterizing the first four decades after World War II, Latin America more fully embraced both democratic principles and free-market economics. The Washington Consensus policies encouraged Latin American regimes to embrace and seek far greater opportunities for international trade than many had done in the past. The establishment of free trade agreements and organizations in the 1990s, highlighted by the European Union, then the North American Free Trade Agreement, pushed Latin America to be more receptive to policies on which it had traditionally vacillated. It bears remembering that the Washington Consensus became the driving term for Latin America's activities at a time when China had few economic links to this region.

LATIN AMERICA'S ECONOMIC DEPENDENCE ON COMMODITY-LED EXPORT GROWTH

Latin America has had a long history of dependence on exports as its comparative advantage in the international system, although many within the region would dispute that characterization, preferring instead the interpretation of the region as being exploited.[10] Part of the historic hesitation to embrace market economics came from the role the state played in Latin America's development; the other aspect was that the region felt that its products were always short-changed by elasticities of demand in global consumption. Dr. Raúl Prebisch's scholarship in the 1940s and 1950s attempted to set into motion policies that would leave the states in the region less vulnerable and more in control of their own development paths, but the import substitution industrialization model, similar to Maoist goals in the early years of the People's Republic, left the region further behind the development level of much of the world, especially the Asian states such as Singapore, Taiwan, Korea, and Japan. Latin America adopted, then rejected, various approaches to economic theory but retained its long-held historical skepticism about the efficacy of genuine global free trade for fear of further exploitation.

By the 1970s, after fits and starts at deciding the appropriate economic development scheme to best change the traditional backward nature of the region, Latin American nations generally found themselves not only far behind other comparable economies from the immediate post–World War II period but saw those other states, such as Korea, Japan, and Taiwan, had leapt far ahead and appeared on an unbroken glide path toward reaching economic prosperity. Latin America in the 1970s and 1980s had the additional burden of massive debt, incurred as a result of poor decisions that led to the tremendous reverse capital flows for debt repayment during the 1980s known as "the Lost Decade" for the region. As the world stumbled toward the end of the Cold War, Latin American economies were weak, political systems shaky, and the region desperately sought a new model that would preclude a repeat of the domestic upheavals resulting from the inability to chart a course for true economic development. More than anything else, Latin America—as had China during the rhetoric of the immediate aftermath of the 1949 Communist victory in the Civil War—wanted to believe it would decide its own future rather than have outsiders make decisions that left it weakened by the vagaries of the international system.[11]

CHINA'S RELATIONSHIP WITH THE REGION

Part of the reason that China's new role in Latin American economies is so noteworthy is that few ties between mainland China and the region predated the turn of the millennium. Chinese works did help build railroads across Peru and Brazil, as true in the United States, but the distance across the Pacific as well as the internal foci of all states involved prohibited greater involvement. Being of a Chinese minority in Latin America was as difficult as in any other part of the world. The Latin orientation for business was either north toward the gringos or northeast to Europe, at least partially because little complementarity of interests existed between struggling areas. China, for the overwhelming majority of the period Latin America has been independent since the 1820s, has been a region in decline rather than expansion beyond its traditional sphere.

Taiwan established the first sustained relations with Latin American countries in the ideologically charged 1940s and 1950s as it sought to accrue allies. This coincided with a period of Latin states turning inward, however, in creating import substitution economies in most states. Taiwan, in alliance with Washington, sought to craft relationships that would reinforce strongly anticommunist regimes. Many leaders within the region, in turn, adopted virulently anticommunist policies that allowed for no possible relationship with Maoist Beijing instead of embracing Chiang Kai-shek's Republic of China.

The Cuban issue illustrated China's place through much of modern Latin American economics. The Cuban regime became anathema to much of the region's leadership with Fidel Castro Ruz's embrace of socialism and links to the Soviet sphere in the early 1960s. Latin governments abhorred the atheism, including Mao's China, of communist governments, fearing they would try to subvert the region as true through the mid-1960s. The region appeared firmly in line with Washington's opposition to global communism and unwillingness to embrace anything other than market regimes.

But, Latin America was instrumental in reopening China's entry to the United Nations in 1971. Salvador Allende Gossens's socialist regime in Santiago first shifted diplomatic relations from Taiwan to the mainland a year before Beijing captured the Security Council seat and the region began following suit until all of the large states of the region had recognized Beijing and rejected Taiwan by 1984.[12] The switch coincided with two ironies that received little attention at the time. One was that the fiercely anticommunist governments in

Brazil, Uruguay, and Argentina were making ties with an avowedly socialist regime and second, this was when Ronald Reagan's regime believed the Cold War was at its hottest point. Taiwan retained diplomatic allies in Paraguay, Costa Rica, Panama, Nicaragua, El Salvador, Guatemala, and Honduras along with a handful of islands in the Caribbean and a few other outposts around the world.

Even with this change, economic ties between the PRC and Latin American governments remained low-key as each side resolved pressing domestic issues. The 1980s were the "lost decade of debt" for much of Latin America, especially important economies in Mexico, Brazil, and Argentina, while China was only beginning its tentative steps toward modernization. None of these states were primed for major expansion across the world for trade and / or investment.

Latin America responded to the end of the Cold War with political and economic reforms of its own that welcomed the outside investment and major trade system taking firm hold of Europe and North America. Mexico, as a founding member of the North American Free Trade Area, became more connected to the United States, in the eyes of many analysts, than Latin America, giving it special advantages in linking its economy to those of partners Canada and the United States. In 1990, President George H. W. Bush actually articulated a desire to create a "free trade zone of the Americas" from Alaska to Tierra del Fuego with his successor Bill Clinton committing at the Miami "Summit of the Americas" in 1992 to have it in place within a decade.[13]

The remainder of the region, however, wrestled with the economic struggles that result from dependence on exporting raw material, resources, and foodstuffs around the world. Cuba kept its status as a centrally controlled political and economic system, one which cast some aspirations on the economic modernization characterizing Beijing's decision of the 1980s and 1990s.

China's twenty years of modernization policies began to drive its behavior abroad by the turn of the century, as did Latin America's general frustration with U.S. trade policy and overall attention. While Mexico had entered NAFTA, other states began anticipating that the free trade zone would open to them. Free trade is not a new aspiration for the region, with the Latin American Free Trade Association created in South America in the early 1960s and the Central American Common Market established at the same time. Neither, however, proved particularly successful as the region saw big economies prosper but smaller economies founder in the face of competition. The Andean Common Market of the late 1960s was a subregional approach to the same but had only marginally better results for Peru, Colombia, Ecuador, Chile (early on), or Venezuela (later added). The PRC economic modernization was significantly more successful for a variety of reasons but it was still an economy focusing on domestic consumption of resources, for the most part, to preclude outside interference in decision-making and because China could meet its own needs.

By the early years of the 2000s, things had changed somewhat on both sides of the Pacific. Latin American societies had felt varying degrees of success with free-market policies and democratic governance. In particular, Venezuela, long seen as a successful democratic, competitive system, had proven less resilient over the long term than anticipated. Argentina was entering a period of chaos as its policies under Carlos Saúl Menem proved impossible to continue, forcing the people of the Argentine Republic to endure five presidents in ten days during late 2001 and early 2002, with Washington showing little sympathy for the socio-economic plight.[14]

China, on the other hand, had been seeing double-digit growth for well over a decade. Fossil fuel and natural resource consumption had risen dramatically, often exceeding domestic reserves. Analysts began talking in Beijing about China being unable to meet its needs, which would undermine growth and, by extension, threaten the Party's hold on power, its primary objective. Additionally, China was feeling more confident in its dealings with foreign partners as it concluded negotiations to join the World Trade Organization in 2002. China, as the Third Generation leadership transitioned to Hu Jintao and the Fourth Generation around the same time, began to go abroad more consistently with Latin America a destination of choice because it met needs China was developing.

It is also important to note that Latin America's relationship with Washington was undergoing one of its periodic troughs. Both North Americans and South Americans had anticipated a renaissance for the region with George W. Bush's election the same year that pro–

free market Vicente Fox Quesada took power from the PRI in Mexico. These hopes were dashed by the 9/11 events as the anticipated attention for the region evaporated as Washington became absorbed in the global war on terrorism and its attendant foibles. But, the problems were deeper, as the U.S.-Latin negotiations for the anticipated free trade zone proved far harder politically for the White House than Presidents Bush and then Clinton had anticipated in the 1990s. Latin American leadership under Brazil in its own expanded trade system began to appear as a counterbalance to hemispheric free trade, which was thought to benefit the United States far more than the rest of the region. Coupled with suspicion about Washington's commitment to trade and to the region in general, political distance began to grow across the hemisphere at the same time that China began exploring relationships around the world.

President Hu Jintao's 2004 visit to Santiago for APEC often appears the most visible shift in China's role in the region, primarily for the visibility, although the swing through several countries had significant outcomes. Jiang Zemin had actually gone to the region in the closing days after the 2000 EP-3 collision between China and the United States, showing a level of confidence on the international scene that China had rarely shown in the modern era. However, Hu also went to Brazil and Argentina as well as Chile, appearing as popular as a rock star with the novelty of a Chinese Communist Party head taking questions from average folk in the streets, making numerous public appearances, and seeming to enjoy the common touch that Latin Americans had believed President George W. Bush should have but did not. Indeed, at the same APEC gathering in Chile, President Bush appeared to have to defend the Secret Service against charges that it was overly protective during this meeting and deciding only to stop at the Colombian coastal city of Cartagena, where he discussed countering narcoguerrillas with his host Álvaro Uribe Vélez, rather than appearing to completely embrace the APEC membership as Hu did.

Hu also came bearing gifts, although they were longer-term commitments. China announced its intention to commit a $100 billion investment in the region over the next decade and to broaden trade relations with the region. Additionally, China would strengthen its "strategic relationship" with Brazil to illustrate the importance of that state while also making clear the crucial nature of its strategic resources to China's economic miracle. The international media welcomed the photographs and showered the Chinese leader with praise that was almost unheard of for the head of a regime pilloried for its treatment of students at Tiananmen Square just over a dozen years earlier.

THE PROOF IN THE PUDDING?

The Latin American experience historically has been one of tremendous disappointment, as these sorts of openings have appeared more than once. Rather than adopting sustained economic modernization in the same manner as China, Latin America has periodically taken dramatic moves that then do not bear fruit, due to either the vagaries of the international economic system or the inability to sustain policies with domestic political upheaval. Indeed, as a 2014 report noted, China has not been successful in all of its commitments, either.[15]

China did, at the turn of the millennium, begin a more substantive approach to engaging with Latin America's economies coincident with pledges to increase trade and investment. The 2004 visit to the region, along with the stated goal of increasing investment over a decade-long period, often misstated as a commitment to increase trade to $100 billion during that period, provided China with higher visibility at a time when Latin American states desperately sought to find an alternative to the more recent decades' economic intertwining with U.S. companies.

Coming at the time when China sought to replenish natural resources that it was using at a rapid pace, Latin America, along with Africa, was an outstanding source for those imports. In particular, Venezuela had petroleum that the Caracas government sought to sell anywhere but to the United States while Brazil had a range of important metals and other natural resources. Chile was a perennial source of copper and Bolivia offered tin. Chinese finance to the region in 2007 ran at roughly $5 billion.[16]

Fully a decade later, China's role in the region has expanded substantially. According to the Inter-American Dialogue and Boston University, bilateral Chinese loans with the region exceeded the combination of Inter-America Development Bank and World Bank finance in 2015, along with $35 billion in investment for infrastructure and associated projects, though primarily where it has longest ties: Venezuela, Brazil, Ecuador, and Argentina.[17] Additionally, investment in energy is substantial and growing, topping $70 billion by 2015.[18] In short, China's financial support is increasingly important to the region as other access points fail to support Latin American's aspirations.

Less commonly considered was the vast improvement in food production that the region had achieved over the prior ten years. The effect of economic modernization on China's domestic agriculture made for less likely sustained commitment to producing the food needed to feed the nation's people. Also, China's concerns about any developments that could adversely affect its ability to protect its foodstuffs made the vast fields of Brazilian and Argentine soybeans a desirable purchase. The reluctance to use genetically modified techniques in the region only made the deal sweeter from Beijing's perspective. Finally, the changing Chinese "palate" as more income and exposure to Western concepts of food consumption made the vast hectares of Argentina and Brazilian beef, along with a tremendous supply of Chilean salmon, much more appealing as well as a status symbol for increasingly affluent Chinese.

Poor infrastructure has been one of the traditional plagues for Latin America, however, partially because of decisions taken by their governments to prioritize other public policy items more highly but also because geography can be a serious impediment to getting goods around in these countries. In any meaningful manner to gain access to the resources, energy, or food of the region, China decided to invest heavily in road building in several parts of the region. The infrastructure projects suffered from some of the same negative reactions from within the region as did similar projects in Africa. The overwhelming aim of the development was to get exports to ports that would then ship them to China rather than projects decided upon through negotiations between Chinese companies and the Latin American host governments or communities.

One concept attracting considerable attention has been that of replacing the Panama canal with something able to carry significantly larger vessels that now characterize global ships. Indeed, the very idea of China having any meaningful ties with the existing canal has raised hackles in the United States for well over a decade as "China skeptics" have feared that the contract with Hong Kong–based Hutchinson Whampoa to manage the Panama Canal really meant that the People's Liberation Army (PLA) and China controlled access to the canal. The implication of this fear was that the People's Liberation Army would be in a position to prevent U.S. Navy vessels from using the canal, in peace or wartime. The argument had problems, however. Hutchinson Whampoa is not controlled by the PLA simply because it is a Hong Kong–based company. More importantly, however, if this were true, it would seem extremely likely that Beijing, in connivance with HW, would force Panama to reject its long-standing recognition of Taiwan as the government of China in favor of Beijing but that has never occurred. Finally, the current canal is small enough now that many U.S. naval vessels cannot transit the body as it is.

Two ideas for a more modern, grander canal have popped up, both with possible Chinese involvement. One is a canal that would, 175 years after first proposed, open the Caribbean to the Pacific across Nicaragua, using Lake Managua as a transit region. Chinese entrepreneur Wang Jing agreed in 2013 to provide funding, through his company HKND, for the task, even though environmental and feasibility questions still plague the project, along with the sheer reality of one of the world's most severe earthquake challenges represented by the 1972 tremor that significantly damaged the Nicaraguan capital city. The cost alone is daunting, estimated at quadruple the Nicaraguan gross domestic project.[19]

From the Nicaraguan perspective, the project appears a tremendous prize. Not only does the $50 billion investment open the possibility of an estimated 25,000 jobs[20] for a country with significant poverty and residual unemployment from decades of internal turbulence seem crucial, but the government of Daniel Ortega Saavedra has long desired ties with anyone except Washington.

Two aspects to this particular project are odd, however. One is that Nicaragua retains diplomatic ties with Taiwan, undermining the argument that China's companies are under Beijing's control as it would seem extremely unlikely that China would tolerate such political affiliation in light of the tremendous benefits this canal could garner for Beijing in highlighting its role as a major infrastructural developer in the world. Additionally, Nicaragua's potential new canal would offer a significant number of jobs bound to go to Chinese workers, not merely local Central Americans. This would seem to undercut the benefits for Nicaragua and the region, but Chinese behavior elsewhere, especially in Africa, has included bringing in their own labor force to the exclusion of both local employees and the other spillover effects for Nicaragua's development.[21] Nicaragua, however, is in no position to affect the Chinese offer as its fragile condition leaves it, along with Venezuela and—to a lesser extent—Argentina, desperate for outside assistance for fear that turning to outside traditional lenders would evoke moves to influence domestic political accountability and openness; China does not do so. While the deal has been announced, there have been few details in the open press. The apparent loss of 80 percent of entrepreneur Wang Jing's estimated $10 billion fortune is the proximate cause cited by some sources,[22] but the entire episode illustrates the tenuousness of some projects and the possibility that China's volatile growth environment can have on foreign projects.

At a 2015 conference in Cartagena, Colombia, an officer from a neighboring state noted that the canal could have

> substantial effect which will be negative for the isthmus. It will be perhaps 15 or 20 years of Chinese involvement but we don't know the details. We don't know the how long it will take and the effects are not immediately clear. It won't so much be security but we can't say without details yet. But, well, it is a theme that we'll have to understand {and} it's more than security. It will affect all of the region. Central America doesn't have the capacity right now to build the thing. Don't have concrete, or workers, or so all of that will have effects. But, we do know that it's something we hope we can work together on instead of driving us apart. We'll see.[23]

The other possible Chinese-inspired canal option is in the northwestern portion, a remote area called the Urabá, of Colombia.

Colombia has not been central to Chinese business interests in the region, probably because of the Republic's exceptionally close relationship with the United States over the past generation. However, China's interest in expanding the existing canal by shifting its path over into Colombia came to the fore in February 2011 when officials announced that exploratory discussions on a land route to move trade between Pacific port Buenaventura and the Caribbean coast were under way.[24] Three years later, the project apparently remains aspirational, even as trade between China and Colombia has increased to more than $5 billion annually.

Taiwan Hovering in the Background

Taiwan retains formal diplomatic relations with six Latin American states—Guatemala, El Salvador, Honduras, Nicaragua, Panama, and Paraguay—thus allowing for a formal relationship with their economies. In each case, these are some of the smaller and more vulnerable economies across the region. These are also some of the least diversified economies, concentrating their exports primarily on agricultural products such as bananas or coffee.

Chile, Colombia, Mexico

Infrastructure has been tremendously important as a target for Chinese investments. Many U.S. observers in the region believe the Chinese ability to establish a vast role for communications equipment through the region, such as Huawei routers, has allowed Beijing to infiltrate the communications of U.S. corporations. When the latter bid for contracts, Chinese companies undercut the bids as a result of material they have seized through using the technology they have in place in these countries. The bids then allow the Chinese to become major providers of infrastructure throughout the region.[25]

China has been notably absent from serious investment in Colombia, and to a lesser extent, Mexico, two countries with strong ties to the United States. In the Colombian case, this is somewhat surprising because of the advancements the country is making after more than half a century of tremendous internal strife. Colombian economic statistics have hovered around 4 percent since the late 2000s, according to the American Chamber of Commerce.[26] The country's single largest export is petroleum, and it produces other minerals and foodstuffs that China increasingly desires.

Argentina and Venezuela

Two of the best-endowed countries in Latin America present some of the greatest quandaries to those analyzing the region. At the beginning of the twentieth century, some viewed Argentina as having the same attributes that China possessed twenty years ago: an increasingly educated population, a work ethic that seemed destined to surpass that of the United States, and an abundance of labor. Instead, the series of economic and political debacles that have plagued the nation since 1930 have resulted in a failing economic system run by a government that is unable to make adjustments that would put the country in sync with the international community, and also unable to sustain a feasible economic program at home.

The latest iteration of this chaotic script has been the Kirchner presidencies of husband Nestor (2003–07) and wife Cristina Fernández de Kirchner from 2007 through 2016 when she left office. The duo attained office as *justicialista*, or members of the Peronist movement, named after nationalist president Juan Domingo Perón who dominated Argentina between his rise in the 1940s and death in July 1974. This political movement has sought to return Argentina to its glory period, prior to 1930, and blames outside forces for subjugating Argentina to exploit its vast resources, open terrain, and relatively educated European-immigrant population.[27]

The Kirchners' rise followed a particularly chaotic period in Argentine history as fellow Peronist Carlos Saúl Menem, who had embraced the George H. W. Bush and Bill Clinton administrations during his tenure, proved unable to sustain an economic program tied to the U.S. dollar, forcing him out of office when he sought a third term as president when his personal standing had fallen dramatically among the electorate. This fall related to the country's deteriorating economic conditions, resulting from Menem's determined attempts to tie the Argentine peso to the U.S. dollar and the accumulating debt that had risen well past $175 billion.

In 2001, as Argentina's plight became increasingly obvious, Secretary of the Treasury Paul O'Neill's statement, "We're working to find a way to create a sustainable Argentina, not just one that continues to consume the money of the plumbers and carpenters in the United States who make $50,000 a year and wonder what in the world we're doing with their money,"[28] reflected a dismissive attitude that illustrated Washington's inability or unwillingness to understand the pain this was inflicting on a traditionally wealthy society. Six months later, when Argentina proved unable to meet its foreign debt obligations, the nation set into motion political theater that ultimately ended up with five presidents in ten days. With the sense that the United States— so obsessed with Afghanistan and the aftermath of the 9/11 attacks— was not the caring strategic partner President Menem had portrayed over his time in office, the frustration only built. O'Neill's comment echoed in the ears of many Argentines who believed they were taking far more than their share of economic medicine and Washington simply did not care. When coupled with a rumored U.S. role in an April 2002 coup attempt against another nationalist government in Caracas, Venezuela, Argentines welcomed any economic ties— trade, infrastructure investment, loans or anything else—that would put distance between the international economic powers (meaning the United States) and Buenos Aires.

China fit the bill nicely, so the ties between the Kirchner government and Beijing were most welcome in Argentina. Argentina offers precisely the products, particularly foodstuffs such as soybeans and beef, as well as natural resources including iron ore that Beijing has been seeking. The Kirchners were delighted to sign agreements with China because it would not impose economic reforms that would further increase pressure on the domestic political landscape. In 2013, *Bloomberg News* quoted China as Argentina's second-largest trading partner behind Brazil with U.S.$17 billion involvement, in one form or another, with the Argentine economy.[29] Further, the Kirchners, with Nestor a former governor with virtual feudal powers in such a position, were accustomed to making arrangements with foreign powers that did not include much domestic political transparency.

Since China's Communist Party similarly ignores transparency, the mutual benefits of China's involvement in Argentina have been significant, growing, and substantial for Buenos Aires' needs such as roads, dams, and rejuvenating its aged railway system built by the British well over a century ago. CCTV America trumpeted the fifteen agreements between Presidents Xi Jinping and Cristina Fernández de Kirchner, putting China much more firmly into Argentina's economy.[30] The Chinese reports did not discuss Kirchner's mocking of the Chinese language in a news conference before formal signing ceremonies in Beijing, something questionable considering Argentina's growing dependence upon the Communist Party's commitments.[31]

Kirchner's successor, Mauricio Macri, has been more guarded in his approach to China, recognizing the pitfalls Beijing created. His interest in reestablishing Argentina's role as a functioning partner with the international economic system has provided the balance to Beijing's involvement so often lacking through much of the past decade. However, as Margaret Myers presciently expressed in February 2016, Washington simply is not paying attention to this region as one might expect.[32]

The country that has stolen most of the limelight with regard to China's role in the region is Venezuela, particularly under the late Hugo Chávez Frías. For the final two decades of his life, Chávez Frías sought to minimize his country's long-standing petroleum ties with the United States, playing the nationalist card to demonize Washington in the region. His "Bolivarian Revolution," hoping to include Bolivia and Ecuador, under Evo Morales and Rafael Correa, respectively, sought to resurrect the vision of early nineteenth-century independence and Venezuelan-born leader Simón Bolívar for a Latin America free and clear of northern influence. From his election in late 1998 to his death in March of 2013, Chávez Frías reached to those partners who would allow him to sell petroleum to anyone but Uncle Sam. With China, he also found a potential partner to deal with his own increasing economic plight as petroleum prices declined and the effects of his Bolivarian Revolution hit the rank-and-file Venezuelan squarely in the pocketbook.

China began its ties with Venezuela as Chávez Frías realized the logic of connections between the two, even if his petroleum would not immediately benefit China's needs. The heavy crude produced in Venezuelan fields does not suit the refinery capabilities currently supplying China's needs but the long-term commitment by Chávez Frías to sell to the Middle Kingdom fit well with China's energy strategy around the globe, one of trying to get long-term connections rather than worry about economically rational commitments.[33] Along with these energy deals, China began offering cash-strapped Venezuela assistance, much of it labeled infrastructure loans.

Between 2008 and 2015, the China Development Bank loaned Venezuela close to $37 billion, with the South American nation offering crude oil as collateral. The loans were to the government agencies and private entities involved in the petroleum sector, thus guaranteeing the collateral.[34] The resulting exports to China averaged above 150,000 barrels daily in 2014 and 2015. Other loans over the same period have focused on infrastructure projects such as transportation expansion and power plants, again in exchange for petroleum products.[35]

By 2015, as the Maduro government found itself unable to recreate the Chávez Frías magic and popular support fell as rapidly as economic prospects, Caracas asked Beijing for more support, such as a January 2015 statement that China would provide $20 billion in additional infrastructure and housing aid, under the China Development Bank. But, the Chinese have remained completely silent on this supposed loan.[36]

As Matt Ferchen has tracked, increased worry in the Chinese capital about the viability of these loans, as well as the overall strategy toward Venezuela, leaves little doubt that Caracas' lifeline from Beijing will be discontinued.[37] All of this has occurred as Beijing's petroleum imports from the Venezuelan market actually *fell* 14 percent in 2014.[38]

In mid-2016, Beijing began renegotiating its $65 billion worth of loans to Caracas while also signaling the reality of having to deal with a post-Maduro government by trying to involve the Venezuelan legislature, run by regime opponents, in the discussions.[39] As Caracas' stability crumbles, Beijing realistically recognizes it has some options to mitigate the pain but it appears highly unlikely that Venezuela can continue under Maduro's chaotic hand for long.

A scenario Beijing probably does not want to ponder is what would happen to Chinese workers, imported as part of this investment scheme and overall involvement in the country, should Venezuela fall further into chaos, resulting in political upheaval and potentially violence. The 2011 evacuation of Chinese workers from Libya was a significant challenge for the Chinese but not one that will be unheard of as Chinese involvement in the new world economy accelerates.

Brazil

The most important relationship within Latin America for China remains that with Brazil, because of what Brazil offers and who it is. Brazil will always be the largest state in population and land mass in the region, with the latter guaranteeing the most diversified and vast supply of natural resources and biodiversity in the world. This supply includes virtually any natural resources and minerals as well as some of the most fertile fields for growing food. Additionally, Brasilia governs a country ranking fifth in both physical size and because of its population of well more than 200 billion.

Brazil embodied the ecstasy of seeing China's new interest in expanding ties around the world when the years between 2004 and 2013 saw a sustained increase in trade between the Chinese and Brazilians. Beginning at U.S.$4.075 trillion in 2004, the bilateral trade flow had reached $77.199 trillion nine years later.[40] While China's imports from Brazil were primary natural resources and various sectors of agribusiness, its exports to Brazil were heavily concentrated in the appliance, small manufacturing, and associated finished-goods sectors. These exports constituted fully 53 percent of Brazil's imports from Asian economies.[41] As the Chinese economic expansion of that period pushed Beijing to sign agreements to promote access to various commodities in Africa, the Middle East, Russia, and Latin America, Brazil played a central role in those agreements. The increase in China's consumption of Brazilian resources hit a snag in 2008–09 as the Chinese economy cooled (slightly compared with that of much of the rest of the world) but has returned to an increasing rate since then.

The 2008 slowdown in Chinese growth, coupled with global debt issues, led to a dramatic drop in the prices for many raw materials and natural resources, precisely as has occurred many times in the past. The confidence voiced by many Brazilian and other Latin American business and political leaders about the region's success at fundamentally recasting its economic growth dissipated considerably as critics asked whether the region had become too dependent upon a single source yet again, albeit one in Asia rather than a Western one. Downturns in a number of indices resulted from both Chinese market volatility and overall economic slowdown as 2016 proceeded.[42]

Brazilians have been generally warm toward the Chinese investment but there have been questions as to whether this has been helpful for Brazil's overall goals of improving the sustained economic growth of the nation. As President Dilma Rousseff's presidency faced more corruption issues, and similar charges reached back to her extremely popular predecessor, Lula da Silva, China's ties with the region fell under scrutiny as another threat to Brazil's ability to grow and take its natural position as a leader in the world.

While Brazil is noteworthy as a founding member of the Asian Infrastructure and Investment Bank (AIIB), Pacific Alliance members Colombia and Chile seek to join the institution.[43] This would dramatically improve China's links with two relatively successful states in the region. Indeed, Chinese interests would improve as it took an even greater role in funding the much-needed infrastructure for Latin American economies. Venezuela also seeks to become a member but its precarious financial and political system would do little to change Beijing's already strong leverage in that state.

PROSPECTS FOR THE FUTURE: IMPERATIVES AND A COUPLE OF SCENARIOS

Two imperatives, geography and transparency, would argue that China's role in the region will never surpass that of the United States. As the past quarter of a century has proven, the international system has few guarantees but the distance would seem somewhat of an unsurmountable obstacle to Chinese dominance in all sectors. Similarly, as Latin American states gradually evolve toward higher standards of accountability and openness, China's apparent rejection of such norms overall in favor of the government's need for secrecy will most likely prevent it from becoming an overwhelming presence whose decisions command absolute direction. Even with an unanticipated "democratic" form of government, China's historic centralization of power in a hierarchical manner would seem a condition that might take a long time to transfer into the increasingly accountable societies appearing across Latin America.

Asked whether he worries about Chinese intervention in the region, one senior U.S. military official at U.S. Southern Command told the author in April 2015, "No, I don't worry about [the Chinese] as they are only interested in economics. The PRC has replaced us as the 'partner of choice' in the economic sphere. They are not involved in military aspects of the region and are pretty much not involved in Colombia."[44] This comment is striking for its implication that economic interests do not imply intervention—a view not widely held in Washington, D.C.—but also for the change this illustrates over the past generation when any "outside" involvement smacked of intervention, if not threat. In March 2015 Senate Armed Services Committee testimony, the U.S. Southern Command combatant commander, General John Kelly, USMC, noted, however, that with more than $100 billion investment in the region over the prior decade, China had "pivoted to the Western Hemisphere" as the United States has done to the Pacific.

The bigger question is whether China will stay involved in this region. If it is true, and the evidence would support this to an extent, that China has moved into the region because the United States has moved away to focus on Asia or the Middle East, then it begs the question whether the United States could reassert itself in the economic importance of this region. At the same time, China is now a global economic force with the same driving forces—fear of resource, food, or energy shortages as well as the desire for global presence—that would seem likely to retain at least a minimal role in the region. What is striking is how similarly China's behavior thus far has been that of the others throughout the region's history. It is a relationship built on the desire to gain something to take home rather than that of building enduring partnerships for mutual benefit, regardless of what the rhetoric says in public settings.

The April 2015 "Summit of the Americas," coming on the heels of the Obama administration's decision to normalize relations with Cuba, may herald heightened U.S. attention toward the region along with greater Latin American receptivity toward the United States. Another possible interpretation of these same events is that China's inroads in the regional economies led this portion of the U.S. government to reevaluate its policies to include the failed attempts over more than half a century to isolate Havana. The success of this intended policy is far from clear.[45] Beyond the bilateral U.S.-Cuban ties, it is conjecture that eradicating the long-standing and growing regional resentment over Washington's ostracizing of a Latin American government in ideological terms from almost sixty years ago will lead to improved economic involvement with the rest of the region.

China's long-term commitment to Latin American economies also remains somewhat opaque. While the need for many of the resources may ebb as China's economic growth stabilizes at a more realistic rate,[46] nationalist sentiment in the PRC will probably still prefer opportunities around the globe to prevent any possibility of a variation on the "Malacca Dilemma," which would be a constraint on Chinese behavior. Latin America may not be the primary focus of China's activities in the future, but nor is it likely to be completely left out of their list of potential partners.

From the region's perspective, the disappointment over China's behavior as a traditional exporting state rather than as a sustaining partner to assist the region's move away from dependency on commodities will continue. Latin America has found China willing to buy but not in any manner of mutual long-term development. Unfortunately, as the weaker of the partners, this trend is likely to continue.

For the states with strong ties to the United States and the global trading regime, Colombia, Chile, and Mexico, the connections with China will continue but produce far less frustration. These states have other options as a result of their economic and political choices. Little is as frustrating as no options as some of their neighbors have discovered, again, in a most painful manner.

CONCLUSIONS

China has made tremendous inroads in a region where it had little recognition, much less substantive connection, three decades ago. This is consistent with other Chinese expansion around the world, meaning it is not a revolutionary change. However, some countries are proving greater economic draws than others, but that may prove problematic for Beijing and exceptionally disappointing to the states involved. Regardless of the rhetoric largely initiated by Hu Jintao's 2004 swing through the region, Chinese investment has been highly concentrated in infrastructure to support transportation of exports to ports because that supports Beijing's interests rather than the region's hopes (and assumptions) this investment would be mutually beneficial. Indeed, Latin America as a region so basically lacked infrastructure that any additional assistance is important. But, the regional analyses in the earliest years of China's engagement included an embedded assumption that China, as a recently developing state, would treat the relationship differently; more contemporary analyses now recognize this is not true and bemoan that. China's involvement in economies throughout the region has *not* left it less vulnerable to commodity price shocks. The effects of the 2008 global economic slowdown proved this harsh reality to governments and business across the region, much to Latin frustration.

What is often lost is that a considerable amount of the investment goes into projects the region desperately needs, such as infrastructure. Latin America has suffered from lack of investment from other sources so it is not surprising to see the leadership there accept assistance from China. Similarly, if Chinese companies provide other assistance, is it so irrational for Latin Americans to accept such?

From China's perspective, Latin America offers opportunities for long-term ties that can prove important but they are also beginning to realize there may be short- to medium-term problems resulting from these engagements. China is far from the largest investor in the region.[47] The states most heavily linked to China, as a result of its advancement over the past decade, include at least two of the least stable political and economic regimes in the region: Caracas and Buenos Aires. The Chinese remain a de facto lifeline to Nicolás Maduro in his increasingly feeble attempts to hold on to power by emulating his late predecessor. China's support through propping up the banks means it cannot avoid watching the ever-cascading problem of internal political dissent and violence that is plaguing the Venezuelan political leader. The petroleum industry, the reason for Beijing to care about the faraway state, is in an ever-increasing state of decay at a time when fracking is putting more petroleum from other sources into the global stream. Venezuela's worth appears far less clear than it did fifteen years ago as Hugo Chávez Frías won his first election and became welcoming of the Chinese option as a significant partner. Whether Beijing will decide to cut the Venezuelans loose is a question beginning to attract serious consideration in Chinese circles.[48] Unspoken is the question of whether China could become a target for a subsequent regime bent on extracting revenge for supporting the increasingly unpopular and hapless Maduro government, something that is not Beijing's image for itself in a new world order.

Similarly, China's support for the erratic Cristina Fernández de Kirschner in Argentina was important for her survival but potentially problematic for the country as it seeks to return as a normal participant in the international system rather than a financial scofflaw. Argentina is a more diversified partner with China, exporting wheat, minerals, and resources, thus making the relationship somewhat more robust. But, Buenos Aires' perpetual shifts in policies and unwillingness / inability to repay debts to external creditors created some nervousness in China. Kirschner did not last forever in power, but the recent exasperating Argentine propensity of populist leaders rejecting outsiders' commitments in favor of keeping domestic support may spell bad news for Chinese investors. Additionally, the possibility of instability leading to poor maintenance of infrastructure will not help China with its own needs. In short, a bigger population and economy in Argentina may spell more significant challenges than Venezuela for China in the long run, at a minimum leading Chinese businesses to reconsider the long-term stability of the country.

China's primary interlocutors in the region remain those regimes whose problems or political orientations are somewhat out of kilter with the mainstream international community. Argentina's inauguration of Macri in late 2015 ended the opening by which Beijing provided major assistance to an otherwise-strapped Kirchner government but the loans and overall financial ties with strongly nationalist outlier governments in Venezuela and Ecuador remain paramount to those governments' survival. Brazil's recent economic turmoil, along with political doubts, also benefited from China's investments and financial engagement but the overall orientation of the Brazilian economy will make it less dependent on Beijing over the long haul. China, in fact, probably has a better chance for deep economic ties with Brazil than with many other states regionally. The key will be how Brazil addresses its internal challenges for restructuring while Beijing cautiously broadens its role in the region.

These are two states where the United States and the international community have kept some distance from the governing leaders, at least partially because of their unwillingness to embrace international financial norms. In the remainder of the region, the Chinese play a role in some aspects of their economies often in healthy competition with U.S. and European firms. China's activities are not guaranteed to win over contracts, nor are U.S. firms completely shut out, but the regional role for the Chinese is certainly much stronger in conjunction with confidence and investment resources than was true only a generation ago.

Finally, as Ambassador Chas Freeman points out about the sense of frustration the region has with highly publicized projects that do not ever come to fruition, there needs be a realistic business case made supporting these efforts. If an announced project does not make business sense, then it is bound to have tremendous trouble.

> After two decades' experience, I can attest that about 90 percent of the apparently attractive and profitable business propositions don't work out for one reason or another. I think . . . discussion of what's going on with China's international commercial activities may be confusing proposals and offers with promises and tenders. In the private sector, a willingness to invest or lend money does not mean that investment or lending will actually occur. This is undoubtedly true also of the mixed public-private sector international transactions in which China engages.[49]

At a minimum, the poor communication and loose use of terminology by high-level Chinese officials is clashing with the expectations and hopes of the Latin Americans, resulting in frustration on both sides of the Pacific. This simple disjuncture goes a long way to explain the disappointment increasingly permeating the views each side has of the other, as is true in other relationships China has around the world, a disappointment often characterizing major power experiences with these weaker economic regions.

As China becomes more involved around the world, it will have both have to temper expectations while recognizing the challenges of such ties. These challenges will include states expecting more "give" by China, much as China has over the decades since it reentered the international system. China often characterizes itself as a developing country, a distinction Beijing hopes will offer it more benefits than the more developed states in some situations. What China is finding is that its new friends around the world do not accept Beijing's answer that it is the developing state, expecting instead that China will make allowances for the weaker states seeking to replicate its amazing rise in economic stature around the globe.

President-elect Trump's concerns about Latin America do not appear to include China's role there. His focus on illegal immigration has meant little recognition of Chinese trade, investment, or a strategic role in this region. Time will tell whether he revises his analysis to include broader strategic issues as he looks at the U.S. bilateral relationships with China and with Latin American states individually.

NOTES

This analysis is personal and does not represent policy on the part of any arm of the U.S. government. The author thanks Drs. Damien Ma, Miles Kahler, Bernard Cole, Jacques de Lisle, Avery Goldstein, and outside reviewers for suggestions on this chapter.

1. Margaret Myers, "Interpreting Chinese Finance to LAC," The-Dialogue.org, February 24, 2016 (www.thedialogue.org/resources/chinese-finance-to-lac-in-2015-2/).

2. Steve LeVine, "How China Is Building the Biggest Commercial-Military Empire in History," *Quartz*, June 9, 2015 (www.defenseone.com /politics/2015/06/how-china-building-biggest-commercial-military -empire-history/114853/?oref=d_brief_nl).

3. Examples include Alexander Gabuev, "Who's Afraid of Chinese Colonization?" (http://carnegie.ru/eurasiaoutlaook/?fa=60515&mkt_tok =3RkMMJWWfF9wsRonva3NNZKXonjHpfsX57uQsW6Sg38431UkwdcjK PmjrlYlERMV0aPyQAgobGp5l5FEIQ7XYTLB2t60MWA 3D%3D); and John Berthelsen, "Trouble Could Be Brewing Over China Development Loans," AsiaSentinel.com, June 19, 2015; and Matt Ferchen "Export Dependence: If China Stops, Then What?" (with Alicia Garcia-Herrero) *China Economic Quarterly* 15, no. 3 (September 2011), pp. 33–37.

4. For example, see Matt Ferchen, "China-Latin American Relations: Long-Term Boon or Short-Term Boom?," *Chinese Journal of International Politics*, January 28, 2011.

5. LeVine, "How China Is Building the Biggest Commercial-Military Empire in History."

6. Jian Zhang, "China's New Foreign Policy Under Xi Jinping: Towards 'Peaceful Rise 2.0?,'" *Global Change, Peace and Security* (http://dx.doi.org/10 .1080/14781158.2015.993958).

7. Dr. Ellis publishes extensively on the individual activities that Beijing engages in. Recent publications include "China-Latin America Military Engagement: Good Will, Good Business, Strategic Position," *Strategic Studies Institute* 25 (August 2011) (http://strategicstudiesinstitute.army .mil/pubs/display.cfm?pubID=1077), and "Strategic Insights: The China-CELA Summit: Opening a New Phase in China-Latin America-U.S. Relations?" *Strategic Insights*, 27 (January 2015) (http://strategicstudiesinstitute .army.mil/index.cfm/articles//The-China-CELAC-Summit/2015/01 /27).

8. Comment to the author, May 20, 2015.

9. There are many histories of the region, but a strong economic history of this period is Leslie Bethell, *Latin America: Economics and Society Since 1930* (Cambridge University Press, 1998).

10. Latin American (as well as many U.S. scholars') elites' attachment to the idea of *dependencia* theory dates to the late 1940s with the work of Argentine economist Raúl Prebisch in his three-part work, the most notable of which was *The Economic Development of Latin America and Its Principal Problems* (New York: United Nations, 1950). Brazilian President Hernando Cardozo, as an academic, embraced this analytical framework.

11. While the *dependencia* school of economics is a Leninist-Marxist term associated with the 1960s and 1970s, the sense of outside exploitation and

vulnerability are fairly pervasive as Latin Americans evaluate their role in the globe.

12. Argentina was the final large state to shift recognition in 1984.

13. See "Summit of the Americas, 1994" (http://www.summit-americas .org/i_summit.html).

14. A statement ascribed to Secretary of the Treasury Paul O'Neill captured the U.S. failure to appreciate the problems when he was to have said, "Argentina needs to take its medicine," suggesting that economic reform and the pain it would inflict was unavoidable.

15. Taotao Chen and Miguel Pérez Ludena, *Chinese Foreign Direct Investment in Latin America and the Caribbean*, Economic Commission for Latin America, January 2014 (www.cepal.org/en/publications/35908-chinese-foreign-direct -investment-latin-america-and-caribbean).

16. Kevin Gallagher and Margaret Myers, "China-Latin America Financial Database," 2015. *The Dialogue: Leadership for Americas* (http://www.thedialogue .org/map_list/).

17. Margaret Myers, Kevin Gallagher, and Fei Yuan, "Chinese Finance to LAC in 2015: Doubling Down," *TheDialogue:Leadership for the Americas, China-Latin America Report,* February 2016 (http://1m1nttzpbhl3wbhhgahbu4ix .wpengine.netdna-cdn.com/wp-content/uploads/2016/02/Dialogue -LoansReport-v4-lowres.pdf).

18. "Interpreting Chinese Finance to Latin America," *TheDialogue: Leadership for Americas* (www.thedialogue.org/resources/chinese-finance-to-lac -in-2015-2/).

19. "A Canal Across Nicaragua: Is this for Real?," *Tico Times*, February 19, 2014 (www.ticotimes.net/2014/02/19/a-canal-across-nicaragua-is-this-for -real).

20. "Company: Nicaraguan Canal to create 25,000 local jobs," *San Diego Union-Telegraph,* January 8.

21. "Company: Nicaraguan Canal to Create 25,000 local jobs," Associated Press, January 8, 2015.

22. Suzanne Daley, "Lost in Nicaragua, a Chinese Tycoon's Canal Project," *New York Times*, April 3, 2016.

23. Remarks made June 11, 2015, but covered by not-for-attribution rules of National Defense University conferences.

24. BBC News, "China and Colombia Announce 'Alternate Panama Canal,'" February 14, 2011.

25. Breakfast conversation with Camilo Reyes Rodríguez at J.W. Marriott in Bogotá, April 15, 2015.

26. Discussion with AMCHAM president Camilo Reyes Rodríguez, April 14, 2015, Bogotá.

27. Argentina has the far-highest percentage of population with roots in Europe of any country in Latin America, primarily Italians who migrated to the Republic between 1880 and 2000.

28. "O'Neill's Candor, Tin Ear often ruffled feathers," *Wall Street Journal*, December 6, 2002.

29. "The Latin America Report" with Katia Porzecanski, Bloomberg.com, February 2015, (www.bloomberg.com/news/videos/2015-02-04/argentina -seeks-chinese-investments).

30. CCTV America, "Strategic Agreements Signed Between China and Argentina," March 10, 2015 (www.cctv-america.com/2015/03/10/strategic -agreements-signed-between-china-and-argentina).

31. Evann Gastaldo, "Argentine President Mocks Chinese Accent while in China for Business Reasons," *Newser*, February 4, 2015 (www.newser.com /story/202225/argentine-president-mocks-chinese-accent.html).

32. Margaret Myers, "Domando al dragón: China, la Alianza del Pacífico y la Asociación Transpacifíca," *Política Exterior*, no. 77 (Summer 2016) (www .politicaexterior.com/articulos/economia-exterior/domando-al-dragon -china-la-alianza-del-pacifico-y-la-asociacion-transpacifica/).

33. Bernard D. Cole, *Sealanes and Pipelines: Energy Security in China* (Westport, Conn.: Praeger Security International, 2008).

34. Prudence Ho, "Venezuela Oil Loans Go Awry for China," *Wall Street Journal*, June 19, 2015, pp. C1–C2.

35. Ibid., p. C2.

36. Ibid., p. C1.

37. Matt Ferchen, "China's Misguided Chavez Love Affair," *The Diplomat*, November 30, 2012; and "Time to Rethink China's Peaceful Development Policy," *Carnegie-Tsinghua Center for Global Policy*, November 6, 2013.

38. Ho, "Venezuela Oil Loans Go Awry for China," p. C2.

39. Lucy Hornby and Andrés Schipani, "China Seeks to Renegotiate Venezuela Loans," *Financial Times*, June 19, 2016 (www.ft.com/content/18169 fbe-33da-11e6-bda0-04585c31b153).

40. China-Brazil Business Council, 2013 (www.cebc.org.br/sites/default /files/cebc_alerta_18_recorde_ingles_pdf.pdf).

41. China-Brazil Economic Council, Informative No. 17, 20 October 2013 (http://www.cebc.org.br/sites/default/files/basket_of_imports.pdf).

42. Jonathan Wheatley, "Emerging Economies Are Coming under 'Even More Pressure,'" *Financial Times*, January 10, 2016 (www.ft.com/content /25fc18d6-b52a-11e5-8358-9a82b43f6b2f).

43. Tom Mitchell, "AIIB Expansion Plans Underscore China's Global Ambitions," *Financial Times*, June 26, 2016 (https://www.ft.com/content /1e53b6fe-3b74-11e6-8716-a4a71e8140b0).

44. Private discussion with senior U.S. Southern Command official in Miami, April 13, 2015.

45. The critics of normalization, overwhelmingly in the legislative branch, vow to retain the policy until the Castro regime embraces democracy. The current relationship will, in fact, be harder to alter than the president's statement indicates as the 1996 congressional actions following the "Brothers to the Rescue" incident where Cuba shot down anti-Cuban forces attempting to assist sympathetic forces on the island. As a result of this incident, Congress passed the Helms-Burton Act codifying steps ungirding the U.S. embargo against the Castro regime.

46. *China Daily*, April 15, 2015, reported that growth rates for the year will be closer to 7 percent percent per annum rather than the double-digit rates recorded over the prior two decades. Well beyond the scope of this work is the debate on whether the "China model" of economic modernization is at a breaking point or will morph into something more sustainable under the current conditions. In any case, the significantly lower growth rate lines up with those of other states, albeit definitely higher.

47. Chen and Pérez Ludena, *Chinese Foreign Direct Investment in Latin America and the Caribbean*.

48. Conversations with U.S. Embassy personnel, March 21–22, 2015, Beijing.

49. E-mail correspondence with author from Ambassador Chas Freeman, June 25, 2015.

SIX

Competing Visions

China, America, and the Asia-Pacific Security Order

JONATHAN D. POLLACK

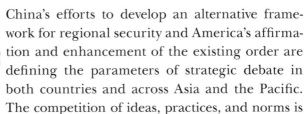 China's efforts to develop an alternative framework for regional security and America's affirmation and enhancement of the existing order are defining the parameters of strategic debate in both countries and across Asia and the Pacific. The competition of ideas, practices, and norms is not overtly confrontational, but reveals pronounced strategic divergence between the United States and China. Both powers are intent on ownership of rival concepts of international relations, with neither prepared to endorse the other's vision. What might these differences imply for Asia and the Pacific? Do realistic possibilities exist for reducing areas of competition and potential conflict?

The United States has long contended that it does not want to exclude China from future international governance and rulemaking, but insists that Beijing pursue its policy goals within an existing framework of rules, institutions, and norms developed under U.S. leadership following the end of World War II. The United States was the dominant actor shaping Asia-Pacific international relations in the aftermath of Japan's defeat; it then created regional security alliances following the Korean War. But the conditions in East Asia did not enable collective security akin to NATO. A "hub and spokes" system of bilateral alliances and a parallel network of less formal defense relationships were (and remain) the primary organizing concepts favored by the United States.

China argues that it is not seeking to overturn the regional order or undermine the continued U.S. political-military presence in Asia and the Pacific. But Beijing has long expressed strong dissatisfaction about U.S. regional policies that it believes impinge on Chinese vital interests. In addition, senior Chinese officials allude regularly to the need for new governance arrangements that more fully reflect shifts in the global distribution of power. Beijing wants other powers (especially the United States) to acknowledge the legitimacy of its security objectives without triggering instability or overt conflict. China also recognizes that coercive behavior will heighten suspicions or outright fears among neighboring states that would reaffirm support for U.S. policies. But a larger realignment of regional order acceptable to both countries remains an elusive goal. The onset of the Trump administration injects additional complexity and uncertainty into the U.S.-China strategic equation.

China was a principal U.S. adversary for more than two decades when it functioned outside the U.S.-led security system, initially within the Sino-Soviet alliance and subsequently as an independent revolutionary state. It actively opposed U.S. containment strategy and the alliances that underpinned it. Even when the United States and China pursued mutual accommodation during the 1970s and 1980s, the relationship was defined largely by shared antipathies to Soviet strategy, rather than by outright congruence of U.S. and Chinese policy goals. China nevertheless had little reason to contest U.S. primacy. The United States paid increased heed to Chinese interests while it sustained existing relations with most U.S. allies and security partners. But China did not possess the economic, military, or political capacity to challenge U.S. security strategy, even if it had wanted to.

The enhancement of China's comprehensive national power over the past two decades has raised renewed questions about the durability of Beijing's accommodation with the American-designed and led order. Appreciable change has been evident in the tone and substance of Chinese external policies under Xi Jinping, which has enabled various policy bureaucracies to more fully pursue their institutional goals. A parallel internal debate about China's capacity for international initiative is also evident, though the policy implications of this latter debate are not always clear.

For the first time in its post-1949 history, China is amassing the economic wherewithal, political and diplomatic resources, and military capacity to influence the region and to contest American power and policy. This does not presume an adversarial competition, but the shift in the relative balance of power between China and the United States is indisputable. To explore these issues more fully, this chapter will assess the premises of regional order, as defined by the United States and China; examine their security implications for the Asia-Pacific region; and ask whether American and Chinese policy conceptions can be reconciled, or at least kept manageable.

THE REQUISITES OF ORDER IN ASIA AND THE PACIFIC

Order is an enduring issue in the theory and practice of international relations. Hedley Bull defined international order as "a group of states, conscious of certain common interests and common values . . . [which presume] a common set of rules in their relations with one another, and share in the working of common institutions. . . . [I]nternational order [implies] a pattern or disposition of international activity that sustains the [underlying] goals of the society of states."[1] By these criteria, order has rarely prevailed in international politics. Acceptance of rules of the game and restraints on state behavior also suggests a strong preference for the status quo among the established powers.

However, the distribution of power within the international system is seldom static. Even as dominant powers seek to retain their position, power transitions exhibit a direction and momentum of their own. Since the 1970s at least three major transformations have occurred in global strategy without triggering acute systemic disruption or the resort to force: the collapse of the Soviet Union and the end of the global adversarial logic of the Cold War; the expansion of international trade and investment based on globalization and the telecommunications revolution; and the simultaneous emergence of the Asia-Pacific economies, especially China's jettisoning of economic autarky. Only the first of these transformations pertained to international security in the traditional sense of the term. So China's reemergence as a comprehensive major power constitutes a fourth such change.

The concept of order is central to the thinking and actions of major powers. Various definitions reveal how states, leaders, and policy bureaucracies articulate their aspirations and goals, hoping to garner legitimacy and acceptance by others. In the contention of power and interests in the international system, how are rules formed and altered? What are the options of less-established powers to realize a larger voice and role?

Members of the international system have three potential paths to enhance their position without directly challenging existing norms or resorting to more coercive strategies: accommodation to existing rules, formulating new rules to supplement or supplant older ones, or enlarging the political and strategic space in which established and aspiring powers can cooperate as well as compete. China's policies encompass elements of all three approaches.

However, simultaneity creates differences and potential contradictions. Chinese conceptions of international order are not always understood in a detailed way. To some observers, Chinese views and policies do not represent an alternative approach to regional order so much as an effort to dilute the singularity of American regional influence. What interests and goals determine Chinese thinking? How does the leadership balance China's domestic policy requirements with the desire for a larger international role? To what extent does China envision active participation and collaboration in facilitating creation of a future order? In what areas does China believe that the existing order can be maintained, as distinct from areas where China deems the status quo disadvantageous to Chinese interests?

A redefined but stable international order presumes rules of the road that upholders of the existing order and aspirants both view as legitimate. Without mutual acceptance, order is illusory. Even as the

United States and China have appreciably broadened the areas of bilateral cooperation, these initiatives touch only minimally on the underlying strategic beliefs and security practices of both countries. China is intent on enlarging its freedom of action, but can it achieve this objective without triggering responses by the United States and neighboring states? This circle cannot be easily squared.

There are also geographic asymmetries between the United States and China. East Asia and the West Pacific have been principal arenas of U.S. regional military involvement for more than a century, and the predominant domain of U.S. economic interests. The sheer expanse of the Asian land mass and of surrounding maritime areas has necessitated choices in U.S. strategy, rendering some locations (in particular, inner Asia) less important for U.S. interests, but of much greater long-term interest to China.

America's use of facilities in Central Asia for transit and logistics following September 11 did not invalidate this judgment. These locations remain far less developed and far less populated than East Asia. Since China does not have to contend with the countervailing power of the United States in Central Asia, it provides readier opportunities for enhancing Chinese influence and outreach. China is what one leading Chinese scholar terms a "state in the middle," and the Asian continent is its natural home. China is thus pursuing a dual strategic identity, entailing maritime and continental dimensions, with the maritime domain the primary arena of U.S.-China competition.

At the close of the Cold War, the United States did not face overt opposition to continued regional primacy. In the early 1990s, some observers argued that the ascendance of Japanese economic and financial power posed a potential challenge to U.S. predominance. But Japan (then and now) was not an autonomous strategic actor, and it soon experienced prolonged economic stagnation that continues to constrain its aspirations. The existing U.S.-led international order was thus largely reaffirmed.[2] No individual state or coalition of states challenged American power and policy, enabling the broad rules of the system to operate in a largely unperturbed fashion. At the same time, bilateralism continued to dominate U.S. regional security policy, especially in Northeast Asia, where nearly all of America's forward-deployed military forces were concentrated.

Like its predecessors, the Obama administration asserted that the U.S. military presence and its leadership role remain integral to upholding regional order.[3] The United States expected that Beijing will accommodate to U.S. policy as its power and interests continue to grow. But an increasingly capable China represents a very different challenge to regional order. It is an autonomous, ascendant strategic actor with a growing array of economic, political, and military capabilities. At least as important, it is now the world's largest trading state, and its financial and economic capacities will enable an appreciable enhancement of China's regional role.

Most regional states continue to express strong support for U.S. economic, political, and military involvement. For nearly all Asia-Pacific states, the United States does not pose a major threat to their underlying strategic interests. Without a credible U.S. presence, most within the region perceive growing risks of uncertainty and (potentially) outright instability. The United States is the only plausible power capable of counterbalancing an ascendant China. But nearly all regional actors voice a parallel desire for a reconfigured regional order acceptable to both states.

Responding to widespread perceptions of American inattentiveness to the region's transformation that antedated the Obama administration, the United States in 2011 enunciated a strategic rebalance toward Asia and the Pacific. The essentials of the strategy were evident from the administration's earliest months in office, but it was only in subsequent years that the strategy was explicitly identified as a defining U.S. goal.[4] The rebalance posited a longer-term shift in the center of economic and strategic gravity to Asia and the Pacific. Journalists and commentators quickly seized on the military dimensions of the rebalance, which derived in large measure from decisions in the Bush administration to assign growing portions of American naval and airpower to the Pacific. But the United States also sought to enhance its economic and diplomatic leverage to complement America's military advantage.

The United States was thus responding to a demand signal from many of China's neighbors; it was also part of the effort to shift American attention away from the open-ended military interventions in the Islamic world following September 11. But preoccupations with upheaval and internal conflict across the Middle East and Southwest Asia continued throughout the Obama administration's time in office, and are now compounded by concerns about a revanchist Russia and a humanitarian crisis and political and economic upheaval within Europe. These crises imposed limits on the time and resources that the United States has been able to devote to Asia and the Pacific. As a result, regional states voiced increased doubts about America's ability to retain its regional advantage as Chinese power continues to grow and some express concern about the possibility of a Sino-American adversarial rivalry.

The emergent fault lines in the regional order are thus apparent. The United States is intent on preserving its regional strategic advantage, combining its military power and a more visible political and diplomatic role with pursuit of new rules governing trade and investment. But China is developing a distinct and appreciably larger voice in economic, diplomatic, and security affairs, utilizing its emergent capabilities to maximum effect. Can these competing national strategies be reconciled? What would be required of the United States and China to realize an outcome acceptable to both states?

INHERITED AND PROSPECTIVE ARCHITECTURES

Chinese policymakers contend that Beijing is not intent on undermining the U.S. regional position or excluding the United States from Asia and the Pacific. Beijing has repeatedly endorsed an "appropriate role" for U.S. power in the region. But Chinese statements lack specificity and operational content. These declarations reveal little about how China conceptualizes the role of American military power in locations contiguous to China's maritime periphery beyond wanting less of it, and perhaps none at all. There is an inescapable duality in Chinese thinking—that is, a commitment to peaceful development while protecting China's "legitimate rights and interests" and a refusal "to sacrifice the state's core interests." This dichotomized conception of Chinese policy will be repeatedly tested in future years.

The enhancement of Chinese military capabilities is a major factor in Beijing's policy equation. Most Asia-Pacific states recognize that

China's rejuvenation will encompass increased military power and presence. But the magnitude and speed of this military transformation and Chinese behavior in contested maritime domains has unsettled many neighbors. In the leadership's view, Chinese military modernization is an appropriate reflection of China's economic and political transition. It is intended to narrow the technological gap between China and the United States, to counter presumed vulnerabilities that Beijing could confront in a crisis, and to protect Chinese economic interests.

However, China's leaders claim that they have no intention of replicating past patterns of great power rivalry. In his first visit to the United Nations, in September 2015, President Xi Jinping emphasized oft-repeated Chinese calls for a multipolar world premised on equal partnerships and multilateral consultation and "a new approach to state-to-state relations [that] . . . seeks partnership rather than alliance" and the abandonment of "Cold War mentality in all its manifestation."[5] Such formulaic renderings seem largely aspirational, and provide few clues about how Chinese leaders envision the role of their increased power, or of how China will justify its future international behavior.

Despite Chinese assurances of peaceful intent, few regional actors are prepared to view the Asia-Pacific future without a substantial American military presence, especially maritime capabilities. But will the role of American military power remain undiminished as Chinese power matures? Does the United States perceive complementarity in U.S. and Chinese views of the regional future? The answers to these questions are far from clear, even as U.S. policymakers insist that an adversarial or quasi-adversarial relationship with China is neither desirable nor inevitable.

At the same time, China's economic and infrastructural activities across continental and maritime Asia are growing very significantly. Beijing contends that there is a natural complementarity between its economic outreach and the development of military capabilities to defend its economic interests. The Asia-Pacific economies and the U.S. economy are already deeply enmeshed with that of China. It is the lead trading partner of nearly all neighboring states, and it has an inherent interest in unimpeded commercial and energy movement across maritime and land borders. China also seeks to enhance its regional economic role through the "One Belt, One Road" (Silk Road Economic Belt and the Maritime Silk Road) initiative of 2013 for trade promotion and infrastructure development; leadership of the Asian Infrastructure Investment Bank; and expanded pursuit of bilateral and multilateral free trade agreements, including with Australia and the Republic of Korea, both important U.S. allies.

Xi Jinping deems the Belt and Road among his major policy priorities, and a primary means to link China to economies across continental and maritime Asia.[6] He appears to believe that China's much-enhanced financial and economic power provides Beijing with newfound comparative advantage. The success or failure of the policy will not be certain for many years. But Xi contends that an Asia-wide development strategy will not generate heightened rivalry. No regional state favors acute security competition or large-scale militarization that would undermine common prosperity, and none want to be compelled to choose definitively between China and the United States. Time will tell.

Longer-term outcomes will also depend on the future of the economic leg of the U.S. rebalance. The Obama administration's advocacy of the Trans-Pacific Partnership envisioned changes that will enhance the U.S. competitive advantage along the Pacific Rim. The TPP specified far more explicit rules and obligations for market access, intellectual property rights, labor standards, and environmental protection among participating states. President Obama depicted the TPP "as more than just a trade pact; it also has important strategic and geopolitical benefits . . . [and] in our shared security and in universal human rights."[7] But President Trump's withdrawal from the TPP and ample wariness of multilateral trade agreements create major uncertainty about America's future trade policies. China has also been conspicuous by its absence from the TPP process. Meanwhile, China's accelerated push for the Regional Comprehensive Economic Partnership (RCEP)—much favored by Beijing—seems a more likely near-term prospect.

President Obama also painted an uncharacteristically zero-sum view of the regional economic future. He argued that "without this agreement, competitors that don't share our values, like China, will write the rules of the global economy. They'll keep selling into our markets and try to lure companies over there; meanwhile they're going to keep their markets closed to us. . . . With this Trans-Pacific Partnership, we are writing the rules for the global economy."[8] The president's statement reflected his evident belief that the rules governing trade and investment will be the driving force in Asia-Pacific international relations in the twenty-first century. The policy trajectories of the United States and China thus address different though not necessarily contradictory goals: China envisions the enhancement of its military capabilities as a natural complement to its growing economic power, whereas the United States views new trade and investment rules as a natural complement to its extant military advantage.

China's initial responses to TPP were decidedly negative, but subsequent statements were more measured. Chinese experts continue to voice wariness about the prospect of U.S.-Japanese leadership over new trade and investment rules that would limit China's economic options. However, as argued in a report prepared by the Ministry of Foreign Affairs think tank, "should TPP be open to China, China may decide on an optimal occasion for joining in the agreement after weighing its overall interests in line with the world economic and political situations."[9] A prominent Chinese official has also contended that ratification of the TPP "could even provide an impetus for China's efforts to deepen its economic reforms [since] it set[s] a higher bar for China in [long-term] global trade and investment."[10] But the rejection of the TPP by the Trump administration reduced this prospect.

International security entails a very different logic than trade and investment. As an autonomous political-military actor with a deep aversion to participation in formal alliances, China is not prepared to undertake binding security obligations toward others, though it has entered into alliance like understandings with a few states, most notably with Pakistan. Beijing also voices increased unease about U.S. efforts to heighten political-military integration with its regional allies and security partners, an issue to which we will return.

The latent possibilities of U.S.-China strategic rivalry are thus apparent. Can adversarial or quasi-adversarial competition be prevented, and what are the consequences for regional order if both states posit a security dilemma? The balance of this chapter will focus primarily on Chinese policy deliberations over these questions. China hopes to reduce its vulnerabilities to American military power and to increase its freedom of action, but can Beijing realize these goals without stimulating a potentially very costly political-military competition? Is it possible to differentiate between security developments that China deems genuinely worrisome, as distinct from actions to which Beijing objects but that do not threaten China's vital security interests?

Chinese researchers have voiced different opinions on these questions, which appear to reflect separate lines of argument within the policy process. Debate in the specialist community about the implications of the country's rise has oscillated between unwarranted optimism and continued caution, if not outright pessimism. Beijing's response to the global financial crisis of 2008–09 provided ample evidence of dichotomized thinking. By avoiding major embroilment in the financial crisis, China was able to sustain double-digit economic growth rates. But some Chinese thinkers saw possibilities of an unexpectedly abrupt realignment of the global order, extrapolating from the U.S. financial meltdown to shifts in the longer-term balance of power.

To more effusive Chinese commentators, divergent American and Chinese economic trajectories evident at the time of U.S. financial crisis highlighted the shortcomings of Western democratic systems and the superiority of a Chinese economic model. These voices have been far less pronounced as Chinese economic growth has slowed and as America's economic recovery has gathered momentum. But some analysts nevertheless still believe longer-term trends will enable a challenge to American predominance; they also raise questions about the continued relevance of Deng Xiaoping's earlier calls for modesty and prudence in Chinese international behavior. Such thinking, unmoored from attention to the risks to China of global financial upheaval, also helped feed the narrative of an "assertive China" among journalists and in strategic circles.[11]

However, divergent assessments among researchers did not prove decisive within the leadership. Throughout Hu Jintao's tenure in power, Dai Bingguo, his senior foreign policy advisor, repeatedly advocated a "peaceful development" strategy favoring enhanced cooperation with the United States. Dai has reaffirmed this strategy in several speeches following his retirement. But these addresses have had a more cautionary character at a time of heightened Sino-American differences, especially over the maritime domain.[12] Some prominent thinkers outside the policy process have voiced dissatisfaction with a lower-profile foreign policy that did not correspond to their belief in China's increased strengths and presumed self-confidence.[13] Moreover, renewed geopolitical competition among major powers and upheaval across much of the Islamic world undermined the capacity of the United States and other major powers to manage global order.[14]

Heightened disruption and instability in the international system have therefore prompted increased attention to China's stake and involvement in global and regional politics. Though Beijing displays no interest in inheriting U.S. global responsibilities, some prominent Chinese scholars have advocated the enhancement of China's role in locations where China is less likely to face head-to-head competition with the United States. For example, Wang Jisi of Peking University has proposed an omnidirectional Chinese strategy that would reduce the risks of a direct competition with the United States in the West Pacific, paying particular attention to a "going west" option. Inasmuch as America's political, economic, and military reach is far less pronounced in Central Asia, Wang's argument seems very much in keeping with Dai Bingguo's earlier policy formulations.[15]

However, advocates of a more forward-leaning foreign policy have viewed China's power ascendance with different goals in mind. Yan Xuetong of Tsinghua University took explicit issue with Deng Xiaoping's formulation of China's international role that has largely governed foreign policy strategy for more than two decades. He argued that a more capable China would be able to assert its interests without risking overt conflict with the United States.[16] By implication, there was a need for a more forceful strategy to address the longer-term U.S.-China competition. China (at least in absolute terms) had advanced from the world's sixth-largest economy to the second largest within a single decade. Even with slowing growth, the absolute economic weight of the United States and China would increasingly differentiate these two countries from all other powers.

To Yan, these altered circumstances warranted a more overt political and diplomatic role, including the cultivation of alliance-like relationships with major U.S. security partners. But other influential voices, including Qin Yaqing of the China Foreign Affairs University, openly challenged the logic of bipolarity, arguing that China was not in a position to compete with (let alone emulate) American power.[17] In Qin's view, China could advance its long-term interests through more gradual options that do not directly challenge American power.

Senior Chinese officials also profess little interest in a coequal strategic relationship with the United States. Yet Chinese observers remain skeptical that the United States is prepared to accord China full legitimacy as a great power in the current international order. The leadership has acknowledged that absolute economic power does not equate with the openness and innovation required to fulfill China's larger development aspirations. But China's "walking on two legs" strategy has combined declaratory adherence to extant international norms while actively pursuing a heightened role that does not adhere to a U.S. script.

Xi Jinping has discussed these possibilities in various policy speeches delivered since 2013. Rather than emulate the United States, Xi sees opportunities to develop indigenous strategic concepts, often without explicit reference to American power.[18] Many of these initiatives have built on concepts first outlined during Hu Jintao's leadership tenure, but under Xi they have assumed increased specificity and momentum. The intent is to capitalize on China's increased economic and financial weight, enabling the nation's fuller entry into global governance, but without opposition to extant norms. As a consequence, China hopes to limit any possibility that regional sentiment might coalesce against it, as well as enable Beijing to make inroads with states closely associated with the United States.

For example, Chinese officials have contrasted Beijing's involvement in finance and infrastructural development with the Marshall Plan, asserting that China is not pursuing its goals with geopolitical interests in mind. As argued by Foreign Minister Wang Yi, "We have worked hard to expand cooperation with foreign countries . . . and have opened a new path of partnership without forging alliances in our contacts with foreign countries. . . . The 'One Belt and One

Road' was born in the age of globalization. It is a product of openness and cooperation rather than a geopolitical tool. We should not treat it with the outdated mentality of the Cold War."[19]

This argument seems highly self-serving. In particular, Wang fails to acknowledge that such policies will advance Chinese interests. His description of Chinese policy focuses entirely on international cooperation, without reference to the more coercive elements of national power. China also continues to deny the legitimacy of U.S. security alliances. By contrast, the Obama administration viewed the reaffirmation of its regional alliances as integral to its Asia-Pacific strategy, especially as regional states that have voiced disquiet about the growth of Chinese power.

Moreover, even as China avers no interest in a bipolar world, such sentiments are not far removed from Chinese or from U.S. thinking. The geographic metaphors utilized by Xi Jinping and by Barack Obama illustrate competing perceptions of Chinese and American power. Xi has stated that "the vast Pacific Ocean has enough space for the two large countries of China and the United States," whereas Obama (quoting the Australian author David Malouf) has characterized the Pacific as a "lake," reflecting "the shrinking of distance . . . of our contemporary world."[20] China is implicitly signaling the need to place limits on the exercise of American power, whereas the United States (notwithstanding its physical distance from the Asian mainland) is staking a claim to operate wherever its interests demand it.

Is there strategic space where the U.S. and Chinese interests can readily coexist, or do the allusions to ocean versus lake prefigure a more antagonistic Sino-American future? Alternatively, will economic and institutional commonalities and growing incentives for international cooperation prove more decisive in emergent conceptions of regional order? What do the pressures and cross currents affecting both countries suggest about the future? Has China already concluded that it must possess the full panoply of political, economic, and military capabilities to inhibit the exercise of American power, and with what objectives in mind?

The United States contends that any modifications of the extant regional order must preclude coercive uses of power, at least as American officials employ this concept. Beijing argues that its assent to the current order must include America's unequivocal acknowledgment of China's standing as a major power and respect for its political institutions and practices. Moreover, China's new National Security Law contains a highly elaborated definition of national security, with explicit reference to "China's political power, sovereignty, unity and territorial integrity, the well-being of the Chinese nation, the sustainable development of the economy and society and other important national interest[s] relatively free of any danger or domestic or foreign threat . . . [including] the ability to maintain a continuously secure state."[21]

Can China's vision be reconciled with American policies and practices and the continued centrality of U.S. power in Asia and the Pacific? This question is a defining issue in future Sino-American relations. It requires a closer examination of the core security precepts espoused by both the United States and China.

CHINA'S STRATEGIC PERIPHERY AND THE ROLE OF U.S. ALLIANCES

Despite Chinese pursuit of economic and political initiatives in Central Asia and in Europe, China's strategic calculations remain heavily focused on East Asia. China's defining security imperatives are within the geographic zone beginning on the Korean peninsula, and extending southward to Japan, the Taiwan Strait, and Southeast Asia. These correspond closely to the locations of predominant U.S. security interest, where the United States deploys the preponderance of its Pacific-based military power.

Notwithstanding U.S. assurances of benign intent and advances in Sino-American military-to-military relations, policymakers in Beijing continue to voice ample wariness toward U.S. military intentions and actions. In China's view, no other power (or states aligned with the United States) has the right to limit Beijing's economic and political objectives, or to place Chinese security interests at risk. China therefore seeks to solidify its economic and political relationships within the region, while also addressing direct threats to its national security.

China's geographic periphery is closely linked to its national security perceptions. When defense of the homeland defined China's principal defense needs, its security calculations were relatively straightforward. But the enhancement of Chinese power and revolutionary changes in defense technology have injected much greater complexity into Beijing's strategic calculations. A prescient assessment by Tang Shiping of Fudan University (published soon after September 11) argued that "there has never been a big power which has been able to maintain its dominance forever." While expressing continued concern about the prospect of U.S. unilateralism Tang also voiced a hope that "if the United States were to adopt a . . . prudent leadership strategy . . . while China maintained its current policy of prudent, defensive realism, and if China and the U.S. . . . were able to reach some degree of relative strategic guarantees, then they could . . . lay the foundation for a more stable strategic understanding."[22]

Unlike in earlier decades, however, China now has far more substantial interests to protect, and far more power with which to protect them. As Li Xiangyang of the China Academy of Social Sciences has observed, "In the process of . . . becoming a global power, China must first become a regional power . . . [and] a participant in the development of international rules. . . . While the United States is not within the scope of China's periphery, all of the contradictions and problems facing China's peripheral strategy are closely related to the United States."[23]

China has enunciated its self-identified rights, but continues to weigh whether they can be achieved without excessive reliance on more coercive policy approaches. Ruan Zongze of the China Institute of International Studies has noted the simultaneous development of China and the United States as the leading powers in the West Pacific. But he has voiced unease about increasing contradictions and an "unstable periphery [that] will necessarily drag down China or disrupt the progress of China's development." In Ruan's view, the U.S. rebalancing strategy has triggered "change in the regional order," thereby emboldening U.S. allies and security partners. While viewing the need for a Sino-American "new consensus on regional order," Ruan has also observed: "The U.S. seems not to have realized the importance and urgency of this issue. . . . [But] China [is not prepared to] sacrifice . . . its core interests. It would be a misjudgment of China's will and ability to resolutely maintain its sovereignty, security, and development interests."[24]

A full understanding of Chinese regional strategy requires a detailed assessment of the posited risks to Chinese security. Most Chinese evaluations do not provide such detail, but recent statements have nevertheless provided more insight into the leadership's longer-term security horizons, with particular attention to the increasing role of maritime power.[25] But Chinese analysts seldom discuss whether China's reach could exceed its grasp. Some Chinese writers, for example, recognize the necessity of avoiding embroilment in unwanted crises that would furnish neighboring states added justification for organizing coalitions to oppose China. But they assert a parallel need to send deterrence signals against others who might challenge China, resulting in an uneasy fit between theory and practice.

These tensions are most evident with respect to Japan, but they are not limited to Japan.[26] Though there have been some modest improvements in Sino-Japanese relations since 2014, the deeper contradictions and differences portend a longer-term power rivalry.[27] Most Chinese observers claim that Japan seeks to upend the postwar order in Asia, which seems a politically safe judgment within Chinese domestic politics, especially as Xi Jinping has sought to curtail more independent assessments within research circles. But some writers still depict Japan as a declining power, whose role in the regional politics and security (absent U.S. consent and encouragement) will continue to diminish. This presumably provides China increased incentive to restrain its actions likely to trigger adverse responses from Tokyo. But its heightened maritime and air activities close to the Senkakus / Diaoyus point in a very different direction, though the Japanese leadership has also been eager to depict its extended political and military reach as a response to Chinese actions.

A different dynamic is at play in the South China Sea, where China claims that U.S. involvement emboldened the Philippines and Vietnam to challenge Chinese interests. But China's extensive if still ambiguously worded maritime claims and its land reclamation efforts on various reefs and shoals have generated strong international opposition and heightened U.S. political-military activities in the South China Sea.[28] China's unambiguous insistence on its claims to territorial sovereignty based on claims of historic rights; its unwillingness to clarify the precise meaning of the nine-dash line; and its refusal to participate in the arbitration proceedings initiated by the Philippines all contributed to outcomes that Beijing presumably wished to avoid.

However, the May 2016 presidential election of Rodrigo Duterte, an intensely nationalistic Filipino politician intent on asserting and pursuing policies independent of the United States, appears to have created possibilities for less confrontational relations between Beijing and Manila. China's provision of substantial economic assistance to the Philippines for infrastructural development and increased trade and investment has provided Duterte with incentives for accommodation with Beijing, presuming this can be achieved without undermining Filipino sovereignty. The new president also expects that China will demonstrate appreciable restraint in its maritime activities in shoals and reefs within Manila's exclusive economic zone. China's readiness to preclude extension of its construction activities to the Scarborough Shoal (Huangyan Island) and permitting access by Filipino fishermen to the location's fishing grounds (systematically blocked by Beijing since 2012) represent the first major tests of a redefined bilateral relationship. These reduce the near-term possibilities of heightened contention between Manila and Beijing, without altering China's repeated objections to U.S. surveillance and reconnaissance activities in the South China Sea.

In various policy addresses, Xi Jinping continues to emphasize non-adversarial conceptions of Sino-American relations and benign, development-oriented policies with neighboring states. But he has also enunciated far more explicit statements of China's determination to defend its self-declared vital security interests. As Xi argued at a Politburo study session on international strategy in early 2013, "We will keep walking on the peaceful development road, but we must not forsake our legitimate rights and interests, [and] must not sacrifice core national interests. . . . No countries should expect us to swallow the bitter fruit that undermines our sovereignty, security and development interests."[29] Can these be reconciled short of incurring substantial damage to Chinese development goals and increasing the risks of a future crisis? This question very much remains unresolved.

Chinese perceptions of continuing disadvantage relative to American power explain much of its thinking. China does not yet occupy a seat at the great power table commensurate with its expectations as a reemergent major power. It argues that the United States is insufficiently attentive to Chinese vital interests. It also confronts American military capacities that far exceed its own. Some Chinese commentators disparage the future of U.S. military power relative to that of China, but authoritative policy circles pay little heed to these arguments, even if these characterizations of U.S. strategy and China's power prospects resonate at a popular level.[30]

The predominant views of Chinese military planners remain much more sober than those conveyed by retired military officers. Despite major advances in Chinese weapons development, its military capacities continue to lag well behind those of the United States and remain entirely unproven in actual combat. China also faces significant limitations in its ability to project military power into the first and second island chains, or beyond. At the same time, China wants to narrow perceived imbalances in power without provoking overt opposition from the United States or the emergence of a regional coalition arrayed against it. This remains the policy needle that China still seeks to thread. But its behavior is eliciting responses from neighbors and from the United States that Beijing cannot possibly see in its interest.

China also wants to maintain as much strategic autonomy as possible. Alliances have long been considered a major constraint on China's freedom of action. Beijing's only extant formal alliance (the China-DPRK treaty of 1961) was a direct outgrowth of the Sino-Soviet rivalry of the early 1960s, and it has been effectively dormant for the last two decades. China contends that alliances embolden smaller states to act beyond the limits of their own capabilities, enabling them to complicate the strategies of bigger powers. At best, alliances are to be tolerated when China lacks the capacity to challenge or undermine them. But there seems little interest or enthusiasm for developing an alliance strategy paralleling that of the United States.

The United States, by contrast, *does* regard alliances as integral to its security interests, furnishing America with lasting political influence in Asia and the Pacific and providing the U.S. with the means to extend its political and military reach to locations far removed from the U.S. homeland. America's alliances first developed in response to immediate exigencies, but now reflect a more diversified set of interests. Without these alliance structures and various less institutionalized security partnerships, it would not be possible for the United States to sustain its national security strategy in the Asia-Pacific region. Former Secretary of Defense Robert Gates, for example, characterized the United States as a "resident power" in Asia and the Pacific, enabling the United States to justify its security role over ample geographic distance.

Can U.S. strategy be maintained apart from extant or prospective threats? The regional security architecture in Asia and the Pacific (including America's base infrastructure and forward military presence) has been enhanced in recent years, particularly the alliances with Korea, Japan, and Australia. There is also increased receptivity in Southeast Asia to less institutionalized security relationships, which derive in substantial measure from regional anxieties about potential imbalances of power. The United States has no interest in forgoing these relationships, perhaps most notably with Vietnam.

Regional circumstances are thus changing appreciably, but not necessarily to China's disadvantage. Unlike that of the Soviet Union, Chinese power is multifaceted, diversified, and closely tied to the regional economies. It has the means and the resources to fashion an external posture that (while mindful of American power and policy) operates apart from it. At the same time, most regional actors (including close U.S. allies) have little interest in strategically alienating Beijing. But this requires China to avoid self-defeating actions.

U.S. alliance strategies therefore remain central issues that Beijing continues to weigh. China contends that America's alliances undermine Chinese interests and inhibit the building of a regional security order that would affirm its enhanced stature and role. By implication, it views security alliances as inherently threat-based, with China as a dominant target. Few Chinese analysts are prepared to acknowledge the assurance and deterrence function of U.S. alliances, or the interest-driven relationships that extend well beyond security ties.

Do America's regional alliances pose an intrinsic threat to the security of China? Aside from deeming alliances "Cold War legacies," Chinese officials and strategists seldom articulate their deeper concerns about how U.S. alliances negatively affect Beijing's security interests. Three seem discernible: (1) alliance actions that directly impinge on important Chinese interests (that is, an ally serving as an adjunct and enabler to American power, with Japan as the operative case); (2) U.S. support for an ally or security partner that embolden it to challenge Chinese interests (for example, the Philippines in recent years, and Taiwan in more historical terms); and (3) alliance policies that enhance U.S. forces both technologically and operationally (for example, heightened collaboration on missile defense between the United States and Japan, and increasingly between the United States and South Korea).

Under all three circumstances, China perceives ample reasons to limit or erode the effectiveness of U.S. alliance relationships. But its ability to do so remains limited. It can voice its objections, but it has a voice rather than a vote, and Chinese policy responses can entail decidedly negative costs to its interests. Beijing's heated objections to the U.S.-Korea July 2016 agreement to deploy a Terminal High Altitude Air Defense (THAAD) missile battery on Korean territory offers an especially apt example. Over the past decade or more but especially since Xi Jinping assumed power, China has made major advances in its relationship with the Republic of Korea, more than with any other U.S. ally. The contrast between China's growing alienation from the DPRK and its ever more diversified economic, political, and institutional relations with the ROK has become increasingly evident. ROK President Park Geun-hye's September 2015 appearance on the Tiananmen podium with Xi Jinping and Vladimir Putin to commemorate the seventieth anniversary of the defeat of Japan revealed the realignment of Chinese interests on the Korean peninsula, and Seoul's willingness to accommodate to Chinese policy preferences.

However, Beijing's harsh responses to the THAAD decision and its far more muted reactions to North Korea's accelerated nuclear and missile development have injected renewed uncertainty into the China-ROK relationship. China first began to object to the possibilities of THAAD deployment when heightened missile defense became a public issue in the ROK in 2014. Xi Jinping and other Chinese officials at first aired their concerns in private discussions. They claimed that the radars linked to a THAAD battery would provide the United States with a surveillance capability against Chinese missiles, thereby purportedly undermining Beijing's strategic weapon capabilities. South Korea repeatedly conveyed that its decision derived exclusively from the need to counter the threat posed by an increasingly diversified North Korean missile capability against the ROK. But China has been wholly unwilling to accept the legitimacy of Seoul's security needs, and it has repeatedly accused South Korea of subordinating ROK interests to U.S. strategic needs.

It is too soon to determine whether China's actions have done lasting damage to its relations with South Korea, but it has undoubtedly undermined personal and political relations between Xi Jinping and Park Geun-hye. In weighing the totality of Chinese interests on the Korean peninsula, fuller acceptance of Seoul's alliance with the United States would have been a far more sensible policy decision. China's unwillingness to consider an alternative course of action raises yet again its ability to achieve a balance between the full spectrum of its interests and the realities of regional security. To consider issues of power and uncertainty in Asia and the Pacific, we need to return to the U.S.-China relationship and its longer-term effects on the region.

THE ROAD AHEAD

Relations between the United States and China will be a decisive factor in the future Asia-Pacific security order. The United States is intent on upholding its long-standing regional interests, but China's

power ascendance is now directly influencing U.S. policy deliberations, triggering an equivalent focus on U.S. strategy in Beijing.
However, there is little uniformity of thinking in either capital.
Neither leadership has yet devised a shared strategy commensurate
with the stakes of both states in mutually productive relations. Both
countries offer words of assurance and peaceful intent that cloak
self-protective tendencies in the two leaderships and in their security bureaucracies. The election of Donald Trump adds measurably
to these uncertainties.

For example, some Chinese thinkers argue that America's global
and regional power position, and hence its presumed hegemonic advantage, will diminish over time. But others are not convinced that
China's increased power will lead to increased security, voicing concern that an excessive focus on hard power will distract attention
from far more consequential transitions within Chinese society and
in internal governance. A more creative vision of an equitable security order upholding the interests of both countries while providing
assurance to regional states remains to be written.

Though Chinese military advances represent an important factor
in U.S. strategy, the enduring issues concern America's willingness to
legitimate China as a comprehensive major power, the ability of both
states to avoid an overtly adversarial rivalry, and Beijing's capacity to
pursue a national security strategy that does not directly challenge the
United States. All these issues are very interactive. Most Chinese strategic specialists argue that the United States wants to inhibit the growth
of Chinese power or contain it outright. At a time of heightened nationalistic sentiment within China, this politically safe judgment posits
more contentious Sino-American relations and an increased emphasis
on malign American intentions.

The gestational elements of a Sino-American strategic competition are thus apparent. Chinese critiques of U.S. political-military
behavior in East Asia are not a new phenomenon, but they have become more pronounced as China's absolute and relative power and
the geographic span of its interests have increased. Most of China's
weapons programs, for example, are designed with U.S. military capabilities and defense strategies in mind, requiring military planners in both capitals to weigh the risks of future crises, and whether

these risks are controllable.[31] The debate within China suggests an increased awareness of the potential consequences, but there is no definitive judgment among Chinese strategists.[32]

In assessing American power, Chinese officials and scholars will continue to pay particular attention to the balance of cooperation, competition, and contention. Beijing is trying to determine whether it can dilute the singularity of U.S. power without provoking an acute crisis or a level of tension that undermines Chinese domestic goals. China also needs to determine whether its underlying differences with the United States are negotiable as its power increases, or if China needs to press for an alteration of the rules of the road written and long dominated by the United States.

There is also a subliminal Chinese debate frequently lost amid various characterizations of Sino-U.S. power rivalry. Beijing does not aspire to explicit participation in a U.S.-led security order. The larger question is whether China is capable of developing a security strategy that is acceptable to neighboring states and does not trigger American counter-strategies. Regional states do not want to be caught in the crosswinds of Sino-American strategic rivalry. The prospect for regional order will depend on simultaneous awareness and self-restraint by both the United States and China, and whether the more competitive elements in bilateral relations can be channeled in productive directions.

Amid political-military uncertainty, persistent and possibly growing distrust, and heightened security debate in both countries, the United States and China need to address first-order strategic questions. Will bounded security competition and increased economic interdependence prove an acceptable outcome to both leaderships? Can they constructively address major issues involving third parties where both countries are deeply invested? What are the risks that either or both leaderships might opt for unilateral actions, regardless of the consequences? Are the major differences negotiable to both sides, and can the possible outcomes gain acceptance within the region? The United States and China are not necessarily on a collision course, but they are also not ships passing in the night. For both countries and for the region, the stakes could not be higher.

NOTES

1. Hedley Bull, *The Anarchical Society: A Study of Order in World Politics* (Columbia University Press, 1977), pp. 13–16.

2. G. John Ikenberry, *After Victory: Institutions, Strategic Restraint, and the Rebuilding of Order after Major Wars* (Princeton University Press, 2001).

3. See, in particular, the speech of U.S. Secretary of Defense Ash Carter to the IISS Shangri-La Dialogue, "A Regional Security Architecture Where Everyone Rises," May 30, 2015. Definitional and semantic overlap exist between the concepts of "security order" and "security architecture." The former term is broader and focuses on the larger patterns of interaction between states, whereas the latter deals primarily with different forms of institutional and operational collaboration between military organizations.

4. Jeffrey A. Bader, *Obama and China's Rise-An Insider's Account of America's Asia Strategy* (Brookings, 2012).

5. Xi Jinping, "Statement of H. E. Xi Jinping at the General Debate of the 70th Session of the UN General Assembly" (New York, September 28, 2015) (http://gadebate.un.org/sites/default/files/gastatements/70/70_ZH _en.pdf).

6. For relevant details, consult *Visions and Actions on Jointly Building Silk Road Economic Belt and 21st Century Maritime Silk Road* (Beijing: National Development and Reform Commission, Ministry of Foreign Affairs, and Ministry of Commerce of the People's Republic of China, with State Council authorization, March 2015).

7. Michael D. Shear, "Refugees Must Not Be Turned Away, Obama Says," *New York Times*, November 21, 2015.

8. Barack Obama, "Remarks of President Barack Obama" (weekly address, The White House, October 10, 2015) (https://www.whitehouse.gov /the-press-office/2015/10/10/weekly-address-writing-rules-global-economy).

9. Jiang Yuechen, Zhang Mei, and Li Xiaoyu, *New Progress of the TPP Negotiations and Strategic Considerations of the Parties Concerned,* No. 8 (Beijing: China Institute of International Studies, October 2015), 46.

10. He Yafei, "China Sees a Chance in TPP to Stimulate Reforms," *China-US Focus* 8 (October 2015), p. 36.

11. For a detailed critique of the "assertive China" hypothesis, especially the role of journalists in adopting the narrative, see Alastair Iain Johnston, "How New and Assertive is China's New Assertiveness?" *International Security* 37, no. 4 (Spring 2013), pp. 7–48.

12. See, in particular, Dai Bingguo, "Adhere to the Path of Peaceful Development" (China Ministry of Foreign Affairs, Xinhua, December 6, 2010);

and *White Paper on China's Peaceful Development* (Beijing: Information Office of the State Council, September 2011). The latter document remains the authoritative statement on Chinese foreign policy; despite evidence of foreign policy activism under Xi Jinping, no other policy paper has yet replaced it. For Dai's more recent, sharper edged views, see "Dai Bingguo's Speech at China Development Forum on Building China-US Relationship" (China Ministry of Foreign Affairs, March 20, 2016); and "Speech by Dai Bingguo at China-US Dialogue on South China Sea Between Chinese and US Think Tanks" (China Ministry of Foreign Affairs, July 5, 2016).

13. For relevant citations, see Dingding Chen and Jianwei Wang, "Lying Low No More? China's New Thinking on the *Tao Guang Yang Hui* Strategy," *China: An International Journal* 9, no. 2 (September 2011), pp. 195–216.

14. For a review of these trends, see Bruce Jones and others, "The State of the International Order," Policy Paper 33 (Brookings, February 2014).

15. Wang Jisi, "Marching Westward: The Rebalancing of China's Geostrategy," in *The World in 2020 According to China*, edited by Shao Binbing (Leiden: Brill, 2014), pp. 129–36. Wang first developed this argument in commentaries published in 2012.

16. See, in particular, Yan Xuetong, "From Keeping a Low Profile to Striving for Achievement," *Chinese Journal of International Politics* 7, no. 2, (2014), pp. 153–84.

17. Qin Yaqing, "Continuity through Change: Background Knowledge and China's International Strategy," *Chinese Journal of International Politics* 7, no. 3, (2014), pp. 285–314. Qin was the featured speaker at a late 2015 Political Bureau study session devoted to the reform of global governance amid "profound changes" in the international balance of power. Xi Jinping also delivered a speech at this event. A report of Xi's remarks is available on Xinhua's domestic service. See, in particular, "Xi Jinping: Promote a More Just and Reasonable Global Governance System" (Chinese), Xinhua, October 13, 2015 (http://news.xinhuanet.com/politics/2015-10/13/c_1116812159 .htm). For a detailed and insightful review of scholarly debate, consult Jinghan Zeng, Yuefan Xiao, and Shaun Breslin, "Securing China's Core Interests: The State of Debate in China," *International Affairs* 91, no. 2 (2015), pp. 245–66.

18. See Xi's speeches (or available summaries of his remarks) at the Political Bureau Study Session, January 29, 2013; to the peripheral Diplomacy Work Conference, October 30, 2013; at the Fourth Summit of the Conference on Interaction and Confidence Building Measures in Asia, May 21, 2014; at the Central Foreign Affairs Work Conference, November 29, 2014; at the Boao Forum for Asia, March 28, 2015; and at the Political Bureau collective study session on global governance, October 14, 2015.

19. Wang Yi, "Foreign Minister Wang Yi Meets the Press," Ministry of Foreign Affairs of the People's Republic of China, March 8, 2015 (www.fmprc.gov.cn/mfa_eng/zxxx_662805/t1346238.shtml).

20. Compare, for example, "Remarks by President Obama and President Xi Jinping of the People's Republic of China before Bilateral Meeting" (Sunnylands Retreat, Calif., June 7, 2013); and "Remarks by President Obama at the University of Queensland" (Brisbane, Australia, November 15, 2014).

21. The National Security Law of the People's Republic of China, Article 2 (2015).

22. Tang Shiping, "China's Peripheral Security Environment in 2010–2015: Decisive Factors, Trends and Prospects" (Chinese), *Zhanlue yu guanli* [Strategy and Management], no. 5 (2002), pp. 35–36.

23. Li Xiangyang, "The Goal of China's Peripheral Strategy and Challenges Faced" (Chinese), *Xiandai guoji guanxi* [Contemporary International Relations] (October 2013), pp. 37–39.

24. Ruan Zongze, "What Kind of Periphery Does China Need to Build," China Institute of International Relations, last modified May 28, 2014 (http://www.ciis.org.cn/english/2014-05/28/content_6942279.html).

25. *China's Military Strategy* (Beijing: Information Office of the State Council, May, 2015) (http://www.china.org.cn/china/2015-05/26/content_35661433.html). See also Dennis J. Blasko, "The 2015 Chinese Defense White Paper on Strategy in Perspective: Maritime Missions Require a Change in the PLA Mindset," *China Brief* 15, no. 12, (2015); and Katherine Morton, "China's ambition in the South China Sea: is a legitimate maritime order possible?" *International Affairs* 92, no.4 (2016), pp. 909–40.

26. See, in particular, Amy King, "Where Does Japan Fit in China's 'New Type of Great Power Relations?,'" *Asan Forum*, March 20, 2014 (www.theasanforum.org/where-does-japan-fit-in-chinas-new-type-of-great-power-relations/).

27. Zhang Tuosheng, "Building Trust between China and Japan: Lessons Learned from Bilateral Interactions in the East China Sea," Policy Brief (SIPRI, February 2015); Hu Lingyuan and Gao Lan, "Proactive Pacifism: A Blessing for the Japan-US Alliance?," *China International Studies*, (May–June 2015), pp. 68–82.

28. See *Asia-Pacific Maritime Security Strategy* (Washington, D.C.: U.S. Department of Defense, 2015), especially pp. 5–8.

29. Xi's comments appear in *People's Daily*, January 30, 2013, as cited in Jian Zhang, "China's New Foreign Policy under Xi Jinping: Towards 'Peaceful Rise 2.0?," *Global Change, Peace & Security*, January 28, 2015.

30. For one recent illustration, see Edward Wong, "A Chinese Colonel's Hard-Line Views Gain Currency," *New York Times*, October 3, 2015.

31. Avery Goldstein, "First Things First: The Pressing Danger of Crisis Instability in U.S.-China Relations," *International Security* 37, no. 4 (Spring 2013), pp. 49–89.

32. Zhang Tuosheng, "Crisis Management and China-US Mutual Trust," *China-US Focus*, April 9, 2015 (http://www.chinausfocus.com/foreign-policy /crisis-management-and-china-us-mutual-trust/).

SEVEN

Is There Something Beyond No?

China and Intervention in a New Era

ALLEN CARLSON

 Over the last several years the issue of intervention has once more risen to prominence on the world stage. This process has been driven by the intensification of internal conflicts in various parts of the globe, especially as many of these wars have generated humanitarian crises that cross national boundaries. While such places are geographically distant from China's borders, the nation has been far from an indifferent bystander to these events. Rather, Beijing has played an important role in influencing the types of intervention that have occurred.

This chapter explores emerging trends in how China perceives the phenomenon of intervention by focusing on new writings about the subject among Chinese foreign policy elites (individuals connected to China's foreign policy establishment, but who operate primarily within the country's university and think tank system). In other words, those persons discussed here do not make policy, but their views on intervention are worthy of close consideration; they offer a more open window into China's approach to the subject than can be found in official statements. Such commentary is an important barometer, enabling others to assess recent Chinese thinking on international intervention. Here I interpret the concept of intervention to mean both humanitarian operations as well as blunter episodes of unilateral military intervention. To do otherwise would be to place artificial constraints on this survey and lead to an incomplete sense of the direction in which Chinese considerations of intervention have been heading in recent years.

Chinese discussions about intervention are quite divided. On the one hand, a number of analysts have openly decried the rise of what they dismissively label the "new interventionism" (*xin ganshezhuyi*) in international politics and have warned of the dangers of such a trend. On the other hand, some within China have forwarded more sanguine analyses. Most notably, two high-profile elites, Yu Xiaofeng and Wang Yizhou, have suggested the need for China to develop more innovative responses to new challenges within the international system, and in so doing they have staked out a rather flexible position on the possible merits of multilateral cooperation and intervention. Their observations in this regard have been complemented by a number of commentaries that have generally looked favorably on the concept of the "responsibility to protect" (*baohu de zeren*) and the manner in which it has led to a modification in the role of the principle of nonintervention in international politics.

Such differences in thinking within Chinese elite circles cuts against the grain of the conventional wisdom about China's stance on intervention, which continues to posit that China basically just says no. The differences also reveal that a Janus-like divide exists among Chinese foreign policy elites regarding the extent to which they look out at the world via retrospective lenses colored by fear and uncertainty versus prospective ones that envision Beijing as a global power.

The remainder of this chapter develops these observations in two parts. The first section outlines the main contours of China's official stance on intervention, and then briefly demonstrates the growing focus on intervention among Chinese foreign policy elites. The second explores the substance of such analysis, and in so doing describes the factors that are driving such writing. The conclusion of the chapter considers the likely implications of such findings for China's future approach to intervention.

CHINA'S POST–COLD WAR APPROACH TO INTERVENTION

The regions of the world in which interventions have occurred over the last two and a half decades have been rather distant from China's borders. Thus, it would not be unreasonable to think that Beijing would have little interest in such episodes because they do not impinge on the country's core national security concerns. In practice, however, China has paid close attention to interventions wherever they occur and has actively sought to shape the when, where, and how of such operations.

As emphasized in my earlier work, Beijing has done more than simply say no to these activities. Rather, during the 1990s and the first part of the next decade, China's leaders developed a pragmatic modus operandi for dealing with the prospect of intervention in other parts of the world. First, they unfailingly championed the principle of nonintervention and questioned the need to ever transgress it. Second, they generally did not actively stand in the way of operations by refraining from using the country's veto power in the United Nations Security Council. Third, with few exceptions, they also managed to avoid explicitly endorsing intervention by abstaining on key resolutions that operationalized such endeavors. Fourth, they also acceded to a limited number of interventions, while contending that none of these created new international precedence. Finally, they gradually, and incrementally, built up their technical and financial support for certain aspects of these endeavors.[1]

During much of the first decade of the new century the era of humanitarian intervention on the world stage appeared to be ending. Since then, however, it has experienced a rather dramatic rebirth. In response, Beijing has largely continued to follow the same pattern of behavior it established during the 1990s: a blend of dogmatic rhetorical opposition to intervention, coupled with a more pragmatic acceptance of certain of these operations. In order to analyze various competing views of intervention by Chinese elites, a four-step process was followed. First, a survey of the China National Knowledge Infrastructure's list of Chinese academic publications was conducted. This list is part of CNKI's China Academic Journals Full-text Database. Articles with the term "interference" (*ganshe*) in their titles and published between 2008 and 2015 were aggregated within the "Politics / Military Affairs / Law" section of the site. This search yielded a total of 170 articles, and, as the list below demonstrates, such analysis grew in volume during this time period:

2009	24	2011	20	2013	30
2010	23	2012	50	2014	23

Second, in order to uncover the main characteristics of such analysis, certain terms were searched for in each article's full text. Specifically, articles were isolated that contained at least three references to three separate terms related to different aspects of intervention: "new interventionism," "responsibility to protect," and "major operations other than war" (*fei zhanzheng junshi xingdong*). The last of these terms yielded a null set. In other words, there was no cognitive overlap between Chinese analysis of intervention and the emerging discussion within Chinese security circles regarding the development of new operational responsibilities (at home and abroad) for the People's Liberation Army. In contrast, twenty-one articles contained at least three references to "new interventionism," and twenty-four made similar mention of the "responsibility to protect." While three articles used both of these terms, the rest of these two lists were mutually exclusive, and thus suggestive of rather distinct points of emphasis within the analysis forwarded within them. While neither of these terms occupied a majority of the analysis surveyed for this chapter, no other concept appeared with similar frequency within these journals, and as such they indicate the two main points of reference within this work.

Alongside this survey of publications within the CNKI database, a third, broader search of the term "interference" was conducted using both English- and Chinese-language search engines, with an eye toward isolating the commentary that was most prevalent on such sites. Finally, the survey focused especially on the work of the two scholars mentioned above, Yu Xiaofeng and Wang Yizhou, particularly prominent voices in the field.

CONSIDERATIONS OF INTERVENTION—DIVIDED ANALYSIS, CONTRASTING POINTS OF EMPHASIS

This four-step process uncovered marked differences within recent Chinese elite writing about intervention. More specifically, it revealed two distinct clusters of analysis of this issue. On the one hand, a number of analysts have pointedly condemned the rise of what they see as a new round of interventionist policies in global politics as both a continuation of older patterns of hegemonic activity in this sphere and a dangerous step backward within international relations. On the other hand, some scholars have forwarded analysis of intervention that is much less critical of the trend. In particular, Wang Yizhou and Yu Xiaofeng have argued that China has nothing to fear from intervention, and is, on the contrary, uniquely positioned to make a positive contribution toward shaping its development (should it have the confidence and poise to do so). In addition, a handful of Chinese elites have engaged the "responsibility to protect" concept as a vehicle to raise question about their country's attachment to the principle of nonintervention.

Opposing New Interventionism: Old Fears, New Concerns

The more defensive side of the Chinese discussion about interventions fits neatly with the continuing conventional wisdom about the country's steadfast opposition to such operations. Contributors to this strand of Chinese analysis find very little of merit in any given episode of intervention and much of concern within the overall reinvigoration of what they view as an insidious trend on the world stage within which powerful states (especially the United States) bully weaker ones in the name of preventing humanitarian crises. Such analysts put virtually no stock in the rhetoric that has accompanied most multilateral interventions over the last decade, and instead find a great deal of evidence within the patterns of such operations of great power politics and hegemonic behavior. There are three main variants of this type of argument within Chinese elite analysis, each of which is distinct, but all of which are unified by concerns about what is portrayed as America's destructive attachment to hegemonic behavior (and what this might mean for China).

Attempts to Reveal the True Nature of the New Interventionism

Shen Dingli and Qian Wenrong are two of the leading Chinese voices opposing the development of the new interventionism in international politics. Of the two, Shen is the better known (both inside China and internationally) because he has an extensive publication record (in both English and Chinese) and has long been a fixture at Fudan University, more specifically its Institute of International Studies.[2] In 2012 he penned a short, but quite blunt, piece on intervention that appeared in *Renmin luntan* (People's Forum).

This article directly challenged the legitimacy of America's intervention in Libya the previous year, while overlooking the fact that Beijing had not stood in the way of such an operation. It also warned of the dangers that the rise of new interventionism posed to the world. Indeed, the subtitle of Shen's article emphasized that U.S. behavior was moving from a regional focus to one of "global intervention" (*quanqiu ganshe*).[3] Such a tendency, he wrote, was nothing new, but given its acceleration, it was something that "people cannot but be on alert about" (*zhe bu you shi ren tigao jingti*).[4]

This sharp opening to the article was followed by a series of references to America's purported role in stirring up instability in the Middle East and Africa during the "Arab Spring." Moreover, Shen viewed all such activities as sharing a number of common characteristics. First, they were grounded in attempts by the United States to find justification for such actions within the "humanitarian protection clauses" (*rendaozhuyi baohu tiaokuan*) of the UN Charter. However, Shen contended that these moves were no more than baseless attempts to find "gaps" (*que kou*) within the UN system within which Washington could pretend to be acting for the benefit of others when in practice it was just engaging in "provocative" (*you yiding shandongli*) behaviors. Second, he acknowledged that the United States normally sought authorization for its intervention from the UN Security

Council, but added that this body did not always go along with American mandates. As a result, Shen argued that the third trait of the new interventionism stemmed from the fact that when UN approval was not forthcoming, the supporters of intervention simply looked to strike at targeted states in an attempt to "force regime change" (*poshi qi gengdie zhengquan*).

What appears to have been most galling to Shen about such actions was they are not novel; rather they are little more than a case of Washington attempting to dress up its old tendencies in new clothing. He specifically charged that Washington has repeatedly attempted to justify intervention with a Rolodex of self-serving excuses ranging from promoting regional stability, to countering terrorism, to protecting human rights. Yet, regardless of which words the United States uses, it is clear that what America's leaders are really attempting to do is "abuse the Security Council's right to authorize action" (*lanyong anlihui shouquan*), while working "to create the negative precedent to use military force to subvert political authority of other states" (*wuzhuang dianfu qita guozhengquan de erlie*).[5]

Qian Wenrong's 2013 analysis, which appeared in the pages of *Heping yanjiu* (Peace Studies), stopped short of Shen's veritable call to arms against the United States, but also found nothing of merit within America's support of intervention.[6] The international legal scholar charged that Washington has repeatedly made use of the "excuse" (*jiekou*) of promoting democratic values and humanitarianism in the service of using arms to "hasten regime change" (*shixing zhengquan gengdie*), when in practice it was only attempting to preserve America's role as a global hegemon.[7] Moreover, since 2011, he contended that events in northern Africa, particularly Libya, have revealed that the United States has become even more expansive in its pursuit of such goals. While America succeeded in bringing Gaddafi down, and did so in the name of preserving peace, Qian noted that in practice such actions "create even larger humanitarian disasters and harm both regional and global peace" (*zhizao xin de gengda de rendaozhuyi zainan, weihai dequ he shijie heping*).[8] Moreover, Washington has continued down such a path despite the concentrated efforts of other members of the international system to blunt such a drive. Given such a context, the Chinese scholar concluded that America's ongoing attachment to "intervention" may now be "included within the scope of being both war crimes and crimes against humanity" (*jun yinglie renfan you zhan-zhengzui, weihai renlei zui de fanwei zhi*).[9]

In a subsequent *Heping yu fazhan* (Peace and Development) article, Qian returned to these themes and dwelled at greater length on the extent to which propping up hegemonism was the real driving force behind American humanitarian efforts throughout the globe (especially in northern Africa and the Middle East). More specifically, he charged the United States with carrying out a savage bombing campaign in Libya, while its efforts to enact sanctions against Iran were akin to the work of "the old colonists' right of extraterritoriality" (*lao zhiminzhuyi de zhiwai faquan*), now put into the service of preserving "international hegemony and great power politics" (*guoji baquan he qiangquan zhengzhi*).[10] According to Qian, such an approach grew out of underlying American pathology about the country's exceptional place within world history, a view that has empowered Washington to feel justified in fermenting "unrest and regime change" (*zhizao dongluan he cehua zhengquan gengdie*) around the globe.[11]

Beyond High-Profile Elites, Commentary Even More Shrill

While Shen Dingli and Qian Wenrong are the most established Chinese elites (in terms of seniority, publishing record, and visibility outside China) to have recently written about new interventionism, they are far from the only ones who in recent years have published pieces on this topic within China. On the contrary, during this period a stream of critical analysis of new interventionism has appeared in the country's academic journals that focus upon international relations and national security. For example, a 2012 article in *Beijing daxue xuebao* (Journal of Beijing University) pessimistically reported that the world is still a place of "great power politics," and within such a structure the United States has continued in its attempts to cloak its baser motives in the cloth of promoting "humanitarianism" (*rendazhuyi*). The authors of the piece then called on China to more actively push for a correction to such a trend by utilizing its influence within the United Nations especially via a continuing defense of the superiority of sovereignty's role within international politics. Failing to do so, they warned, will result in the "creation of even greater humanitarian crises" (*zaocheng geng da de rendaozhuyi zainan*) around the globe.[12]

The following year, as questions regarding intervention in Syria and the Ukrainian crisis became more prominent, many Chinese commentators became even more suspicious of what they saw as the motives and goals that underlay U.S. efforts to promote intervention in such conflicts. For example, Jiang Xiaoran asserted that the continued U.S. drive in support of "neo-interventionism was spurring the acceleration of terrorism around the world, and undermining peace, and even the pace of economic development." Jiang added that it was clear the United States had no qualms about using the language of human rights in order to put others in their place. This trait showed that "America's globalizing interests are the underlying rationale of the new interventionism" (*Meiguo liyi quanqiuhua shi xinganshezhuyi de shen cengci yinsu*).[13] Moreover, Jiang claimed that such behavior is "inseparably related" (*youzhe buke fenshou de guanxi*) to the rise of terrorism.[14] More broadly, America's obstinate promotion of intervention appears to have one ultimate target: China, the only country with the potential to stand in the way of the United States on the world stage.

An article published the same year by Li Jingzhi echoed this claim and the degree to which it posed a threat to China. Indeed, Li contended that it has already "caused losses for China" (*dui woguo suo zaocheng de sunshi*).[15] More specifically, in places like Libya it has damaged Chinese investments. Even more directly the United States has, under the banner of human rights, "used a variety of means to interfere in China's internal affairs" (*butong de xingshi ganshe zhongguo neizheng*), including supporting the Dalai Lama and other Tibetan and Xinjiang separatist elements, and even propping up Taiwanese independence.[16]

Intervention's Real Goal—Challenging Beijing's Maritime Claims

While the analysis discussed so far has been quite blunt in its condemnation of the United States, such sentiments are rather consistent with earlier, critical Chinese commentary on intervention. In this sense it is to be expected. What was, however, surprising within Chinese analysis was the extent to which some Chinese writers have begun to see insidious linkages between the resurgence of interventionism worldwide and an emergent threat to Chinese maritime security. More specifically, a small number of elites have started to express concerns about the threat of intervention by the United States to China in the South and East. Such work tends to make direct mention of Secretary of State Clinton's 2010 statement regarding U.S. opposition to unilateral actions in the oceans south of China. Some Chinese elites have subsequently linked this comment to the topic of intervention more broadly.

The earliest such analysis was located within the nebulous world of Chinese cyberspace. For example, when keyword searching the term "new interventionism" on Sina.com and Baidu.com, as well as Google, one of the first articles that consistently turned up on the first page of each of these sites is a blog post by Zhang Jingwei. A self-described "finance columnist" (*caijing zhuanlan zuojia*), who is affiliated with the Harbin branch of the Chinese Academy of Social Sciences (CASS), Zhang appears to have had nearly 5 million visits to his site, and has contributed a number of columns to Chinese newspapers.

This particular post was entitled "America's 'New Interventionism' Toward China" (*Meiguo duihua xinganshezhuyi*). Startlingly, the article began, "America is experimenting with 'new interventionism' and its main target is China" (*Meiguo ye zai shiyan ganshezhuyi erqie zhuyao zhendui Zhongguo*).[17] More specifically, Zhang charged that in recent years the United States had been taking an increasingly combative attitude toward China, one that was intended to "set off a wave of territorial disputes" (*xiangqile yibobo de lingtu zhengduan*) in Asia, especially in the South and East China Sea.[18] Along China's southern flank Zhang contended that for over a decade China had been working assiduously to develop a peaceful relationship with Vietnam. However, this situation was disrupted in 2010 when, according to the author, Clinton's incendiary remarks pushed their territorial conflict into a more "intense period" (*jilie qi*).[19] Zhang also charged that Washington had concurrently accelerated the militarization of the Sino-Japanese dispute in the East China Sea by placing conflicted territory there within the scope of the U.S.-Japan Security Treaty.

Zhang also accused the United States of a litany of other efforts intended to undermine Chinese territorial claims in both maritime regions. Such actions revealed the "typical nature" (*xiangdang di-anxin*) of America's "new interventionist" approach to China.[20] Indeed, Zhang lambasted the United States for attempting to make use of "geography, neighbors, sovereignty, nuclear (issues), cross-Strait relations, as well as trade and finance, in an increasingly desperate attempt to control China."[21]

This refrain was reiterated in 2014 in an article written by Zhang Yuquan (affiliated with *Zhongshang Daxue* [Sun Yat-sen University]) in *Guoji anquan yanjiu* (Journal of International Security Studies). This journal is published by *Guoji Guanxi Xueyuan* (University of International Relations), and as such has a level of reputability that far exceeds any blog post, as it is on a par with China's leading academic publications in the field. The article began with a bevy of references to the work of other Chinese scholars and called attention to the fact that such writing makes it clear that "America's policies on the South China Sea conflict have never left the principle of interventionism . . . it is just that under different historical conditions the specific content of American intervention has changed somewhat."[22] Moving beyond such a statement, Zhang explained that his use of the term "intervention" was an expansive one as "apart from military and humanitarian intervention, it includes aspects of economic and diplomatic pressure," which are utilized with the intention of undermining a state's sovereignty.[23]

Working within such a broad conceptualization of "intervention," Zhang reiterated that the United States has always sought to interfere in the South China Sea. However, he added that since the end of the Cold War such activities have escalated as Washington has made increasing use of multilateral maritime regimes in the region. As these policies are the product of a combination of American economic and security interests, as well as an underlying cultural predisposition toward intervening, they are unlikely to change.

Seeing Opportunity Where Others Find Threat

While it may seem that fear of U.S. power and worries about Chinese weakness are pervasive in analysis such as that of Zhang, and by extension appear to be deeply entrenched within the country's foreign policy establishment, this is only part of the recent Chinese view of intervention. Two of China's more accomplished students of international relations, Wang Yizhou and Yu Xiaofeng, have a more expansive and flexible approach, especially informed by the potentially positive role of the responsibility to protect concept within international politics.

Wang and Yu have devoted considerable attention in recent years to the issue of intervention. Both have carved out positions on intervention that are quite innovative and have done so primarily with reference to China's expanding international profile.

Wang received his Ph.D. from the CASS in 1988 and became one of the leading researchers at CASS's Institute of World Economics and Politics (*shijie jingji yu zhengzhi yanjiusuo*) during the following decade. Most significantly, for much of this period he was chief editor of *World Economic and Politics*, which has long been considered one of China's leading international relations journals. In 2009 Wang moved from CASS to Peking University's School of International Studies, where he currently serves as an associate dean. Virtually all of Wang Yizhou's work has revolved around a central theme: transnational forces are growing more pronounced within the contemporary international system, and while they are not so strong as to surpass its Westphalian foundations, they have significantly modified such fundamental structures.

The touchstone for Wang's most recent discussions of these issues can be found in his fascinating 2011 book *Creative Involvement: Chinese Foreign Policy's New Orientation* (*Chuangzaoxing jieru: Zhongguo waijiao quxiang*).[24] On this publication's pages, Wang lays out a broad argument in favor of China moving forward in regard to its approach to the international system. Indeed, he posits that making such a move will be good for both China and the rest of the international system as it will allow the country to move past some of the contentious issues it faces while becoming a model for other countries as well.

According to Wang the pursuit of "creative involvement" is characterized by three broad factors. First, it is premised upon the belief that the overall trend in the world continues to be one of peace and development. Second, given such continuity, China's orientation toward the world should be one of leading, constructing, and actively participating in the international system in accord with attempts to promote international norms and standards that are beneficial to both China and other international actors. Third, it is in "opposition to a continuation of traditional ideological modes" (*ta jujue chengwei xiguan sixiang he zuofa*) and embraces the concept that in periods of difficulty it is essential not to fall back on "simple oppositional methods for resolving problems" (*jiandan de duikang jiejue fangfa*).[25] This involves a willingness to cultivate a positive attitude toward the international system that is developed in accord to "eastern culture and history" (*dongfang wenhua yu lishi*).[26] Such moves have to be done with respect for the principle of sovereignty; however, this norm's role within international politics is not static and unchanging. Rather, according to Wang, it is constantly evolving. More specifically, in the post–Cold War era if a state abuses its sovereign status, it can "give up its sovereign interests, lose its international standing, and even be changed."[27] He then concludes that China cannot pretend that such changes have not occurred, on the contrary it should pursue a creative involvement approach to the world that "pays attention to this type of development."[28]

Wang then directly applied such concepts to the issue of intervention in a 2013 *Guoji zhengzhi yanjiu* (International Politics Studies) article. He began this piece with a defense of China's ongoing attachment to the principle of nonintervention, but quickly pivoted to arguing that "in order to be more in line with the changing characteristics of a new period" and "in accordance with China's own situation," it is increasingly urgent for the country to reconsider this approach. According to Wang as the world has changed, so too has the role that nonintervention should play in international politics. More specifically, "the damage caused by internal conflicts is not limited to those living within the areas in which they take place" (*hen you keneng bujin shanghai benguo diqu de renmin*).[29] While it is essential that involvement in such conflicts respect the UN Charter and the principle of noninterference, it is also increasingly the case that they demand "a high level of international involvement in the internal crises of states" (*guoji shehui canyu gebie guojia neibu weiji*).[30] Such a trend has increasingly required China to "play a new role" (*banyan de xin juese*) in these situations. It cannot afford to woodenly, "mechanically" (*jixiehua*) take a stance on noninterference.[31]

Yu Xiaofeng, the father of nontraditional security studies in China, has expanded on Wang's writings in this regard in a pair of recent, well-placed articles within China.[32] The longer of these two pieces appeared in *Guoji anquan yanqjiu* (Journal of International Security Studies) at the start of 2014 and stands in rather stark contrast to Zhang Yuquan's analysis of intervention that appeared in the very same journal. Unlike Zhang, Yu finds nothing to be particularly defensive about when it comes to the topic of intervention. On the contrary, within the context of his sweeping study of the contribution China might make to the development of the concept of "shared security" (*gongxiang anquan*) Yu urges China to think more creatively about the international system. In so doing he shows no sign of misgivings about how the United States might manipulate the concept of security. Instead, Yu takes stock of what those in the "West" are saying about how various aspects of globalization have created the need for all nations to think more collectively about their individual security.

Building on such a foundation Yu emphasizes that the basic sovereign-centric nature of the international system is unchanging, but he also notes that new developments have already had an impact on what can, and should, be considered as within the legitimate scope of the international community's right to intervene. Given China's own experiences and cultural predispositions, and what Yu sees as the positive aspects of its involvement in other parts of the world, he feels the country is uniquely positioned to help shape such trends.[33]

Later in 2014 Yu made a more direct link between these themes and the issue of intervention in a *Guoji guanxi yanjiu* (Journal of International Studies) article. After reiterating the claims he had previously made about the growing importance of collective security, he took note of China's ongoing attachment to the principle of noninterference. However, he then added that such a fixation has become counterproductive. More specifically, Yu observed, "China must consider giving up a traditional approach to stiffly and unconditionally not intervening" (*Zhongguo dou bixu kaolu bingqi jiangying de wutiao-*

jian bu jieru de chuantong zuofa), and instead give consideration to how to create the conditions to "intervene in a creative way" (*jieru fanshi*)."[34]

Importantly, Yu does not believe he is the only Chinese scholar promoting such a change in perspective. On the contrary, he sees facets of such thinking in the work of many Chinese foreign policy elites, including Yan Xuetong, Zhao Tingyang, Zhu Mingquan, Wang Yiwei, Su Changhe, Li Dongyan, among others. According to Yu, all of these scholars are exploring ways in which aspects of Chinese culture and civilization may help guide the country's rise on the world stage.

R2P: Not Such a Threat to China

The threads within Wang and Yu's writing on intervention have reverberated within a wave of new Chinese writing on "the responsibility to protect" concept. The origins of such a norm can be found in the humanitarian interventions that occurred (and those that did not) during the 1990s, and in the work of the International Commission on Intervention and State Sovereignty in 2000, as well as the Secretary General's 2009 report on the concept. In a general sense both of these documents place an emphasis on all states' obligations to protect their own populations, the international community's commitment to assist in the development of such capabilities, and its right to intervene when states fail in this regard. In other words, the "responsibility to protect" concept constitutes a sustained consideration of the degree to which states' sovereign rights need to be adjusted and modified within the contemporary international order.

Not surprisingly, Chinese analysts have approached such a concept with caution as it inherently challenges Beijing's promotion of the principle of noninterference in any country's internal affairs. However, unlike Chinese discussions of the new interventionism, elite analysis of R2P has had more than one note to it. In other words, while Chinese analysts have expressed reservations about the potential misuse of the concept on the international stage by certain powers, they have also found some merit in the idea that within today's international system sovereignty should not be treated as sacrosanct.

A leading example of such analysis is contained within an article that Yuan Juanjuan, a legal scholar at Peking University, contributed to the journal *Hebei faxue* (Hebei Law Journal) in 2012. The piece began with an acknowledgment that the concept of R2P had "opened a breach" (*dakaile tupokou*) between the principles of sovereignty and nonintervention.[35] Yuan then noted that due to such a development it is possible that sovereignty's role in international politics has gone from a stage of being "limited" to one in which international society has been empowered to use "non-compulsory means of intervening" (*guoji shehui caiqu qiangzhi shouduan ganyu*) in a manner that has caused a "derogation of sovereignty" (*zhuquan de jiansun*) within the contemporary international system and may now be on the verge of entering a period in which international society has the right to "use coercive intervention" (*caiqu qianzhi shouduan ganyu*), with the expectation that all members of the international system actively cooperate with such a development.[36]

Rather than denigrate this trend as an artifact of U.S. manipulation, Yuan takes note of the extent to which China, in its position as a permanent member of the UN Security Council, has played a positive role in articulating its limits. Thus, on the issue of the responsibility to protect "China and international society have kept pace with one another" (*Zhongguo yu guoji shehui baochi tongbu*) in a way that is indicative of the increasingly responsible role the country is playing within international politics.[37]

Such a sentiment was echoed in a contribution by Yang Zewei, a scholar affiliated with Wuhan University's Law School, in *Falu kexue* (Legal Science). The piece began with an overview of the development of the humanitarian intervention norm and then turned to a consideration of how China's new position as a global power has "made it increasingly difficult for China to abide to the principle of non-intervention" (*shi Zhongguo keshou bu ganshe neizheng yuanze mianlin xuduo kunnan*).[38] Indeed, this trend has developed to such an extent that it has become "entirely necessary for China to re-consider the principle of non-interference" (*chongxin dingwei bu ganshe neizhang yuanze*). Yang then stops short of calling for a jettisoning of this cardinal tenet of Chinese foreign policy, but, advocates for the promotion of "protective intervention" (*baohuxing ganyu*).[39]

In short, China should support intervention in cases in which there are serious humanitarian crises, or, importantly, when China's national interests are severely threatened or damaged." Or, as Yang writes, the principle of protective intervention pertains under two conditions, first in cases of extreme threats to humanity, second "when China's national interests are threatened" (*er shi Zhongguo de guojia liyi shoudao weixie*).[40] Such a turn should assist the country in its efforts to make a more positive contribution to international society and do so in a manner that should strengthen its ability to "maintain" (*weihu*) its own interests as well.[41]

In 2014 a third article focusing on "the responsibility to protect" concept reiterated the claims previously made by Yuan and Yang. The piece was published in *Guoji wenti yanjiu* (Journal of International Studies) by the pair of Fudan University scholars, Zhen Ni and Chen Zhimin. It emphasized that while China should continue to uphold the principle of nonintervention in international politics, the manner in which it interprets such a position, and puts it into practice, should be flexible and pragmatic. More specifically, they note that to date the country has "agreed that in instances when a country experiences massive humanitarian crises or wide spread human rights abuses" the UN should get involved with the discussion of internal politics within such a sovereign state, and China should show much "flexibility" (*linghuoxing*) in such situations.[42]

In sum, neither in the work of Wang or Yu, nor in the Chinese analysis focused on R2P, is there an emphasis on an incipient threat to China lurking beneath the surface of the renewed round of interventions in international politics. On the contrary, such work suggest that it is China's own unease on this score that has prevented it from playing a more constructive, influential role in shaping how such operations are conceptualized and carried out. In this regard the enemy is less to be found in Washington and more located within the tendency of so many within China to think about such developments in "traditional" and outmoded ways that accentuate the dangers they pose.

CONCLUSION: IS THERE SOMETHING BEYOND NO?

The dichotomy within Chinese elite writing about intervention is suggestive of two pointedly different futures within China's stance on such episodes. First, the discordant chorus of naysayers to intervention within China may very well be a forerunner to the development of a much more muscular and assertive Chinese stance in opposition of intervention. Such a resolve would stand at the nexus of swelling Chinese pride in the country's growing international influence, coupled with underlying unease about America's intent to derail such a development. In other words, elite chest-thumping and gnashing of the teeth over infringements upon Libyan, or Syrian, sovereignty reveals more about the way those within the Chinese foreign policy establishment think about their own country (and its changing relationship with the United States) than it does about North Africa or the Middle East.

On this score, it is clear that many Chinese elites are incredibly wary of the degree to which they feel America is likely to cling to its hegemonic status (regardless of the price of such an action). As a result, they are deeply dis-settled by the extent to which Washington may be able to exploit Chinese weaknesses at home to undermine the current power structure there. While it is entirely possible that the United States is attempting to shape events in and around China, it also seems rather far-fetched to jump to the conclusion that Washington is actively looking to interfere in the region. Thus, Chinese sensitivities on this front are more a reflection of an almost Cybil-like pairing of confidence and anxieties than they are a product of American policies. As such, the actions Washington takes within such a Chinese narrative are almost irrelevant, as whatever the United States does will be interpreted in a negative light, and, decried as both hegemonic and a threat to China.

Extending such a hostile worldview forward, one can expect that China's stance on intervention is likely to grow increasingly truculent in the coming years. Bluntly stated, Beijing will become more reticent to go along with operations that are viewed within China as little more than the death rattles of a failing hegemon bent on preventing the country from attaining its rightful position as a major power on the world stage. While it may not behoove Beijing to oppose all interventions in the short term (or even be necessary), we should expect to see an ever-decreasing Chinese willingness to show flexibility on this front. China will say no more often, and at a much louder decibel, than has previously been the case, and in so doing seek to put an end to this new era of intervention. This, though, is not the only possible future into which China is heading. On the contrary, analyses like Wang and Yu's hint at the likelihood of a rather different scenario. Within their worldview China is also rising, but its rise is not nearly as fraught with dangers as other Chinese elites suggest.

Chinese foreign policy elites operating within this perspective are less alarmed by the manner in which the international system is changing. On the contrary, they generally take a positive perspective on the patterns of deepening interdependence, the erosion of state sovereignty, and the rise of new international norms, which appear to be unfolding on the global stage. Indeed, such trends have had a beneficial impact on both the world and China. In so doing they have not altered the fundamentals of the existing international order, but have modified states' interests through creating the space for enhanced levels of multilateral cooperation between states. While America may be behind such developments, and has attempted to utilize them to its own benefit, they have now extended well beyond Washington's control, and become part of the warp and weft of a new international order.

Rather than disparage this shift as those elites who rail against the "new interventionism" have done, Chinese analysts such as Wang and Yu accept that change has occurred, and take note of the degree to which China has benefited from these changes. The country's rise on the world stage has coincided with it; to ignore this is to misunderstand how China's relationship with the rest of the international system has changed over the last two decades. More importantly, a knee-jerk attachment to the defense of the principle of noninterference in response to such developments runs counter to two underlying aspects of China's emerging role as a global power.

First, whereas the United States is weighed down by its own hegemonic position and the baggage it has produced, China's own stature on the world stage is buoyed by the degree to which it is new to great power politics and enhanced by historical and civilizational foundations that make it more inclined to seek out cooperative and relational solutions to complex problems. In other words, China is poised to more actively shape the world in a way that is more consistent with its own interests and cultural heritage, but the process of creating such an order will not be particularly disruptive. Beijing can afford to go along with intervention because it faces no real challenge from such operations.

Second, it will potentially retard the manner in which the country responds to the types of responsibilities and obligations that have developed as China has become a major power. In other words, as the country's global footprint has expanded, so too have its needs to protect such a position, and defend aspects of its national interest that are geographically distance from China and located within the territory of other sovereign states. Given such an expanding presence on the world stage China should place a premium on molding the parameters under which intervention may be justified and legitimized, rather than simply stand in opposition to all such episodes.

In the short term, there are simply not enough cases of intervention (or proposed interventions) to determine in which of these two directions China's stance on intervention is heading. On the one hand, China's stance on Libya is more consistent with the flexibility on intervention seen in Wang and Yu's work. On the other hand, its use of veto power to stop similar operations in Syria resonates with the elite voices that oppose intervention under almost any conditions. However, it is difficult to say which of these two cases carry more weight. As such, the next major humanitarian crisis in the globe may very well offer a crucial bellwether data point that will allow us to garner a better sense of which side in the Chinese debate on intervention is winning, whether or not Beijing is still willing to play by the rules of an international game not of its own making, or if it is going to begin to rewrite this playbook in a manner that is more consistent with its own perceived needs and interests.

NOTES

1. See Allen Carlson, "Helping to Keep the Peace (Albeit Reluctantly): China's Recent Stance on Sovereignty and International Intervention," *Pacific Affairs* (Spring 2004), pp. 9–27.

2. Shen's full biography can be found at www.cas.fudan.edu.cn/view profile.en.php?id=66.

3. Shen Dingli, "*Meiguo xin ganshezhuyi dongxiang guancha*" [A survey of trends in the new American interventionism], *Renmin luntan* [People's Forum] 10 (2012), p. 4.

4. Ibid.

5. Ibid.

6. For decades Qian served as a correspondent for the Xinhua News Agency, most notably as the Director of its office at the United Nations. Moreover, beginning in the 1990s, he moved into a number of advisory and analyst positions within China's expanding think-tank community. This includes affiliations with the United Nations Association of China and the China Foundation for International Studies. A short bio for Qian Wenrong can be found at http://english.cri.cn/7146/2011/10/25/2001s664332.htm.

7. Qian Wenrong, "*Xin ganshezhuyi dui guoji zhixu de chongqi*" [The impact of new interventionism on the international order], *Heping yu fazhan* [Peace and Development] 1 (2013), p. 23. Please note that this journal also carries English-language versions of much of its content. However, for this essay the Chinese version of Qian's writing was utilized.

8. Ibid., p. 25.

9. Ibid., p. 27.

10. Qian Wenrong, "*Meiguo liweilun shi Meiguo baquanzhuyi duiwai zhengce de sixiang jichu*" [American exceptionalism is the ideological foundation for america's hegemonic foreign policy], *Heping yu fazhan* [Peace and Development] 6 (2013), p. 35.

11. Ibid.

12. He Zhaoyu and and Shen Xiaoruo, "*Shilun rendaozhuyi ganshe yu Zhongguo duice*" [On humanitarian interventionism and China's countermeasures] *Beijing daxue xuebao* [Journal of Beijing University] 13, no. 4 (2012), p. 64.

13. Jiang Xiaoran, "*Meiguo xinganshezhuyi ji yinxiang*" [The influence of the new American interventionism], *Shang* [Trade] 9 (September 2013), p. 168.

14. Ibid., p. 167.

15. Li Jingzhi, "*Jingti xinganshezhuyi yousuo shangsheng*" [Watch out for the new interventionism], *Sixiang lilun jiaoyu dao kan* [Leading Journal of Ideological & Theoretical Education], 3 (2013), p. 57.

16. Ibid., p. 58.

17. Zhang Jingwei, "*Meiguo dui hua 'xinganshezhuyi'*" [America's 'new interventionism' toward China], May 5, 2012 (http://blog.sina.com.cn/s/blog_40758f8c0102dzoc.html).

18. Ibid.

19. Ibid..

20. Ibid.

21. Ibid.

22. Zhang Yuquan, "*Ganshezhuyi shijiao xia de Meiguo nanhai zhengci luoji ji Zhongguo de yingdui celue*" [The policy logic of the South China Sea from the perspective of interventionism and China's countermeasures], *Guoji anquan yanjiu* [International Security Studies] 5 (2014), p. 82.

23. Ibid., p. 84.

24. Wang Yizhou, *Chuangzaoxing jieru: Zhongguo waijiao quxiang* [Creative involvement: Chinese Foreign policy's new orientation] (Beijing University Press, 2011).

25. Ibid., p. 5.

26. Ibid., p. 21.

27. Ibid., p. 99.

28. Ibid., p. 100.

29. Wang Yizhou, "*Chuangxin bu ganshe yuanze, jiada baohu haiwai liyi de lidu*" [An innovative approach to the principle of non-interference, will increase the protection of overseas interests], *Guoji zhengzhi yanjiu* [International Politics Studies] 2 (2013), p. 3.

30. Ibid.

31. Ibid., p. 4.

32. Yu established one of the first, and the most well-known, centers for nontraditional security studies at his home institution, Zhejiang University, over a decade ago. He has published a long list of articles on the topic of NTS; been a visiting scholar at CASS, Oxford, and Harvard; and won a series of academic awards and honors within China for his writing. His CV can be found at www.cpa.zju.edu.cn/eng/show.aspx?id=173&cid=9.

33. Yu Xiaofeng, "*Gongxiang anquan: feichuantong anquan yanjiu de Zhongguo shiyu*" [Shared security: Chinese perspectives on non-traditional security], *Guoji anquan yanqjiu* [International Security Studies] 1 (2014), pp. 4–34.

34. Yu Xiaofeng, "*Lun Zhongguo ruhe canyu quanqiu anquan jian*" [On China's participation in global security], *Guoji guanxi yanjiu* [International Security Studies] 2 (2014), p. 9

35. Yuan Juanjuan, "*Cong ganshe de quanli dao baohu de zeren*" [From the right to interfere to the responsibility to protect], *Hebei faxue* [Hebei Law] 8 (2012), p. 47.

36. Ibid., p. 51.

37. Ibid., p. 53.

38. Yang Zewei, *"Guoji shehui de minzhu he fazhi jiazhi yu baohu xing ganyu"* [The democratic and legal values within the international community and the principal of protective intervention], *Falu kexue* [Legal Science] 5 (2012), p. 45.

39. Ibid.

40. Ibid.

41. Ibid., p. 46.

42. Zhen Ni and Chen Zhimin, *"Bu ganshe neizheng yuanze yu lengzhanhou Zhongguo zai anlihui de toupiao shijian"* [The principle of non-interference in internal affairs and China's voting practice in the security council after the cold war], *Guoji wenti yanjiu* [International Studies] 3 (2014), p. 27.

EIGHT

The Rise of the Chinese Navy

From Regional Naval Power to Global Naval Power?

ROBERT S. ROSS

 After nearly forty years of post-Mao economic reforms and sustained economic development and military modernization, China is developing advanced military capabilities that extend its strategic reach beyond the East Asian mainland and Chinese coastal waters. The People's Liberation Army (PLA) Navy has achieved gains vis-à-vis the U.S. Navy, narrowing the capabilities gap between the U.S. and Chinese navies. China's modernizing submarine and surface fleets now command the attention of the U.S. Navy operating in the western Pacific Ocean and the South China Sea and increasingly challenge the security of countries throughout maritime East Asia.

The Chinese Navy has yet to reach parity with the U.S. Navy in East Asia, but it has not shown any tendency to slow the rate of its naval development program. If, over the next two decades, the Chinese economy continues to develop at approximately 7 percent annually, or even 3 to 5 percent annually, it will generate increasing funds for naval expansion that will permit continued development of Chinese maritime capabilities, generating greater Chinese power projection capabilities throughout East Asia and challenging U.S. dominance of maritime East Asia.

But Chinese naval modernization and security interests suggest that China's maritime ambitions may not be limited to achieving the power to rival the United States in East Asian waters. Its long-term plan to construct multiple aircraft carriers suggests an interest in developing global power projection capabilities that would enable China to influence strategic developments outside East Asia.[1] The development of the Indian Navy could elicit Chinese interest in developing naval power that could contend for influence in the East Indian Ocean. And as a trading nation with an interest in global markets and access to distant natural resources, China may seek naval capabilities that can defend distant sea lanes of communication and that can ensure that resource-rich developing countries will not disrupt Chinese access to their resources. China's global maritime ambitions have become official policy. The PLA's 2015 Defense white paper "China's Military Strategy" reported that China's "traditional mentality that land outweighs sea must be abandoned, and great importance has to be attached to managing the seas and oceans and protecting maritime rights and interests." Thus, China's navy "will gradually shift its focus from 'offshore waters defense' to the combination of 'offshore waters defense' with 'open seas protection.'"[2]

This chapter's analysis of Chinese naval expansion and the implications for U.S.-China naval balance does not assume a "best case" scenario for the Chinese economy and political system. It does not assume that China will sustain GDP growth of 7 percent and it does not assume that the Chinese Communist Party will be able to resolve the societal challenges to its legitimacy and security. Rather, it makes less demanding assumptions regarding China's future. It assumes that the Chinese Communist Party will be able to repress significant challenges to its authority and to social stability, that it will continue to dominate the Chinese political system, and that the Chinese leadership will be able to sustain at least moderate economic growth that will enable increased funding for the Chinese Navy.

The first part of this chapter examines the necessary geopolitical prerequisites that create a permissive environment for great powers to develop great power naval capabilities. The second part of this chapter examines China's contemporary geopolitical conditions and whether it can permit Chinese development of a great power navy. The third part of this chapter evaluates Chinese progress toward development of great power naval capabilities. It assesses the Chinese Navy's contemporary capabilities vis-à-vis the United States. The fourth part of this chapter assesses the implications of the current regional naval balance for Chinese security and its naval deployments. The fifth part of the chapter examines the likely trend in the U.S.-China naval competition and whether the emerging regional balance of forces will allow for the significant expansion of Chinese naval activities outside of East Asia so that China can transition from being simply a naval great power to become a global naval power, and the implications of the emerging balance of forces for U.S. status as a global naval power. The chapter's conclusion briefly considers the likely implications of the rise of Chinese naval power for great power competition in East Asia, for great power stability in other regional systems, and for the global maritime order.

THE GEOPOLITICAL PRECONDITIONS TO DEVELOPING A GREAT POWER NAVY

Global military powers possess naval capabilities that allow them to exercise great power influence in distant waters and that affect distant regional balances of power and the outcome of military conflicts. Such global naval power contributes to the great power's military influence over the security of the coastal waters of distant states and over the security of distant sea lanes of communication, and it can support the great power's development of expeditionary forces that can project power onto distant continents.

There have been few global military powers over the past 200 years. In fact, there have been only two—Great Britain and the United States. Only Great Britain and the United States have succeeded in establishing the great power naval capabilities that could influence the balance of power in distant regions. On occasion France tried to challenge British naval power in European waters, but it could not overcome the prohibitive costs of its continental defense requirements.[3] In the late 1850s it engaged in a brief arms race with Great Britain and deployed ships in Britain's coastal waters.[4] In the 1890s, France challenged the British Navy in the Mediterranean Sea. In both cases it conceded defeat.[5] Similarly, in 1912 Germany ceded victory to Great Britain, ending the pre–World War I Anglo-German naval arms race.[6] Japan was an East Asian naval power for a brief period, but during World War II it was unable to contend with U.S. naval capabilities. The Soviet Union made a brief bid to be a global naval power in the mid-1970s and rival U.S. maritime power, but this was a short-lived effort that did not survive the onset of the Soviet Union's decline in the mid-1980s.

None of these unsuccessful contenders for naval great power status lacked sufficient funding and the advanced technologies necessary to build a large navy. They all possessed large defense budgets and advanced economies. Nor did they lack the necessary "naval tradition" or "strategic culture." From its founding until the early twentieth century, the United States, for example, had been a continental power with a continental strategic perspective.[7] Its strategic perspective only evolved in the late nineteenth century, reflected in the major expansion of the U.S. Navy through the William McKinley and Theodore Roosevelt presidencies, when the United States first developed significant distant blue-water naval capabilities.[8] The onset of U.S. naval power only then fostered its "naval culture," rather than a U.S. naval culture fostering the development of its naval power. Had past pretenders for naval great power status succeeded in developing the required capabilities, their strategic cultures would have evolved to complement their enhanced naval capabilities.

Adequate funding and technology are necessary but insufficient to enable development of great power naval capabilities. Geopolitical environments create necessary permissive conditions enabling the development of great power naval capabilities. The past contenders for great power naval status possessed sufficient funding and technology; they failed because they had to divide their resources to fund both a great power army and a great power navy to contend simultaneously with maritime and continental security challenges. In the 1860s France gave up the quest for naval power to rival the Royal Navy in recognition of British possession of superior naval resources and in the aftermath of the French defeat in the Franco-Prussian War and then the growing German continental challenge in the 1870s.[9] In the 1890s it conceded to British maritime dominance following the 1898 Fashoda Crisis and as it confronted the emerging German military challenge.[10] In 1912 Germany gave up its challenge to British naval power in the context of its preparation for simultaneous land wars against Russia and France.[11] During World War II Japan's maritime capabilities suffered from its costly effort to establish simultaneously a land empire throughout China and an East Asian maritime empire.[12] Russia's effort to develop naval power while maintaining a continental army led to maritime defeats, first in war with Great Britain in the Crimean War, and then in war with Japan in the Russo-Japanese War.[13] And the Soviet Union's effort to contend both with NATO forces in Europe and Chinese ground forces in East Asia constrained its naval development.

The only states that that have achieved great power naval status have enjoyed the prospect of long-term unchallenged territorial security, reflecting either an insular geography or their strategic domination over their continental neighbors, and thus the luxury of concentrating their resources on naval power. For Great Britain, its insular geography enabled it to maintain a small standing army, which permitted funding of its global naval capability. During the nineteenth century, for example, Great Britain only mobilized its territorial defense capabilities during periods of heightened threat perception from French naval expansionism.[14] For the United States, by the late nineteenth century British forces in Canada could not challenge U.S. territorial security, and the U.S. Army had defeated both the Native American tribes throughout the continent and the Mexican Army. In these strategic conditions, the United States could allocate significant funds to the Roosevelt administration's ambitious ship-building program and to U.S. naval expansionism.

THE GEOPOLITICAL CONTEXT OF CHINA'S
NAVAL PROGRAM

China's economy will continue to grow and develop advanced technologies, providing the PLA with the sufficient funds and technology
necessary to build a sophisticated and capable navy. Similarly, China
will likely be able to maintain the domestic preconditions for expansion of naval power. The Chinese leadership faces considerable challenges from multiple societal sources of regime instability and its
effort to maintain domestic stability will likely require a costly and
protracted effort. Nonetheless, the challenges of domestic instability
will not likely require significant financial resource allocation that
could constrain funding for Chinese naval power.[15] Thus far, the
growing budget for China's para-military People's Armed Police has
not prevented the PLA from enjoying double-digit budget increases
for the past fifteen years.[16]

But will China enjoy the long-term domination of its territorial
neighbors to permit stable funding of its ground forces and large-
scale increases in its naval budget? Simply put, will Chinese political
geography more closely resemble British and U.S. political geographies
or the French, German, and Russian / Soviet political geographies?

The Chinese Army confronts multiple border challenges. China
has fourteen territorial neighbors; only Russia borders this many
countries. Four of China's neighbors possess nuclear weapons—
Russia, North Korea, Pakistan, and India. Moreover, many Chinese
border regions are occupied by disaffected religious and ethnic minorities that challenge Chinese political control and that seek independence. Many of these separatist groups could draw support from
sympathetic religious sympathizers in neighboring countries. Cross-
border terrorism poses a potential challenge to Chinese domestic
security.

Nonetheless, in the aftermath of the Cold War, China has experienced better border security than any time since 1839 and the onset
of the Opium War. China filled the strategic "vacuum" created by
the collapse of Soviet power. It now dominates its borders with North
Korea, the Russian Far East, Mongolia, Kazakhstan, Tajikistan, Kirgizstan, and Afghanistan. It similarly dominates its borders in South

Asia and Indochina with Pakistan, Bhutan, Nepal, Burma, and Laos. Vietnam chafes at Chinese influence over Indochina, but it cannot pose a credible challenge to Chinese security. Despite the high cost of its 1979 war with Vietnam, China achieved its military and political objectives. Since then, China's military superiority over Vietnam has significantly increased.[17]

China's contemporary geopolitical circumstances are likely to endure and enable long-term development of Chinese naval power. Only a territorial threat by a rival great power and the corresponding Chinese long-term budget emphasis on the PLA forces could constrain Chinese naval ambitions.

India is a great power in South Asia bordering Chinese territory. Nonetheless, India's inability to sustain economic development rivaling Chinese growth suggests that it is not a likely potential great power rival requiring extensive long-term Chinese preparation for a major land war. Since the end of the Cold War, the economic gap between China and India has grown. The "rise of India" has failed to meet expectations.[18] Recently India's GDP growth rate has surpassed China's GDP growth rate. But because China's GDP is five times the size of India's GDP, even should China's GDP growth maintain the relatively "slow" rate of 7 percent and India maintain 8 percent GDP growth through 2020, China will add another "three Indias" to its GDP.[19] Similarly, in contrast to developments in the Chinese PLA, there has been minimal indigenous modernization of the Indian armed forces; trends in Chinese and Indian military modernization continue to favor Chinese security. Overall, contrasting developments in Indian and Chinese trajectories have contributed to declining relative Indian capabilities vis-à-vis rising China. Moreover, the Himalayan Mountains present an imposing geopolitical impediment to major Sino-Indian hostilities, thus mitigating against a significant Indian military threat to Chinese territorial security.

The more recent significant development favoring the expansion of Chinese naval power has been the dramatic and enduring decline of Russian military power. After the Cold War, the greatest potential long-term threat to Chinese territorial security was the revival of Russian military power. For many years after the Cold War, China remained suspicious of Russia's potential to challenge Chinese security

in Central Asia and in Northeast Asia. Chinese leaders did not dismiss Russia's ability to restore its traditional ground force capability
that had been such a potent force vis-à-vis China during the late
nineteenth century and the late twentieth century.

Nonetheless, in recent years a combination of factors has reduced
the likelihood that Russia will be able to regain its great power status
in Northeast Asia. First, the infrastructure in the Russian Far East
has continued to erode. The region lacks adequate electricity and
roads to support economic development and substantial military deployments. Second, since the demise of the Soviet Union, the region's
population has declined significantly to approximately 6 million
people.[20] Third, Russia's inability to carry out significant reforms of its
military has led to a continued relative decline in Russia's capabilities
vis-à-vis the PLA. The Russian Navy has been in serious decline since
the end of the Cold War and consists primarily of Soviet era ships. Its
long-term shipbuilding plans focus on construction of small coastal
defense ships, leading to further erosion of Russian blue-water capabilities.[21] Fourth, Russia has yet to reform its economy. It has been
content to rely on oil revenues to sustain economic growth. Fifth,
the combination of new international sources of gas and oil and the
resulting drop in world energy prices and NATO's economic retaliation against Russian intervention in the Ukraine have brought on an
earlier-than-expected Russian recession that is likely to endure for
many years, thus further postponing Russia's ability to field a strong
military. Sixth, Russian intervention in the Ukraine and subsequent
NATO renewed ground force and naval exercises on Russia's periphery have compelled Russia to concentrate its limited force capabilities
on the growing U.S. / NATO challenge to Russian security, thus further weakening the Russian strategic presence in the Far East.[22] To
sustain its support for the opposition forces in the Ukraine and coerce
Ukraine compliance with Russian demands, Moscow has had to transfer much of its professional ground force units in the Far East to the
Ukraine conflict.[23]

Unremitting Russian decline suggests that Russia's Cold War status as an East Asian great power was an anomaly in East Asian international politics and that Russia is returning to its historical norm as
simply a European power.[24] Many Chinese have concluded that well

into the twenty-first century, Russia will not be able to challenge Chinese security. Russia's enduring domestic problems and its preoccupation with European security affairs and deteriorating U.S.-Russian relations have not only reduced it to a second-rank East Asian power, at best, but also requires Moscow to cooperate with Chinese security interests to avoid costly Sino-Russian conflict.[25]

In Northeast Asia, Russia increasingly affects Chinese security the way that Canada affects U.S. security. For China, Russia is an under-populated northern neighbor that requires minimal strategic attention to maintain Chinese border security. Many Chinese observers believe that China can now substantially increase its naval budget while making minimal annual increases to its army budget.[26] Thus, China's geopolitical environment increasingly resembles more closely the geopolitical environments of insular Great Britain and continental United States, rather than the geopolitical environments of France, Germany and Russia / Soviet Union. In the twenty-first century, China will enjoy both the necessary permissive economic and geopolitical conditions for the development of great power naval capabilities.

CHINESE NAVAL MODERNIZATION AND THE U.S.-CHINA BALANCE OF FORCES

Over the past decade China has been rapidly expanding its modern naval fleet. It is replacing its older platforms, including submarines, destroyers, attack ships, and amphibious ships, with contemporary platforms that possess greater firepower and sea-worthiness than their predecessors. While some of these platforms have been purchased from Russia, China is developing the indigenous ability to manufacture advanced submarines, aircraft, and surface ships.[27] It is developing an indigenous aircraft carrier capability that, when fully developed with support ships and advanced aircraft, will contribute to enhanced PLA Navy power projection and expeditionary capabilities.[28] Simultaneously, the PLA has been developing reconnaissance and targeting capabilities that will endow its more modern platforms with sophisticated firepower capabilities.[29] Together, these next-generation platforms and weapon systems have contributed to greater Chinese naval capability to target enemy ships and wage war against modern navies, including against the U.S. Navy operating in the West Pacific and the South China Sea.

Outside its coastal waters, in which Chinese surface ships enjoy the deterrent capability and air support from Chinese coastal-based surface-to-air missiles and advanced war planes, the Chinese Navy has yet to develop parity with the U.S. Navy. United States aircraft, destroyers, submarines, and anti-submarine warfare capabilities are all superior to advanced Chinese capabilities in both quantity and quality.[30] U.S. Navy and Air Force communication and electronic warfare capabilities are also superior to Chinese capabilities, contributing to both the offensive capabilities of U.S. forces in East Asia and to the U.S. Navy's ability to defend against Chinese offensive systems.[31] Equally important, the Chinese Navy has yet to develop the training and leadership necessary for advanced wartime naval operations. The experience of China's anti-piracy operations in the Gulf of Aden reveals that, despite the improvements in its operational sophistication, the PLA Navy suffers from protracted logistical weaknesses and the significant constraints on its ship commanders' operational autonomy.[32]

Moreover, East Asia's maritime geography contributes to U.S. ability to constrain Chinese naval operations outside of the "first island chain." The narrow maritime passages between South Korea and Japan, through Japan's Ryukyu Islands, and between Taiwan and the Philippines enable the United States to detect and intercept Chinese submarines and surface ships sailing toward the West Pacific Ocean to engage the U.S. Navy.[33] The United States thus retains the ability to operate safely its air and naval forces in the West Pacific Ocean in close proximity to the region and to project air power against the Chinese Navy operating in the East China Sea and the South China Sea.

China's development of anti-satellite and cyber warfare capabilities contributes to its ability to degrade U.S. advanced communication technologies. But these capabilities are not asymmetric "silver bullets" or "assassin's maces" that enable China to offset U.S. maritime advantages to wage war confidently against U.S. forces. Generally, the attack capabilities of cyber technologies are greatly exaggerated.

Equally important, China's advanced weapons and surveillance capabilities that pose the greatest challenge to U.S. naval operations, including perhaps its in-development anti-ship ballistic missile, are as vulnerable to U.S. cyber warfare capabilities as U.S. advanced military technologies are vulnerable to Chinese cyber warfare capabilities, so that the quality of traditional platforms and advanced weapons systems remain crucial to an assessment of the U.S.-China balance of forces.[34]

Further offshore, outside the range of its coastal-based air-support capabilities, China's navy is much less capable. Its surface ships remain vulnerable to attack from U.S. aircraft and ship-based missiles. Despite making progress, the PLA Navy's ship-based cruise missiles suffer from persistent reconnaissance and targeting problems and from their vulnerability to U.S. electronic warfare technologies.[35] In 2015 the U.S. Navy's Office of Naval Intelligence reported that China's C4ISR capabilities face a "formidable challenge" before they can support the PLA Navy's more sophisticated munitions, including its cruise missiles.[36] Meanwhile, the United States has continued to develop its defensive and offensive capabilities, including naval "stealth" technologies, ship-based rail guns, directed energy weapons, ship-based reconnaissance and attack unmanned aerial vehicles (UAVs), and long-range ship-based anti-ship missiles.[37] Despite Chinese ongoing military modernization, U.S. relative advantages in developing new advanced technologies contribute to U.S. ability to offset Chinese military advances.[38]

Nonetheless, the advances in Chinese naval capabilities are evident and significant for U.S. security and regional affairs. Chinese advances has been most significant for the U.S.-China balance of forces in the Taiwan theater. In 1995 the United States could send an aircraft carrier through the Taiwan Strait with no concern for its safety; China could not even detect the presence of a carrier.[39] But by 2015, the advances in Chinese coastal weaponry and surveillance capabilities had made such an exercise highly risky. Whereas Taiwan was once considered an "unsinkable aircraft carrier," by the 2000s Taiwan's proximity to the Chinese coastal warfare capabilities made it useless as a U.S. base and as a platform for power projection capabilities. Moreover, China's coastal capabilities have significantly raised the cost to the United States of war with China. For Taiwan, China's medium-range ballistic missiles and advanced aircraft have undermined U.S. ability to defend Taiwan from the cost of war, regardless of the outcome of such a war, weakening Taiwan's resolve to challenge Chinese determination to oppose Taiwan independence.[40]

Beyond the Taiwan Strait, the rise of the Chinese Navy is gradually restoring "normalcy" to great power relations. U.S. post–Cold War worldwide near absolute naval supremacy was destined to erode as inevitable resistance to unchecked U.S. maritime hegemony would result in a greater equilibrium of international capabilities. The rise of China has been the critical force in this emerging greater equilibrium in the great power balance. The United States has retained absolute naval superiority over much of the world, but in East Asia, the central great power theater in twenty-first century international politics, the rise of China has contributed to the determined erosion of U.S. global maritime power.

This trend in the East Asian balance of forces has affected U.S. global capabilities throughout the world. Since the late 1990s, following the 1996 Taiwan Strait confrontation and the ongoing rise of the Chinese Navy, the United States has transferred much of its air force and naval capabilities to East Asia, thus reducing its capabilities in other theaters. It also deployed each new weapon system to East Asia, including F-22 aircraft, littoral combat ships, Virginia-class submarines, and converted Ohio-class SSGN submarines. The Obama's administration's "pivot" to East Asia thus reaffirmed U.S. intent to concentrate its naval forces in East Asia.[41]

The emerging U.S.-China naval balance increasingly resembles the nineteenth-century naval balance. Throughout the nineteenth century, Great Britain enjoyed undisputed global maritime superiority. All of its potential adversaries understood that they would lose a naval war with Great Britain. The Royal Navy's "two-power standard" assured Great Britain of victory against even a coalition of naval powers. Nonetheless, at no time in the nineteenth century did British leaders believe that a war with France, for example, would be easy or cost-free. For perhaps the next two decades the United States will retain superiority over the Chinese Navy. But great power war has always been costly and dangerous, and China's emerging naval capabilities and its challenge to U.S. maritime hegemony is restoring normalcy to great power relations.

THE EAST ASIAN MARITIME BALANCE AND CHINESE MARITIME SECURITY

The prerequisite for extended and large-scale Chinese naval deployments outside of East Asia waters will be the prior ability of the Chinese Navy to guarantee Chinese security on its immediate maritime perimeter. But the contemporary U.S.-China naval balance continues to pose a significant challenge to Chinese security and naval operations in East Asian waters. Not only does the United States possess superior military capabilities, but its basing facilities near China's coastal waters and along the perimeter of China's "near seas" enable the U.S. Navy to exercise naval superiority against the PLA Navy in proximity to Chinese coastal bases. In 2015, the Chinese Navy, despite its extensive modernization and expansion, lacked the ability to defend its sovereignty claims in maritime East Asia against U.S.-supported allies and to deter U.S. initiation of hostilities against the Chinese Navy.

U.S. air and naval access to military bases and facilities in South Korea, adjacent to the Yellow Sea, in Japan, adjacent to the East China Sea, and on Guam and Singapore, along the perimeter of the South China Sea, contribute to U.S. encirclement of Chinese coastal waters. Combined with the reach of U.S. carrier–based aircraft and munitions and China's unfavorable maritime geography, the United States can pressure the PLA Navy along its coastal perimeter. Moreover, in recent years the U.S. has been expanding its naval and air force access to facilities in Malaysia and the Philippines. In 2014 the United States revealed that it had access to Malaysian facilities for its antisubmarine warfare operations in the South China Sea.[42] In 2015, U.S. air force surveillance aircraft operated out of Clark Air Force Base in the Philippines to observe Chinese land reclamation activities in the South China Sea.[43] The United States has also been cooperating with Australia to expand U.S. force deployments and communication and surveillance capabilities in West Australia and to expand Australia's military facilities on Cocos Island, south of Indonesia.[44]

Given the present vulnerability of its navy and its near seas to U.S. forward deployment of its superior air and naval capabilities, China's maritime strategic priority must be continued concentration of its naval forces in East Asia, rather than deployment of a global navy.

China's maritime vulnerability to the U.S. Navy has encouraged U.S. allies and other local powers to challenge Chinese maritime claims, including its sovereignty claims to disputed islands and its delimitation of its exclusive economic zones.[45] Confident that China would not use force to enforce its claims for fear that the United States would retaliate against the Chinese Navy in defense of its allies and of its region-wide credibility, Japan and the Philippines and, to a lesser extent, Vietnam, have continued to allow fishing and they have continued to search for energy resources in disputed waters and to enhance their presence on disputed islands. Chinese dispersal of its limited naval capabilities to distant waters and its engagement in distant conflicts could further embolden the other territorial claimants to challenge Chinese claims.

China must also be concerned that heightened tension with local powers over disputed waters and islands could escalate into maritime hostilities between China and a U.S. ally. In these circumstances, China must rely on the regional deployment of its naval capabilities to deter U.S. intervention and possible U.S. preventive use of force against the Chinese Navy. Chinese observers have expressed concern that as a rising naval power, the PLA Navy must be particularly concerned that the United States might use a local conflict as a pretext to carry out a "Copenhagen," a preventive attack, on China's rising naval capabilities.[46] Throughout the Anglo-German naval arms race, a British preventive attack during the "danger zone," before Germany established naval parity, was a persistent fear among German officials. Indeed, British Admiral of the Fleet John "Jackie" Fisher more than once recommended to King Edward VIII such an attack on the German fleet.[47] Given China's disadvantages in the East Asian naval balance, dispersal of its limited naval forces to distant regions could significantly undermine its deterrent capability.

Similarly, China must be concerned that a U.S.-China crisis over freedom of navigation within China's 200-mile exclusive economic zone or over U.S. air surveillance activities near Chinese coastal waters could escalate and lead to naval hostilities with the U.S. Navy. Once again, China would have to depend on the immediate presence in its coastal waters of its full-strength naval capability to deter a debilitating U.S. preemptive or preventive attack on the Chinese Navy.

China's navy is developing greater experience in operating in distant waters. Chinese naval forces conduct sophisticated, large-scale, and extended training exercises at increasing distances from Chinese territory in the West Pacific Ocean and in the Indian Ocean.[48] The Chinese Navy's participation in anti-piracy operations in the Gulf of Aden has given the navy valuable experience in distant waters. Nonetheless, given U.S. naval superiority, its ongoing advantage in arms innovation, and its substantial forward presence on China's maritime periphery, the Chinese Navy has yet to develop the relative capabilities necessary to deploy a global navy to defend its interests and exercise influence in distant waters and also deter hostilities in East Asian waters.

TOWARD A GLOBAL CHINESE NAVY?

China possesses the necessary geopolitical conditions that allow for the development of a large great power navy able to contend with any other naval power in its own region. It also has the financial and technological resources required to sustain its long-term naval development program that has already begun to challenge U.S. naval capabilities in East Asia. Should it sustain this program for the next ten to twenty years, it may well develop naval power that could rival the U.S. Navy.

To establish a maritime equilibrium of power in East Asia, China will require sea-based defense capabilities that will enable its ships to operate far from shore. Its long-term aircraft carrier program will, in part, contribute to this capability. Chinese development of ship-based antiship and antiair missiles will also contribute to its development of naval security in distant waters. These capabilities are not beyond China's reach. With regard to quantity, China will benefit from its location in East Asia. Because its naval facilities are in the region, its ships spend less time in transition to and from deployments than U.S. ships based in the United States, so that equal ship quantities would amount to in situ Chinese numerical superiority.[49] The United States might well respond with increased home-porting of its ships in allies' facilities, but there will be limits to this possibility. Moreover, U.S. naval access to port facilities on China's maritime perimeter will become increasingly vulnerable to Chinese land-based ballistic missiles.

Over the next decades, China's will likely have the ability to achieve these capabilities. The pace of China's shipbuilding program has been impressive. Since 2000, China has replaced most of its pre-reform platforms with "modern" platforms. In 1996 only 3 percent of its submarines were modern; in 2016 nearly 70 percent were modern. Even at reduced rates of GDP growth, China's shipbuilding program will add significant numbers to the quantity of it modern naval platforms, including attack submarines, destroyers, and smaller, fast-attack ships armed with anti-ship cruise missiles. According to one estimate, assuming that China's naval budget will grow commensurate with the rate of its GDP growth, in less than fifteen years the Chinese Navy will possess well over four hundred surface combat ships and nearly one hundred submarines. All of these ships will make significant contributions to relative Chinese naval capabilities in the East China Sea and the South China Sea, and they will contribute to improved Chinese capabilities in the West Pacific Ocean.[50]

In contrast, the United States will confront considerable difficulty in allocating sufficient financial resources to enable the navy to realize its 2015 shipbuilding plan and to simply maintain the current size of the U.S. Navy. According to the Congressional Budget Office, for the U.S. Navy to fulfill its plan to operate a 308-ship navy in 2044, its annual budget will have to be nearly one-third larger than its average budget since 1985. Should the navy simply be able to maintain the levels of past funding, the size of the navy will shrink to 237 ships. As president-elect, Donald Trump called for a 350-ship navy without clarifying how the new administration would secure the huge increase in the Navy's budget this buildup would require.[51]

Although the capabilities of Chinese naval platforms may not reach the level of U.S. naval platforms and the Chinese Navy may not achieve parity with the U.S. Navy, especially given ongoing U.S. technological innovations, the combination of likely significant Chinese superiority over the United States in the number of modern ships with its in-region basing facilities may pose a significant challenge to the security of the U.S. fleet in East Asia.[52]

Thus, the continued long-term development of the Chinese Navy will likely enable the Chinese Navy to challenge U.S. naval supremacy in East Asia. But the combination of a permissive geopolitical environment and the resources necessary to sustain long-term naval development are insufficient to allow a regional maritime great power navy to become a global maritime great power. Equally necessary are trends in great power competition and the implications for a great power's maritime defense priorities and the corresponding scope of its naval operations.

Great Britain was a global naval power because great power competition on the European mainland inhibited the continental European states from developing naval capabilities that could challenge the British Isles. Unchallenged British maritime security in European waters enabled Great Britain to deploy its navy in distant waters, including in the Caribbean Sea, South Asia, and East Asia. But in the early twentieth century, after first France and Russia and then Germany developed and deployed enhanced naval capabilities in European waters, challenging Britain's two-power standard, Britain reduced its distant security commitments and concentrated its own naval forces in the European theater.[53] The 1902 Anglo-Japanese Treaty reflected British recognition of both Japanese security interests in Northeast Asia and of the necessity to cooperate with Japan against the Russian expansionism in Northeast Asia.[54] Similarly, in the mid-1890s Great Britain accommodated U.S. interests in the Caribbean, reflected in its nod to the legitimacy of the Monroe Doctrine.[55] Thus, in the decade prior to World War I, despite significant increases in the Royal Navy's budget, due to the emerging naval challenges in its home theater, Great Britain had become a declining global naval power. British preoccupation with its European challenges and the retrenchment of its global maritime capabilities contributed to the 1942 Japanese victory over the isolated British Navy based at Singapore.

Great Britain's decision to concentrate its naval forces in Europe was a necessary condition for the emergence of the global U.S. Navy. U.S. economic development and continental security enabled the United States to develop a large navy, but the absence of an adversarial navy in the Western Hemisphere enabled the United States to deploy its navy in distant waters to participate in great power politics throughout the world. Thus, in 1898 the expansion of the U.S. Navy enabled the United States to first annex Hawaii and then, in the Spanish-American war, to defeat the Spanish Navy, "liberate" Cuba, and take possession from Spain of the Philippines.[56] Had the British Navy remained a powerful force in the Western Hemisphere, the U.S. Navy would have stayed close to home in the West Atlantic Ocean, both to defend U.S. coastal security and shipping interests and to deter a British attack on a concentrated U.S. coastal fleet. In the twenty-first century, the United States does not deploy its navy in the Western Hemisphere to defend U.S. coastal security.

Trends in great power naval competition will similarly affect China's long-term ability to develop global naval power. Outside of the Western Hemisphere, the foremost U.S. security interest is preventing hegemony in both Europe and East Asia, its "flanking regions." As a new state in the eighteenth and nineteenth centuries, U.S. security and continental expansion benefited from European rivalries. But once it became a great power, the United States participated in European and East Asian great power politics to assure that the regions would remain divided. Its participation in World War I in Europe and in World War II and the Cold War in both Europe and East Asia reflected this U.S. preoccupation with the balance of power in these regions.[57]

In the early twenty-first century, the greatest challenge to U.S. interest in opposing hegemony on its flanks is the rise of China in East Asia, so that the East Asian theater is the foremost strategic priority for the U.S. Navy. In November 2014, U.S. president Barack Obama observed that the world is getting smaller, and that for the United States, "even the Pacific has become a lake."[58] Thus, as the Chinese Navy continues to expand and achieve relative gains vis-à-vis the U.S. Navy, the United States will engage in heightened naval competition with China and it will be compelled to deploy an ever-larger share of its naval capabilities in East Asia. Since the 1996 U.S.-China confrontation over Taiwan and heightened U.S. concern for possible U.S.-China hostilities over Taiwan, the United States has deployed an increasing share of its naval platforms to East Asia.[59] In 2012, U.S. Secretary of Defense Leon Panetta announced that the U.S. Navy would deploy 60 percent of its fleet in East Asia.[60] Should China continue to achieve relative gains in its naval capabilities, the United States will likely deploy an even greater share of its naval capabilities to East Asia.

Heightened U.S.-China naval competition will impede China's ability to develop global maritime influence, regardless of the growth of the Chinese fleet. If the United States, at minimum, responds to China's naval rise with sufficient resolve to maintain regional naval parity, China will continue to concentrate its naval forces in East Asia to defend Chinese coastal security and its regional shipping interests and to prevent a U.S. attack on a dispersed Chinese fleet.

In this respect, growing concern for China's developing access to port facilities in the India Ocean and East Africa is misplaced.[61] The strategic utility of access to distant naval facilities requires a priori naval capabilities that can forge distant stable strategic partnerships and can enable wartime naval access to those facilities. Thus, for the Chinese Navy to secure access to port facilities in distant waters, it will first have to develop a global naval presence. But this will depend not only on absolute Chinese naval capabilities, but also on the trend in the regional U.S.-China naval competition.

U.S. commitment to prevent Chinese regional hegemony will drive the United States to resist Chinese naval supremacy and to concentrate its naval forces in East Asia. Thus, the likely implication of the rise of a Chinese great power navy is not the emergence of Chinese global naval power, but rather the erosion of U.S. global naval power. China will have to concentrate its naval forces in East Asia to ensure the security of its fleet against the U.S. Navy. The United States will have to concentrate its fleet in East Asia waters to sustain the regional balance of power and ensure the security of its fleet against the Chinese Navy. Similar to the experience of Great Britain in the early twentieth century, the United States will not be able to remain a global naval power and also contend with a rising naval power in a region critical to its security. Whereas in the early nineteenth century Great Britain ceded influence to the United States and Japan in distant regions, in the twenty-first century the United States will look to its European allies to enhance their ground force capabilities to provide for their own security and to keep Europe divided.[62]

CONCLUSION

In the twenty-first century, both China and the United States will possess the necessary economic and geopolitical conditions that will enable them to prioritize their respective naval capabilities. This will enable China to develop a navy that rivals U.S. naval capabilities, and it will enable the United States to maintain an East Asian power equilibrium vis-à-vis a rising China. But the determined development of U.S.-China naval parity will not lead to the emergence of two global naval powers. Rather, it would lead to the absence of any global naval power.

Because of the continental geopolitical conditions in the Western Hemisphere and on the East Asian mainland, both China and the United States can prioritize development of their respective naval capabilities. In these circumstances, the rise of the Chinese Navy and heightened U.S.-China maritime competition will consolidate the importance of the East Asian theater as the central great power theater in the twenty-first century global balance, just as the European theater was the central theater in the U.S.-Soviet Cold War global balance of power. This trend will compel the United States to concentrate its global naval forces in East Asia, thus forsaking its status as a global naval power, and it will compel China to keep its naval forces in East Asia.

The likely outcome of sustained heightened U.S.-China regional competition will be a U.S.-China naval competition that will generate a prolonged U.S.-China East Asian power equilibrium that will prevent both countries from becoming a global naval power. It is thus unlikely that the rise of the Chinese Navy will foster great power naval competition and instability outside of East Asia. Rather, the rise of the Chinese Navy will contribute to global instability because it will erode the contribution of global U.S. great power naval dominance to global stability. With U.S. forces concentrated in East Asia to contend with the rise of China, the U.S. Navy's global power projection and expeditionary capabilities will decline, affecting local power stability in continental regions stretching from Europe through North Africa, the Middle East and the Persian Gulf and into Central Asia. The European members of NATO have been concerned about this possibility, reflected in their preoccupation over the long-term implications of the U.S. concern for the rise of China for European security.[63] Similar concerns over U.S. policy have been expressed regarding stability in the Middle East.[64] Moreover, with the concentration of U.S. naval forces in East Asia, the U.S. Navy's ability to maintain maritime stability of critical sea lanes of communication will likely decline.

The rise of China will bring about the demise of both U.S. global "unipolarity" and the era of global superpowers. In its place will emerge a traditional bipolar great power competition over the regional balance of power. For the China, for the United States, for East Asia, and for much of the world, this will likely be a costly development that may result in in less, not more, security.

NOTES

1. On China's aircraft carrier plans, see Ronald O'Rourke, *China Naval Modernization: Implications for U.S. Navy Capabilities*, CRS Report RL33153 (Washington, D.C.: United States Library of Congress, 2015), pp. 18–20 (https://www.fas.org/sgp/crs/row/RL33153.pdf.

2. For the text of the white paper, see Xinhua, May 26, 2015 (http://news.xinhuanet.com/english/china/2015-05/26/c_134271001.htm). For an analysis, see Dennis Blasko, "The 2015 Chinese Defense White Paper on Strategy in Perspective: Maritime Missions Require a Change in the PLA Mindset," *China Brief* 15, no. 12 (May 2015) (http://www.jamestown.org /programs/chinabrief/single/?tx_ttnews%5Btt_news%5D=43974&tx _ttnews%5BbackPid%5D=25&cHash=929d41649db48810d4e9257ba57d17 44#.VXWotNJVhHx).

3. Paul M. Kennedy, *The Rise and Fall of British Mastery* (Atlantic Highlands, N.J.: Ashfield Press, 1986), pp. 124–33, 145, 167–68.

4. C. I. Hamilton, *Anglo-French Naval Rivalry, 1840–1870* (Oxford University Press, 1993), pp. 79, 83, 88, and table 3, 327–28; James Baxter III, *The Introduction of the Ironclad Warship* (Annapolis: Naval Institute Press, 2001), pp. 100–101, 151; Andrew Lambert, "Politics, Technology, and Policy-Making, 1859–1865: Palmerston, Gladstone and the Management of the Ironclad Naval Race," *Le Marin du Nord* [The Northern Mariner], 8, no. 3 (July 1998), p. 10.

5. Arne Røksund, *The Jeune Ecole: The Strategy of the Weak* (Boston: Brill, 2007).

6. Peter Padfield, *The Great Naval Race: Anglo-German Naval Rivalry 1900–1914* (Edinburgh: Birlinn, 1974), pp. 297–99, 311–12; Holger H. Herwig, *"Luxury" Fleet: The Imperial German Navy, 1888–1918* (Amherst, N.Y.: Humanity Books, 1980), pp. 78–79.

7. Cf. Colin S. Gray, *The Geopolitics of Super Power* (University Press of Kentucky, 1988), chaps. 5, 6.

8. Harold Sprout and Margaret Sprout, *The Rise of American Naval Power, 1976–1918* (Princeton University Press, 1939), pp. 207–13; George W. Baer, *One Hundred Years of Sea Power: The U.S. Navy, 1890–1990* (Stanford University Press, 1993), pp. 21–22, 40; Mark Russell Shulman, *Navalism and the Emergence of American Sea Power, 1882–1893* (Annapolis: Naval Institute Press, 1995), pp. 113, 117–18; Samuel P. Huntington, "National Policy and the Transoceanic Navy," *United States Naval Institute Proceedings* 80, no. 5 (May 1954), pp. 485–87. See the table of the history of the commissioning of U.S. Navy ships at http://www.navy.mil/navydata/ships/battleships/bb-list.asp. For an examination of the underlying political and institutional sources of U.S. development of great power naval capabilities, see Fareed Zakaria, *From Wealth to Power: The Unusual Origins of America's World Role* (Princeton University Press, 1998), chap. 5.

9. Kennedy, *The Rise and Fall of British Naval Mastery*, pp. 173–74; Baxter, *The Introduction of the Ironclad Warship*, p. 140; Hamilton, *Anglo-French Naval Rivalry*, pp. 84, 90–93, 304; Baxter, *The Introduction of the Ironclad Warship*, p. 139; Lambert, "Politics, Technology, and Policy-Making, 1859–1865," pp. 12, 28.

10. Kennedy, *The Rise and Fall of British Naval Mastery*, pp. 179, 206–8.

11. Padfield, *The Great Naval Race*, pp. 297–99, 311–12; Herwig, *"Luxury" Fleet*, pp. 78–79.

12. James William Morley, *The Fateful Choice: Japan's Advance into Southeast Asia, 1939–1941* (New York: Columbia University Press, 1980), pp. 121–22; John Mueller, "Pearl Harbor: Military Inconvenience, Political Disaster," *International Security* 16, no. 3. (Winter 1991–1992).

13. Donald W. Mitchell, *A History of Russian and Soviet Sea Power* (New York: Macmillan, 1974), pp. 204–10, 216–33; chaps. 11, 12.

14. Hamilton, *Anglo-French Naval Rivalry*, pp. 19–22; David Brown, "Palmerston and Anglo-French Relations, 1846–1865," *Diplomacy and Statecraft* 17, no. 4 (December 2006), p. 683; Lambert, "Politics, Technology, and Policy-Making, 1859–1865, pp. 10, 19–22; Robert H. Welborn, "The Fortifications Controversy of the Last Palmerston Administration," *Army Quarterly and Defence Journal* 112, no. 1 (1982), pp. 50–61.

15. For this author's earlier examination of the long-term geopolitical obstacles to Chinese development of a global blue-water navy, see Robert S. Ross, "The Geography of the Peace: Great Power Stability in Twenty-First Century East Asia," *International Security* 23, no. 4 (Spring 1999).

16. On the Chinese defense budget, see Adam P. Liff and Andrew S. Erickson, "Demystifying China's Defense Spending: Less Mysterious in the Aggregate," *China Quarterly* 216 (December 2013); Dennis J. Blasko and others, *Defense-Related Spending in China: A Preliminary Analysis and Comparison with American Equivalents* (Washington, D.C.: The United States–China Policy Foundation, 2007) (www.uscpf.org/v2/pdf/defensereport.pdf).

17. On the military aspects of the 1979 Sino-Vietnamese war, see Zhang Xiaoming, *Deng Xiaoping's Long War: The Military Conflict between China and Vietnam, 1979–1991* (University of North Carolina Press, 2015).

18. For an early optimistic assessment of India's great power potential, see the special issue "The Rise of India," *Foreign Affairs* 84, no. 4 (June 2006).

19. Yoolim Lee and William Mellor, "India Rising, China Slowing Doesn't Mean Modi Wins," *Bloomberg Business,* June 16, 2015; "Catching the Dragon: India's Economy Is Now Growing Faster than China's," *The Economist,* February 9, 2015.

20. Nicholas Eberstadt, "The Dying Bear: Russia's Demographic Disaster," *Foreign Affairs* 90, no. 6 (November–December 2011).

21. Dmitry Gorenburg, "Tracking Developments in the Russian Military," January 14, 2015 (https://russiamil.wordpress.com/2015/01/14/russian-naval-capabilities-and-procurement-plans/).

22. Lance M. Bacon, "Joint Exercises Put U.S. Navy at Russia's Doorstep," *Navy Times,* April 4, 2015 (www.navytimes.com/story/military/2015/04/04/russia-navy-exercises-aggression/25265193/).

23. Igor Sutyagin, *Russian Forces in Ukraine* (London: Royal United Services Institute, 2015) (www.rusi.org/downloads/assets/201503_BP_Russian_Forces_in_Ukraine_FINAL.pdf).

24. For a discussion of nineteenth- and early twentieth-century Russian frustration in trying to overcome the geographic obstacles to expansion into the Far East, see John J. Stephan, *The Russian Far East: A History* (Stanford University Press, 1994) pp. 57, 84–85; David Wolff, "Russia Finds Its Limits: Crossing Borders into Manchuria," in *Rediscovering Russia in Asia: Siberia*

230 ROBERT S. ROSS

and the Russian Far East, edited by Stephen Kotkin and David Wolff (Armonk, N.Y.: M. E. Sharpe, 1995), p. 42; Walter A. McDougall, *Let the Sea Make a Noise: A History of the North Pacific from Magellan to MacArthur* (New York: Basic Books, 1993).

25. Author's interviews with Chinese foreign policy analysts, January–June 2014.

26. Ibid.

27. Andrew S. Erickson, "Rising Tide, Dispersing Waves: Opportunities and Challenges for Chinese Seapower Development," *Journal of Strategic Studies* 37, no. 3 (2014); Andrew Erickson and others, *Research, Development, and Acquisition in China's Aviation Industry: The J-10 Fighter and Pterodactyl UAV* (La Jolla, Calif.: Institute on Global Conflict and Cooperation University of California, 2014) (file:///C:/Users/Robert/Desktop/eScholarship%20UC%20 item%200m36465p.pdf).

28. Robert S. Ross, "China's Naval Nationalism: Sources, Prospects, and the American Response," *International Security* 34, no. 2 (Fall 2009).

29. Dennis M. Gormley, Andrew S. Erickson, and Jingdong Yuan, *Low-Visibility Force Multiplier: Assessing China's Cruise Missile Ambitions* (Washington, D.C.: Institute for National Strategic Studies, National Defense University, 2014) (http://oai.dtic.mil/oai/oai?verb=getRecord&metadataPrefix =html&identifier=ADA602350).

30. William S. Murray, "Underwater TELs and China's Antisubmarine Warfare: Evolving Strength and calculated Weakness"; and John Patch, "Chinese Houbei Fast Attack Craft: Beyond Sea Denial," in *China's Near Seas Combat Capabilities,* China Maritime Study No. 11, edited by Peter Dutton et. al. (Newport: U.S. Naval War College, 2014), pp. 4–9. Also see Michael S. Chase and others, *China's Incomplete Military Transformation: Assessing the Weaknesses of the People's Liberation Army (PLA)* (Santa Monica, Calif.: RAND, 2015).

31. Jonathan Greenert "Sea Change: The Navy Pivots to Asia," *Foreign Policy,* November 14, 2014.

32. Andrew S. Erickson and Austin M. Strange, *No Substitute for Experience: Chinese Antipiracy Operations in the Gulf of Aden* (Newport, R.I.: China Maritime Studies Institute, U.S. Naval War College Newport, 2013) (www.usnwc .edu/Research---Gaming/China-Maritime-Studies-Institute/Publications /documents/CMS10_Web_2.aspx).

33. Owen R. Cote Jr., "Assessing the Undersea Balance," SSP Working Paper WP11-1 (Cambridge, Mass.: Massachusetts Institute of Technology, 2011) (http://web.mit.edu/ssp/publications/working_papers/Undersea%20 Balance%20WP11-1.pdf).

34. Jon R. Lindsay, "The Impact of China on Cybersecurity: Fiction and Friction" *International Security* 39, no. 3 (Winter 2014–15).

35. On the targeting issues, see Cote Jr., "Assessing the Undersea Balance," pp. 12–14.

36. *The PLA Navy: New Capabilities and New Missions for the 21st Century* (Washington, D.C.: Office of Naval Intelligence, 2015), p. 24 (www.oni.navy .mil/Intelligence_Community/china_media/2015_PLA_NAVY_PUB _Print.pdf). Also see Cote Jr., "Assessing the Undersea Balance," pp. 12–14.

37. See, for example, Ronald O'Rourke, *Navy Shipboard Lasers for Surface, Air, and Missile Defense: Background and Issues for Congress* (Washington, D.C.: Congressional Research Service, 2015); Bryan G. McGrath and Timothy A. Walton, "The Time for Lasers Is Now," *Proceedings of the U.S. Naval Institute* 139, no. 4 (April 2013) (www.delex.com/data/files/The%20Time%20for%20 Lasers%20Is%20Now.pdf).

38. China has improved its ability in "downstream" defense innovation, using existing foreign technologies to develop new products, but it has yet to be able innovate new advanced technologies. See, for example, Tai Ming Cheung, "The Chinese Defense Economy's Long March from Imitation to Innovation," *Journal of Strategic Studies* 34, no. 3 (2011), pp. 327–33; Edward S. Steinfeld, "Scale-up Nation: China's Specialization in Innovative Manufacturing," *World Development* 54 (February 2014); Thomas Barlow, *Between the Eagle and the Dragon: Who Is Winning the Innovation Race?* (Sydney: Barlow Advisory, 2013).

39. Central News Agency, January 27, 1996, in *Foreign Broadcast Information Service*, China, January 29, 1996, p. 83; Department of State daily press briefing, January 26, 1996; author interviews with former assistant Secretary of Defense Joseph Nye, NSC Director of Asian Affairs Robert Suettinger, and other administration officials.

40. Robert S. Ross, "Taiwan's Fading Independence Movement," *Foreign Affairs* 85, no. 1 (March–April 2006).

41. Robert S. Ross, "US Grand Strategy, the Rise of China, and US National Security Strategy for East Asia," *Strategic Studies Quarterly* 7, no. 2 (Summer 2013), p. 20.

42. Jane Perez, "Malaysia Risks Enraging China by Inviting U.S. Spy Flights," *New York Times*, September 13, 2014.

43. See the CNN report of the overflight at Jim Sciutto, "Behind the Scenes: A Secret Navy Flight over China's Military Buildup," May 26, 2015.

44. Bates Gill and Tom Switzer, "The New Special Relationship: The U.S.-Australia Alliance Deepens," *Foreign Affairs*, February 19, 2015.

45. M. Taylor Fravel, "China's Strategy in the South China Sea," *Contemporary Southeast Asia* 33, no. 3 (December 2011).

46. Interviews, Beijing, April 22, 2007, April 24, 2007; Ni Lexiong, "Haiquan yu Zhongguo de fazhan" [Naval power and China's development], in *Zhanlüe*

yanjianglu [Lectures on strategy], edited by Guo Shuyong (Beijing: Daxue Chubanshe, 2006), p. 116. "Copenhagen" refers to Great Britain's 1807 preventive attack on the Danish fleet to prevent it from falling to Napoleon. For a discussion of repeated preemptive "Copenhagens" and enduring rising powers' concern for "Copenhagens," see George H. Quester, "Two Hundred Years of Preemption," *Naval War College Review* 60, no. 4 (Autumn 2007).

47. Jonathan Steinberg, "The Copenhagen Complex," *Journal of Contemporary History* 1, no. 3, (July 1966), p. 38; Jonathan Steinberg, "The Novelle of 1908: Necessities and Choices in the Anglo-German Arms Race," *Transactions of the Royal Historical Society*, 5th Series, vol. 21 (1971), pp. 26–28; Margaret MacMillan, *The War That Ended the Peace: The Road to 1914* (New York: Random House, 1914), pp. 129–30.

48. For a discussion of the growing sophistication of China's far-seas naval exercises, see Christopher H. Sharman, *China Moves Out: Stepping Stones Toward a New Maritime Strategy* (National Defense University Press, 2015).

49. The issue of regional powers possessing advantages over distant powers in deploying naval forces affected the naval arms control negotiations during the inter-war period. See Robert Gordon Kaufman, *Arms Control During the Pre-Nuclear Era: The United States and Naval Limitation Between the Two World Wars* (Columbia University Press, 1990).

50. For a discussion of the pace of China's modern shipbuilding program, see James E. Fanell and Scott Cheney-Peters, "The 'China Dream' and China's Naval Shipbuilding: The Case for Continued High-End Expansive Trajectory," paper presented to the conference on China's Naval Shipbuilding: Progress and Challenges, sponsored by the China Maritime Studies Institute, U.S. Naval War College, May 19–20, 2015, pp. 5–6, 28; Eric Heginbotham et al., *The US-China Military Scorecard: Forces, Geography, and the Evolving Balance of Power, 1996–2017* (Santa Monica, Calif.: RAND Corporation, 2015), chap. 13 (pp. 321–42) (http://www.rand.org/content /dam/rand/pubs/research_reports/RR300/RR392/RAND_RR392 .pdf); Michael McDevitt, ed., *Becoming a Great "Maritime Power": A Chinese Dream* (Washington, D.C.: Center for Naval Analyses, 2016); O'Rourke, *China Naval Modernization*, p. 2.

51. *An Analysis of the Navy's Fiscal Year 2015 Shipbuilding Plan* (Congressional Budget Office, December 15, 2014), pp. 17–18 (https://www.cbo .gov/publication/49818); "Trump's Navy Buildup Would Cost $25 Billion Per Year, CBO Says," *Gazette,* January 4, 2017 (http://m.gazette.com/trumps -navy-buildup-would-cost-25-billion-per-year-cbo-says/article/feed /436848).

52. For a discussion of how China may use quantitative advantages to challenge U.S. operations, see Martin N. Murphey and Toshi Yoshihara,

"Fighting the Naval Hegemon: Evolution in French, Soviet and Chinese Naval Thought, *Naval War College Review* 68. no. 3 (Summer 2015), pp. 31–33.

53. MacMillan, *The War That Ended the Peace*, p. 122.

54. Aaron L. Friedberg, *The Weary Titan: Britain and the Experience of Relative Decline, 1895–1905* (Princeton University Press, 1988); Ian Nish, *The Anglo-Japanese Alliance: The Diplomacy of Two Island Empires, 1894–1907* (Althlone Press, University of London, 1966); John King Fairbank, Edwin O. Reischauer, Albert M. Craig, *East Asia: Tradition and Transformation* (Boston: Houghton Mifflin, 1978), pp. 555–56.

55. Dexter Perkins, *A History of the Monroe Doctrine* (Boston: Little, Brown, 1941), pp. 175–85.

56. Julius W. Pratt, *Expansionists of 1898: The Acquisition of Hawaii and the Spanish Islands* (Johns Hopkins University Press, 1936), chap. 8; Richard Hofstadter, "Manifest Destiny and the Philippines," in *America in Crisis: Fourteen Crucial Episodes in American History*, edited by Daniel Aaron (New York: Alfred A. Knopf, 1952), pp. 173–75.

57. Samuel Flagg Bemis, *A Diplomatic History of the United States* (New York: Henry Holt, 1936); Nicholas John Spykman, *America's Strategy in World Politics: The United States and the Balance of Power* (New York: Harcourt Brace, 1942), chap. 15. For the importance of this grand strategy for contemporary U.S. policy in East Asia, see Ross, "US Grand Strategy."

58. "Remarks by President Obama at the University of Queensland," November 15, 2014 (https://www.whitehouse.gov/the-press-office/2014/11/15/remarks-president-obama-university-queensland).

59. Shirley A. Kan, *Guam: U.S. Defense Deployments* (Washington, D.C.: Congressional Research Service, 2014).

60. William Wan, "Panetta, in Speech in Singapore, Seeks to Lend Heft to U.S. Pivot to Asia," *Washington Post*, June 1, 2012.

61. See, for example, Christopher D. Yung and Ross Rustic, *"Not an Idea We Have to Shun": Chinese Overseas Basing Requirements in the 21st Century*, China Strategic Perspectives, No. 7, Center for the Study of Chinese Military Affairs, Institute for National Strategic Studies (National Defense University Press, 2014).

62. For an early discussion of this trend, see Robert S. Ross, "The Rise of Russia, Sino-Russian Relations, and U.S. Security Policy," in *Perspectives for a European Security Strategy Towards Asia: Views from Asia, Europe and the US*, edited by Gustaaf Geeraerts and Eva Gross (Brussels: Academic & Scientific Publishers, 2011).

63. See, for example, Øystein Tunsjø, "Europe's Favourable Isolation," *Survival* 55, no. 6 (2013); Peter Herrly and Hugo Meijer, eds., *The US "Rebalance" Towards Asia: Transatlantic Perspectives*, CERI Strategy Papers, no. 16, July 25,

2013 (file:///C:/Users/Robert/Desktop/SSRN-id2315165.pdf); Doug Stokes And Richard G. Whitman, "Transatlantic Triage? European and UK 'Grand Strategy' After the US Rebalance to Asia," *International Affairs* 89, no. 5 (September 2013); Gideon Rachman, *The Pivot: Test of Europe as a Security Actor?*, Policy Brief, The German Marshall Fund of the United States, June 16, 2013 (www.gmfus.org/publications/pivot-test-europe-security-actor).

64. See, for example, Yoel Guzansky and Miriam Goldman, "America Can't Abandon the Middle East," *National Interest*, March 18, 2013; "Obama's Steps on the Path of the Nixon Doctrine," *Javan* (Tehran), June 5, 2014, at LexisNexis (www.lexisnexis.com.proxy.bc.edu/lnacui2api/results/docview /docview.do?docLinkInd=true&risb=21_T21805511713&format =GNBFI&sort=RELEVANCE&startDocNo=51&resultsUrlKey=29 _T21805511717&cisb=22_T21805511716&treeMax=true&treeWidth=0&csi =10962&docNo=53); Naofumi Hashimoto, "The US 'Pivot' to the Asia-Pacific and US Middle East Policy: Towards an Integrated Approach," Middle East Institute, March 15, 2013 (www.mei.edu/content/us-pivot-asia-pacific-and-us -middle-east-policy-towards-integrated-approach).

NINE

China's Territorial and Maritime Disputes in the South and East China Seas

What Role for International Law?

JACQUES DELISLE

International law has failed to offer much help in addressing the territorial and maritime disputes between China and its neighbors in the South China Sea and the East China Sea. International law has not merely been ineffective—a fate it often suffers. It has been part of the problem. In the peculiar historical, geographic, and political contexts of the South and East China Seas, international law issues invitations, and creates incentives, to arguments and actions—and responses from other interested parties—that increase friction and risk conflict. International law could play a more productive role, offering mechanisms to help manage—perhaps even settle—the disputes. But effective use of those legal means requires political will from interested states that has not been forthcoming, with the 2013–16 arbitration case brought by the Philippines against China over South China Sea issues being a partial exception that proves this rule.

Disputes over rights in the South and East China Seas involve high stakes. The South China Sea—almost all of which is the object of Chinese claims that overlap with those of several of its neighbors—includes some of the world's richest fishing grounds, which provide livelihood and sustenance for many throughout the region. The East China Sea is home to fisheries that are important to China, Japan, and Korea. With climate change, key fishing stocks are expected to migrate north, shifting the balance of value somewhat toward the East China Sea. Fish resources in both areas are in severe peril absent effective regulation, which is more difficult because of the conflicting and unresolved international legal claims.

Beneath both seas lie possibly large if still uncertain oil and gas resources, as well as mineral wealth. In recent years, one major trigger for problems in the South China Sea has been rival claimant states' undertaking or authorizing surveys of hydrocarbon reserves. In the East China Sea, a short-lived cooperative agreement to develop energy resources in an area claimed by China and Japan collapsed. Absent treaty-like agreements or other definitive allocations of legal rights, development of resources is unlikely and episodes of confrontation are more probable.

The South China Sea is a crossroads for world trade. About one-quarter of all cargo shipping and one-third of all maritime traffic passes through the area. Its sea lanes are the pathway for oil and other inputs for the dynamic but resource-poor economies of industrial East Asia. The same sea lanes are the channels through which many of the region's exports—including nearly one-third of China's—pass on their way to Europe and other markets. The East China Sea is an important avenue for global trade as well, not least because it is a route for Japanese and Korean trade that passes through the Taiwan Strait and the South China Sea.

Areas with such economic significance usually are politically important, and the two seas are no exception. Rights of access, or to restrict others' access, to these maritime zones and the airspace above them matter for the economic and national security interests of states abutting the two seas, the United States as the principal underwriter of the regional order, and other states beyond the region. Recently, the South and East China Seas have again become flashpoints and relatively likely foci of conflict among powers, great and lesser, with interests in the region.

International law is a part of this story. Assessing disputes from the perspective of international law shows how legal doctrines that generally track norms and rules of international politics, and that usually support regional stability, can produce perverse results in the unusual circumstances of the South and East China Seas. An international law–focused analysis provides a distinctive perspective for interpreting China's interactions with rival claimants and thus understanding past behavior and future prospects. Therein lie possible lessons about China's approach to issues beyond the South and East China Sea cases, and reasons to give credence to both relatively optimistic and pessimistic scenarios for China's relations with its neighbors and the United States.

CONTEXT AND BACKGROUND

Throughout the period since the People's Republic recommenced its engagement with the outside world in the 1970s, China has made strong claims to "indisputable" sovereignty over areas along its maritime periphery. These claims have coexisted with a relative lack of Chinese control over the areas and much fluctuation in relations between China and rival claimants. With the former British colony of Hong Kong and the former Portuguese colony of Macao having reverted to China in the 1990s, and relations between the Mainland and Taiwan having warmed since 2008 (albeit with a retrenchment to a "cold peace" after the 2016 change in Taiwan's ruling party from Ma Ying-jeou's Kuomintang to Tsai Ing-wen's Democratic Progressive Party), concern over sovereignty-related issues for China has shifted to the South and East China Seas. The islands, rocks, other marine features, and nearby waters in the two seas have been the objects of increased tension, provocative actions, and sharpened legal disputes between China and other interested states.

The recent discord is far from the first, or the most serious. In the South China Sea, China's seizure of much of the Paracel Islands from Vietnam in the middle 1970s involved a battle with at least dozens of casualties. Confrontations between the two neighbors spiked again with military clashes in 1988 leading to scores of fatalities as Chinese forces took and secured control over disputed reefs in the South China Sea, and resurged on a much smaller scale in 2014 after China deployed a large oil exploration platform in a contested area near the Paracels. There have been incidents between China and the Philippines as well, including those relating to China's erection of structures on the allegorically named Mischief Reef in the 1990s, recurring forcible measures by each side to prevent the other's fishing boats from operating in disputed waters, and China's taking control of the area surrounding Huangyan Island / Scarborough Shoal in 2013, which precipitated the Philippines' filing of an international arbitration claim that produced a legal victory (albeit an at least initially hollow one) for Manila in 2016.[1] In 2014, China began island-building projects—literally laying the groundwork for more robust occupation and possible militarization—at several small marine formations in the southern reaches of the South China Sea, causing further, and ongoing, alarm in neighboring states, Washington, and beyond. Incidents at sea, including intentional collisions among coast guard and civilian vessels from China and rival claimant states in disputed waters, have recurrently contributed to tensions in the region.

Beginning in the early 2010s, tensions with the United States over the region began to rise with bellicose articles in nationalist PRC media, a disputed statement attributed to State Councilor Dai Bingguo that warned the U.S. Secretary of State, Hillary Clinton, that China considered the South China Sea a "core interest" (a phrase generally understood to mean interests to be defended with force), and Chinese deputy foreign minister Cui Tiankai's warning that the United States was "playing with fire" through its involvement in the South China Sea disputes.[2] Frictions escalated anew with China's land reclamation projects in 2014–15. As China built up and more densely occupied several maritime features in the South China Sea and appeared to be contemplating an Air Defense Identification Zone (ADIZ), the United States responded, sending navy ships and planes into adjacent areas, over sharp Chinese objections.[3] The Philippines-China arbitration case made more pointed recurrent U.S. calls—earlier pressed by then–Secretary of State Clinton—on China to follow international law, including the outcome of what the United

States regarded as a procedurally proper arbitral decision.[4] Increased friction may lie ahead, given incoming President Donald Trump's tweet denouncing China's "build[ing] a massive military complex in the middle of the South China Sea," calls for building up the U.S. Navy, and generally tough tone on China policy, and given China's subsequent moves to station weapons on the newly built-up land forms, seize a U.S. surveillance drone, and send China's lone aircraft carrier through the East and South China Seas.

In the East China Sea, the unraveling of the 2008 agreement between China and Japan for joint development of energy resources in a zone claimed by both states marked the beginning of a return to discord.[5] In September 2010, friction rose sharply when a Chinese fishing trawler near the Diaoyu/Senkaku islands was confronted by, and rammed, a Japanese coast guard ship, leading to the arrest of the Chinese captain and threats of retaliation by China.[6] Beginning in 2012, confrontation over the islands escalated after China reacted to the Japanese government's acquisition of privately owned land in the islands. Over the following months, fishing boats, coast guard ships, and military craft from both sides engaged in a tense standoff.[7] In November 2013, Beijing declared an ADIZ taking in the airspace over the disputed islands, asserted unusually broad powers to regulate foreign aircraft overflight, and threatened extraordinary forcible measures to enforce China's rules.[8]

Before and between these moments of serious friction or crisis have been relatively long stretches of stability and signs of limited cooperation. In relatively recent times, for example, China and the Association of Southeast Asian Nations (ASEAN) forged the 2002 Declaration on the Conduct of Parties in the South China Sea, with an eye to a legally binding Code of Conduct, and the ASEAN-China Free Trade Agreement. Until tensions began to rise in the late 2000s, China pursued what many observers regarded as a "charm offensive" and soft power–based agenda toward its southeastern neighbors.[9] Even after 2010, heightened tensions have been interspersed among periods of quiet and more moderate approaches, including, for example, revived calls from Beijing to set aside territorial disputes while pursuing common development, respect for international law, and the elusive South China Sea Code of Conduct.[10]

Before the 2010s, and despite popular nationalist sentiments on both sides concerning the Diaoyu / Senkaku issue, the East China Sea had not been a focus of crisis between China and Japan during most of the postwar period.[11] The two countries had forged the seemingly promising joint development agreement for the Chunxiao / Shirakaba gas field in 2008. Despite the conflicts of 2012–14 and China's suspicions about the more nationalist Liberal Democratic Party leadership that came to power in Japan at the end of 2012, the APEC summit in Beijing in November 2014 brought a handshake (albeit an awkward one) between Chinese president Xi Jinping and Japanese premier Abe Shinzo, and a joint statement pledging efforts to avoid, or at least manage, disputes over the islands.[12] Still, the calm remained precarious: despite a second brief meeting between the two heads of government at the G-20 meeting in Hangzhou, several incidents renewed tensions in 2016, including Chinese fishing and coast guard vessels and military aircraft entering Japanese-claimed waters and airspace very near the islands.

Many factors contribute to these patterns. Among them are the incentives created by international law. In the unusual context of the South and East China Sea disputes, international law encourages actions and reactions by China, and other claimants, that are conducive to sporadic, sometimes serious, and potentially escalatory, conflict.

AN INVITATION TO CONFLICT: INTERNATIONAL LAW, HISTORY, AND PRACTICE IN AN EXCEPTIONAL SETTING

International legal rules typically track the underlying norms of a state-centric international system and promote stability or orderly change. On issues of territorial sovereignty, international law tends to support stability and order by grounding rights in long-standing and ongoing exercises of the powers of governance, occupation by people who are the nationals of a sovereignty-claiming state, and so on. On matters of jurisdiction over maritime zones, international law provides relatively clear and coherent rules, embodied in an especially robust treaty—the United Nations Convention on the Law of the Sea (UNCLOS)—and received into customary international law (partly by virtue of the near-universal accession to the treaty). This regime for the law of the sea ties into the usually stability-promoting regime of territorial sovereignty. It allocates largely geographically determined, and in many cases clearly rule-dictated, rights over maritime zones on the basis of sovereignty over adjacent land. This legal arrangement is most succinctly captured in the law of the sea adage that "the land dominates the sea." International law also provides general and context-specific methods to facilitate and solemnize agreements that states reach, or judgments international bodies render, to determine or rearrange rights to territory and adjacent maritime zones.

In the South and East China Sea contexts, however, these legal rules have failed to prevent chronic friction and periodic crises. Indeed, they have encouraged moves that increase conflict over territorial sovereignty and maritime rights. They have provided occasions to stretch, test, or contest existing law and interpretations thereof. With China as the most powerful, generally the most assertive, and arguably the most legally revisionist of the rival claimants, China's arguments and actions have been especially prominent and significant.

China's approach to issues of sovereignty over landforms and marine features, and rights in maritime zones in the South and East China Seas, interacts with international law (as well as other states' approaches to these issues) in at least five problematic respects. These include, in roughly ascending order of systemic significance, the nature or content of assertions of sovereignty; invocation—and rejection—of history as a basis for sovereignty (or similar rights); moves seeking to extend control over disputed territory and waters; basing claims to vast and valuable maritime rights on vulnerable claims to modest territorial sovereignty; and assertion of jurisdictional or regulatory rights in maritime zones that, although purporting to conform with existing rules (or legitimate interpretations of them), may be incipiently or implicitly revisionist.

Asserting Sovereignty

Reflecting the politics of a state-centric international order, international law emphasizes sovereignty—and particularly territorial sovereignty—as a core attribute from which many other valuable rights follow. Where sovereignty is disputed and reasonably disputable, as it is in the South and East China Seas, international law can be conducive to rival claimants' making politically provocative assertions, as has occurred with China and its maritime neighbors. China asserts "indisputable" sovereignty over the contested South and East China Sea islands and maritime features—something that is predictably offensive and vexing to other claimant states, which in some cases have made similarly conclusory claims about their own rights to the same areas. China makes its claims of indisputable sovereignty highly visibly and in consistent terms in many fora, including declarations to international bodies, domestic laws, white papers from PRC government entities, a position paper issued in connection with the international arbitration brought by the Philippines, and many statements by officials and in official media.

The PRC's Declaration on the Territorial Sea (1958) proclaimed that all of the features in the South China Sea—the Nansha / Spratly Islands, the Xisha / Paracel Islands, Dongsha Islands / Pratas Reefs, Zhongsha Islands / Macclesfield Banks, and Huangyan Island / Scarborough Shoal (which, in some contexts, is folded into the Zhongsha grouping)—"and all other islands belonging to China" (a category not explicitly including the Diaoyu / Senkaku islands in the East China Sea)—are "China's territory."[13] In a Law on the Territorial Sea and the Contiguous Zone (1992), as reaffirmed in a Declaration on Ratification of the United Nations Convention on the Law of the Sea (1996), China maintained that the "land territory of the People's Republic of China"—that is, territory over which China has sovereignty—includes "the Diaoyu [Senkaku] Islands" (as islands "appurtenant to Taiwan"—*Taiwan ji qi baokuo Diaoyudao zai nei de fushu ge dao*), plus the four major island groups in the South China Sea, as well as "all other islands belonging to the People's Republic of China" (*yiji qita yiqie shuyu Zhonghua Renmin Gongheguo de daoyu*).[14]

Although the PRC was excluded from the San Francisco Peace Conference that produced the treaty ending the Second World War in the Pacific, the principal media organ of the Chinese Communist Party, *Renmin ribao* (People's Daily), called for a treaty provision by which Japan would acknowledge the PRC's "complete sovereignty" over all four island groups in the South China Sea.[15] The much more recent White Paper on the Diaoyu Islands (2012) proclaims that these islands are China's "inherent territory" (*guyou lingtu*).[16] China's formal submissions to the United Nations Commission on the Limits of the Continental Shelf (2009, in response to rival claimants' submissions) describe the islands within the nine-dash line on the PRC's map of the South China Sea as areas over which China has "indisputable sovereignty."[17] The same claim in the same terms appears in other official statements by China's Ministry of Foreign Affairs concerning some or all of the South China Sea island groups across three and a half decades, up through a Position Paper issued at the end of 2014 rejecting the arbitration panel's jurisdiction over law of the sea claims brought by the Philippines.[18]

China has combined its textual declarations with graphic supplements. For the South China Sea, the locus classicus of China's claims is a map with what PRC sources call the dotted line (*duanxu xian*) enclosing the bulk of the South China Sea, including all of the disputed landforms and marine features.[19] China's submissions to the Commission on the Limits of the Continental Shelf directed recipients to "see attached map," which included the standard PRC depiction of the nine-dash line to illustrate the "islands in the South China Sea and the adjacent waters" over which China has sovereignty (as well as "relevant" waters and seabed over which China "enjoys" sovereign rights).[20]

For the East China Sea, Chinese official sources similarly have long proffered conjoined texts and maps depicting a demarcation that gives China the Diaoyu / Senkaku Islands. China's submission to the Commission on the Limits of the Continental Shelf declared the landforms to have been "inherent territory of China since ancient times," and placed them on the Chinese side of a dividing line that assigns China most of the area between China and Japan.[21]

The ADIZ Beijing declared over the East China Sea in 2013 necessarily presumed that the islands are part of Chinese territory. Amid resurgent tensions over the South China Sea, against the backdrop of China's accelerated "island-building," and in the wake of China's denunciation of the arbitration process that produced a judgment favoring the Philippines, concerns have increased that China would proclaim a similar South China Sea ADIZ, adding another formal and particularly provocative expression of China's claims to disputed landforms in that sea.[22] An equivalent assertion of sovereignty over landforms is inherent in China's declaration of baselines—from which territorial seas and exclusive economic zones adjacent to a state's sovereign territory are drawn—surrounding the Paracel group in the South China Sea in 1996 and the Diaoyu / Senkaku in the East China Sea in 2012.[23]

Making assertions of sovereignty—often strong ones—is what states do in the context of territorial disputes. Still, the PRC's position is notable for the rather strident use of "indisputable," particularly when juxtaposed with the absence of the usual indicia of the exercises of sovereignty demanded by the international law of territorial sovereignty. In keeping with the position that China's claims are "indisputable," Chinese sources reject Vietnam's claims that there is a dispute over the PRC-controlled Xisha / Paracels and chafe at Japan's claim that there is no dispute over the Japanese-controlled Diaoyu / Senkaku.[24]

Denial that a rival has claims rising to the level of disputes that have to be addressed or engaged is at least modestly conducive to conflict—perhaps generally, but more so in light of relevant international legal principles. Absent acknowledgment of a dispute, claimant states are more likely to resist the (limited) pressure that international law imposes through affirmative obligations to resolve international "disputes" peacefully.[25] The claim that there is no legitimate dispute was a complicated part of the subtext of China's refusal to participate in the arbitration initiated by the Philippines.[26] The view that there was such a dispute underpinned the partly China-reproaching U.S. call on all parties to resolve their disputes in the South China Sea peacefully.[27] At times, Chinese policy has sought to moderate this source of strife, through expressions of willingness to "set aside" sovereignty questions and engage in informal, nonbinding bilateral discussions, or to pursue the long-pending binding code of conduct for the South China Sea.[28]

Bold and unequivocal declarations of sovereignty over contested areas typically lead to arguments about the basis for the asserted rights and thus political disputes that are deeply entangled with legal claims. The South and East China Seas cases have been no exception. In addition to generating sharply clashing assertions of sovereignty, they have given rise to at least four other aspects of contentious and tension-generating interactions among international legal rules and China's and its rivals' claims in the two seas.

How Thin and Troubled History Does, and Does Not, Matter

International law generally accords history a significant role in determining territorial sovereignty and thus invites history-invoking arguments. This is especially problematic in the South and East China Sea contexts, where history—and, specifically, the history relevant to questions of sovereignty—is complex, disputed, and rife with old wounds and unsettled scores. China's claims to sovereignty over landforms and maritime features in the South and East China Seas, and the maritime rights that follow therefrom, rely significantly on history. China's positions give some aspects of the regions' complicated and contested history an outsized role, reject the relevance of other aspects of that history, and rely—selectively—upon a history that is especially neuralgic for China and, thus, all the more conducive to international discord.

Chinese sources point to Chinese "discovery" of territories in the two sea regions, as recorded in contemporaneous official documents and reflected in archaeological evidence, in "ancient" times—as far back as the Han dynasty for South China Sea islands,[29] and the Ming for the Diaoyu / Senkaku.[30] With long-ago discovery, thinly documented contacts, and at best sporadic activities generally seen as insufficient to establish sovereignty under contemporary international law, Chinese sources implicitly rely on the doctrine of "intertemporal law," under which claims are judged by the law in effect when a purported right arose. Arguably until at least the eighteenth century and perhaps the early twentieth century, discovery was a colorable ground for sovereignty, at least over *terra nullius*—that is, land belonging to no state.[31] This position, however, is awkward for Beijing and links the South and East China Sea issues to fraught aspects of China's history of external relations. China in other contexts—most notably the "unequal treaties" that ceded Hong Kong to Britain and Taiwan to Japan—rejects as invalid agreements purportedly affecting territorial sovereignty that were arguably lawful under the international legal rules of the time.[32]

China's arguments invoke a second aspect of history: China's earlier-than-rival-claimants' "occupation" of the contested landforms, which is a sturdier basis for sovereignty under modern international law.[33] Principal official Chinese statements stress the roles of Chinese people in the modest economic development and exploitation of the Nansha / Spratly Islands in the South China Sea at least since the Ming dynasty. For the Diaoyu / Senkaku, China's arguments grapple with the lack of significant occupation by Chinese people by asserting that the islands have "always" (*yizhi*) been "affiliated" (*fushu*) with Taiwan (at least geographically), thus piggybacking claims to the East China Sea islands on China's more hearty—if hardly uncontroversial—history-based claims to sovereignty over Taiwan.[34]

Chinese claims invoke a third, closely related, but, for China's claims, problematic aspect of history that matters more under contemporary international law: the "exercise" of sovereignty or jurisdiction over territory. Chinese official accounts argue that the territories were placed under formal and sometimes somewhat effective Chinese jurisdiction (variously, under a Chinese province, country or prefecture), starting during the Yuan (and perhaps the Tang) for the Nansha / Spratly group in the South China Sea,[35] and the Ming and Qing (and specifically under Taiwan's provincial jurisdiction during the Qing) for the Diaoyu / Senkaku.[36] For both seas, these Chinese sources also point to Chinese assertions of formal jurisdiction and invoke legal actions (including a nineteenth-century Sino-French treaty) and broader practices to indicate early acquiescence in China's claims by rival claimants, including Japan in the East China Sea, and France (as the colonial power in Vietnam) in the South China Sea. These are, at most, thin and formal—and in some respects disputed—exercises and evidence of Chinese sovereignty from long ago.

Problems with Chinese arguments based on the historical exercise of sovereignty deepen—and China's arguments shift to reject some aspects of history as irrelevant—when Chinese sources address the treaty-based transfer of the Diaoyu / Senkaku (along with Taiwan) to Japan after the war between China and Japan in 1894–95, and the loss of the South China Sea islands to expanding imperial Japan during the first half of the twentieth century (and also, earlier, France, as Vietnam's predecessor in title). These events undercut the already limited legal and practical significance, for sovereignty today, of China's earlier, weak exercises of sovereignty.

One prominent strand in Chinese analyses argues that any purported formal transfers of sovereignty, despite their seeming legality under the international law of the time, did not do—or could not have done—anything to vitiate China's sovereignty. A long, and in some cases ongoing, history of other states' exercise of sovereignty (which is itself also very thin) is irrelevant, on this view, because any nominal cessions by China were the products of "unequal treaties" that were void ab initio and thus had no legal effect. In the Chinese account, the same was true, and even clearer, in the case of the unlawful taking, without benefit of a treaty, of the South China Sea islands by foreign powers. As Zhou Enlai put it in connection with the San Francisco Peace Treaty, and as official Ministry of Foreign Affairs accounts reiterated, the four island groups in the South China Sea have "always" been Chinese territory. From comments at the San Francisco Conference by China's then-surrogate the Soviet Union, through the white papers and similar documents of recent years, the PRC has claimed that the disputed islands are inalienable territory or have always been under Chinese sovereignty.[37]

In the alternative, Chinese sources make a less radical legal claim that attributes importance to selected aspects of history—that these territories, even if lost, were returned to Chinese sovereignty through: Japan's 1937 invasion of China in violation of the Treaty of Shimonoseki (which had purported to cede the Diaoyu / Senkaku, along with Taiwan, in return for peace); the Cairo and Potsdam Declarations (by which the Allied Powers during the Second World War legally bound themselves to return the territories illegally taken by Japan, including the Diaoyu / Senkaku, and Japanese-occupied islands in the South China Sea—as well as Taiwan); and the ROC's resuming sovereign authority formally over the Diaoyu / Senkaku (as a part of Taiwan) when it resumed governance on Taiwan in 1945, exercising the rights of the Chinese state, which, since 1949, have been in the hands of the PRC.[38]

Concerning the postwar period, Chinese sources make other history-based claims that other regional states (and, in the South China Sea, their European colonial rulers) consistently acquiesced in China's assertions of sovereignty—a type of argument that Chinese sources also raised with respect to much earlier periods but which is more difficult to make in the context of contemporary, mainstream international law's rather skeptical views of, and exacting standards for, claiming title by prescription or lesser forms of acquiescence. For the South China Sea, China claims, Vietnam (as successor to France) was bound by the French colonial authorities' acknowledgment of Qing China's sovereignty; North Vietnam (and by extension unified Vietnam) formally accepted Chinese sovereignty when it accepted China's claims to a Paracels-based set of territorial waters in 1958;[39] Japan renounced claims to the islands (leaving them to return to China) in the San Francisco Peace Treaty;[40] and the several Southeast Asian claimant states "did not challenge" China's already long-standing claims to the islands until the 1970s, when the prospect of rich fossil fuel deposits made the area suddenly potentially valuable.[41] For the East China Sea, China supplements its claims about earlier Japanese acquiescence with references that characterize Japan's postwar renunciation of sovereignty over territories "stolen" from China as extending to the Diaoyu / Senkaku. On this view, Vietnam, the Philippines, and Japan were stopped by their earlier acknowledgements and acquiescence when they later sought to claim sovereignty.

None of this produced a situation in which the PRC enjoyed—over most of the disputed landforms—the most powerful, history-based foundation for claiming sovereignty under international law: the actual exercise of sovereignty for an extended (and preferably ongoing or, at least, recent) period. This lacuna in the Chinese claim has encouraged Chinese arguments that complain about how other states—including rival claimants to sovereignty over the territories, and the United States as well—have violated international legal rules and obligations to China by impeding China's actual control. This argument, too, dates to the early days of the PRC, with the Soviet Union's Foreign Minister Andrei Gromyko arguing at the San Francisco Peace Conference that the U.S.-UK draft for an accord with Japan "completely violates the indisputable right of China to recover its inalienable territories" including the Xisha/Paracel Islands, and "other islands which the Japanese militarists carved out of China."[42]

In more recent years, Chinese arguments have complained of failures of the United States and Second World War allies to live up to the promises of Cairo and Potsdam, and violations by Japan of obligations to return stolen territories. On the Chinese view, the two declarations bound the United States as a matter of international law to return the islands to China, especially once the U.S. occupation regime assumed control over East China Sea islands from Japan after the war. On Beijing's account, the United States further violated its duties to restore China's historic sovereignty when it returned administrative power over those islands to Japan under the 1971 Okinawa Reversion Agreement, which the PRC denounced as "a blatant infringement on China's territorial sovereignty that is intolerable for the Chinese people" and an act that "cannot change the People's Republic of China's sovereignty right" over those islands.[43] In the Chinese view, the United States made matters still worse with affirmations that the U.S.-Japan Security Treaty extends to protecting the status quo of Japanese administration over the Diaoyu/Senkaku.[44] Similar Chinese complaints extend to Vietnam, the Philippines, Japan, and others for actions—military presences, economic exploitation, or implementation of state regulations—on or in the vicinity of the contested landforms that China views as inconsistent with China's sovereign jurisdiction and rival states' obligations (based partly on their prior acquiescence in China's claims).

China's arguments about the relevance of history to sovereignty are, thus, complex and at times in seeming tension with one another. They also are conducive to friction with rival claimants and the United States. Many of China's history-based arguments entangle China's claims to sovereignty over islands with some of the most painful and nationalism-stoking moments in modern Chinese history. (Incidents at the end of 2016 underscored this link and its volatile politics: in a tweet, Trump linked objections to China's militarization of the South China Sea with possible reconsideration of the United States' long-standing "one China policy" concerning Taiwan; and China, not for the first time, sent military aircraft to fly along the nine-dash line in the South China Sea and the "tenth dash" east of Taiwan, and sailed China's aircraft carrier past the Taiwanese controlled Dongsha islands.) The parts of the disputed territories' complicated histories that appear unfavorable to China's claims have led China to rely on arguments that complain bitterly about other states' having wronged China by violating international legal obligations to respect China's sovereignty and territorial integrity. The apparent weak points in China's history-invoking case have given China reasons to adopt views on relevant legal rules that depart from mainstream international legal doctrine to lay claims to territories that are now, and often have been, beyond China's actual control and, under conventional analyses, beyond China's legal authority. China's explicit or implicit legal claims thus include some that are unconventional and that—in at least three respects, including moves to alter actual control, claims to vast maritime rights based on small landforms, and unconventional arguments about the law of the sea—make China's positions look more assertive to other interested states. This, in turn, feeds a broader, discord-promoting and distrust-fostering narrative that China is an expansionist and revisionist power.

Contending and Thin Exercises of Sovereignty over
Rocks and in Hard Places

Because prevailing international legal doctrine on territorial sovereignty emphasizes the actual, durable, and ongoing *exercise* of sovereignty, and because maritime rights mostly derive from territorial sovereignty, rival claims in the South and East China Seas make crucial the answer to the question of which state has what degree of de facto control over the contested terrain. Usually, the international legal rules are conducive to stability. In ordinary contexts, one state has been exercising and continues to exercise the powers of government over a territory populated by persons who are the nationals of the governing state and members of the same "people" (in the sense of having common communal traits) who are the people (or, at least, a people) of that state. One state's or government's assertion that it has sovereignty over territory that it does not control and that is not populated by its people ordinarily has little weight. Changes in the status quo of "thick" exercises of sovereignty do not happen often or easily. When they occur as the result of coercion or other nonconsensual means, they will often run afoul of other fundamental international legal rules—including the prohibition against the use of force or threat of force, especially to take territory—that also reflect and reinforce state-centric and stability-favoring norms of international politics.[45]

In the South and East China Seas, however, international law invites provocative moves, and risks escalation toward serious conflict. Where exercises of sovereignty are thin and title is disputed, as they are in the South and East China Seas, answering the vital international legal question of the actual exercise of sovereignty requires a *comparative* inquiry as well as a judgment about whether a claimant clears a minimal threshold.[46] Because the ordinary means of exercising sovereignty—presence of a significant population of a state's citizens or performance of ordinary functions of government—are impossible on the tiny, disputed landmasses and lesser marine formations in the South and East China Seas, claimant states can achieve only very weak forms of sovereign-like control, such as adopting and purporting to apply laws to the disputed areas, deploying coast guard or navy patrols near the rocks and reefs, stationing small contingents of troops, and so on. In these factual and legal circumstances (and notwithstanding Beijing's occasional assertions that exercises of actual control cannot affect sovereignty), China and its rivals have incentives not only to accrue whatever attributes of governing powers they can, but also to prevent others from doing the same. Any party's act that marginally ups its claims to govern or control or populate disputed territory is a significant challenge because another claimant's small moves can surpass one's own thin governance, control, or occupation. Simply, every claimant has reason to push the envelope through small-scale actions reinforcing its own claims, and to have a hair trigger in responding to analogous moves by others.

Worsening tensions and periodic crises unsurprisingly have followed moves to assert or increase actual control in recent years. When Chinese ships strung a net across the mouth of Huangyan Island / Scarborough Shoal in 2012 in the wake of steadily rising frictions with the Philippines, this was a qualitative increase in China's control of access to a landform-adjacent maritime area—an attribute associated with the exercise of sovereignty over the relevant landform—where the Philippines had previously exercised significant control, including in the form of repelling or arresting Chinese fishing boats operating in the area.[47] The Philippines reacted with sharp protests and a high-profile, high-stakes, and (at least initially) conflict-exacerbating international arbitration claim.

In a similar, but less fraught, set of actions and reactions, Chinese Navy vessels impeded the resupply of a handful of Filipino marines stationed on the rusting ship *Sierra Madre* aground on the disputed Second Thomas Shoal.[48] In another, earlier, more serious incident in 1995, China built rickety structures and stationed a handful of troops on Mischief Reef (one of the seven landforms on which China undertook land reclamation two decades later). Possibly responding to the more modest assertion of sovereignty implicit in the Philippines' issuing a resource exploration permit for a nearby area, China's move was a more vigorous exercise of the limited achievable powers of sovereignty, and it provoked a correspondingly high level of concern from other South China Sea claimants, especially the Philippines.[49]

Beginning in 2012, confrontation in the East China Sea escalated sharply after China reacted to the Japanese government's "acquisition" (in the Japanese characterization) or "nationalization" (in the Chinese characterization) of land in the Senkaku / Diaoyu that was owned by Japanese citizens, and that was at risk of being purchased, and put to more provocative use, by nationalists associated with the governor of Tokyo.[50] China rejected Japan's portrayal, and cast the Japanese government's act as a redoubled assertion of Japan's sovereignty over the islands (notwithstanding the logic of Japan's position that private Japanese citizens' previous ownership of the land entailed a similar assertion of Japan's sovereignty as the precondition to their having such property rights). However one interprets Japan's motives and the legal implications of its actions, China's responses undermined the prior status quo of essentially exclusive Japanese exercise of the very limited powers associated with sovereignty that could be exercised over the islands.

During the following months, Chinese fishing boats, civilian maritime law enforcement vessels, and Chinese Navy ships squared off with their Japanese counterparts near the islands. In November 2013, Beijing declared the ADIZ that included the airspace over the islands (and thereby reaffirmed China's claim of territorial sovereignty), and initially threatened to impose more severe notice requirements and possible restrictions on entry by foreign aircraft than are ordinarily imposed in these common—if legally questionable—zones. Incidents of Chinese encroachment into Japan's claimed territorial sea, contiguous zone, and superadjacent airspace—all challenging Japan's once-predominant exercise of thin sovereignty-related rights (and taxing Japan's military resources)— have continued to occur frequently since the passing of the initial crisis.

These developments echoed and amplified another incident that followed from actions that had appeared to pose a more modest challenge to the status quo: Japan's moves to enforce its maritime laws against a Chinese civilian boat that entered waters near the Diaoyu/Senkaku in 2010.[51] When the Chinese trawler rammed a Japanese coast guard vessel, leading to the arrest of the Chinese captain, China's threats of painful economic retaliation against Japan, and, ultimately, the release of the detained ship's captain, the implications concerning the exercise of sovereign powers made the incident especially volatile. The Japanese coast guard was enforcing Japan's claimed right to regulate fishing (a maritime jurisdictional right that implied Japanese territorial sovereignty over the islands, or, at least, the absence of effective or accepted rights based on territorial sovereignty held by China or other states). For Japan to acquiesce in the Chinese ship's implicit claim of a right to operate in the area thus risked undermining Japan's already thin exercise of sovereignty. The prosecution of the captain would have represented a fairly strong— within the narrow limits possible in the Diaoyu/Senkaku context— exercise of sovereign powers, in the form of enforcement of domestic Japanese criminal laws prohibiting interference with law enforcement activities.

When China dispatched a giant oil exploration rig to waters near the Paracels in 2014,[52] it was part of another escalatory cycle. China's initial move threatened to—and, at least for a time, did— raise the absolute and relative level of China's exercise of the attributes of sovereignty in the contested area, through the presence of the Chinese-authorized platform, the related, assumed right to regulate resource exploitation in the area, and the use of force to repel Vietnamese ships that arrived to challenge the Chinese presence. Here, too, there were echoes of earlier, more violent precedents: China's seizure of islands in the Paracels group in the middle 1970s (following actions and responses on both sides) and the two states' armed skirmishes, and China's seizure of reefs, in the Spratlys in 1988 (following a spiral of escalation from Chinese construction of a survey station and observation post on one of the marine formations).[53] As these instances illustrate, efforts to alter the balance of who exercises the few achievable, thin attributes of sovereignty can bring dangerous, potentially spiraling conflict.

China's large-scale land reclamation and construction of naval facilities and airstrips since 2014 on marine features that it controls in the South China Sea is a recent, tension-generating example of the same general pattern. China's moves, which greatly exceed similar activities previously undertaken by rival claimants, have caused alarm and provoked confrontation, most notably with the U.S. Navy when the United States has dispatched ships and aircraft to adjacent waters and airspace. China's efforts created "islands" that exceed in area the largest naturally occurring landform in the Spratly group (Taiping Island / Itu Aba) and that have seen ongoing, incremental increases in China's military presence (which China has characterized as legitimate, legal, and normal). China's moves hold the potential— not yet fully realized, but widely recognized—to increase dramatically China's own position, and thus far surpass rival claimant states' postures, in the competition to hold and use the powers (limited in this context) associated with having sovereignty over the territories.[54]

A problematic cycle is at work: building up land area, constructing infrastructure, and stationing personnel and matériel are exercises of the typical attributes of sovereignty, which can enhance China's claims of sovereignty in a context where no state exercises much sovereignty. Under color of this behavior-enhanced claim of sovereignty over the landforms and marine formations, China can more strongly assert sovereignty-conferred legal rights, and resulting political advantage, to reclaim more land, build structures, and post people, thereby undertaking more extensive exercises of attributes of sovereignty and strengthening its claim to sovereignty.[55]

These dynamics are a law-related parallel to features discerned in more political- and security-focused analyses of China's behavior toward territorial disputes: China generally becomes more assertive when it sees its position as weak or weakening; and China is prone (as sometimes are rival claimants) to "retaliatory escalation" in the South and East China Sea disputes.[56]

Less tension-producing or crisis-provoking measures to exercise the thin attributes of sovereignty that can be wielded over the disputed landforms and marine features (and to outstrip others' exercises of those powers) have been in the mix as well. The PRC has reprised and extended imperial Chinese practices of placing the territories formally under the authority of regional units of the Chinese state. The PRC put all of the South China Sea island groups except the Dongsha under the jurisdiction of Guangdong province and, when Hainan became a separate province in 1988, under Hainan province.[57] China acknowledges that the Dongsha are under the authority of Taiwan, but Beijing regards Taiwan for these purposes as a Chinese provincial government. For the East China Sea, the PRC continuously has asserted that the Diaoyu / Senkaku have remained a part of Taiwan.[58]

In 2012, China superseded a relatively notional county government for the three South China Sea island groups (excluding the Dongsha) with the higher, prefectural-level city of Sansha. Sansha came complete with an elected municipal people's congress, mayor, and city government, headquartered (as the prior county government had been for more than fifty years) on Yongxing Island in the Xisha / Paracel group and with a mandate to serve as "an important base to safeguard China's sovereignty."[59]

China also has asserted legal regulatory authority over maritime zones adjacent to the contested landforms in ways that imply or assume sovereignty over the landforms (because that is the most—and arguably the only—plausible basis under international law for the asserted regulatory powers) and that attempt to counter or preempt similar moves by rival claimants. China has adopted, and declared applicable to the waters around the contested landforms in both seas, several laws asserting authority to regulate economic, scientific, and other maritime activities in the categories covered by UNCLOS's EEZ provisions, as well as UNLCOS's territorial sea provisions.[60] Since 1999, China has imposed seasonal fishing bans in waters around South China Sea islands, sometimes coinciding with parallel limits issued by other states.[61] The purported, territorial sovereignty-based authority to regulate fishing is a legal underpinning for conflict-generating behavior, such as the Chinese Navy and coast guard ships driving off or seizing fishing boats from Vietnam and the Philippines in contested waters, China's extension of control (through nets and coast guard and naval patrols) over the waters adjacent to Scarborough Shoal / Huangyan Island, and analogous (if frequently smaller and less effective) actions by rival claimant states toward Chinese fishing vessels, often in furtherance of those states' own laws.

In much the same vein, Beijing has long purported to regulate fishing activities in the waters near the Senkaku / Diaoyu, as has Japan. Practice in the East China Sea has resembled that in the South China Sea, with China and Japan (and Taiwan) claiming regulatory authority, at least implicitly grounded in territorial sovereignty. Here, too, Chinese fishing boats have entered waters claimed by Japan and faced Japanese moves to exclude or detain them. This was the pattern that produced the 2010 trawler incident and that escalated (amid the quarrel over Japanese "nationalization" of land in the islands) in 2012–13 to flotillas of ostensibly private fishing vessels, civilian maritime enforcement authorities (coast guards), and, at further remove, navy vessels from China and Japan—and some ships from Taiwan as well—swarming around the islands and feeding fears of escalation to armed clashes.

In the East China Sea, interactions have had another, less simply conflictual legal dimension. China and Japan entered into bilateral fishing agreements in 1975 and 1997 that allowed each side to preserve its assertion of sovereignty over the disputed islands and possession of related maritime rights, while arguably winning from the other side an implicit recognition of a colorable claim to rights in the relevant zones. The appeal to China of this (tepidly) sovereignty-affirming approach to an area over which China had not exercised control is further suggested by Beijing's relatively calm reaction to Taiwan's forging an analogous agreement with Japan in 2013, with

China merely cautioning Japan that such an agreement does not signal a lack of acceptance of China's insistence that Taiwan is not a sovereign state distinct from China (but rather is an entity negotiating over Chinese rights).[62] Tellingly, all of the agreements did notably little to address the particularly charged, sovereignty-related issue of fishing areas that would fall within a Diaoyu / Senkaku territorial sea.

Much the same pattern has extended to the other principal area of economic regulation, oil and gas exploration and development. Exercising maritime rights that stem from asserted territorial sovereignty, China and rival claimants in the South China Sea have authorized or undertaken offshore energy surveying and exploitation, and have opposed—sometimes with force—parallel moves by one another. China's dispatch in 2014 of the large exploration platform to waters also claimed by Vietnam, ensuing incidents with Vietnamese ships, and the removal and subsequent redeployment of the rig, is one especially highly charged example of a broader, recurring pattern.[63]

As with East China Sea fisheries, hydrocarbon resources in the South and East China Seas have been the focus of international agreements that allow all parties to maintain assertions of sovereignty over the contested landforms and enjoyment of related maritime rights, while arguably extracting from other parties implicit acknowledgment of the potential legitimacy of one's own claims. The Chunxiao / Shirakaba Joint Development Agreement with Japan in 2008 and the tripartite accord for joint marine seismic surveys among China, Vietnam, and the Philippines in 2005 are principal examples, neither of which ultimately succeeded in preventing unilateral moves to explore or exploit the areas, or other claimants' resistance and denunciations of such actions as unlawful.[64]

China's efforts to exercise powers in disputed maritime zones consistent with legal rights that are derivable from territorial sovereignty appear unlikely to abate and likely to expand. There is likely to be resistance, to varying degrees, or, perhaps, preemptive moves from other states. The predictable results include persistence or increase in the frictions and confrontations that have arisen from past exercises of purported authority by China and other interested states. The PRC's Twelfth (2011–15) and Thirteenth (2016–20) Five-Year Plans have placed unprecedented emphasis on China's "maritime development" and China's becoming a "maritime power," and China has pledged to adopt a comprehensive Maritime Law by 2020—developments that indicate the growing importance China attaches to exerting authority and protecting interests in maritime areas that include the South and East China Seas.[65] Beijing has committed sharply increased resources for offshore surveillance, patrols, and enforcement of its laws governing maritime zones and activities.[66] In 2012, China's Hainan province issued regulations asserting its authority to enforce Chinese maritime laws in disputed zones in the South China Sea.[67]

In 2016, China made clear that it would not accept or implement the international arbitration decision that upheld the Philippines' claims to rights over maritime areas near disputed landforms that China controls in the South China Sea.[68] Whether reflecting the policy choices of the new Duterte administration, or a sober recognition of the limited prospects for achieving China's compliance, the Philippines has not pressed to implement the award and has been open to negotiations with China.[69] As a result, the arbitral decision, despite its formal allocation of rights, has not prompted a major round of moves to change the pattern of exercise of sovereignty-related authority in the contested areas. Still, the gap between the "pro-Philippines" content of the legally authoritative decision and the seemingly still-evolving, much more "pro-China" reality lurks as a source of friction and potential conflict, not least because the tribunal's decision and the contrasting practice chafe against the recurrent U.S. call (which will diminish under Trump) on all parties to observe international law and U.S. concerns (which are sure to persist) about China's growing control over the South China Sea region.

The various crisis-risking moves, the confrontations at sea, the patterns of escalation, the formal assertions of sovereignty-linked legal jurisdiction, and the efforts to enforce restrictions based on such jurisdiction are all examples of China's—and, sometimes, its rivals'—responses to the invitation to conflict that the law of territorial sovereignty and appurtenant maritime rights issues in contexts where the legally crucial attribute of actual—and relative—exercise of sovereignty is inescapably thin and vulnerable to rearrangement.

Small Land, Big Water: Expansive Rights Based on Weak Sovereignty

The street protests that have erupted in Chinese and other claimant states' cities over the disputes in the South and East China Seas, and the links official and popular Chinese sources draw between century-old foreign-inflicted humiliation and those disputes, show that disputes over title to atolls, barren rocks, and tiny islands can be a focus of strident, even virulent, nationalism and international crisis. But, as the quarrels over fisheries and hydrocarbon resources and the deployment of costly and conflict-risking naval and maritime law enforcement assets suggests, much of what makes the tumult over territorial sovereignty worth the costs of potentially crisis-provoking acts for China, as well as its rivals, are the strategically, politically, and economically valuable rights over adjacent maritime areas that the territorial sovereign can assert under international law. Here, too, international law—primarily, UNLCOS and the customary international law with which UNLCOS heavily overlaps—creates problematic incentives with potentially destabilizing consequences.

The maritime rights at stake are vast (especially relative to the small landforms that can generate them in the South and East China Sea contexts) and relatively complex. They include essentially full sovereignty over internal waters within permissibly drawn maritime baselines (which sometimes can enclose significant waters beyond the low-tide marks of sovereign territory); nearly full sovereignty-like rights over a twelve-nautical-mile territorial sea; extensive rights to economic resources of the waters and the seafloor, and to regulate scientific research activities, in an up to two-hundred-nautical-mile Exclusive Economic Zone (EEZ); and rights to prohibit, regulate, or be free from certain activities by other states and their nationals in the various maritime zones.[70] These rights derive from sovereignty over the land territory that constitutes the basis for drawing maritime zones.[71]

Tellingly, China's most formal and high-profile statements claiming sovereignty over the South and East China Sea landforms have come in the context of asserting or resisting claims about rights over maritime zones: Chinese laws concerning baselines, the territorial sea and contiguous zone, the EEZ and continental shelf, and maritime scientific research; the *notes verbales* to the UN Commission on the Limits of the Continental Shelf, countering the claims of Vietnam, Malaysia, and the Philippines in the South China Sea; and the position paper China issued in connection with the arbitral claim concerning South China Sea maritime rights brought by the Philippines—a claim that, under UNCLOS rules, necessarily avoided questions of sovereignty over territory and delimitation of maritime zones but that, in China's view (which was rejected by the arbitral panel), inevitably required addressing territorial sovereignty and maritime zone delimitation and thus lay beyond the tribunal's jurisdiction.[72]

In the context of the South and East China Seas, the UNCLOS-centered international legal regime, and its basic principle that "the land dominates the sea," mean that conflicts concerning sovereignty over the small landforms and lesser marine features "infect" questions of allocating economically and strategically valuable rights over adjacent maritime areas. Because UNCLOS and the broader law of the sea simply do not address issues of territorial sovereignty, they import into the law of addressing claims to maritime zones the problems that plague application of the law of territorial sovereignty in the South and East China Sea settings. Given the capacious maritime rights that law of the sea rules can confer, this increases the stakes and amplifies the problems rooted in the territorial disputes.

But the difficulties extend further. This aspect of international law's invitation to conflict is partly endogenous to the law of the sea when that law is applied in the troublesome setting of the South and East China Seas. Like the law of territorial sovereignty, the UNCLOS-centered law of the sea regime is in many contexts conducive to stability, given its comprehensive and elaborate rules for assigning rights (including generous rights for coastal states over adjacent waters) while protecting broad rights of navigation and other peaceful operations for all states in much of the ocean. This tendency toward stability is less true in the context of the South and East China Seas, where the often-benign ambiguities, compromises, and exceptions embedded in UNCLOS rules loom especially large. In several ways, they have prompted aggressive and provocative interpretations, especially by China.

First, the UNCLOS regime's predominantly geography- and geology-based rules for assigning maritime rights allow limited, but not entirely clear, roles for history-based claims to maritime zones.[73] Chinese claims have seized the seemingly small opportunity offered by this limited deference to history, invoking history-based rights to waters in the South China Sea that, under the general rules of the law of the sea, would not belong to China. "Historic rights" or "historic title" appears to be the principal foundation of the most radical readings of China's long-standing—but persistently legally ambiguous—claim to the area within the nine-dash line: that the lion's share of the South China Sea is for reasons of history the equivalent of a territorial sea or even internal waters.[74]

Chinese arguments concerning historic rights have been more elaborately (if still ambiguously) formulated in the context of China's reaction to the Philippines' arbitration claim, with prominent Chinese analyses asserting historic rights that exist apart from the UNCLOS legal regime and that are purportedly grounded in customary international law that predates and survives the coming into force of UNCLOS (a point purportedly recognized by the UNCLOS preamble's "affirming that matters not regulated by [UNCLOS] continue to be governed by . . . general international law").[75] With the arbitration panel in the Philippines-China case siding with the Philippines and flatly rejecting any Chinese claim of historic rights within the nine-dash line,[76] with the U.S. State Department's analysis having done so as well,[77] with China pointedly rejecting the arbitration decision, and with subsequent bilateral negotiations between China and the Philippines uncertain to produce durable results and unable to address the rights of other states, the question of historic rights to maritime zones is unlikely to disappear as a source of friction and possible instability in the South China Sea.

Second, UNCLOS rules leave room for argument about the extent of rights to maritime zones that might flow from sovereignty over the maritime features that are the foci of the disputes over territorial sovereignty in the South and East China Seas. Although UNCLOS provisions are clear about the types of rights over maritime zones that can be based on "islands" capable of sustaining human habitation and economic lives of their own, lesser "rocks," mere "low tide elevations," and so on, those rules do not eliminate uncertainty or at least, arguably, plausible arguments about the classification of particular small features such as those at issue in the South and East

China Seas.[78] With vastly different rights flowing from contestable taxonomic determinations, the law invites aggressive interpretation and, in turn, conflict among rival claimants.

A robust interpretation of the status of small marine formations has long been a central, if often only implicit, element of China's claims in the South China Sea. Unlike neighboring states, which can base parts of their claims of rights to significant maritime zones on clearly substantial islands over which they have uncontested sovereignty, any territorial sovereignty-based rights China asserts over sea areas must be based on claims to sovereignty over marine formations that do not indisputably qualify as maritime zone-generating islands. Thus, here, again, international law has created incentives for China to take controversial and provocative stands, and for other states to reject them vigorously.

The Philippines-China arbitration brought this feature of China's claims more sharply into focus. The decision in the case, and China's rejection of it, has heightened this point of contention by declaring that the largest island in the hotly disputed Spratly group, Taiping Island / Itu Aba (which has been under Taiwanese and, therefore in China's view, Chinese control), is incapable of generating an EEZ (notwithstanding China's—and Taiwan's—arguments to the contrary), and that several other formations—including sites of China's land reclamation projects—were mere low-tide elevations incapable of generating territorial seas (and, thus, a legal foundation for China's large-scale land-building projects).[79] China's claim that a tiny reef in the South China Sea—James Shoal / Zengmu Ansha—qualifies as potentially marine zone-generating "territory" (and, indeed, is China's southernmost national territory) has faced equally pointed, if less authoritative, criticism.[80]

Third, similar problems arise from UNCLOS rules permitting states to draw straight baselines along crenelated coastlines or around clusters of islands, in effect treating the enclosed waters as internal waters and the equivalent of a landmass from which maritime zones extend.[81] Because small and widely scattered features and tiny marine formations proximate to larger landforms are prevalent in the South and East China Seas, UNCLOS's indeterminate or potentially malleable language, here again, creates potent incentives to take steps that can spawn discord and conflict. China has drawn baselines that are expansive (taking in substantial areas in the South China Sea and the East China Sea) and controversial (provoking sharp pushback from rival claimants and the United States).[82]

Fourth, international law of the sea rules do not provide clear, reliably outcome-determinative rules for allocating jurisdiction over maritime zones where application of the ordinary rules result in two or more states having overlapping zones. Claims to overlapping zones are ubiquitous in the South and East China Seas, with much of the overlap at least partly rooted in China's claims to sovereignty over small marine formations near the larger islands and main coasts of other states. Here, international law encourages, or at least tolerates, self-serving claims that invoke rival, yet legitimate, legal norms.

A possible basis for China's nine-dash line in the South China Sea is the application of a principle of equidistance between marine formations that China claims as its sovereign territory and the nearby, generally much larger landforms of other states (although China's nine-dash line does deviate a little from midpoints between potentially relevant formations). But international law does not mandate a rule of simple equidistance in cases where the parties cannot, as UNCLOS prefers, agree on delimitation. In recent years, international law has been less receptive to claims to maritime zones based on one state's territorial sovereignty over a small land formation near a much more substantial landmass and coastline of another state. Geological features (in the case of continental shelf delimitation—a key point of contention between China and Japan), equitable division, and, perhaps, historical usage can matter as well.[83] In the complex setting of the South and East China Seas, analyses that emphasize one or another of these factors serve the interests of various claimants and thus give the contending parties room, and reason, to press irreconcilable—and not easily resolved—legal arguments.

Fifth, international law gives China and its rivals ample latitude to reject formal mechanisms that could provide legal clarity. They thus sustain disputes and risk recurrent tension and conflict. In practice, legal pressure to seek definitive resolution is all the weaker where—as is the case with some of the South and East China Sea controversies—one side or the other denies that a legal dispute exists. Even where parties acknowledge a dispute, the obligations international law generally imposes on states to take affirmative steps, including submission to adjudication or arbitration, are very weak. UNCLOS sought to ameliorate this problem by providing multiple options for mandatory adjudication or arbitration. But opt-outs are allowed. Permissibly under UNCLOS, China declared that it would not pre-commit to submit to binding resolution by an international tribunal any disputes concerning delimitation of maritime zones, historic bays or titles, military activities, law enforcement activities in exercise of sovereign powers, or matters in which the Security Council had taken action.[84] This reservation provided the basis for China's argument (later rejected by the panel, but not obviously implausible) that the Philippines-China arbitral panel lacked jurisdiction over the case.[85]

The Philippines did succeed in finding a pathway to international arbitration through artful pleading of UNCLOS-based claims, convincing the tribunal that its claims could be resolved without deciding questions of territorial sovereignty, maritime zone delimitation, and other matters that were placed off-limits by UNCLOS generally or China's declaration to UNCLOS concerning dispute resolution.[86] Yet, the aftermath has not been promising: with China so thoroughly rejecting the decision and, more pointedly, the tribunal's authority to issue it; with the Philippines foregoing obviously futile efforts to enforce the decision and, under a new leader, seeking amicable bilateral negotiations in which the decision would play at best a marginal role; with Vietnam and other rival claimants understandably uneager to reprise the Philippines' empty, even pyrrhic, victory; and with the United States unable to do much to promote adherence to the outcome of a legal process that it had championed. Against this background, prospects seem bleak for formal international legal dispute resolution procedures as a means to resolve conflicts, or even to manage them, or avoid exacerbating them, in the South and East China Seas.

The pattern of indeterminate or interpretable legal rules, the problematic and high-stakes application of those legal rules to complex, disputed, and sometimes-shifting factual circumstances in the South and East China Seas, and claimants' leeway to refuse to submit the issues to authoritative judicial or arbitral resolution have been, and are likely to remain, conducive to friction, tension, and potential crisis and conflict between China and its neighbors (and the United States as well) in the South and East China Seas.

Toward Law of the Sea Revisionism?
China's "UN-Conventional" Lawfare

Doctrinal indeterminacy and institutional weaknesses in international law foster a more distinctively law-focused form of conflict, including measures that fall within the vague category of "lawfare." Where ostensibly rights-determining doctrines are vague, or uncertain, or, at least, subject to conflicting not-implausible interpretations, as has been the case for the law of sovereignty and the law of the sea in the South and East China Sea contexts, disputants have opportunities, and good reasons, to cast assertive or questionable positions as consistent with existing law and proper application of that law. Because international law lacks legislative institutions and, absent disputants' consent (which has not been forthcoming in the South and East China Sea contexts), effective judicial or quasi-judicial institutions, states that disagree with, or are ill-served by, established, prevalent, or rival readings of international law can, and do, try to change rules through behavior and argument that do not openly challenge the status quo regime but purport to conform to it. The possibility or perception that a rival state is engaged in such ambiguous or surreptitious revisionism fosters distrust, pushback, and potentially escalating conflict over legal rules and the valuable rights they recognize.

China's interpretation and application of international law in the South and East China Seas fit this pattern.[87] China makes geographically and jurisdictionally expansive claims that it frames and defends as consistent with law of the sea rules when applied to the peculiar and difficult factual circumstances of the South and East China Seas. The legal bases China explicitly or implicitly relies upon are in conflict with relevant legal principles as interpreted by many states (including the principal status quo power, the United States) and are sufficiently in tension with established legal norms that they may signal significant challenges to them.[88]

When China claims that it has sovereignty over all of the disputed landforms and lesser formations within the nine-dash line in the

South China Sea and in the Senkaku / Diaoyu group in the East China Sea (including the majority that are, long have been, or until recently were, more under the control of other states), China presses one or more views of international law that are highly controversial. It asserts that international law is consistent with flatly asserted "indisputable" Chinese sovereignty over highly disputed territories. Or China gives extraordinary, decisive weight to some aspects of history and some international agreements while dismissing others, without providing a clear, persuasive, or widely accepted legal argument for the mix of reliance and rejection. Or China marginalizes the usually crucial (although, in the South and East China Sea context, highly problematic) issue of the actual exercise of attributes of sovereignty, even as China takes assertive and provocative steps to increase its exercise of those powers (sometimes in response to, and recently greatly exceeding, analogous actions by rival claimants).

When China claims rights under the law of the sea to large maritime zones, especially in the South China Sea, China relies upon readings of international law that are similarly controversial. It assigns the status of EEZ-generating island or territorial sea-generating rock to marine features, many of which are so small that they, at best, test the limits of the language in relevant UNCLOS provisions, and some of which the Philippines-China arbitration panel determined to be of lesser status than China claims. China asserts a construction of international law that permits China to draw expansive straight baselines (or archipelagic baselines) around small and scattered landforms and marine features that mainstream analyses and official U.S. positions regard as impermissible.[89] China adopts a principle of equidistance (or a standard even more favorable to China) in allocating jurisdiction over waters between small marine formations claimed by China and larger landmasses belonging to other states, even though that position is hard to square with recent decisions by international tribunals and has faced a sharp critique in official U.S. analyses.[90] China invokes the ambiguous and generally secondary criterion of "natural prolongation" to trump the usual standard of equidistance and give China a disproportionate share of the East China Sea continental shelf, despite the absence of a clear and strong geological basis for China's position. China asserts a notion of historic rights that puts under Chinese jurisdiction (and, perhaps, sovereignty) maritime areas that would be beyond its reach under the ordinary application of UNCLOS rules—a position specifically rejected by the Philippines-China arbitration panel concerning areas inside the nine-dash line in the South China Sea, and by an extensive official U.S. legal analysis, as well as other sources.[91]

China's claims are jurisdictionally (in terms of the extent of legal rights claimed) as well as geographically (in terms of the physical area claimed) expansive. And China's jurisdictional claims have legal or "lawfare" characteristics akin to those of its geographic claims. When Chinese analysts envision, and official Chinese sources demur when asked to repudiate definitively, claims to sovereign waters—which may include internal waters–like or dry land–like rights—in significant areas in the South China Sea (perhaps as a form of historic rights or title), they must rely on an ostensible principle of international law that is not effectively articulated in China's own official arguments, not widely accepted in international law, and sharply at odds with the views of many states, including the United States.[92]

When China asserts, and orthodox Chinese sources argue, that China enjoys "historic rights" in maritime zones, the underlying international legal positions provoke pointed resistance and are plausibly understood as challenges to established law. Here, too, the precise contours of the rights China claims are ambiguous, but many Chinese analyses clearly reject the internationally widely held view that the UNCLOS-centered regime is the exclusive, or nearly exclusive, source of law governing rights over maritime areas. Although adopted to implement China's obligations under UNCLOS, China's EEZ law pointedly states that the legislation "shall not affect" (*bu yingxiang*) China's "historic rights" (*lishixing quanli*) to sea areas, including those adjacent to the disputed South and East China Sea islands that the same law declares to be part of China's sovereign territory.[93] According to recent, prominent Chinese analyses, these rights are rooted in customary international law that has remained in effect despite the advent of the UNCLOS regime.[94] This view, too, has faced pointed repudiation, including from the Philippines-China arbitration tribunal (which rejected the claim that China could enjoy "historic rights" inside the nine-dash line that were more than those conferred by the ordinary UNCLOS rules governing rights in maritime zones) and the United States (which rebuffed Chinese claims with a detailed argument that the international law of the sea sets a high bar for historic rights and imposes narrow geographic limits).[95]

When China claims extensive legal authority to regulate other states' activities in the various maritime zones recognized in UNCLOS and the customary international law of the sea, it adopts positions on legal issues that are, at best, highly controversial, enjoying support from a minority of states but facing opposition from many others, including major maritime states. China's positions thus raise concerns about legal revisionism and prompt pointed rejoinders, especially from the United States.

From China's initial declaration of a territorial sea in 1958 through its UNCLOS-linked Law on the Territorial Sea and Contiguous Zone, and in many official statements, China has asserted a legal right to require other states' military ships to give notice of, or seek permission for, innocent passage through its claimed territorial seas.[96] This position was not accepted in the UNCLOS process because of a lack of consensus, and has been strongly rejected by the United States in statements asserting that the law of the sea authorizes innocent passage without notice or permission, and through freedom of navigation operations that the U.S. Navy has conducted in Chinese-claimed waters, including areas near the maritime features in the Spratly group where China has been building islands and near islands in the Chinese-controlled Paracel group.[97]

In its claimed EEZs, China has asserted far-reaching rights to regulate activities of foreign militaries (in practice, principally the U.S. Navy) on several legal grounds, including broadly requiring those engaging in navigation or overflight in EEZs to obey "the laws and regulations" of the PRC as well as international law (implicitly, as interpreted by China);[98] interpreting the "maritime scientific research" that UNCLOS allows coastal states to regulate in EEZs as extending to surveillance activities by foreign military vessels (including those of the U.S. Navy);[99] and characterizing the shadowing and harassment of U.S. Navy ships as "routine" and "appropriate and legal" enforcement of China's international law–conforming laws (including China's legal authority to prohibit military surveillance activities in its EEZs);[100]

and perhaps attempting to revive a notion of coastal states' "security rights" in EEZ areas.[101] (A concept of security rights over the EEZ appears to have underpinned China's approach to the 2001 collision of a Chinese military jet with a U.S. EP-3 reconnaissance plane.)[102] These Chinese positions on the law are, variously, supported by only relatively few states, were considered and excluded from the UNCLOS regime (in the case of EEZ security rights), and have been pointedly challenged and rejected in word and deed by the United States.[103]

In declaring an Air Defense Identification Zone over the East China Sea in November 2013 and reportedly considering the establishment of an ADIZ over the South China Sea, China was, at one level, merely asserting an international legal right of possibly dubious status to do something akin to what its neighbors and the United States have done in proclaiming their own ADIZs. But, here, too, China pressed further, contemplating an ADIZ far beyond any substantial landforms or populations under its governance (in the South China Sea), and purporting to impose unusually extensive restrictions on freedom of overflight (in the East China Sea), including by applying requirements of notice, identification, and continuous contact to planes not intending to enter Chinese airspace, and threatening "defensive emergency measures" against those who failed to comply. Here, as well, conflict over legal rules and their application escalated, with Japan and the United States, among others, denouncing overreaching Chinese controls and the United States flying B-52s through the area without complying with China's rules.[104]

China also relies upon expansive constructions of international legal rights to regulate, or be free from, actions of foreign militaries on the high seas (with, again, the practical concern being principally the activities of the United States). This position has not been very clearly or consistently articulated, but Chinese challenges to the legality of some U.S. Navy operations on the high seas (or in China's claimed EEZs when Chinese complaints appear not to be linked to the areas' status as EEZs) appear to claim that U.S. behavior violates international legal obligations, such as those to exercise law of the sea rights, including high seas freedoms, without abusing such rights and with "due regard" for China's interests;[105] to use the high seas only for "peaceful purposes";[106] and, perhaps, not to transgress the general international legal proscriptions on threatening or using force.[107] Sometimes, China has eschewed engaging the legal issues while acting in ways that imply a right to impede U.S. Navy activities on the high seas, with the most dramatic recent example being the PLA Navy's December 2016 seizure of an ostensibly unidentified surveillance drone attached to the USS *Bowditch*, operating outside the nine-dash line.[108] Chinese positions have been firmly, thoroughly, and consistently rejected by the United States, and strain the text and challenge widely shared understandings of international legal rules.[109]

China has sought to soften the perceived implications of its legal positions, and thus limit political consequences, by insisting that it would never interfere with freedom of navigation in the South and East China Sea. But there remains in international law—and, therefore, at least potentially in international politics—a fundamental difference between China saying that it will not interfere with such freedoms (a policy choice that is, in principle, reversible) and China acknowledging that it has no right to do so.

Because the interactions of legal rules governing rights over maritime zones and the facts of the South and East China Seas are so complex, and because China's legal arguments are so numerous, varied, and under-articulated, there is room for disagreement about how status quo–challenging or revisionist China's positions are on legal issues at stake in the disputed ocean regions. Yet, here again, international law tends to raise the stakes and thus the risks of friction and conflict.

First, international legal argument invites generalization, or analogical extension, of claims made in one setting to other, related contexts. China's arguments about how distant and recent history, treaties, actual control, formal assertions of sovereignty, and patterns of acquiescence in others' exercises of authority determine sovereignty over territory (and, in turn, rights to vast maritime zones) are not limited to the South and East China Seas. Chinese arguments about the two maritime regions closely parallel China's claims about Hong Kong, Macao, and Taiwan and thus appear to reflect China's more general views about the law of sovereignty over contested territory. So, too, China's positions on the maritime-zone-generating status of particular landforms and maritime features, historic rights within the nine-dash line, complaints about U.S. Navy infringements, and so on have emerged in the South and East China Sea disputes. But the legal arguments about China's rights to, and in, maritime zones are not easily—or, in many cases, plausibly—limited to the particular geographic areas of the South China Sea or the East China Sea.

Second, the politics of international law tend to produce assumptions that a state's approach to one aspect extends to other areas of international law and, in turn, international order. Where legal questions affect major economic and security interests and where legal doctrines involve a major field of international law—as is the case with the South and East China Sea disputes, these assumptions are likely to be stronger still. Thus, China's assertive and heterodox approach to law-related issues in the South and East China Sea disputes creates concern—among China's neighbors, the United States, and other stakeholders in the international system—about whether China is challenging established international law and, more broadly and more importantly, the status quo international order.

China is, of course, not unique in stretching existing law, challenging, sub rosa, established understandings of international law, or rejecting other states' contrary interpretations—generally or in the areas of law most germane to the South and East China Sea disputes. The United States has not joined UNLCOS, but claims the benefit of most of its substantive content as binding customary international law. Washington long preceded Beijing in declaring ADIZs. China's rivals in claiming territorial sovereignty and rights to maritime zones in the South and East China Seas have made their own questionable legal claims and undertaken legally questionable actions to support and further those claims.

Nonetheless, many of China's actions and arguments appear to reflect or imply challenges to—and possibly revisionist postures toward—prevalent legal rules and, more clearly, interpretations embraced by the United States and its allies, and the legitimacy of the U.S. security role in the region. Moreover, Beijing's stances on international legal principles concerning territorial sovereignty and maritime jurisdiction come against the backdrop of Chinese arguments that can feed a penchant for revisionism. Chinese official and orthodox sources have long emphasized that China had been excluded from the formulation of many international legal rules that the

United States and China's neighbors seek to impose on China, and they now argue further that a more powerful China should take its rightful place in shaping those rules.[110]

INTERNATIONAL LAW IN THE SOUTH AND EAST CHINA SEA DISPUTES—RETROSPECT AND PROSPECT

International law has not been effective in avoiding discord and risks of conflict over territorial and related maritime claims in the South and East China Seas. In several ways, international law has contributed to heightened tensions among China and its neighbors and between China and the United States. Yet the picture is not necessarily as bleak as the foregoing account may suggest, and international law's roles are not inevitably so weak or perverse. Although chronically crisis-prone and intermittently crisis-ridden, the South and East China Seas have not be been the foci of large-scale, sustained conflict. International law may deserve some of the credit.

International law can limit conflict and facilitate cooperation, even when it fails to resolve underlying disputes over sovereignty and maritime rights if rival claimants find the will to seek the accommodations that law offers. International law can encourage disputants to channel interest-based or nationalism-driven agendas into assertions of legal rights. This enables parties to articulate legal arguments that can help protect claims from erosion and thus encourage patience by extending the time frame parties perceive for pursuing an acceptable resolution. At least arguably, this characterization applies to much of the way China and its neighbors have handled their rival claims over the South and East China Seas.

International law's analytic distinction between having rights and exercising rights—and between choosing or agreeing not to exercise rights and ceding rights or conceding a lack of rights—aligns with what has been a seemingly assertive yet, in practice, conflict-containing mind-set in Beijing: because China's sovereignty is indisputable and non-derogable, Chinese sovereignty and related rights are unaffected by long periods of control over disputed areas by other states. Therefore, other states' long-term exercises of the attributes of sovereignty can be tolerated and need not trigger measures—possibly forcible ones—to bring actual control into line with claimed rights, at least until sometime in the possibly distant future.[111]

International law recognizes and supports parties' preserving incompatible rights claims (such as those to territorial sovereignty) while agreeing to allocate or rearrange lesser included rights (such as the use or regulation of resources under disputed ownership). As official Chinese sources have noted, this aspect of international law resonates with Deng Xiaoping's venerable and, in orthodox Chinese views, still-enduring dictum to "set aside sovereignty" and seek cooperation on practical matters.[112] This legal logic is reflected in, and facilitates, some of the conflict-abating and stability-supporting measures that rival claimants have adopted in the two seas, including the notable—if ill-fated—China-Japan joint development project for the Chunxiao / Shirakaba gas field, the short-lived bilateral and multilateral accords to permit oil and gas exploration in the South China Sea, and fisheries agreements covering waters in the East China Sea. It also may underlie the otherwise curiously calm reactions to other states' imposing simultaneous and overlapping limits on fishing in maritime zones claimed by multiple states. It also perhaps was reflected in the aftermath of the China-Philippines arbitration decision, when China sought post-decision negotiations with the Philippines despite rejecting the decision as a mere "scrap of paper," and the Philippines, under its new president, indicated that it was open to bilateral negotiation, consigning the tribunal's judgment to "the back seat" while not conceding that the decision lacked binding legal effect.[113]

International law offers means, if the parties are willing, to submit disputes to binding and relatively predictable legal resolution by impartial tribunals, or to settlement through accords that bind in law and may hold in practice. This more benign and vibrant role for international law has had dim prospects in the South and East China Seas. That is the evident lesson from China's treaty-based reservations limiting formal dispute resolution under UNCLOS and its aversion to formal legal means for resolving international disputes more generally; from Beijing's and Tokyo's reluctance to acknowledge formally the existence of legitimate territorial disputes with, respectively, Vietnam over the Paracels and China over the Diaoyu / Senkaku;

and from China's refusal to participate in the arbitral proceedings initiated by the Philippines and its pointed rejection of the tribunal's decisions on jurisdiction and on the merits. The long-running failure to move forward from the 2002 nonbinding Declaration of Conduct for the South China Sea to a legal obligation–imposing Code of Conduct, and the lack of progress in bilateral negotiations among claimants in the two seas, do not augur well for treaty-like arrangements as solutions to the disputes.

As this account of the past and possible future roles for international law in the South and East China Sea disputes reflects, it is uncertain whether international law will become more significantly helpful—and not be harmful—in the pursuit of stability and peace in the region. Prospects depend on several factors, not least the views and behavior of China. In one scenario, the relatively near future may resemble the relatively recent past. China—and rival claimants as well—may continue to see international law as often offering incentives or creating imperatives to undertake provocative actions and escalatory reactions to advance national interests and pursue policy goals in the disputed South and East China Sea regions.

Alternatively, if China's rise in power and influence continues, Beijing will be in a stronger position not just to adopt heterodox and self-serving interpretations of legal rules, or at times to flout them, but also to challenge them openly and reshape them in ways that serve China's aims and interests. China's hitherto mixed or ambiguous approach may ripen into a more robust revisionism that could undermine what have been relatively clear, stable, and pro–open-seas rules of the law the sea. These rules have generally been conducive to international peace and stability (notwithstanding their problematic effects in the South and East China Seas), have served U.S. security interests, and have helped provide international public goods in a vital region.

On the other hand, a China that is more fully risen or more deeply integrated in international institutions may come to hold preferences and discern interests that more closely resemble those of the United States today. China may leave behind the mentality—rooted in history but nurtured by the regime's rhetoric—of a victim or potential victim of foreign encroachment and depredation. China would become less inclined to incur the reputational costs and the distrust from neighbors that come with appearing to challenge the legal (and other) norms that have underpinned a largely peaceful and stunningly prosperous postwar order in East Asia. Beijing might develop preferences more typical of a force-projecting major power, deploying a formidable navy with global missions to protect far-flung national interests and therefore favoring weaker coastal state rights. Some signs already point to incipient adjustments in behavior and attitude: PLA Navy thinkers, especially among the rising generation, talk in these terms; PLAN vessels increasingly venture far from China's shores, toward U.S. coasts and the polar regions; and the 2016 South and East China Sea deployment of the *Liaoning* aircraft carrier was accompanied by an explicit official assertion of China's entitlement to freedom of navigation and overflight under international law that all parties should respect.[114] But a fundamental and operationally decisive shift in that direction is, at best, likely too far off to affect China's near-term agendas in the chronically and recently tension-filled South and East China Seas. In the relatively near term, conflicting and unresolved claims to territorial sovereignty and maritime rights, and the problematic interaction of international law and the geography and politics of the South and East China Sea regions, are likely to produce recurrent tensions and occasional crises between China and its maritime neighbors and between China and the United States.

NOTES

1. South China Sea Arbitration (Philippines v. China), PCA Case No. 2013-19 (July 12, 2016).

2. Long Tao, "A Good Time to Take Military Action in the South China Sea," *Global Times*, September 28, 2011; Michael D. Swaine, "China's Assertive Behavior, Part One: On 'Core Interests,'" *China Leadership Monitor* no. 34 (2011); "The True Story behind Huangyan Island Dispute in the South China Sea," Xinhua, May 9, 2012; "Hillary Clinton Presses Beijing on South China Sea," Associated Press, July 12, 2012; Deputy Foreign Minister Cui Tiankai's News Briefing, June 22, 2011(www.mfa.gov.cn/chn/gxh/tyb /wjbxw/t83291.htm); Edward Wong, "Beijing Warns U.S. about South China Sea Disputes," *New York Times*, June 21, 2011.

3. Jim Sciutto, "Behind the Scenes: A Secret Navy Flight over China's Military Build-Up," CNN, May 26, 2015 (www.cnn.com/2015/05/26/politics /south-china-sea-navy-surveillance-plane-jim-sciutto/); Jane Perlez, "U.S. Admiral, in Beijing, Defends Patrols in South China Sea," *New York Times*, November 3, 2015; Ben Blanchard and Andrea Shalal, "Angry China Shadows U.S. Warship Near Man-made Islands," Reuters, October 28, 2015; Sam LaGrone, "U.S. Destroyer Comes within 12 Nautical Miles of South China Sea Artificial Island, Beijing Threatens Response," USNI News, October 27, 2015 (https://news.usni.org/2015/10/27/u-s-destroyer-comes-within-12-nautical -miles-of-chinese-south-china-sea-artificial-island-beijing-threatens -response); Jane Perlez, "U.S. Sails Warship Near Island in South China Sea, Challenging Chinese Claims," *New York Times*, May 10, 2016.

4. U.S. Department of State, "Comments by Secretary Clinton in Hanoi, Vietnam," July 23, 2010; Decision in the Philippines-China Arbitration, Press Statement by John Kirby, Assistant Secretary and Departmental Spokesman, Bureau of Public Affairs, U.S. Department of State, July 12, 2016.

5. Xinjun Zhang, "Why the 2008 Sino-Japanese Consensus on the East China Sea Has Stalled," *Ocean Development and International Law* 42, no. 1 (2011), pp. 53–65.

6. Sheila Smith, "Japan and the East China Sea Dispute," *Orbis* 56, no. 3 (2012), pp. 370–90; International Crisis Group, *Dangerous Waters: China-Japan Relations on the Rocks* (April 2013).

7. See International Crisis Group, *Dangerous Waters*; see also Martin Fackler, "Chinese Patrol Ships Pressuring Japan over Islands," *New York Times*, November 3, 2012.

8. The East China Sea ADIZ is addressed later in this chapter.

9. Joshua Kurlantzik, *Charm Offensive: How China's Soft Power Is Changing the World* (Yale University Press, 2007); Yanzhong Huang and Sheng Ding, "Dragon's Underbelly: An Analysis of China's Soft Power," *East Asia* 23, no. 4 (2006), pp. 22–44; Jacques deLisle, "Soft Power in a Hard Place," *Orbis* 54, no. 4 (2010), pp. 493–524.

10. For a summary, see M. Taylor Fravel, "All Quiet in the South China Sea," *Foreign Affairs*, March 22, 2012; Edward Wong, "China Hedges over Whether South China Sea Is a 'Core Interest' Worth War," *New York Times*, March 30, 2011.

11. See, generally, M. Taylor Fravel, "Explaining Stability in the Senkaku (Diaoyu) Islands Dispute," in *Getting the Triangle Straight: Managing China-Japan-US Relations*, edited by Gerald Curtis, Ryosei Kokubun, and Wang Jisi (Tokyo: Japan Center for International Exchange, 2010); Erik S. Downs and Phillip C. Saunders, "Legitimacy and Nationalism: China and the Diaoyu Islands," in *The Rise of China*, edited by Michael E. Brown, Owen R. Coté, Sean M. Lynn-Jones, and Steven E. Miller (MIT Press, 2000).

12. Jane Perlez, "For China and Japan, a New Effort to Improve Relations Produces a Chilly Scene," *New York Times*, November 10, 2014; Japan Ministry of Foreign Affairs, "Regarding Discussions Toward Improving Japan-China Relations," November 7, 2014 (www.mofa.go.jp/a_o/c_m1/cn/page4e _000150.html); Ministry of Foreign Affairs, People's Republic of China, "Xi Jinping Meets Japanese Prime Minister Shinzo Abe," November 10, 2014 (www.fmprc.gov.cn/mfa_eng/topics_665678/ytjhzzdrsrcldrfzshyjxghd /t1209092.shtml).

13. Declaration of the Government of the People's Republic of China on China's Territorial Sea (September 4, 1958), para. 1 (hereafter, "Territorial Sea Declaration").

14. Law of the People's Republic of China on the Territorial Sea and the Contiguous Zone (1992), art. 2 (hereafter, "Territorial Sea Law"); Declaration of the People's Republic of China upon Ratification of the United Nations Convention on the Law of the Sea, China (1996) (hereafter, "UNCLOS Ratification Declaration").

15. *Renmin ribao* [People's Daily], September 9, 1951.

16. Information Office, State Council of the People's Republic of China, "The Diaoyu Islands Are Inherent Territory of China" (2012) (hereafter, "Diaoyu White Paper").

17. People's Republic of China, *Note Verbale to the Secretary General of the United Nations with Regard to the Joint Submission Made by Malaysia and Vietnam to the Commission on the Limits of the Continental Shelf,* CML/17/2009, May 7, 2009 (hereafter, "*Note Verbale* [2009]"); and People's Republic of China, *Preliminary Information Indicative of the Outer Limits of the Continental Shelf Beyond 200 Nautical Miles of the People's Republic of China,* May 11, 2009; see also People's Republic of China, *Note Verbale to the Secretary-General of the United Nations with regard to the Republic of Philippines' Note Verbale* No.000228, CML/8/2011, April 14, 2011 (hereafter, "*Note Verbale* [2011]").

18. Ministry of Foreign Affairs of the People's Republic of China, *China's Indisputable Sovereignty over the Xisha and Nansha Islands* (1980) (hereafter, "China's Indisputable Sovereignty"); Ministry of Foreign Affairs of the People's Republic of China, *The Issue of the South China Sea* (June 2000) (hereafter, "South China Sea White Paper"); Ministry of Foreign Affairs of the People's Republic of China, "Position Paper of the Government of the People's Republic of China on the Matter of Jurisdiction in the South China Sea Arbitration Initiated by the Republic of the Philippines," sec 2 (December 7, 2014) (hereafter, "Position Paper").

19. On the line's origins, see Li Jinming and Li Dexia, "The Dotted Line on the Chinese Map of the South China Sea," *Ocean Development and International Law* 34, nos. 3–4 (2003), pp. 287–95; see also Zou Keyuan, *Law of the Sea in East Asia* (New York: Routledge, 2005), chapter 3.

The line had eleven dashes in the original version issued by the Republic of China in 1947. The PRC version mostly follows the contours of the ROC map, but it has used slightly different locations for its dashes, and the nine dashes have been placed in slightly different locations in various PRC versions of the map. The two dashes on the eleven-dash map nearest Vietnam were dropped after China deemed the maritime border with Vietnam in the Gulf of Tonkin settled. In recent years, a tenth dash has appeared to the east of Taiwan. While such variations can undermine claims of a stable, unchanging position by China, they do not materially alter the geographic scope of the Chinese claim.

20. *Note Verbale* (2009); *Note Verbale* (2011).

21. Communication from the People's Republic of China to the UN Commission on the Limits of the Continental Shelf, CML/001/2013 (January 7, 2013) and CML/017/2013 (August 5, 2013); "China Submits East China Sea Islands Claim to UN," BBC News Asia, December 14, 2012.

22. Zheng Wang, "China's Puzzling ADIZ Decision Making," *The Diplomat,* December 18, 2013; Chico Harlan, "China Creates New Air Defense Zone in East China Sea amid Dispute with Japan," *Washington Post,* November 23, 2013; "Experts Worry China May Soon Establish South China Sea ADIZ," *Voice of America,* July 29, 2015 (www.voanews.com/content/experts-concerned -china-may-soon-establish-southern-adiz/2882795.html); Roncevert Almond, "Mandate of Heaven: An ADIZ in the South China Sea," *Diplomat,* July 20, 2015 (http://thediplomat.com/2015/07/mandate-of-heaven-an-adiz -in-the-south-china-sea/).

23. Declaration of the Government of the People's Republic of China on the Baselines of the Territorial Sea of the People's Republic of China, May 15, 1996 (concerning Paracels); Statement of the Government of the People's Republic of China on the Baselines of the Territorial Sea of the Diaoyu Islands and Affiliated Islands, September 10, 2012. China's proclamation of baselines and their implication are discussed in a later section of this chapter.

24. See, for example, "Letter Dated 24 July 2014 from the Permanent Representative of China to the United Nations Addressed to the Secretary General," UNGA A/68/956 ("The Xisha Islands are China's inherent territory, a fact over which there is no dispute"); Foreign Ministry spokesman Hong Lei's regular press conference on September 21, 2012 ("Japan's claim that there is no sovereignty dispute over the Diaoyu Islands shows total disregard of historical facts and jurisprudential evidence and is absolutely untenable").

25. See, generally, UN Charter, art. 2(3) and chapter 7.

26. Position Paper, paragraphs 18–22 (denying arbitration tribunal's jurisdiction over Philippines' claims because they required determination of

territorial sovereignty, which the tribunal could not address and which belonged to China).

27. See, for example, U.S. Department of State, "Comments by Secretary Clinton in Hanoi, Vietnam."

28. Ministry of Foreign Affairs of the People's Republic of China, "Set Aside Dispute and Pursue Joint Development," undated (www.fmprc.gov.cn /mfa_eng/ziliao_665539/3602_665543/3604_665547/t18023.shtml). See also Position Paper, section 3 (arguing that the Philippines arbitration claim was barred by bilateral agreement to settle disputes through negotiations).

29. See, for example, South China Sea White Paper, section II.1.

30. Diaoyu White Paper, section I.1.

31. Island of Palmas (Netherlands v. United States), *Reports of International Arbitration Awards* 2 (1928), pp. 829, 845.

32. See, generally, Dong Wang, "The Discourse of Unequal Treaties in Modern China," *Pacific Affairs*, 76, no. 3 (2003), pp. 399–425; Tieya Wang, "International Law in China: Historical and Contemporary Perspectives," Hague Academy of International Law, *Recueil des cours*, 221 (1990-II), pp. 237–62.

33. Arbitral Award on the Subject of the Difference Relative to the Sovereignty over Clipperton Island (Mexico v. France) (1931), *American Journal of International Law* 26, no. 2 (1932), pp. 390–94.

34. Daioyu White Paper, section IV and passim; South China Sea White Paper, section II.

35. South China Sea White Paper, section II.3.

36. Diaoyu White Paper, section I.1–2.

37. "Text of Gromyko's Statement on the Peace Treaty," *New York Times*, September 8, 1951; China's Indisputable Sovereignty, sections II–III (concerning lack of significance for territorial sovereignty of illegal seizure of South China Sea islands); Jerome A. Cohen and Hungdah Chiu, *People's China and International Law* (Harvard University Press, 1974) pp. 344–45. The Diaoyu White Paper, section IV, argues that the Diaoyu have always been affiliated to Taiwan and thus implicitly invokes one line of argument in the white papers concerning Taiwan (discussed below) that China never lost sovereignty. See Jacques deLisle, "The Chinese Puzzle of Taiwan's Status," *Orbis* 44, no. 1 (2000), pp. 39–41.

38. PRC State Council, Taiwan Affairs Office, "The Taiwan Question and the Reunification of China" (1993) (hereafter, "1993 Taiwan White Paper"), section 1; South China Sea White Paper, sections I, III.3; Diaoyu White Paper, section III.2; "South China Sea: Controversies and Solutions—Interview with Liu Nanlai," *Beijing Review*, June 4–10, 2009.

39. China asserts that this was done through a diplomatic note from Vietnamese Premier Pham Van Dong to PRC Premier Zhou Enlai. Chinese

sources still invoke this history in addressing contemporary disputes with Vietnam. See "China Urges Consensus with Vietnam on South China Sea Issue," Xinhua, June 28, 2011.

40. The Treaty of Taipei confirmed that the Spratly and Paracel groups were included in Japan's renunciation. The San Francisco Treaty does not mention them specifically. PRC official and orthodox sources generally avoid relying on the Treaty of Taipei because it would imply recognition of the Republic of China's capacity to enter into a treaty relating to Chinese territory in 1952—three years after the ROC ceased to exist as the government of China, in the PRC's view.

41. See, for example, "China Opposes Attempts to Internationalize South China Sea Issue: Military," Xinhua, June 14, 2011; "Chinese Experts Call for Talks on South China Sea Issue," Xinhua, June 24, 2011.

42. Xinhua News Agency Dispatch, September 8, 1951; Tass News Agency Dispatch, September 7, 1951, reprinted in *Chinese Law and Government*, 46, nos. 3–4 (2013), p. 12.

43. Agreement between the United States of America and Japan Concerning the Ryukyu Islands and the Daito Islands, June 17, 1971; PRC Foreign Ministry Statement, December 1971, quoted in Diaoyu White Paper, section III.3.

44. Satoshi Ogawa, "Official U.S. View: Senkakus Fall Under the U.S.-Japan Security Treaty," *Yomiuri shimbun*, March 5, 2009; "Q&A: Japan's Yomiuri Shimbun Interviews President Obama," *Washington Post*, April 23, 2014; Department of State, Hillary Rodham Clinton Joint Press Availability with Japanese Foreign Minister Seiji Maehara, October 27, 2010.

45. See, for example, UN Charter, art. 2(4).

46. See, generally, Legal Status of Eastern Greenland (Denmark v. Norway), 1933 P.C.I.J. (Ser A/B) No. 53 (1933); Western Sahara, International Court of Justice Advisory Opinion, October 16, 1975; Island of Palmas Case.

47. M. Taylor Fravel, "China's Island Strategy: 'Redefine the Status Quo,'" *The Diplomat*, November 1, 2012; Jason Miks, "China, Philippines in Standoff," *The Diplomat*, April 1, 2012; Jane Perlez, "Alarm as China Issues Rules for Disputed Area," *New York Times*, December 2, 2012; M. Taylor Fravel, "Redefining the Status Quo," *The Diplomat*, November 2, 2012.

48. Jeff Himmelman, "A Game of Shark and Minnow," *New York Times Magazine*, October 27, 2013; Jane Perlez, "Philippines and China in Dispute over Reef," *New York Times*, March 31, 2014.

49. Daniel J. Dzurek, "China Occupies Mischief Reef in Latest Spratly Gambit," *IBRU Boundary and Security Bulletin* (April 1995), pp. 65–71; Michael Richardson, "Chinese Gambit: Seizing Mischief Reef without a Fight," *New York Times*, February 17, 1995.

50. See International Crisis Group, *Dangerous Waters*; see also Fackler, "Chinese Patrol Ships Pressuring Japan over Islands"; Scott Cheney-Peters, "How Japan's Nationalization Move in the East China Sea Shaped the U.S. Rebalance," *National Interest*, October 26, 2014 (http://nationalinterest.org /feature/how-japans-nationalization-move-the-east-china-sea-shaped -11549).

51. Smith, "Japan and the East China Sea Dispute"; International Crisis Group, *Dangerous Waters*.

52. Ankit Panda, "China's HD-981 Oil Rig Returns, Near Disputed South China Sea Waters," *Diplomat*, June 27, 2015 (http://thediplomat.com/2015 /06/chinas-hd-981-oil-rig-returns-to-disputed-south-china-sea-waters/); "China and Vietnam Clash over Oil Rig in South China Sea as Tensions Escalate," *Washington Post*, May 7, 2014.

53. Toshi Yoshihara, "The 1974 Paracels Sea Battle," *Naval War College Review*, 69, no. 2 (2016), pp. 41–65; Brian Kalman, "Two Case Studies that Illustrate the Growing Militarization of the South China Sea," *South Front*, April 18, 2016.

54. Edward Wong and Jonathan Ansfield, "To Bolster Its Claims, China Plants Islands in Disputed Waters," *New York Times*, June 16, 2014; Elizabeth Shim, "Ashton Carter: Beijing Should End Activities in the South China Sea," UPI, September 16, 2015; "Remarks by President Obama and President Xi of the People's Republic of China in Joint Press Conference," September 25, 2015, (www.whitehouse.gov/the-press-office/2015/09/25/remarks -president-obama-and-president-xi-peoples-republic-china-joint) (Obama "conveyed . . . significant concerns over land reclamation, construction and the militarization of disputed areas"). Li Xiaokun, "Island Defenses 'Legitimate, Legal,'" *China Daily*, December 16, 2016 (quoting statements by Defense Ministry and Foreign Ministry); Chris Buckley, "China Suggests It Has Placed Weapons on Disputed Spratly Islands in South China Sea," *New York Times*, December 15, 2016.

55. The Philippines-China arbitration decision has made this issue more complicated for China or, perhaps more accurately, made clear the complexity and difficulty of this issue for China. Significant land reclamation around a rock capable of generating a twelve-nautical-mile territorial sea (when undertaken by or with the permission of the state holding sovereignty over that landform) is permissible. For a mere low-tide elevation (one not sufficiently near a more substantial territory) or for an artificial island constructed on such a marine formation, only a minimal "safety zone" is permissible—a maritime area too small to allow room for land reclamation. The arbitration panel ruled that some of the sites where China has been undertaking land reclamation are mere low-tide elevations, some not located sufficiently close

to rocks generating entitlements to territorial seas. Philippines v. China, paragraphs 382–84; UNCLOS, art. 60.

56. See International Crisis Group, *Dangerous Waters* (concerning the escalation dynamic); Fravel, "Redefining the Status Quo"; M. Taylor Fravel, *Strong Borders, Secure Nation: Cooperation and Conflict in China's Border Disputes* (Princeton University Press, 2008).

57. See, for example, State Council Information Office, People's Republic of China, "China Adheres to the Position of Settling through Negotiation the Relevant Disputes between China and the Philippines in the South China Sea" (July 13, 2016), paragraphs 35–38 (hereafter, "Settling through Negotiation"); South China Sea White Paper, section III.3.

58. Diaoyu White Paper, sections I.2, I.5; 1993 Taiwan White Paper, section 1.

59. "China Establishes Sansha City," Xinhua, July 24, 2012; "Administrative Level Status of Islands Raised," *China Daily*, June 22, 2012.

60. Ronald O'Rourke, "Maritime Territorial and Exclusive Economic Zone (EEZ) Disputes Involving China," Congressional Research Service Report 7-5700; Territorial Sea Law; Law of the People's Republic on the Exclusive Economic Zone and Continental Shelf (1998) (hereafter, "EEZ Law"); Fisheries Law of the People's Republic of China (2000, 2004, 2013); "Statement by the Government of the PRC concerning the Baselines for the Territorial Sea Surrounding Diaoyu and Appurtenant Islands," Xinhua, September 10, 2012.

61. "South China Sea Fishing Ban 'Indisputable': Foreign Ministry Spokesman," Xinhua, June 9, 2009; "Fourth Fishing Ban on South China Sea to Begin," Xinhua, May 29, 2002.

62. See, for example, Oscar Chung, "One Step Forward to Peace," Taiwan Info, June 1, 2013 (http://taiwaninfo.nat.gov.tw/ct.asp?xItem=204966&ctNode =124); James Manicom, "The State of Cooperation in the East China Sea," *NBR Analysis Brief*, April 30, 2013 (www.nbr.org/publications/analysis/pdf /brief/043013_Manicom_EChinaSea.pdf).

63. Chau Boa Nguyen, "With China's Oil Rig Back in the South China Sea, What's Vietnam's Play?" *East Asia Forum*, July 24, 2015 (www.eastasiaforum .org/2015/07/24/with-chinas-oilrig-back-in-the-south-china-sea-whats -vietnams-play/); "China Opposes Vietnam Oil, Gas Exploration in China's Jurisdictional Sea Area: FM Spokeswoman," Xinhua, May 28, 2011. See also Liselotte Odgaard, *Maritime Security between China and Southeast Asia* (Aldershot: Ashgate, 2002), pp. 84–86.

64. Gao Jianjun, "A Note on the 2008 Cooperation Consensus Between China and Japan in the East China Sea," *Ocean Development and International Law* 40, no. 3 (2009), pp. 302–3 (text of the agreement).; CNOOC, Petro-Vietnam, PNOC, "Joint Statement on the Signing of a Tripartite Agreement

for Joint Marine Seismic Undertaking in the Agreement Area in the South China Sea," March 14, 2005 (http://ph.china-embassy.org/eng/zt/nhwt /t187333.htm).

65. Twelfth Five-Year Plan for National Economic and Social Development of the People's Republic of China (2011–15) Part III, chapter 14, section 2; Outline of the 13th Five-Year (2016–20) Plan for National Economic and Social Development of the People's Republic of China (2016); Ryan D. Martinson, "The Thirteenth Five-Year Plan: A New Chapter in China's Maritime Transformation," *China Brief*, vol. 16, no. 1 (January 2016); "China to Make Maritime Law in Five Years," Xinhua, March 5, 2016.

66. See "Maritime Forces to be Beefed Up amid Disputes," *China Daily*, June 17, 2011 (60% expansion from 2011 to 2015 in China's offshore surveillance fleet and personnel); "China Starts Regular Patrols of South China Sea," Xinhua, April 25, 2010.

67. See, generally, Li Minjiang and Zhang Hongzhou, "Restructuring China's Maritime Law Enforcement: Impact on Regional Security," RSIS Commentary No. 050/2013 (April 1, 2013); M. Taylor Fravel, "Hainan's New Maritime Regulations: A Preliminary Analysis," *The Diplomat*, December 1, 2102; Jane Perlez, "Alarm as China Issues Rules for Disputed Area," *New York Times*, December 2, 2012; Hainan Provincial People's Congress Standing Committee, Hainan Coastal Border Security Regulations (2012).

68. Settling through Negotiation, § V; "China Remains Committed to Peaceful Settlement of Disputes in the South China Sea through Negotiations and Consultations—Keynote Speech by Mr. Liu Zhenmin, Vice Foreign Minister of China," March 25, 2016, (www.fmprc.gov.cn/mfa_eng /wjbxw/t1350776.shtml).

69. Joint Statement of the Republic of the Philippines and the People's Republic of China, October 21, 2016 (www.philstar.com/headlines/2016 /10/21/1635919/full-text-joint-statement-philippines-and-china); Benjamin Kang Lim, "Philippines' Duterte Says South China Sea Arbitration Case to Take 'Back Seat,'" Reuters, October 19, 2016.

70. UNCLOS, arts. 2–32, 55–85, 17–45.

71. Ibid., arts. 3–15, 33, 48, 57, 76.

72. Position Paper, section II.

73. UNLCOS, arts. 7(5), 10(6), 15, 46–47, 51, 62, 70, 71 (concerning: history of economic uses in context of baselines; "historic bays" permitting departures from usual rules, primarily concerning baselines; "historic title" in context of territorial seas; areas "historically . . . regarded" as archipelagos; accommodation in EEZ and archipelagic waters context of interests of other states whose nationals have "habitually" fished in the area or whose economies have been extensively dependent on fishing in those areas).

74. See, for example, Peng Guangqian, "China's Maritime Rights and Interests" in *Military Activities in the EEZ: A U.S.-China Dialogue* (U.S. Naval War College, 2010), pp. 15–22; Peter Dutton, "Three Disputes and Three Objectives," *U.S. Naval War College Review* 64, no. 4 (2010), pp. 45–48; "New Map Boosts China's Claim in South China Sea," *South China Sea Bulletin* 2, no. 8 (2014) (describing map as highlighting China's "historic title" consistent with UNCLOS).

75. UNCLOS, preamble, paragraph 8. These arguments are discussed more fully in the next section of this chapter.

76. Philippines v. China, section V.

77. Office of Ocean and Polar Affairs Bureau of Oceans and International Environmental and Scientific Affairs, U.S. Department of State, "China: Maritime Claims in the South China Sea," *Limits in the Seas* No. 143, December 5, 2014, pp. 10–13, 15–22.

78. UNCLOS, arts. 6, 13, 60, 121, 259, 260.

79. Philippines v. China, section VI.

80. Zhao Lei, "Combatant Ships Patrol Southernmost Point," *China Daily*, May 27, 2013; Bill Hayton, "How a Non-Existent Island Became China's Southernmost Territory," *South China Morning Post*, February 9, 2013.

81. UNLCOS, arts. 7–10, 14, 47.

82. *Limits in the Seas* No. 143, p. 13; Office of Ocean and Polar Affairs Bureau of Oceans and International Environmental and Scientific Affairs, U.S. Department of State, "Straight Baselines Claim: China," *Limits in the Seas* No. 117, July 6, 1996; see also the discussions earlier in this chapter of China's declarations of baselines, and of U.S. and PRC actions and reactions concerning U.S. Navy close-in approaches to the Paracel Islands and the marine features in the Spratly Islands where China has undertaken land reclamation.

83. UNLCOS, arts. 59, 74, 83; North Sea Continental Shelf Cases (Federal Republic of Germany v. Denmark, Federal Republic of Germany v. Netherlands), 1969 I.C.J. 3; Guyana v. Suriname Arbitral Award (September 17, 2007); Territorial and Maritime Dispute (Nicaragua v. Colombia), 2012 I.C.J. 624.

84. Declaration of the People's Republic of China to UNCLOS UNCLOS, August 25, 2006 (www.un.org/Depts/los/convention_agreements/convention_declarations.htm#).

85. Position Paper, section II; Statement of the Ministry of Foreign Affairs on the People's Republic of China on the Award of 12 July 2016 of the Arbitral Tribunal in the South China Sea Arbitration Established at the Request of the Republic of the Philippines, July 12, 2016 (hereafter, "Ministry of Foreign Affairs Statement on South China Sea Arbitration Award").

86. Philippines v. China, section IV.

87. Dean Cheng, "Winning without Fighting: Chinese Legal Warfare," *Heritage Foundation Backgrounder* No. 2692 (May 18, 2012); Qiao Liang and Wang Xiangsui, *Unrestricted Warfare* (Beijing: PLA Literature and Arts, 1999); Peter Dutton, Statement at Hearing before the Senate Subcommittee on East Asian and Pacific Affairs, Committee on Foreign Relations, United States Senate, 111th Congress, 1st Session, July 15, 2009, pp. 19, 23.

88. See generally, Ren Xiaofeng and Cheng Xizhong, "A Chinese Perspective," *Marine Policy* no. 29 (2005), pp. 139ff; Peter Dutton and John Garofano, "China Undermines Maritime Laws," *Far Eastern Economic Review*, April 2009, pp. 44–47; Jacques deLisle, "Troubled Waters: China's Claims and the South China Sea," *Orbis*, 56, no. 4 (2012), pp. 608–42.

89. See Hong Nong, Li Jianwei and Chen Pingping "The Concept of Archipelagic States and the South China Sea: UNLCOS, State Practice, and Implication," *China Oceans Law Review*, no. 1 (2013), pp. 209–39; Daniel J. Dzurek, "The People's Republic of China Straight Baseline Claim, *IBRU Boundary Security Bulletin*, 4, no. 2 (1996), pp. 77–89; *Limits in the Seas* No. 117.

90. *Limits in the Seas* No. 143, pp. 5, 14–15; see also the discussion of equidistance and maritime delimitation in the preceding subsection of this chapter.

91. See the discussion of historic rights earlier in this chapter and later in this subsection. On the tensions between Chinese positions and mainstream interpretations of relevant laws, see, generally, deLisle, "Troubled Waters," pp. 628–35; Ren and Cheng, "A Chinese Perspective," pp. 139–46; Dutton and Garofano, "China Undermines Maritime Laws."

92. See deLisle, "Troubled Waters," pp. 615–16, 618–19; Statement of Scott Marciel, Deputy Assistant Secretary of State, Statement at Hearing before the Senate Subcommittee on East Asian and Pacific Affairs, Committee on Foreign Relations, United States Senate, 111th Congress, 1st Session, July 15, 2009, p. 5; *Limits in the Seas* no. 143, pp. 14–15; Dutton, "Three Disputes," pp. 45–48.

93. EEZ Law, art. 14; see also Zou Keyuan, "China and Maritime Boundary Delimitation," in *Conflict Management and Dispute Settlement in East Asia*, edited by Ramses Amer and Keyuan Zou (Farnham: Ashgate, 2011), pp. 161–62; Yann-huei Song and Zou Keyuan, "Maritime Legislation of Mainland China and Taiwan," *Ocean Development and International Law* 31, no. 4 (2000), pp. 318–19.

94. Zhiguo Gao and Bing Bing Jia, "The Nine-Dash Line in the South China Sea: History, Status and Implications," *American Journal of International Law* 107, no. 1 (2013), pp. 98–123; Position Paper, paragraphs 8, 68, 92–93; Li and Li, "The Dotted Line," pp. 290–93; Zhang Haiwen, "Indisputable

Sovereignty," *Beijing Review,* June 7, 2011; Foreign Ministry Spokesperson Jiang Yu's Regular Press Conference on September 15, 2011(http://vancouver .china-consulate.org/eng/fyrth/t860126.htm) (asserting that UNCLOS "does not restrain or deny a country's right which is formed in history and abidingly upheld").

95. Philippines v. China § V; *Limits in the Seas* No. 143, pp. 21–22; see also Office of Ocean and Polar Affairs Bureau of Oceans and International Environmental and Scientific Affairs, U.S. Department of State, "United States Responses to Excessive National Maritime Claims," *Limits in the Seas* No. 112 (March 9, 1992), p. 13.

96. Territorial Sea Declaration; UNCLOS Ratification Declaration; Territorial Sea Law, arts. 6, 12; Zhao Jianwen, "On the Interpretive Declarations by the State Parties to United Nations Convention on the Law of the Sea concerning the Issue of Innocent Passage of Warships through the Territorial Sea," *China Oceans Law Review,* no. 2 (2015), pp. 282–310; compare UNCLOS, arts. 17–32; Mu Xuequan, "China Urges U.S. Not to Undermine Mutual Trust," Xinhua, January 30, 2016; Sam LaGrone, "China Upset over 'Unprofessional' U.S. Freedom of Navigation Operation," USNI News, February 1, 2016 (http://news.usni.org/2016/01/31/china-upset-over -unprofessional-u-s-south-china-sea-freedom-of-navigation-operation).

97. See, for example, *Limits in the Seas* No. 112, pp. 51–61; Ashley Roach and Robert W. Smith, "Territorial Sea," *International Law Studies* 66 (1994) (https://www.usnwc.edu/Research---Gaming/International-Law/New -International-Law-Studies-(Blue-Book)-Series/International-Law-Blue -Book-Articles.aspx?Volume=66); see also the discussion of U.S. freedom of navigation operations in the "Context and Background" section of this chapter. Sam LaGrone, "U.S. Destroyer Challenges More Chinese South China Sea Claims in New Freedom of Navigation Operation," USNI News, January 30, 2016 (http://news.usni.org/2016/01/30/u-s-destroyerchallenges -more-chinese-south-china-sea-claims-in-new-freedom-of-navigation -operation%3B); "Full Statement of US Dept of Defense on USS Curtis Wilbur's FONOP Past Triton Island," South China Sea Research, January 31, 2016 (https://seasresearch.wordpress.com/2016/01/31/full-statement-of-us -dept-defense-on-uss-curtis-wilburs-fonop-past-triton-island/); Idrees Ali and Matt Spetalnick, "U.S. Warship Challenges China's Claims in South China Sea," Reuters, October 21, 2016.

98. Territorial Sea Law, art. 8; EEZ Law, art. 11; compare UNCLOS, arts. 30, 58.

99. Surveying and Mapping Law of the People's Republic of China, art. 7 (1992, 2002); EEZ Law, art. 9; Guifang Xue, "Maritime Scientific Research and Hydrographic Survey in the EEZs," in *Freedom of Seas, Passage*

Rights and the 1982 Law of the Sea Convention, edited by Myron H. Nordquist, Tommy T. B. Koh, and John Norton Moore (Leiden, Netherlands: Brill, 2009), pp. 209–25.

100. "China Demands U.S. Navy End Surveillance Missions," Sina.com, March 12, 2009 (http://english.sina.com/china/2009/0311/225194.html) (Defense Ministry Spokesperson Huang Xueping); see also Danh Duc and H. Trung, "Just Another 'Chicken Game' on the Sea," March 12, 2009 (Foreign Ministry Spokesperson Ma Zhaoxu); Raul Pedrozo, "Close Encounters at Sea: The USNS Impeccable Incident, *U.S. Naval War College Review* 62, no. 3 (2009), pp. 101–11; Ji Guoxing, "The Legality of the Impeccable Incident," *China Security* 5 (2009), pp. 16–21.

While much of the discussion has focused on incidents involving the *Impeccable* and the *John McCain* in the South China Sea in 2009, similar incidents have occurred against U.S. Navy ships elsewhere and on other occasions, including harassment of the guided missile cruiser *Cowpens* by a Chinese Navy ship in the South China Sea in 2013, "unsafe" intercepts of U.S. reconnaissance aircraft by Chinese jets over the South China Sea in 2016, a Chinese submarine's surfacing amid the *Kitty Hawk* carrier battle group near Japan in 2007, Chinese naval ships harassing or trying to drive off the *Bowditch* in the Yellow Sea in the 2000s, and seizing of a U.S. Navy drone in 2016.

101. See Jing Geng, "The Legality of Foreign Military Activities in the Exclusive Economic Zone under UNCLOS," *Merkourios* 28, no. 74 (2012), pp. 22–30; Raul Pedrozo, "Preserving Navigational Rights and Freedoms: The Right to Conduct Military Activities in China's Exclusive Economic Zone," *Chinese Journal of International Law* 9 (2010), para. 32.

102. "Spokesman Zhu Bangzao Gives Full Account of Collision between U.S. and Chinese Military Planes" (www.china-un.ch/eng/premade/11437/spokesman040401.htm); Ren and Cheng, "A Chinese Perspective," § V; "U.S. Plane Grossly Violated International Law," *People's Daily*, April 4, 2001; Eric Donnelly, "The United States-China EP-3 Incident: Legality and Realpolitik," *Journal of Conflict and Security* 9, no. 1 (2004), pp. 25–42; W. Allan Edmiston III, "Showdown in the South China Sea," *Emory International Law Review* 16, no. 2 (2002), pp. 639–88.

103. Tallies of states' views on rights in the EEZ find fewer than twenty to at most two dozen states fully siding with China and well over one hundred siding with U.S.-favored views. Dutton, Statement before Senate Subcommittee, p. 24; Moritaka Hayashi, "Military and Intelligence Gathering Activities in the EEZ: Definition of Key Terms," *Marine Policy* 29, no. 2 (2005), pp. 123–37; Raul Pedrozo, "Military Activities in the Exclusive Economic Zone: East Asia Focus," *International Law Studies* 90 (2014), pp. 514–39.

104. Ministry of National Defense, People's Republic of China, Statement by the Government of the People's Republic of China on Declaring the East China Sea Air Defense Identification Zone, November 23, 2013; Ministry of National Defense, People's Republic of China, Announcement of Aircraft Identification Rules for the East China Sea Air Defense Identification Zone of the PRC, November 23, 2013; Michael D. Swaine, "Chinese Views and Commentary on the East China Sea Air Defense Identification Zone," *China Leadership Monitor*, no. 43 (2014); Statement by Secretary of Defense Chuck Hagel on the East China Sea Air Defense Identification Zone, November 23, 2013 (zone a "destabilizing attempt to alter the status quo" and "will not in any way change how the United States conducts military operations"); "Shinzo Abe: China New Air Defence Zone Move 'Dangerous,'" BBC, November 25, 2013 (quoting Japanese Premier Abe statement that zone had "no validity"); Jane Perlez, "China Explains Handling of B-52 Flight as Tensions Escalate," *New York Times*, November 27, 2013.

105. Ren and Cheng, "A Chinese Perspective" section V; Zhang, "Indisputable Sovereignty"; UNCLOS, arts. 58, 87.

106. Mu, "China Urges U.S. Not to Undermine Mutual Trust"; "U.S. Plane Grossly Violated International Law"; UNCLOS, arts. 88, 141, 143, 301; United Nations Charter, arts. 1, 2(3).

107. deLisle, "Troubled Waters," pp. 632–35; Ji, "Legality of the Impeccable Incident" (U.S. actions were "threat of force" against "China's territorial integrity and political independence"); "Chinese General Says U.S. Military Drills in South China Sea 'Inappropriate,'" Xinhua, July 11, 2011 (PLA Chief of General Staff Chen Bingde); "Intensive U.S.-Led War Games Detrimental to Asia-Pacific Stability," Xinhua, August 5, 2012; Blanchard and Shalal, "Angry China Shadows U.S. Warship"; UNCLOS, arts. 119, 39, 301, United Nations Charter, art. 2(4).

108. Terri Moon Cronk, "Chinese Seize U.S. Navy Underwater Drone in South China Sea," DoD News, December 16, 2016 (https://www.defense.gov/News/Article/Article/1032823/chinese-seize-us-navy-underwater-drone-in-south-china-sea); Helene Cooper, "U.S. Demands Return of Drone Seized by Chinese Warship," *New York Times*, December 16, 2016.

109. For descriptions of U.S. positions, see "Chapter 10: Air, Sea and Space Law," *Operational Law Handbook* (Washington: Library of Congress, 2015), pp. 173–77; James W. Houck and Nicole M. Anderson, "The United States, China, and Freedom of Navigation in the South China Sea," *Washington University Global Studies Law Review* 13, no. 3 (2014), pp. 443–47.

110. On earlier criticisms or rejections of international law, see Hungdah Chiu, "Communist China's Attitude toward International Law), *American Journal of International Law* 60, no. 2, (1966), pp. 245–67; Jacques deLisle,

"China's Approach to International Law," *American Society of International Law Proceedings*, 94 (2000), pp. 272–73. On the Xi Jinping-era call for greater influence, see Eighteenth Central Committee of the Chinese Communist Party, Fourth Plenum, Decision Concerning Some Major Questions in Comprehensively Promoting Governing the Country According to Law (October 23, 2014) § VII (7) (calling for China to "vigorously participate in the formulation of international norms . . . strengthen our country's discourse power and influence in international legal affairs, use legal methods to safeguard our country's sovereignty, security and development interests").

111. This is similar to the approach that Beijing has taken toward cross-strait relations in the period of calm that began under Hu Jintao and progressed when Ma Ying-jeou came to power on Taiwan. The view is most formally and ingeniously expressed in the Anti-Secession Law. See Jacques deLisle, "Legislating the Cross-Strait Status Quo?" in *Economic Integration, Democratization and National Security in East Asia*, edited by Peter C.Y. Chow (Cheltenham: Edward Elgar, 2007), pp. 101–38.

112. Ministry of Foreign Affairs, People's Republic of China, "Set Aside Dispute and Pursue Joint Development," July 9, 2016 (www.fmprc.gov.cn /mfa_eng/ziliao_665539/3602_665543/3604_665547/t18023.shtml); Ministry of Foreign Affairs, Japan, "Senkaku Islands Q&A" (mofa.go.jp/region /asia-paci/senkaku/qa_1010.html) (quoting Deng Xiaoping's remarks at joint press conference with Prime Minister Fukuda Takeo, October 25, 1978).

113. Ministry of Foreign Affairs Statement on South China Sea Arbitration Award; "Foreign Ministry Spokesman Lu Kang's Regular Press Conference on October 27, 2016," October 27, 2016 (www.fmprc.gov.cn/mfa_eng /xwfw_665399/s2510_665401/t1410179.shtml); Benjamin Kang Lim, "Philippines' Duterte Says S. China Sea Arbitration Case to Take 'Back Seat,'" Reuters, October 19, 2016.

114. Foreign Ministry Spokesperson Hua Chunying's Regular Press Conference on December 26, 2016 (http://www.fmprc.gov.cn/ce/cedk/eng/fyrth /t1426902.htm); Javier C. Hernandez, "China Deploys Aircraft Carrier to Disputed South China Sea," *New York Times*. December 27, 2016.

TEN

China and the International Human Rights Legal Regime

Orthodoxy, Resistance, and Legitimacy

PITMAN B. POTTER

Human rights conditions in the People's Republic of China continue to elicit criticism and debate.[1] Systematic normative and operational analysis has been useful in building understanding about human rights in the PRC in the context of international standards.[2] This paper builds on that work, offering a thematic approach focused on themes of orthodoxy, resistance, and legitimacy. The orthodoxy of the PRC subordinates human rights to the authority of the Communist Party of China (CPC) and the policy priorities of the Party/state. As a result, the PRC government has consistently resisted the application of international standards on human rights in China. Yet increasing citizen activism over human rights abuses raises questions about regime legitimacy, as does increasing support for such activism internationally.

HUMAN RIGHTS ORTHODOXY: PARTY LEADERSHIP, CONDITIONALITY, AND DEVELOPMENT

The human rights orthodoxy of the PRC Party / state sets the boundaries for determining the nature and beneficiaries of human rights in China. Beginning with the PRC Constitution and extending to other instruments of governance, human rights orthodoxy in the PRC embraces doctrines of Party leadership, conditionality of rights, and the imperative of economic development.

Party Leadership

The sanctity of CPC leadership has remained relatively unchanged in China's approach to human rights over the past thirty years. The 1982 PRC Constitution enshrined as imperatives of governance Deng Xiaoping's "Four Cardinal Principles": (1) socialism; (2) the people's democratic dictatorship; (3) the leadership of the CPC; and (4) "Marxism-Leninism Mao Zedong thought."[3] The imperative of CPC leadership is the most fundamental of the Four Cardinal Principles and underscores the monopoly of Party leadership over governance activities and institutions—inviting concern over the permitted scope of activities and discourses (including human rights) that are not endorsed by the Party. While policy innovation in China's economic and social transformation has caused many to question the consistency and continued vibrancy of the themes of socialism, democratic dictatorship, and ideological tradition,[4] the imperative of Party leadership has remained a core constitutional principle, despite variations in immediate policy priorities.[5] Speaking to the 2004 Amendments to the PRC Constitution, NPC Standing Committee vice chair Yang Jingyu indicated that retaining the Four Cardinal Principles and especially the principle of Party leadership in the Preamble ensured their permanence regardless of subsequent amendments to the Constitution itself.[6] To do otherwise, Yang said, would "shake the foundations of the state" (*dongyao guojia de genben*). The Four Cardinal Principles were enshrined yet again in the 2012 revisions to the CPC Constitution.[7]

Party control extends to the socialist legal system, gradually replacing the focus on class struggle with the need to maintain stability and protect the Party / state. While Mao's critique of formal law and regulation had been grounded in ideas about continued class struggle and the need for permanent revolution,[8] the determination by the 3d Plenum of the 11th CPC Central Committee in November–December 1978 that class struggle had been largely resolved indicated a tentative step away from Maoist doctrine and laid the foundation for legal and economic reform.[9] At the 13th National Party Congress in 1987, General Secretary Zhao Ziyang asserted that China was in the preliminary stage of socialism, suggesting that class struggle had declined yet further, raising the prospect for greater autonomy and authority for the legal system, particularly in civil and economic affairs.[10]

Nonetheless, the imperative of Party leadership remained. Following the disastrous Tiananmen massacre in 1989, Deng Xiaoping's 1992 Southern Tour (*nanxun*) supported "deepening reform," which combined market reforms in the economy with resistance to political reform under the guise of maintaining stability.[11] This orthodoxy continued under Deng Xiaoping's successors Jiang Zemin and Hu Jintao.[12] Despite increased professionalism and autonomy among judicial personnel and institutions, Party-led adjudication committees (*shenpan weiyuanhui*) in the People's Courts ensured CPC leadership over judicial appointments and decisions.[13] A 2010 Supreme Court opinion on reforming and improving adjudication committees provided,

> Reforming and improving the adjudication committee system must uphold the "three supremes" (*sange zhishang*) as the guiding thought in people's court work, uphold the leadership of the Party regarding people's court work, consciously accepting the supervision of the NPC, consciously safeguarding the seriousness and authority of the Constitution and laws, consciously upholding lawful powers of the people, insist on proceeding from the facts of adjudication work, and progress positively and reliably according to law.[14]

Under Xi Jinping, the assertion of Party leadership over the legal system has included a renewed emphasis on maintaining stability as a prerequisite for economic development.[15] The 4th Plenum of the

18th Central Committee in October 2014 emphasized that the socialist legal system would remain bound by the Constitution and thus by the principle of Party leadership:

> The position of leadership of the CPC is written into China's Constitution. Upholding the Party's leadership is fundamental to socialist rule of law; it is the foundation and lifeblood of both the Party and the country, affects the interests and well-being of people of all China's ethnic groups, and is an integral part of our efforts to comprehensively advance the law-based governance of the country. The Party's leadership is consistent with socialist rule of law: socialist rule of law must uphold the Party's leadership, while the Party's leadership must rely upon socialist rule of law.[16]

The organizational features of Party leadership over the socialist legal system were brought into sharp relief when the Politburo Standing Committee received reports on Party organization work at leading legal and judicial organs:

> One very important system of the Party Central's unified leadership over the NPC Standing Committee, State Council, CPPCC, Supreme People's Court and Supreme People's Procuracy is the establishment of Party organs (*dang zu*) in these institutions. Party organs are organizational institutions established in leadership offices of non-Party organizations by the Central Committee and by local Party committees at various levels, and are an important organizational form and systemic guarantee for realizing Party leadership over non-Party organs. The work of the Central Politburo Standing Committee receiving reports from the Party organs of the NPC Standing Committee, State Council, CPPCC, Supreme People's Court and Supreme People's Procuracy is a systemic arrangement for ensuring the collective unified leadership of the Party Central, it is of surpassing significance, and has demonstrative significance of great importance for the whole Party.[17]

Thus, subordination of law and legal institutions to Party leadership is not simply an abstract ideological principle, but rather is thoroughly entrenched in the organization and operation of the PRC Party/state. This has significant implications for issues of judicial independence, autonomy of legal relationships, and the consistent enforcement of the rule of law.

Conditionality of Rights

Entrenched principles on Party leadership complement principles of conditionality in the exercise of human rights. Article 33.2 of the Constitution conditions the extension of legal and civil rights on performance of the "duties prescribed by the Constitution and the law," which according to the Four Cardinal Principles include "upholding Party leadership."[18] This provision retains its effect despite the addition in 2004 of Article 33.3 that "the State respects and ensures human rights." The explanatory speech on the 2004 amendments specified that the CPC Politburo Standing Committee exercised "direct leadership" over the revisions, which then could hardly be seen as imposing limits on Party authority.[19] Indeed the insertion of the human rights provision following the conditionality rule of Art. 33.2 underscored that human rights would remain subject to the same limitations as apply to rights expressed elsewhere in the constitution and the legal system generally.[20]

Echoing the Constitutional language of Art. 33.2, the 2012 amendments to the Criminal Procedure Law (CPL) included in Article 2 a reference respecting and ensuring human rights (*zunzhong he baozhang renquan*).[21] Yet the repeated references in the CPL to the Constitution and the law entrench principles of Party leadership and the conditionality of rights:

> *Article 1* This Law is enacted in accordance with the Constitution and for the purpose of ensuring correct enforcement of the Criminal Law, punishing crimes, protecting the people, safeguarding State and public security and maintaining socialist public order.

Article 2 The tasks of the Criminal Procedure Law of the People's Republic of China are to ensure the accurate and prompt discovery of criminal facts, the correct application of law, the punishment of crimes, and the protection of the innocent from criminal prosecution; to educate citizens to comply with the law and to fight crimes; to maintain the socialist law and order, to respect and ensure human rights, and to protect citizens' rights to person, rights to property, democratic rights and other rights; and to guarantee smooth progress of the cause of socialist development.

The reference in CPL Article 1 to the Constitution and by extension the Four Cardinal Principles, clarifies the pre-eminence of Party authority in determining how purposes of "ensuring correct enforcement of the Criminal Law, punishing crimes, protecting the people, safeguarding State and public security and maintaining socialist public order" will be carried out. Similarly, the orthodoxy of Party supremacy infuses Article 2's summary of CPL's goals regarding "correct application of law," the need to "abide by the law" and "safeguard the socialist legal system," and "to guarantee smooth progress of the cause of socialist development." Requirements in Art. 3 that the courts, procuracy and public security organs (extended in Art. 4 to state security organs) "strictly observe this Law . . . and other laws" do not allow for derogation from Party leadership. Similarly, references to independence of the courts and the procuracy (Art. 5) and the universal application of law (Art. 6) still remain subject to the supremacy of the Party. Thus, despite superficial changes, the revised Criminal Procedure Law does little to dilute the power of the Party / state over the justice system.[22] Similar constitutional references appear in other PRC laws for matters such as judicial review (for example, Administrative Litigation Law, Article 1); civil rights (for example, General Principles of Civil Law, Article 1); and economic relations (for example, Property Rights Law, Article 1),[23] making clear that all rights (including human rights, whether of the civil and political; or the economic, social, and cultural variety) remain dependent upon the imperatives of the Party / state.

The Imperative of Economic Development

Building on principles of Party leadership and conditionality of rights, China's human rights orthodoxy enshrines the discourse of the "right to development."[24] Although many international law scholars challenge the notion that a right to development can take precedence over other human rights,[25] China's 1991 human rights white paper stressed the right to subsistence as the primary right from which all other rights derive.[26] In explaining the 1991 white paper, the Director of the State Council Information Office stressed the primacy of the state's management of economic conditions as the basis for development: "[W]e enable our people to have the economic foundation upon which they can enjoy political rights."[27] China's assertions that the right to development should take precedence over civil and political rights was reiterated through Beijing's support for the 1993 Bangkok Declaration on Human Rights, in which the participants underscored a range of principles resisting the application of international human rights standards that might challenge the authority of national governments.[28] The 1995 Human Rights white paper repeated the regime's commitment to the primacy of economic development over other human rights issues,[29] while the 1997 white paper reiterated the theme that subsistence and development were paramount human rights.[30]

Achievements in satisfying human rights to subsistence and development were given prominence yet again in the 2000 Human Rights white paper, which put "the rights to subsistence and development in the first place under conditions of reform, development and stability."[31] The white paper articulated a sequential time-table for human rights development in which economic development must precede construction of democracy and the legal system, which in turn are aimed to ensure that, "the Party and the government control political power and administer the country according to law. . . . Socialism with Chinese characteristics is . . . the only road which can effectively promote human rights in China."

While academic human rights specialists in China acknowledge the importance of individual freedoms (including freedom of thought and expression) in human rights protection, these are still thought

298 PITMAN B. POTTER

to rest ultimately on different conditions of development.[32] China's 2009 white paper continued the emphasis on the rights to subsistence and development,[33] while China's 2012 Human Rights Action Plan equated human rights with development and social harmony.[34] This pattern continued with China's Human Rights white papers in 2014 and 2015.[35] Thus, civil and political rights continue to be subordinated to the economic development goals of the Party/state and its focus on stability maintenance.

In summary, human rights orthodoxy in the PRC proceeds from the governance principle of Party leadership as expressed in the Constitution to generate a doctrine subordinating rights to the authority of the Party/state. The Party's policy imperative of economic development then stands as the primary condition through which human rights are identified and protected. China's human rights orthodoxy of Party leadership, conditionality of rights, and economic development cannot be divorced from human rights conditions for which China is criticized, such as abuse of criminal process for political purposes,[36] suppression of religious freedoms,[37] denial of labour rights,[38] the use of surveillance technology to suppress freedom of communication and expression,[39] and treatment of minority nationalities.[40] In the wake of the awarding of the Nobel Peace Prize to dissident writer Liu Xiaobo in October 2010, and the circulation of anonymous calls for a "jasmine revolution" in China following Arab Spring events of early 2011 in Tunisia and Egypt, human rights activists around the country faced disappearances, arrests, and prosecution on "state security" related charges.[41] The sham trial and life sentence imposed on moderate economics professor Ilham Tohti for alleged separatism confirms that the PRC Party/state will continue to confine human rights protection to an orthodoxy of Party rule, conditionality of rights, and the priority of economic development.[42] Such repression has continued into 2016, with continued arrests and abuse of human rights lawyers and NGO workers and ongoing state directives to suppress public expression with which the regime disagrees.[43] Even where human rights abuses (such use of the death penalty,[44] torture and abuse of prisoners,[45] and discrimination against women[46]) can be attributed to the failure of local authorities to comply with central government dictates, the slow pace of reform suggests an unwillingness to commit political capital to achieve meaningful change.

RESISTANCE TO INTERNATIONAL STANDARDS

China's human rights orthodoxy encourages resistance to international standards, even while appropriating human rights language embodied in those standards. As a signatory of the Universal Declaration of Human Rights, China is bound to the principles of the Declaration on such matters as freedom of thought, conscience, and religion (Art. 18); freedom of opinion and expression (Art. 19); freedom of peaceful assembly and association (Art. 20); the right to form and join trade unions (Art. 23), and others.[47] The Declaration expressly limits the authority of states to restrict the exercise of these rights or to undermine them: "Nothing in this Declaration may be interpreted as implying for any State, group or person any right to engage in any activity or to perform any act aimed at the destruction of any of the rights and freedoms set forth herein." (Article 30).

China is also bound by various international human rights treaties it has ratified and/or acceded to, including the International Covenant on Economic, Social, and Cultural Rights (ICESCR), the Convention on Elimination of All Forms of Discrimination Against Women (CEDAW), the Convention on Elimination of All Forms of Racial Discrimination (CEAFRD) the convention against slavery, and the anti-torture convention.[48] China has signed but not ratified the International Convention on Civil and Political Rights ("ICCPR). In anticipation of the 12th National People's Congress in early 2013, more than one hundred intellectuals in China petitioned the NPC to ratify the ICCPR.[49] Although China began a policy review process on the ICCPR and has sent delegations to North America and Europe to collect information on expectations about compliance,[50] so far, ratification has not been forthcoming.

Despite these commitments, China's human rights white papers confirm a pattern of resistance to international criticism and assert China's authority to set its own human rights standards. Thus, the 1995 white paper condemned "unwarranted charges (*heng jia zhi se*) against the internal affairs of some developing countries" purportedly lodged by the United States and other Western countries,[51] while editorials in state-controlled media expressly rejected Western notions of civil and political rights.[52] Orthodox commentators have championed the primacy of state sovereignty, claiming that the United States and other Western countries have engaged in "new interventionism" (*xin ganshe zhuyi*) by asserting that human rights take precedence over sovereignty.[53] Commentators who see a more complementary relationship between human rights and sovereignty still assert that international human rights standards represent a challenge by the West to the sovereignty of China and other developing countries.[54]

Even when the importance of international human rights documents is acknowledged, defensiveness over China's human rights practices continues. China's 2004 human rights white paper suggested that China's practices were undiminished by international treaty standards:

> The Chinese government cherishes the important role of international instruments on human rights in promoting and protecting human rights. . . . Realization of full human rights is a common pursuit of all countries in the world. It is also an important target of China's all-round construction of a well-off, harmonious socialist society. Together with the international community, China will, as always, make persistent efforts in promoting continuous progress of human rights in China and healthy development of international human rights.[55]

While language such as on the "important role of international instruments," and "common pursuit of all countries," suggests recognition of international standards, elsewhere the white paper expresses continued resistance. Language on "as always" and "persistent efforts in promoting continuous progress" suggests resistance to criticism while the reference to "healthy development of international human rights" suggests an effort to adjust international standards to China's liking.[56]

Five years later, coinciding with the sixtieth anniversary of the Universal Declaration, China's 2009 white paper focused on performance of China's international obligations and the need for "fair" assessments of China's human rights practices:

China is an active participant in the work of UN's human rights agencies, and it plays a constructive role in order to encourage countries around the world to handle human rights issues fairly. . . . China's efforts and progress made in the sphere of human rights have been recognized by many countries. . . . China, as always, upheld the basic tenets and principles stipulated in the Charter of the United Nations, performed its duties conscientiously, and proactively participated in reviews and discussions of the human rights issues. The full realization of human rights is an important goal for China in its efforts to build a moderately prosperous society in an all-round way as well as to build a harmonious society. Working closely with other countries, China will, as always, spare no efforts and contribute its due share to ensure the continuous progress of China's human rights, as well as the healthy development of human rights in the rest of the world and the building of a harmonious world with lasting peace and common prosperity.[57]

Language such as "handle human rights issues fairly" suggests that China has been unfairly criticized for its human rights practices. The reference to upholding "the basic tenets and principles stipulated in the Charter of the United Nations" suggests a primary commitment to the Charter's emphasis on state sovereignty and relations between states rather than human rights conditions within them. References to performing China's duties and participating in reviews and discussions suggest a formalistic approach to treaty obligations on human rights that elides questions about actual practice. The reference to China's "due share to ensure the continuous progress of China's human rights" distorts the doctrine of progressive realization[58] to justify restrictions on human rights. Moreover, as the doctrine of progressive realization is not included in the International Convention on Civil and Political Rights, China's focus on it suggests further emphasis on economic, social, and cultural rights rather than civil and political rights.

Resistance to international standards is also evident in China's 2009 presentations to the UN Human Rights Council under the

Universal Periodic Review (UPR) process.[59] China's UN submission offered a recitation of purported achievements in promoting democracy, guaranteeing judicial independence, supporting civil society and ethnic equality and autonomy and social welfare, each of which remained constrained by the imperative of Party leadership enshrined in China's constitution and laws. Pursuant to the UPR process, UN members submitted responses and recommendations, which varied from praise from allies such as Iran and Myanmar to measured critiques from some European members and Australia.[60] China's response to recommendations on treatment of detainees (Germany); combating child labor (Finland); protection of ethnic minorities' religious, civil, socioeconomic and political rights (Australia); and protection of the right of minorities to exercise human rights to preserve cultural identity (Austria) asserted that measures on these issues were already being implemented or already had been implemented and therefore no further action was necessary.[61] China agreed to revisit recommendations on issues such as discrimination (Portugal, Argentina); reduction in the number of crimes carrying the death penalty (Australia, Canada); and domestic violence (Brazil).[62] However China rejected a wide range of recommendations involving minority nationality policy and opening up of minority areas to foreign journalists, reforming arbitrary detention records and providing greater transparency and information reporting on detention and torture; ratification of the ICCPR; expansion of media freedoms; and protection of the rights of lawyers to defend their clients free from harassment.[63] As if to emphasize China's limited engagement with the UPR process, official media reports in China gave scant attention to the numerous criticisms raised, focusing instead on praising China's human rights record.[64]

The process of Human Rights Council reviews—referred to by critics as a "mutual praise society"[65]—seems unlikely to induce China to make significant changes. Indeed at the time of the UPR, China continued to deny that the government censors news, claimed that citizens are free to express their opinions in the press without fear of retribution, and denied persecuting those who challenge the state in the Internet or in print.[66] Yet on the eve of the UN Human Rights Council meeting, security forces increased their repression of dissent—arresting a group of petitioners seeking redress for local corruption.[67] The government also launched a publicity campaign extolling the virtues of China's "democratic" system over those associated with the "western multiparty system."[68] In advance of the UN Human Rights Council meetings, China flat-out rejected recommendations and findings from the UN Committee against Torture that alleged "routine and widespread use of torture and ill treatment of suspects in police custody, especially to extract confessions or information to be used in criminal proceedings."[69]

Resistance to international standards is also evident in China's 2013 UPR responses.[70] China dismissed as "already implemented" recommendations on protection of human rights lawyers, legal rights to appeal, treatment of detainees, protection of religious belief and ethnic minorities, and protection against arbitrary detention and torture.[71] China rejected recommendations involving minority nationality policy, arbitrary detention and torture; ratification of the ICCPR; freedoms of belief and expression; and protection of the rights of lawyers.[72]

Soon after its first UPR review, China released its first National Human Rights Action Plan.[73] The Plan covered three main thematic areas: economic, social and cultural rights; civil and political rights; and the rights of particular groups, including women, ethnic minorities, the elderly, children, and people with disabilities. The Action Plan framed protection of human rights as a project to be undertaken through the existing structure of Party rule: "Since the founding of the People's Republic of China in 1949, under the leadership of the Communist Party of China, the Chinese government, combining the universal principles of human rights and the concrete realities of China, has made unremitting efforts to promote and safeguard human rights."[74]

China's 2012–15 Human Rights Action Plan asserted that human rights remain subject to China's national conditions: "The Chinese government respects the principle of universality of human rights, but also upholds proceeding from China's national conditions and new realities to advance the development of its human rights cause on a practical basis."[75] This contradicts core provisions of the Universal Declaration of Human Rights (Art. 2)[76] and the Vienna Declaration and Programme of Action (Article 5),[77] both of which China signed, to the effect that national conditions are not a justification for the denial of human rights. The Action Plan's provisions that civil and political rights should be balanced against economic, social and cultural rights under the principle of "coordinated development," and that individual rights should be balanced against collective rights under the principle of "balanced development" contradict widely accepted human rights principles of indivisibility.[78]

China's 2014 human rights white paper claimed that China's progress on human rights should be clear to unbiased observers and that human rights in China should properly depend on domestic political arrangements:

> The pursuit of the improvement of human rights never ends, for there is always room for better human rights conditions. China's progress in its human rights undertaking is there for everybody to see, and every unbiased and reasonable observer can draw a fair conclusion. At the same time, China is still a large developing country, with conspicuous problems of unbalanced, uncoordinated and unsustainable development. Therefore, greater efforts are needed to bring higher standards to human rights protection. It has been proved that only by adhering to the socialist path with Chinese characteristics can China's human rights undertaking achieve better development, and the Chinese people realize more comprehensive development.[79]

By conditioning human rights on China's status as a developing country, the 2014 white paper contradicts the principles of the Vienna Declaration Article 10 ("While development facilitates the enjoyment of all human rights, the lack of development may not be invoked to justify the abridgement of internationally recognized human rights").[80] The statement that human rights improvements in China can be achieved "only by adhering to the socialist path with Chinese characteristics" indicates a continued commitment to the orthodoxy of CPC leadership, which contradicts the provisions of the Universal Declaration: "The will of the people shall be the basis of the authority of government; this will shall be expressed in periodic and genuine elections which shall be by universal and equal suffrage and shall be held by secret vote or by equivalent free voting procedures."[81] Finally, while noting the need for continued improvement, the white paper also suggests that critics of China's human rights record are biased and unreasonable.

Thus, official statements on China's human rights policy and practice suggest a pattern of resistance to international standards. Early on, China's human rights white papers asserted China's compliance with international human rights standards under the rubric of the right to development and prosperity, with implications for domestic stability maintenance. Gradually there has emerged a pattern of appropriation and selective adjustment of human rights principles that privileges China's local conditions and policy preferences and asserts that China has achieved compliance with its international human rights obligations. While China's accession to the GATT/WTO in 2001 along with increased globalization of China's economy and society have suggested the potential for better human rights protection,[82] the pattern of resistance to international standards continues undiminished.

LOCAL RESISTANCE AND REGIME LEGITIMACY

Human rights resistance is not limited to China's defense of Party/state orthodoxy in the face of international human rights standards, however. Emerging conditions of citizen activism illustrate resistance of another kind, while also raising questions for regime legitimacy. Concepts of legitimacy owe much to the work of Max Weber—particularly his typologies of traditional, rational-legal, and charismatic authority.[83] While Weber treated these as independent typologies with neither developmental nor operational linkages between them,[84] in China today we find each present in efforts by the Xi Jinping regime to assert the authority of the Party/state. Traditional authority is evident in claims about CPC authority grounded in principles of neo-Confucianism.[85] Reliance on rational-legal authority is evident in references to the socialist rule of law.[86] Finally, Xi's "China Dream" discourse along with his anti-corruption and reform initiatives embody the messianic sensibility emblematic of Weber's model of charismatic authority.[87] Yet each of these elements in Xi Jinping's legitimacy discourse remains weak for the same reasons as articulated in Weber's original typologies. The failure to confront CPC history on matters such as the post–Great Leap Forward famine, the Cultural Revolution, and the 1989 Tiananmen massacre prevent discussion and consensus over what exactly is the tradition that is proposed as a basis for contemporary legitimacy.[88] The inability of the legal system to overcome formalism and CPC intrusion undermines claims to rationality and legitimacy.[89] The failure to institutionalize Xi Jinping's "China Dream" embodies the dilemmas of routinization of charisma that impede long-term legitimacy.[90]

Where legitimacy discourses turn from the abstract toward questions of regime performance,[91] ongoing criticisms of PRC human rights policies and practices continue to pose a challenge. Party / state orthodoxy conflating human rights with notions about development invites analysis of conditions of development in China. The Chinese Academy of Social Sciences' 2008 report on China's social conditions provided stark evidence on declining disposable income, increasing unemployment, increasing income gaps between the richest and poorest in society.[92] Continued disparities of wealth, environmental degradation, expanding costs (and resulting inaccessibility) of housing and health care, and deteriorating labor conditions all raise questions about the capacity of the Party / state to actually deliver conditions of development that are meaningful for the vast majority of people.[93] Under these circumstances, law becomes a resource for resistance against government authority, as workers seek payment of wages, villagers seek compensation for illnesses and injuries resulting from pollution and environmental degradation, military veterans seek payment of pensions, and neighborhood residents in urban areas seek redress for allegedly unlawful relocation and expropriation of housing.[94] Members of society seem increasingly willing to use the law as a mechanism for resistance in the more explicitly political realm as well, as legal conflicts with the government emerge on issues such as corruption in the 2008 Sichuan earthquake,[95] the legacy of the Tiananmen massacre,[96] and challenges to local election processes.[97]

As was always possible since the beginning of the legal reform effort in the late 1970s, once law becomes accessible to the public, the state's monopoly on legal interpretation is at risk along with its ability to control the outcome of legal processes. The development of the PRC legal regime has seen a new generation of legal professionals emerge who are invested in the specialized vernacular and organizations of the legal system.[98] A new category of lawyers known as "rights defenders" (*weiquan*) suggests an emerging phenomenon of "cause lawyering"[99] that has expanded steadily over the past ten years.[100]

For its part, the government has consistently suppressed the use of law to protect rights that challenge the authority of the Party/state. Revisions to the Lawyers Law in 2007 imposed on lawyers and legal advisors more stringent requirements to uphold the interests of the Party/state.[101] Building on a set of regulatory pronouncements aimed at curbing legal representation for collective disputes and protesters,[102] the revised Lawyers Law reinforced government efforts to restrict the use of law to challenge official policies and practices. Even as academic commentators in China have relied on the Lawyers Law to critique practices by public security organs denying lawyers access to their client defendants,[103] provisions of the Criminal Law (Art. 306) and the Criminal Procedure Law (Art. 38) prohibiting submission of false evidence continue to be used to intimidate defense counsel.[104] The "Lawyers' Code of Practice" required by the All China Lawyers Association imposes requirements for "loyalty to the Party, the nation, the people, and the Constitution and laws" in effect prohibiting lawyers from challenging the Party/state.[105]

Statutory measures have been matched by institutional efforts restricting popular resistance through law. Even as public concern has increased over material living conditions (equated with human rights under the right to development discourse), the Supreme Court revoked its decision permitting citizens to bring constitutional cases to the courts.[106] The imbroglio involving the escape from extra-legal detention by legal advocate Chen Guangcheng, highlighted the penalties imposed on public interest lawyers for challenging the

Party/state and its local officials, but also suggested the resiliency of legal activists.[107] The detention of lawyers such as Gao Zhisheng and Pu Zhiqiang who have challenged regime orthodoxy by pursuing human rights cases,[108] ongoing arrests of citizens challenging the government's human rights plan,[109] and continued harassment of journalists[110] reflect the Party/state's commitment to suppress popular resistance.

Local resistance poses a significant dilemma for a regime that has based its legitimacy to a considerable extent on a purported commitment to the rule of law.[111] If the governing regime is seen to fail in honoring its commitments around the rule of law, this will have important implications for the legitimacy of governance orthodoxy domestically and internationally. As an increasing number of court cases and legal submissions challenge the Party/state to live up to the promises of the socialist rule of law, and as lawyers and judges take positions contrary to the parochial interests of local officials, attempts to repress such challenges undermine the legitimacy and authority of the legal system and the Party/state of which it is a part.

The 4th Plenum Decision of 2014 seemed to recognize this by its claim to "comprehensively advance the rule of law."[112] By insisting on a rule of law that continues to privilege a governance orthodoxy of Party leadership, conditionality of rights, and the primacy of economic development, the PRC regime attempts to insulate itself from criticism even as its method of doing so erodes its legitimacy. Attacks on lawyers and civil rights activists have tended to reinforce the very criticisms that China has hoped to avoid, as international human rights groups have become increasingly vocal in publicizing and challenging regime efforts to silence reformers.[113] Governments too have intensified their criticisms even in the face of continued resistance from the PRC government.[114] Thus, China's legitimacy deficit involves both domestic resistance and the ways in which this contributes to legitimacy challenges internationally. Neither seems likely to be addressed in the near term as challenges to legitimacy generated by human rights activism are linked inextricably with the orthodoxy of the Party/state and its resistance to international human rights standards.

SUMMARY

The backdrop of orthodoxy, resistance, and legitimacy provides useful context for understanding ongoing tensions over China's human rights record and possible international responses. Certainly China's human rights orthodoxy suggests limits to regime efforts at legal reform generally and human rights protection more specifically. Yet there are possibilities for positive engagement. The human rights orthodoxy of Party leadership, conditionality of rights, and the imperative of development, and the policies and practices that result, will likely continue but may also present possible opportunities for engagement on issues such as government accountability (coordinated with PRC efforts to increase central controls over lower level units through transparency efforts[115]), rights protection (coordinated with expanded opportunities for public interest litigation[116]), and socio-economic equity (such as collaborative efforts on corporate social responsibility).[117] While resistance by the regime to adoption and enforcement of international human rights standards with which it disagrees will continue to be driven by and dependent upon the conditions of local orthodoxy, cooperative legal reform efforts may help to change these conditions. While citizen resistance in the form of human rights activism does not appear yet to have diminished the Party/state's continued reliance on its particular human rights orthodoxy in resistance to international standards, the challenges raised for regime legitimacy are significant inviting consideration of further possibilities for reform.[118] Thus the themes of orthodoxy, resistance, and legitimacy are useful not only for considering human rights in China, but also for considering international responses.

NOTES

1. See, for example, Human Rights Watch, "World Report 2014: China," January 21, 2014 (www.hrw.org/world-report/2014/country-chapters/china); Congressional Executive Committee on China, "Annual Report 2014," October 9, 2014 (www.cecc.gov/sites/chinacommission.house.gov/files/2014%20 annual%20report_0.PDF).

310 PITMAN B. POTTER

2. This paper builds upon parts of Pitman B. Potter, *Assessing Treaty Performance in China: Trade and Human Rights* (Vancouver, B.C.: UBC Press,
2014).

3. See Peng Zhen, "Report on the Draft of the Revised Constitution of the
People's Republic of China," November 26, 1982, pp. 398–99 (www.e-chaupak
.net/database/chicon/1982/1982e.report.pdf). Also see Deng Xiaoping,
"Jianchi sixiang jiben yuanze" [Uphold the four cardinal principles], *Deng
Xiaoping wenxuan 1975–1982* [Collected works of Deng Xiaoping 1975–1982],
vol. 2 (Beijing: People's Press, 1983), p. 144. For discussion, see, generally,
Stanley B. Lubman, *Bird in a Cage: Legal Reform after Mao* (Stanford University
Press, 1999), especially pp. 126–30.

4. See, for example, Qian Gang, "Shenhongse celiangchi: 'Sixiang jiben
yuanze'" [Measurements of redness: The Four Cardinal Principles], *New
York Times China Edition*, September 18, 2012 (http://cn.nytimes.com/china
/20120918/cc18qiangang1/).

5. See, for example, "Yang Jingyu yi 82 xianfa zhiding: Sixiang jiben yuanze shifou ruxian cun zhengyi" [Yang Jingyu on enactment of the 1982
Constitution: The existing controversy over whether the Four Cardinal
Principles are part of the Constitution], *Zhongguo xinwenwang* [China News
Net], September 11, 2014 (www.chinanews.com/gn/2014/09-11/6579284
.shtml). Yang, responsible member of the Legal Affairs Committee of the
10th NPC (2003–2008), asserted, "The 18th CPC Congress pointed out,
'Most fundamental in the development of socialist democratic governance is
the need to unify upholding Party leadership, people being masters of their
own country, and ruling the country according to law.' This can be said to be
the legacy and development of the inclusion of thinking on democracy and
the legal system of the first generation of revolutionaries, including Peng
Zhen." For discussion of Peng Zhen's role in the development of the socialist
legal system, see Pitman B. Potter, *From Leninist Discipline to Socialist Legalism:
Peng Zhen on Law and Political Authority in the PRC* (Stanford University Press,
2003). Peng Zhen's oft-quoted phrase "the Party leads the people in enacting
the law and leads the people in respecting the law" (*Dang lingdao renmin zhiding falu, ye lingdao renmin zunzhong falu*) remains a key theme.

6. Yang Jingyu, "Renzhen xuexi xianfa, zengqiang xianzheng yishi"
[Conscientiously study the Constitution, strengthen awareness of constitutional governance], in *Xianfa he xianfa xiuzhengan fudao duben* [Guidance
reader on the constitution and constitutional amendments] (Beijing: Legal
System Press, 2004), pp. 93–111, at p. 101.

7. "Constitution of the Communist Party of China" (rev. November 14,
2012) (www.china.org.cn/china/18th_cpc_congress/2012-11/16/content
_27138030.htm). Also see "Full Text of Hu Jintao's Report to the 18th Party

Congress," November 27, 2012 (www.china-embassy.org/eng/zt/18th_CPC _National_Congress_Eng/t992917.htm).

8. Graham Young, "Mao Zedong and the Class Struggle in Socialist Society," *Australian Journal of Chinese Affairs* 16 (July 1986), pp. 41–80.

9. Zhongguo gongchandang di shiyi jie zhongyang weiyuanhui di san ci quanti huiyi gongbao" [Communique of the Third Plenary Session of the 11th Central Committee of the Communist Party of the People's Republic of China], December 22, 1978 (http://cpc.people.com.cn/GB/64162/64168 /64563/65371/4441902.html).

10. Wu Guoguang, "Democracy and Rule of Law in Zhao Ziyang's Political Reform," in *Zhao Ziyang and China's Political Future*, edited by Wu Guoguang and Helen Landsdowne (London: Routledge 2013), pp. 34–36.

11. See, generally, John Wong and Zheng Yongnian, eds., *The Nanxun Legacy and China's Development in the Post-Deng Era* (Singapore University Press and World Scientific Press, 2001).

12. Jamie Horsley, "Pushing the Limits of Party Rule," in *China Today China Tomorrow: Domestic Politics, Economy, and Society*, edited by Joseph Fewsmith (Lanham, Md.: Rowman & Littlefield, 2010), pp. 51–70.

13. He Xin, "Black Hole of Responsibility: The Adjudication Committee's Role in a Chinese Court," *Law and Society Review* 46, no. 4 (December 2012), pp. 681–712.

14. See "Zuigao renmin fayuan guanyu gaige he wanshan renmin fayuan shenpan weiyuanhui zhidu de shishi yijian—fafa 2010 3 hao" [Provisional opinion of the Supreme People's Court concerning reforming and improving the system of people's court adjudication committees— court issue no. 3 of 2010], *Wendang zhijia* [Archivist] (www.doczj.com /doc/62dfafc32cc58bd63186bdb8.html). Also see Susan Finder, "2010 Reforms in the Chinese Courts: Reforming Judicial Committees," *Bloomberg Law Reports* 3, no. 5 (2010) (https://chinaspc.files.wordpress.com/2014 /12/reforming-judicial-committees.pdf). The concept of *sange zhishang* refers to Hu Jintao's 2007 remarks to the December 26, 2007, conference of representatives of the national political legal work committee, national senior judges, and national senior procurators, asserting the imperative of putting the Party's cause, the interests of the people, and the constitution and laws above all else. See "Sange Zhishang" (Three supremes), *Baidu/Baike* [Baidu Encyclopedia] (http://baike.baidu.com/view/1838760.htm). Also see Wang Shengyu, "Zhichi 'sange zhishang' tuidong renmin fayuan gongzuo kexue fazhan" [Uphold the three supremes in promoting scientific development of peoples' court work], *Fazhi wang* [Legal System Net], December 14, 2009 (www.legaldaily.com.cn/index_article/content/2009-12/14/content _2004336.htm).

15. Ye Du, "The 'Stability Maintenance System' versus the Rule of Law," *The PEN Report: Creativity and Constraint in Today's China*, May 3, 2013 (www .pen-international.org/wp-content/uploads/2013/05/The-PEN-Report -Creativity-and-Constraint-in-Todays-China.pdf).

16. "Communique of the Fourth Plenary Session of the 18th Central Committee of the Communist Party of China," October 23, 2014 (www.china.org .cn/china/fourth_plenary_session/2014-12/02/content_34208801.htm).

17. "Zhengzhiju changweihui tingqu Renda Guowuyuan deng dangzu gongzuo huibao" (Politburo Standing Committee hears reports on work of Party organs at NPC, State Council, etc.), *Xinwen zhongxin* [Sina], January 16, 2015 (http://news.sina.com.cn/c/2015-01-16/195331409709.shtml). New CPC regulations would require establishment of "Party organs" in all government departments. "Shehui zuzhi lingdao jiguan yao sheli dangzu" [Leadership organs in social organizations must establish Party organs], *Beijing News*, May 30, 2015 (www.bjnews.com.cn/news/2015/05/30/365259 .html).

18. "Zhonghua renmin gongheguo xianfa" [Constitution of the People's Republic of China] (rev. 2004) (www.gov.cn/gongbao/content/2004/content _62714.htm); Constitution of the People's Republic of China (rev. 2004) (www.npc.gov.cn/englishnpc/Constitution/node_2825.htm).

19. Wang Yaoguo, "Guanyu 'Zhonghua renmin gongheguo xianfa xiuzhengan (caoan)' de shuoming" [Explanation on the draft amendments to the constitution of the People's Republic of China] (March 8, 2004), in *Xianfa he xianfa xiuzhengan fudao duben* [Guidance reader on the constitution and constitutional amendments] (Beijing: Legal System Press, 2004), pp. 81–89 at pp. 82–83.

20. See Xin Chunying (Vice Chair NPC Legislative Affairs Committee), "Zunzhong he baozhang renquan, shixian shehui quanmian jinbu" [Respect and ensure human rights, achieve overall progress in society], in *Xianfa he xianfa xiuzhengan fudao duben* [Guidance reader on the constitution and constitutional amendments] (Beijing: Legal System Press, 2004), pp. 218–30, at p. 230. Xin's concluding comment that "[i]ncluding 'the State ensures and protects human rights' in the Constitution embodies the basic spirit of our constitution and laws" underscored that the human rights provision remains subject to the same principles as guide the rest of the socialist legal system— including the imperative of Party rule.

21. "Zhonghua renmin gongheguo xingshi susongfa [2012 nian xiuzheng] (quanwen)" [Criminal procedure law of the People's Republic of China 2012 Revision (complete text)], edited by Xinhua, 2012 (www.china .com.cn/policy/txt/2012-03/18/content_24922812_2.htm): Li Zhengxuan, "Working Translation of Amendments to the Criminal Procedure Law of

the People's Republic of China, March 14, 2012," *Danish Institute for Human Rights*, March 14, 2012 (http://lawprofessors.typepad.com/files/130101 -crim-pro-law-as-amended-en.pdf). Also see Wendy Zeldin, "China: Amendment of the Criminal Procedure Law," Library of Congress, April 9, 2012 (www.loc.gov/lawweb/servlet/lloc_news?disp3_1205403080_text).

22. Danish Institute for Human Rights, "Legal reforms in China," September 9, 2014 (www.humanrights.dk/news/legal-reforms-china); Wendy Zelden, "China: Amendment of Criminal Procedure law," Library of Congress, April 9, 2012 (www.loc.gov/lawweb/servlet/lloc_news?disp3_1205403080 _text); "China's New Criminal Procedure Law: 'Disappearance Clauses' Revised," *Dui Hua Human Rights Journal,* March 19, 2012 (www.duihuahrjournal .org/2012/03/chinas-new-criminal-procedure-law.html); Stanley Lubman, "China Criminal Procedure Law: Good, Bad and Ugly," *China Real Time,* March 21, 2012 (http://blogs.wsj.com/chinarealtime/2012/03/21/chinas -criminal-procedure-law-good-bad-and-ugly/).

23. See, generally, Pitman B. Potter, *The Chinese Legal System* (Cambridge: Polity Press, 2013); *Xianfa gongmin quan xiao quanshu* [Small compendium on constitutional and civil rights] (Beijing: Law Press China, 2010).

24. United Nations General Assembly, "Declaration on the Right to Development," A/Res/41/128, December 4, 1986 (www.un.org/documents/ga /res/41/a41r128.htm).

25. Jack Donnelly, "In Search of the Unicorn: The Jurisprudence and Politics of the Right to Development," *California Western International Law Journal* 15 (1985), p. 473.

26. "Text of Human Rights white paper," *FBIS Daily Report: China (Supplement),* November 21, 1991.

27. "Interview with Zhu Muzhi, Director of the State Council Information Office," Xinhua, November 2, 1991, in *FBIS Daily Report: China,* November 4, 1991, p. 16.

28. United Nations General Assembly, "Final Declaration of the Regional Meeting for Asia of the World Conference on Human Rights," A/CONF.157/ ASRM/8 A/CONF.157/PC/59, April 7, 1993 (www.unhchr.ch/Huridocda /Huridoca.nsf/TestFrame/9d23b88f115fb827802569030037ed44 ?Opendocument).

29. Xinhua Domestic Service, "The Progress of Human Rights in China," December 27, 1995, in *FBIS Daily Report: China,* December 28, 1996, pp. 8–26.

30. Information Office of the State Council, "Progress in China's Human Rights Cause in 1996," March 1997 (www.china.org.cn/e-white /prhumanrights1996/index.htm).

31. State Council Information Office, "White Paper: Fifty Years of Progress in China's Human Rights," 2000 (www.china-embassy.org/eng/zt

/ppflg/t36624.htm). Also see Human Rights Watch, "China: White Paper a 'Whitewash,'" April 11, 2001 (www.hrw.org/news/2001/04/09/china-white -paper-whitewash).

32. See, for example, Ji Yanping, *Renquan yu fazhi* [Human rights and the rule of law] (Jinan: Shandong People's Press, 2003), pp. 79–80, 94–101; Lin Zhe, *Gongmin jiben renquan falu zhidu yanjiu* [A study of the legal institutions of citizens fundamental human rights] (Beijing University Press, 2006), pp. 97–99.

33. State Council Information Office, "Progress in China's Human Rights in 2009," September 2010 (http://english.gov.cn/official/2010-09/26/content _1709982.htm).

34. State Council Information Office, "National Human Rights Action Plan of China (2012–2015)," June 11, 2012 (www.china.org.cn/government /whitepaper/2012-06/11/content_25619560.htm).

35. State Council Information Office, "Progress in China's Human Rights in 2013" May 26, 2014 (http://news.xinhuanet.com/english/china/2014-05 /26/c_133361505.htm); and "Progress in China's Human Rights in 2014" (June 2015) (http://english.gov.cn/archive/white_paper/2015/06/08/content _281475123202380.htm).

36. Congressional Executive Committee on China, "China: List of Political Prisoners Detained or Imprisoned as of October 11, 2016 (1,433 cases)" (http://www.cecc.gov/sites/chinacommission.house.gov/files/documents /CECC%20Pris%20List_20161011_1433.pdf).

37. Congressional Executive Committee on China, "Annual Report 2014," October 9, 2014, pp. 90–99 (www.cecc.gov/publications/annual-reports /2014-annual-report); U.S. Department of State, "International Religious Freedom Report 2013: China" (n.d.) (www.state.gov/j/drl/rls/irf /religiousfreedom/index.htm?year=2013&dlid=222123); Council on Foreign Relations, "Religion in China," May 16, 2008 (www.cfr.org/china /religion-china/p16272).

38. Congressional Executive Committee on China, "Annual Report 2014," October 9, 2014, pp. 71–80 (www.cecc.gov/publications/annual-reports /2014-annual-report); Bureau of Democracy, Human Rights and Labor, "Country Reports on Human Rights Practices for 2013," Section 7 (www .state.gov/j/drl/rls/hrrpt/humanrightsreport/index.htm?year=2013&dlid =220186).

39. Congressional Executive Committee on China, "Annual Report 2014," pp. 61–70; Xu Beina, "Media Censorship in China," Council on Foreign Relations, September 25, 2014 (www.cfr.org/china/media-censorship -china/p11515); Bureau of Democracy, Human Rights and Labor, "Country Reports on Human Rights Practices for 2013," Section 2a.

40. Congressional Executive Committee on China, "Annual Report 2014," pp. 100–2; Bureau of Democracy, Human Rights and Labor, "National /Ethnic Minorities" in "Reports on Human Rights Practices for 2013: China, Section 6" (www.state.gov/j/drl/rls/hrrpt/humanrightsreport/#section6na tionalracialethnicminorities); Minority Rights Group International and Human Rights in China, "China: Minority Exclusion, Marginalization and Rising Tensions," April 25, 2007 (www.hrichina.org/content/4081).

41. Thomas Lum, *Human Rights in China: Trends and U.S. Policy.* (Washington, D.C.: Congressional Research Service, July 18, 2011) (https://www .fas.org/sgp/crs/row/RL34729.pdf); Tania Branigan, "Crackdown in China Spreads Terror Among Dissidents," *The Guardian*, March 21, 2011; Amnesty International, "China: New Generation of Internet Activists Targeted," March 23, 2011 (www.amnesty.org/en/news-and-updates/china -new-generation-internet-activists-targeted-2011-03-23).

42. Human Rights Watch, "China: Uighur Scholar's Trial a Travesty of Justice," September 15, 2014 (www.hrw.org/news/2014/09/15/china-uighur -scholar-s-trial-travesty-justice); Ian Johnson, "They Don't Want Moderate Uighurs," *New York Review of Books—Blog*, September 22, 2014 (www.nybooks .com/blogs/nyrblog/2014/sep/22/trial-ilham-tohti-they-dont-want -moderate-uighurs/).

43. See, for example, "Chinese lawyer Who Exposed Baby Milk Scandal Jailed for Subversion," *The Guardian* August 4, 2016; "Chinese Democracy Veteran Hu Shigen Jailed for Subversion," *South China Morning Post*, August 3, 2016 (www.scmp.com/news/china/policies-politics/article/1998638 /second-activist-sentenced-subversion-charges-after-huge); Zhai Minglei, "Beijing Gonganju: Wo he ni weiyi de gongtong yuyan shi falu" [Beijing Public Security Bureau: The law is our only common tongue], in *Hong Kong University China Media Project*, January 6, 2015 (http://xgmyd.com/archives /11561).

44. Robin Hood and Carolyn Hoyle, "Capital Punishment in China: Room for Cautious Optimism?" *Oxford Human Right Hub*, January 12, 2015 (http://ohrh.law.ox.ac.uk/capital-punishment-in-china-room-for-cautious -optimism/).

45. "Courts Slow to Throw Illegally Collected Evidence Out of Trials," *Caixin (Finance) English Service*, January 8, 2105 (http://english.caixin.com /2015-01-08/100772276.html). Also see Committee Against Torture, "Concluding Observations of the Committee Against Torture: China," CAT/C/ CHN/CO/4, November 21, 2008; Congressional Executive Committee on China, "Annual Report 2010," October 10, 2010, pp. 86–98 (www.cecc.gov /publications/annual-reports/2010-annual-report); Margaret K. Lewis, "Controlling Abuse to Maintain Control: The Exclusionary Rule in China,"

Working Paper, September 2010 (http://works.bepress.com/cgi/viewcontent .cgi?article=1000&context=margaret_lewis); UN Commission on Human Rights, "Civil and Political Rights, Including the Question of Torture and Detention: Report of the Special Rapporteur on Torture and Other Cruel, Inhuman, or Degrading Treatment or Punishment, Manfred Nowak—Mission to China," E/CN.4/2006/6/Add.6, March 10, 2006.

46. See Human Rights in China, *Implementation of the Convention on the Elimination of Discrimination Against Women (CEDAW) in the People's Republic of China*, July 2006 (www.hrichina.org/content/4124); CEDAW, "Concluding Comments of the Committee on the Elimination of Discrimination Against Women: China," CEDAW/C/CHN/CO/6, August 25, 2006; Human Rights in China et al., "Report on the Implementation of CEDAW in the People's Republic of China," 1998; Jonathan Mirsky, "The Bottom of the Well," *New York Review of Books*, October 6, 1994, pp. 24–28.

47. United Nations, ed., "Universal Declaration of Human Rights, " 2015 (www.un.org/en/documents/udhr/index.shtml).

48. "Human Rights Library," University of Minnesota, 2015 (www.umn.edu /humanrts/research/ratification-china.html). China's ratification of the IC-ESCR was made subject to reservations that preserve China's policy preferences on labor rights. See generally, Yang Songcai, Tai Li, Guo Xianghe, eds., *Jingji, shehui, he wenhua quanli guoji gongyue ruogan wenti yanjiu* [Study of several questions on the International Covenant on Economic, Social, and Cultural Rights] (Changsha: Hunan People's Press, 2009).

49. Chris Buckley, "Chinese Intellectuals Urge Ratifying Rights Treaty," *New York Times*, February 26, 2013. A text of the petition appears in David Badurski, "Open Letter to NPC on Human Rights," *China Media Project*, February 26, 2013 (http://cmp.hku.hk/2013/02/26/31531/.

50. "China amends laws for ICCPR," Xinhua, July 14, 2011 (www .chinadaily.com.cn/china/2011-07/14/content_12904570.htm); Yang Yu-guan, "Pizhun 'Gongmin quanli he zhengzhi quanli guoji gongyue' xiang-guan wenti yanjiu" [A study of issues related to ratification of the "International Covenant on Civil and Political Rights"], *Gansu shehui kexue* [Gansu Social Studies], no. 4 (2008), pp. 2–5, 209; Shi Jiangtao, "Beijing reviews key human rights treaty," *South China Morning Post*, September 6, 2005.

51. Xinhua Domestic Service, "The Progress of Human Rights in China," December 27, 1995, in *FBIS Daily Report: China*, December 28, 1996, pp. 8–26.

52. See, for example, Ren Jiyu, "Weihu renquan fazhan renquan" [Safeguard human rights, develop human rights] and Zhu Muzhi, "Zhongguo zai renquan wenti shang de lichang" [China's stance on human rights issues], both in *Zhongguo renquan de jiben lichang he guandian* [Basic stance

and concepts of China human rights], edited by Zhongguo renquan fazhan jijinhui [Foundation for Development of China Human Rights] (Beijing: New World Publishers, 2003), pp. 9–10 and pp. 11–19; "Freedom Loser When Democracy Wins," *China Daily*, December 6, 1995, p. 4.

53. Zhu Muzhi, "Sha 'renquan gaoyu zhuquan' " [Rejecting "human rights take precedence over sovereignty"], in *Renquan yu zhuquan* [Human rights and sovereignty], edited by Zhongguo renquan fazhan jijinhui [Foundation for Development of China Human Rights] (Beijing: New World Publishers, 2003), pp. 1–6.

54. Liu Nanlai, "Zhuelun renquan yu zhuquan de guanxi" [Brief thoughts on the relationship between human rights and sovereignty], in ibid., pp. 61–66.

55. State Council Information Office, "China Progress in Human Rights in 2004," April 2005 (www.china.org.cn/e-white/20050418/index.htm).

56. For discussion of ongoing efforts by the PRC government to shape international human rights discourses, see Sonya Sceats and Shaun Breslin, "China and the International Human Rights System," *Chatham House*, October 12, 2012 (www.chathamhouse.org/sites/files/chathamhouse/public/Research/International%20Law/r1012_sceatsbreslin.pdf).

57. State Council Information Office, "Progress in China's Human Rights in 2009," September 26, 2010 (www.china.org.cn/government/whitepaper/2010-09/26/content_21007490.htm).

58. The principle of "progressive realization" is set forth in Article 2.1 of the International Convention on Economic, Social and Cultural Rights (parties to the Convention must take steps . . . to the maximum of its available resources, with a view to achieving progressively the full realization of the rights recognized in the present Covenant by all appropriate means, including particularly the adoption of legislative measures). United Nations Treaty Collections, "International Covenant on Economic, Social and Cultural Rights," G.A. res. 2200A (XXI), 21 U.N.GAOR Supp. (No. 16) at 49, U.N. Doc. A/6316 (1966), 993 U.N.T.S. 3, *entered into force* January 3, 1976.

59. UN Human Rights Council, *Draft Report of the Working Group on the Universal Periodic Review: China A/HRC/WG.6/4/L.11*, February 11, 2009.

60. Human Rights in China, "Summary Chart of UPR Recommendations Accepted by the People's Republic of China," February 11, 2009 (http://hrichina.org/sites/default/files/oldsite/PDFs/Submissions/Summary_Chart_of_Accepted_UPR_Recommendations.pdf).

61. Human Rights in China, "Summary Chart of UPR Recommendations 'Already Being Implemented' by China," February 11, 2009 (http://hrichina.org/sites/default/files/oldsite/PDFs/Submissions/Summary_Chart_of_UPR_Recommendations_Already_Implemented.pdf).

62. Human Rights in China, "Summary Chart of UPR Recommendations to Be Examined by China," February 11, 2009 (http://hrichina.org/sites /default/files/oldsite/PDFs/Submissions/Summary_Chart_of_UPR _Recommendations_to_Be_Examined.pdf).

63. Human Rights in China, "Summary Chart of UPR Recommendations Rejected by the People's Republic of China," February 11, 2009 (http:// hrichina.org/sites/default/files/oldsite/PDFs/Submissions/Summary _Chart_of_Rejected_UPR_Recommendations.pdf).

64. "China's human rights achievements highlighted at UN review," Xinhua, February 9, 2009 (http://news.xinhuanet.com/english/2009-02/10 /content_10791017.htm).

65. UN Watch, "Mutual Praise Society," February 6, 2009 (www.unwatch .org/site/c.bdKKISNqEmG/b.4967647/k.7162/Mutual_Praise_Society .htm); UN Watch, "U.N. Delegates Laud China for Death Penalty and Restricting Internet," February 9, 2009 (www.unwatch.org/site/apps/nlnet /content2.aspx?c=bdKKISNqEmG&b=1316871&ct=6751847).

66. Frank Jordans, "China Denies Censorship, Persecuting Activists," Associated Press, February 9, 2009 (http://seattletimes.com/html/nationworld /2008723649_apununchinarights.html).

67. "China Hammers Dissent Despite Looming UN Review," *Associated Press/International Herald Tribune*, February 7, 2009 (www.highbeam.com /doc/1A1-D966H9QG1.html). Also see Willy Lam, "Beijing Sets Out on Chaos Offensive," *Asia Times*, February 11, 2009 (www.atimes.com/atimes /China/KB11Ad01.html).

68. "Woguo juebuneng gao Xifang de duodangzhi" [We will never adopt the Western multi-party system], *Renmin ribao* [People's Daily], February 13, 2009.

69. Compare "UN Committee says China 'Should Take Immediate Steps to Prevent Acts of Torture,'" *HRIC*, November 23, 2008, with "China Rejects UN Report on Torture, Calling Allegations 'Untrue and Slanderous,'" Associated Press, November 22, 2008.

70. UN Human Rights Council, *Report of the Working Group on Universal Periodic Review: China*, A/HRC/25/5, December 4, 2013 (www.hrichina.org /sites/default/files/outcome_report_of_the_working_group_on_upr.pdf). For text and discussion of China's 2009 UPR, see UN Human Rights Council, "Universal Periodic Review—China" (www.ohchr.org/EN/HRBodies /UPR/Pages/CNSession4.aspx); Human Rights in China, "China's UN Human Rights Review: New Process, Old Politics, Weak Implementation-Prospects" (www.hrichina.org/en/content/246).

71. Human Rights in China (HRIC), "Summary Charts: China's Responses to Recommendations Advanced by Human Rights Council Member and Observer States 2nd Universal Periodic Review of China" (n.d.) (www

.hrichina.org/sites/default/files/upr_2013_recommendations_and_chinas
_responses.pdf).

72. Ibid.

73. United Nations Human Rights Council, *Report of the Working Group on Universal Periodic Review: China, A/HRC/11/25*, October 5, 2009; Ariana Eunjung Cha, "China Tells U.N. Panel that It Respects Rights," *Washington Post*, February 10, 2009, p. A12; "China to Outline First National Action Plan to Protect Human Rights," Xinhua, November 4, 2008.

74. Information Office of the State Council, "National Human Rights Action Plan of China" (2009–2010) (www.china.org.cn/archive/2009-04/13/content_17595407.htm); "China to outline first national action plan to protect human rights," Xinhua. Also see Human Rights Watch, "Promises Unfulfilled: An Assessment of China's National Human Rights Action Plan," January 11, 2011 (www.hrw.org/en/reports/2011/01/11/promises-unfulfilled-0).

75. State Council Information Office, "National Human Rights Action Plan of China (2012–2015)," June 11, 2012 (www.china.org.cn/government/whitepaper/2012-06/11/content_25619560.htm).

76. Universal Declaration of Human Rights, Article 2: "Everyone is entitled to all the rights and freedoms set forth in this Declaration, without distinction of any kind, such as race, colour, sex, language, religion, political or other opinion, national or social origin, property, birth or other status. Furthermore, no distinction shall be made on the basis of the political, jurisdictional or international status of the country or territory to which a person belongs, whether it be independent, trust, non-self-governing or under any other limitation of sovereignty."

77. Vienna Declaration, Article 5: "While the significance of national and regional particularities and various historical, cultural and religious backgrounds must be borne in mind, it is the duty of States, regardless of their political, economic and cultural systems, to promote and protect all human rights and fundamental freedoms."

78. The 1993 Vienna Declaration and Programme of Action on human rights (www.ohchr.org/EN/ProfessionalInterest/Pages/Vienna.aspx) provides in Article 5, "All human rights are universal, indivisible and interdependent and interrelated." See Foreign Affairs, Trade and Development Canada, "What Are Human Rights?" November 28, 2014 (www.international.gc.ca/rights-droits/human_rights-droits_personne.aspx?lang=eng). For a critical review, see Daniel J. Whelan, *Indivisible Human Rights: A History* (University of Pennsylvania Press, 2010).

79. State Council Information Office, "Progress in China's Human Rights in 2013," May 26, 2014 (http://news.xinhuanet.com/english/china/2014-05/26/c_133361505.htm).

80. This approach was also evident in China's 2015 white paper that asserts China "is taking the correct path of human rights development that suits its national conditions" (http://english.gov.cn/archive/white_paper/2015/06/08/content_281475123202380.htm).

81. Universal Declaration of Human Rights, Article 23.

82. See, generally, Sylvia Ostry, Alan S. Alexandroff, and Raphael Gomez, eds., *China and the Long March to Global Trade: The Accession of China to the World Trade Organization* (New York: Routledge, 2002).

83. See Max Weber, *Economy and Society*, edited by Guenther Roth and Klaus Wittich (University of California Press, 1978), part 3.

84. See, generally, Reinhard Bendix, *Max Weber: An Intellectual Portrait* (University of California Press, 1977), part 3.

85. See, for example, Perry Link, "What It Means To Be Chinese: Nationalism and Identity in Xi's China," *Foreign Affairs*, April 20, 2015.

86. See, for example, "Xi Says China Adheres to Socialist Path in Rule of Law," *Global Times*, October 28, 2014 (www.globaltimes.cn/content/888703.shtml).

87. "Zongguo meng" [Chinese dream], *Baidu Baike* [Baidu Encyclopedia] (http://baike.baidu.com/subview/1817221/9342599.htm).

88. He Qinglian, *The Fog of Censorship: Media Control in China* (New York: Human Rights in China, 2008) (www.hrichina.org/sites/default/files/PDFs/Reports/HRIC-Fog-of-Censorship.pdf).

89. See, generally, Carl Minzner, "After the Fourth Plenum: What Direction for Law in China?" *China Brief* 14, no. 22 (November 10, 2014), pp. 7–10 (www.jamestown.org/uploads/media/China_Brief_Vol_14_Issue_22_1_01.pdf).

90. "Xi Jinping's Anti-Curruption Drive Has Echoes of Putin's," *South China Morning Post*, July 31, 2014 (www.scmp.com/article/1563290/xi-jinpings-anti-corruption-drive-has-echoes-putins); Teng Biao, "Politics of the Death Penalty in China," *China Change*, January 16, 2014 (http://chinachange.org/tag/anti-corruption/).

91. For discussion of legitimacy in terms of pragmatic assessments of the benefits conferred by particular institutional systems, conformity with moral values, and the rational acceptance of the authority of specific regulatory arrangements, see Mark Suchman, "Managing Legitimacy: Strategic and Institutional Approaches," in *Academy of Management Review* 20, no. 3 (1995), pp. 577–85.

92. Lu Xin, Lu Xueyi, and Li Peilin, *Zhongguo shehui xingshi: Fenxi yu yuce* [Chinese society: Analysis and forecasts] (Beijing: Chinese Academy of Social Sciences Press, 2008).

93. Geremie Barme, "The Ten Grave Problems Facing China," *The China Story*, September 8, 2012 (https://www.thechinastory.org/2012/09/the-ten-grave-problems-facing-china/).

94. Eva Pils, "Asking the Tiger for His Skin: Rights Activism in China," *Fordham International Law Journal* 30 no. 4 (2008), pp. 1209–87; Keith J. Hand, "Using Law for a Righteous Purpose: The Sun Zhigang Incident and Evolving Forms of Citizen Action in the People's Republic of China," *Columbia Journal of Transnational Law*, no. 45 (2007), pp. 114–95; May E. Gallagher "Mobilizing the Law in China: 'Informed Disenchantment' and the Development of Legal Consciousness," *Law & Society Review* 40, no. 4 (2006), pp. 783–816; Neil J. Diamant, Stanley B. Lubman, and Kevin J. O'Brien, *Engaging the Law in China: State, Society, and Possibilities for Justice* (Stanford University Press, 2005).

95. Chris Buckley, "China to Try Earthquake Critic on Secrets Charge," Reuters, February 1, 2009 (http://uk.reuters.com/article/2009/02/02 /idUKPEK312306).

96. "Released Tiananmen Prisoner Incarcerated in Psychiatric Institution since Olympics," *Chinese Human Rights Defenders (CHRD)*, January 22, 2009 (http://crd-net.org/Article/Class9/Class10/200901/20090123063047 _13237.html).

97. "Activist Promoting Democracy at Grassroots Disappears, Feared Abducted by Authorities," *China Election Watch*, January 20, 2009 (http://yaolifa .blogspot.ca/2009/01/chrdactivist-promoting-democracy-at.html).

98. Benjamin L. Liebman, "Legal Aid and Public Interest Law in China," *Texas International Law Journal* 34 no. 2 (1999), pp. 211–86.

99. Austin Sarat and Stuart Scheingold, eds., *Cause Lawyering: Political Commitments and Professional Responsibilities* (Oxford University Press, 1998).

100. See, for example, Eva Pils, *China's Human Rights Lawyers: Advocacy and Resistance* (London: Routledge, 2014); Jonathan Benney, *Defending Rights in Contemporary China* (London: Routledge, 2012); Fu Hualing and Richard Cullen, "Climbing the *Weiquan* Ladder: A Radicalizing Process for Rights-Protection Lawyers," *China Quarterly*, no. 205 (2011), pp. 40–59.

101. "Zhongguo lushi fa" [Law of the PRC on lawyers], *Zhongguo Xinwenwang* [China News], October 28, 2007 (www.chinanews.com.cn/gn/news /2007/10-28/1061502.shtml); Human Rights Watch, "'Walking on Thin Ice': Control, Intimidation, and Harassment of Lawyers in China," April 2008.

102. Amnesty International, "Breaking the Law: Crackdown on Human Rights Lawyers and Legal Activists in China" (ASA 17/042/2009, September 7, 2009) (www.amnesty.org/en/library/info/ASA17/042/2009/en); Human Rights Watch, "China: Curbs on Lawyers Could Intensify Social Unrest— New Regulations Cast Doubt on Legal Reforms," December 12, 2006 (www .hrw.org/news/2006/12/11/china-curbs-lawyers-could-intensify-social -unrest).

103. See, for example, Zhang Bufen, "Shili 4: Lushi yiju xin lushi fa huijian dangshi ren zaoju shijian" [Example No. 4: Events around the rejection

of a lawyer relying on the new lawyers law to meet with the client], in *2008 nian Zhongguo shida xianfa shili pingxi* [Critical analysis of ten major examples of constitutional governance in China in 2008], edited by Hu Jinguang (Beijing: Law Publishers, 2009), pp. 58–75.

104. "Editorial: 'Big Stick 306' and China's Contempt for Law," *New York Times*, May 5, 2011.

105. China Law and Practice, "All China Lawyers Association, Code of Practice for Lawyers (2d Revision)," November 9, 2011 (www.chinalawand practice.com/Article/3002784/Channel/9952/All-China-Lawyers -Association-Code-of-Practice-for-Lawyers-2nd-Revision.html). Also see China Law Translate, "ACLA Explanation of Reforms to the Lawyers Code of Conduct," June 22, 2014 (http://chinalawtranslate.com/en/acla -explanation-of-reforms-to-the-lawyers-code-of-conduct/); China Law and Practice, "The All China Lawyers Association, Lawyers Code of Practice (Trial Implementation)," March 20, 2004 (www.chinalawandpractice.com /Article/1692834/Channel/9934/The-All-China-Lawyers-Association -Lawyers-Code-of-Practice-Trial-Implementation.html).

106. Donald Clarke, "Supreme People's Court Withdraws Qi Yuling Interpretation," *Chinese Law Professor's Blog*, January 12, 2009 (http:// lawprofessors.typepad.com/china_law_prof_blog/2009/01/supreme -people.html).

107. "China Lacks Rule of Law, Chen Guangcheng Warns," *The Guardian*, May 20, 2012. For further reports, see www.guardian.co.uk/world/chen -guangcheng.

108. Human Rights in China, "HRIC Urges Independent Observers at Upcoming Trials of Lawyers and Activists in China" (August 5, 2016) (www .hrichina.org/en/press-work/statement/hric-urges-independent-observers -upcoming-trials-lawyers-and-activists-china); Human Rights Watch, "China: Release Leading Rule of Law Activists," January 22, 2015 (www.hrw .org/news/2015/01/22/china-release-leading-rule-law-activists); Tania Branigan, "Chinese Lawyers Warn of Crackdown After Arrest of Pu Zhiqiang," *The Guardian*, June 17, 2014; Jerome A. Cohen and Beth Schwanke, "The Silencing of Gao Zhisheng," *Wall Street Journal*, May 31, 2010; Human Rights in China, "Human Rights Lawyer in Arbitrary Detention," February 2, 2009 (https://www.hrw.org/news/2009/02/02/china-human-rights-lawyer -arbitrary-detention).

109. "Beijing Cao Xunli deng duo ren zaice yaoqiu canjia 'Guojia renquan xingdong jihua' beizhua" [Beijing Cao Xunli and many others arrested for demanding once again to participate in the "state human rights action plan"], *Boxun*, February 6, 2009 (http://peacehall.com/news/china/2009 /02/200902061559shtml).

110. "Beijing to Introduce Journalist 'Black List,'" Reuters, February 13, 2009.

111. Pitman B. Potter, "Riding the Tiger—Legitimacy and Legal Culture in Post-Mao China," *China Quarterly*, no. 138 (June 1994), pp. 325–58. Also see Stanley B. Lubman, "Riding the Tiger: China's Struggle with Rule of Law," *China Real Time*, December 18, 2013 (http://blogs.wsj.com/chinarealtime /2013/12/18/riding-the-tiger-chinas-struggle-with-rule-of-law/).

112. "CPC Key Meeting Lays Down Major Tasks for Advancing 'Rule of Law,'" Xinhua, October 23, 2014 (http://news.xinhuanet.com/english/china /2014-10/23/c_133737939.htm).

113. See, for example, Law Society of Upper Canada, "Letter to Xi Jinping," September 5, 2014 (www.lsuc.on.ca/uploadedFiles/Equity_and_Diversity /Human_Rights_Monitoring_Group/Tang_Jingling.pdf); Human Rights Watch, "China: End Nationwide Crackdown on Activists," January 29, 2014 (www.hrw.org/news/2014/06/29/china-end-nationwide-crackdown-activists); Amnesty International, "Against the Law: Crackdown on China's Human Rights Lawyers Deepens," 2011 (www.amnesty.org/en/library/asset/ASA17 /018/2011/en/20ed6bf3-aaa9-4da5-8220-6c07615e531b/asa170182011en .pdf).

114. See, for example, U.S. Department of State, "Press Conference Following U.S.–China Human Rights Dialogue," August 2, 2013 (www.state .gov/j/drl/rls/rm/2013/212667.htm), in which the leader of the U.S. delegation said: "we specifically called into question the pattern of arrests and extra-legal detentions of public interest lawyers, internet activists, journalists, religious leaders and others who challenge official policies and actions in China. We noted that such actions are contrary to China's international obligations and indeed, in most cases, China's own laws and constitution." Campbell Clark, "China Turns Chilly on Human Rights Dialogue," *Globe and Mail*, January 6, 2011 (www.theglobeandmail.com/news/world/china-turns -chilly-on-human-rights-dialogue/article560756/.

115. See, for example, Beijing University Public Participation Research and Support Centre, *Zhongguo xingzheng toumingdu guancha baogao—2010– 2011*[Investigation report on administrative transparency in China—2010– 2011] (Beijing: Law Press, 2012).

116. Susan Finder, "Supreme People's Court's environmental public interest litigation regulations," *Supreme People's Court Monitor*, January 6, 2015 (http://supremepeoplescourtmonitor.com/2015/01/06/environmental -public-interest-litigation-regulations-issued/).

117. See, for example, Canada China Business Council, "CSR Roundtable— Building Responsible Business," March 10, 2011 (www.ccbc.com/events/csr -roundtable-building-responsible-businesses/).

118. Sophia Woodman, "Human Rights as 'Foreign Affairs': China's Reporting Under Human Rights Treaties," *Hong Kong Law Journal* 35, part 1 (2005), pp. 179–204; Leila Choukroune, "Justiciability of Economic, Social, and Cultural Rights," *Columbia Journal of Asian Law* 19, no. 1 (2005), pp. 30–49.

ELEVEN

Leaders, Bureaucrats, and Institutional Culture

The Struggle to Bring Back China's Top Overseas Talent

DAVID ZWEIG

Leaders matter. According to the author Valerie Bunce,[1] the impact of new leaders on public policy is significant in both democratic and authoritarian systems. Given the potentially contentious nature of policies facilitating inbound migration—where various groups of locals may feel threatened by the inflow of talent—one might assume that the role of leaders is important when governments change their migration regimes. This phenomenon may be particularly true in authoritarian regimes, where public opinion plays a minimal role in policy deliberations. But even in democracies, such as the United States, presidential leadership is important in overcoming congressional resistance to immigration reform.[2]

In most cases, the link between leadership and migration arises as opposition forces use anti-immigration policies as a plank to challenge the ruling party. Nigel Farage and his UK Independence Party (UKIP) used anti-immigrant policies to win seats in the

May 2014 elections for the European Parliament and, due to its opposition to migration from the EU, the UKIP became the second most popular party in Great Britain.[3] Similarly, in 2010, President Merkel criticized Germany's immigration policies to court her coalition's right wing.[4]

In today's knowledge economy, the world is engaged in intensive competition for highly skilled talent.[5] And governments are often actively involved in introducing strategic policies to enhance the attractiveness of their country as a destination for such international talent. Yet, given the importance of reverse migration of highly skilled talent in today's competition for national development, one would expect more discussion of the role national leaders play in generating reverse migration. Bang certainly saw President Pak Chung Hee as the driving force behind South Korea's 1975 reverse migration policy.[6] However, in a typology of key variables affecting reverse migration, one of the world's leading specialists on the topic did not allude to the role of leaders, even though many reasons that overseas nationals refuse to return home are due to internal problems that leadership must overcome.[7]

Yet leaders have been critical players in China's reverse migration, which has seen thousands of Mainland academics, scientists, and entrepreneurs who went abroad for advanced degrees return. Leaders have overcome negative forces that stall the return of China's top overseas talent, including bureaucratic resistance, institutional "bias," a scientific culture that does not mesh with the values of overseas scholars, political and economic crises that triggered conservative reactions, as well as the refusal of overseas students to return to a society that does not afford them the academic security of life overseas. Thus, when the domestic situation changed and reverse migration slowed, leaders of the Chinese Communist Party (CCP) proposed innovative policies showing that, in the face of administrative obstructionism and domestic hostility toward returnees and foreign influence, leadership activism is essential if more developing societies wish to trigger their own "brain gain."

LEADERSHIP AND REVERSE MIGRATION

Countries that wish to trigger a reverse migration of highly skilled labor must invest heavily in scientific infrastructure, as the quality of laboratories and equipment are likely to be better in Organization for Economic Cooperation and Development (OECD) countries.[8] Thus Savaria and Miranda argue that "when real opportunity exists within the context of coherent internal policies and investments in science and technology, returning to the home country becomes an attractive option for emigrants."[9] Yet, perhaps more important is to improve their country's "soft environment," that is, the legal, cultural, and interpersonal environment to which people return. According to Newland, to facilitate circular migration, governments must create an "enabling environment in the country of origin. The most fundamental (and most difficult) elements of this are establishment of the rule of law, property rights, open and transparent government, lack of corruption and other attributes of good governance, including dual citizenship or eliminating visa requirements for members of the diaspora who are citizens of another country."[10] Such dramatic reforms, which challenge the authority of bureaucrats, would be quite difficult without the support of top leaders. Similarly, keeping a developing country politically stable is quite a challenge, as is convincing members of the diaspora to return after a domestic political crisis.

The income gap between developed (host) societies and developing (home) ones is another key problem. Tax breaks, housing subsidies, higher salaries, easy access to loans, liberal usage of grant monies, and so forth, are incentives for overseas talent to return. However, while subsidies for returnees increase the average quality of returnees, rewards for returnees push people to go abroad, increasing the supply of talent overseas, which in turn drives down wages paid to returnees.[11] Subsidies also generate hostility among talented locals who feel that their societal contributions are not appropriately appreciated and rewarded.[12] Locally trained people may see highly talented returnees as threats to their jobs.[13] Also, because they relocate in a few cities, returnees exacerbate regional inequality in the home country.[14]

Third, the relocation of people, values, talent, information, and knowledge across international borders into the home country can alter the distribution of power, ideas, status, and resources within it.[15] According to Cerase, returnees see themselves as "carriers of change."[16] Yet their ability to affect change may be limited "because of the resilience of strong power relations and vested interests which prevent innovators from undertaking any initiatives that could jeopardize the established situation and the traditional power structure."[17] Solingen sees "firewalls" in the home country limiting external influences,[18] such as dominant norms about how to do business.[19] Entrenched power holders may also resist new ideas brought by returnees which challenge justifications for the extant distribution of power and resources. Rather than confront these "firewalls," overseas talent may simply choose not to return.

Yet, by refusing to return, overseas talent can press for policy changes through the "diaspora channel."[20] Because the state wants to utilize their "transnational capital,"[21] their refusal to return—what Hirschman calls "exit"—or their "voicing" of concerns through petitions, protests, or lobbying from abroad,[22] may force leaders to innovate new policies to attract them back.[23]

Top Chinese leaders responded to these problems. They introduced subsidies and special policies for overseas talents. They prioritized the role of talent in national development and invested heavily in scientific and academic institutions. China's leaders learned to allow talent to flow freely, recognizing that, to learn from the West, people must go abroad. While resisting dual citizenship, the government introduced long-term "green cards," simplifying cross-border flows. While historically and contemporarily China's leaders mistrust foreign values, some leaders advocated adopting Western academic and scientific norms to make China more competitive.[24] Similarly, China's leaders accepted the idea that Mainlanders who remain abroad can contribute to national development without returning full-time.[25] Finally, central leaders encourage localities to recruit overseas talent through various incentives and, in the late 2000s, pressured them to do so.

Still, strong forces within China resist many of these policies. Chinese officials historically have seen overseas study as ideologically loaded and politically contentious. In the mid-nineteenth century, conservative bureaucrats within the Qing government argued that foreign subjects, such as mathematics, would destroy China's "essence,"[26] and in 1885 pressured the emperor to call back all overseas students.[27]

Similarly, the CCP tightly controls its "culture and education sector," seeing universities as key battlegrounds to combat foreign values that could undermine CCP control. Moreover, the culture and education sector attracted conservative officials who tightened transnational flows when the unintended consequences of the policy on overseas study emerged. As a result, openings to the outside world were often followed by constrictions, only to be driven forward again by national leaders who pushed the policy and found supporters within organizations and localities who saw benefits from transnational flows.[28]

But the biggest problems lie *within* organizations, where returned scientists and academics have their strongest impact, but where they confront bias at the working level on a daily basis. Initially in China, this confrontation pitted foreign-trained Ph.D.s against domestic Ph.D.s who felt betrayed by the privileges proffered to those who had returned.[29] Surveys by Zweig and Chen in 2002 and 2004 showed that local academics were much more likely than returnees to believe that the state "overemphasized the role of returnees" (10 percent vs. 3 percent), that the state promoted returnees faster (19 percent vs. 2 percent), gave returnees better housing (14 percent vs. 2 percent), and more research money (19 percent vs. 3 percent).[30] Similarly, locals in the Chinese Academy of Sciences felt that the housing for returnees was "much better" than their own conditions (18 percent vs. 4 percent), that returnees got more research money (29 percent vs. 18 percent), that they were promoted faster (28 percent vs. 12 percent) and that overall the state's emphasis on returnees was "too high" (21 percent vs. 16 percent).[31]

Today, a generation of earlier returnees, who went abroad for one or two years as visiting scholars twenty to thirty years ago, now lead many scientific and academic institutions. They battle with those returning under current programs who are heralded as the very top mainland researchers in the diaspora. Also, the CCP's desire to promote these later returnees to leadership posts threatens the current administrators' power.

Finally, issues related to reverse migration—from passport renewals, residence permits, schooling for children, scientific entrepreneurship and technology transfer, tax and import issues, and jobs for spouses—covered a gamut of bureaucratic responsibilities and government organizations. Yet before 2008, no "overall encompassing coordinating ministry" controlled the policy.[32] Only in 2008 did Li Yuanchao, then-director of the Organizational Department of the CCP, reinvigorate the Leadership Small Group on Talent (LSGT), which drove the policy for several years.

DECONSTRUCTING THE STATE

China's policy-making and implementation system on reverse migration is composed, at the apex, of an overlapping circle of approximately twenty-five to thirty-five leaders in the Politburo and / or the State Council (that is, the Cabinet),[33] who establish national development strategies and initiate new programs. In the early 2000s, the Director of the Organization Department of the CCP took the lead on this issue. Other key ministries or agencies involved in this policy include: Personnel, Education, Science, Public Security, Foreign Affairs, and Overseas Chinese Affairs, along with the LSGT, which includes representatives from key ministries and CCP committees. The Chinese Academy of Sciences (CAS), a ministerial-level organization, manages 115 scientific research institutes nationwide and, along with a few top science universities, was the prestigious landing point for returning scientists. It has played an enormous role in attracting overseas talent since the policy began in 1978, although recently it has lost ground to the best universities in terms of the quality of the returnees under its program.[34]

Most state bureaucrats fulfill their bureau's mandate and implement state policies. Long-term interactions by the author with people working on policies to encourage people to study overseas and return demonstrate a strong commitment to this policy. Yet some bureaucrats privilege their own interests over recruiting overseas talent. In the face of unintended consequences, or when China's political climate turned frosty, the Ministry of Education (hereafter MOE) reined in overseas study, undermining reverse migration. The Overseas Chinese Office of the State Council, concerned that Chinese abroad will be accused of dual loyalties, staunchly opposes dual citizenship for ethnic Chinese holding foreign passports. And today, some administrators in CAS and China's top universities oppose the privileges granted under the Thousand Talents Program to returnees so they oppose directly funding these world-class returnees.[35]

The central government also encourages research institutes, universities, and Chinese state-owned enterprises (SOEs) to recruit overseas talent by downloading money and authority to the MOE and CAS. Under the "985 Program," announced by then General Secretary of the CCP, Jiang Zemin, in May 1998, 20 percent of the funds given to China's top nine universities were to be used to import overseas talent. Under the CAS "Hundred Talents Plan," awardees receive 2 million renminbi (RMB) with which to start a laboratory, buy equipment and hire technical personnel; importantly, 20 percent of the funds can supplement their salary. SOEs have become active recruiters, particularly China's Fortune 500 companies, which need talent with international experience to find markets and resources overseas.[36]

To recruit people from abroad successfully, leaders must understand the global environment, as those living abroad respond to China's policies and enticements based largely on their situation overseas. Deng Xiaoping, who worked in France; Jiang Zemin, who had studied in the Soviet Union; and Li Yuanchao, who studied at Harvard's Kennedy School, seemed attuned to the views of overseas students. In fact, the launching of the "Thousand Talents Program" in December 2008 may have been more than happenstance, as leaders understood that the West's financial crisis had created a cohort of Chinese global talent willing to relocate.[37]

CHINESE LEADERS AND CHINA'S REVERSE MIGRATION

The historical descriptions below highlight the role played by top leaders in the establishment, renewal, and development of the policy to send students abroad and then entice them to return. They reflect shifting global conditions, policies in China, and the ways in which new leaders responded to a changing China in a changing world.

Deng Xiaoping and the Decision to Send Students Abroad

Deng Xiaoping worried about the scientific gap between China and the West, so in spring 1978 he affirmed the role of learning from other countries in China's transformation into a powerful socialist country. On June 23, 1978, he pressed the MOE to set up a special group to manage overseas study and criticized the previous policy on overseas students as "too inflexible," arguing that "independence does not mean shutting the door on the world, nor does self-reliance mean blind opposition to everything foreign."[38] According to Huang, "Deng Xiaoping's personnel intervention in policy matters concerning education and science in 1977 [and 1978] were of crucial importance in the shaping of later policies."[39] But in August 1979, when Deng proposed that China send 10,000 students abroad each year, the MOE cut the quota to 3,000 a year for five years.[40]

Before 1981, all students and scholars going abroad were approved and funded by the MOE and CAS. But in 1980, a "self-paying" category allowed Overseas Chinese to help Mainland relatives study abroad. However, in March 1982, after too many children of high-ranking officials used the self-paying category to go overseas, the Central Committee restricted this category.

Zhao Ziyang: Decentralizing Controls over Channels Overseas, 1984–85

In mid-1984, Zhao Ziyang and Hu Yaobang, the reformist PM and General Secretary of the CCP, respectively, liberalized the flow overseas.[41] A new policy allowed universities to set up bilateral exchanges with foreign schools; their students could now apply directly for overseas scholarships. As of November 1984, "anyone" [except current graduate students] who could get foreign financial support could study overseas. Self-paying students no longer needed MOE permission to leave, only the approval of their local Public Security Bureau, triggering a dramatic rise in the outflow of students.[42]

In spring 1985, more reforms decentralized authority over finances, exchanges, curriculum, student enrolment, and capital construction to organizations,[43] while a new Natural Science Foundation for China (NSFC) began accepting applications for funding in the sciences, specifically from returnees. Thereafter, spouses of overseas students were allowed to join their partners abroad. The return rate slowed dramatically, as many former M.A. students shifted into Ph.D. programs, supported by their spouses who now worked overseas.[44]

1987–1991: The MOE Tightens Up

Student protests in December 1986, the subsequent crackdown in January 1987, and the removal of the reformer, Hu Yaobang, as CCP General Secretary, increased hostility between the CCP and students at home and abroad. In late January 1987, 1,000 overseas students in the United States signed an open letter to the General Office of the Central Committee, protesting Hu's dismissal and expressing their "deep sense of mission about the motherland's future."[45]

In response to these events, and data in mid-1987 showing that most students sent abroad for Ph.D.s after 1983 were not returning to China, He Dongchang, a conservative vice-chair of the State Education Commission (the SEDC had replaced the MOE), led a delegation to the United States which announced plans to increase the proportion of short-term visiting scholars, who were more compliant, while at the same time decreasing the share of graduate students.

In late 1987, the SEDC tried to cut the flow of students to the United States where it believed "anti-China" forces were strong. A CCP Central Document, supported by Deng Xiaoping, cut the number of students to the United States from 68 to 20 percent and pressured students in the United States to return.[46] The SEDC created one application form for the United States and another for all other countries, but then printed very few of the former. However, the State Science and Technology Commission (SSTC), which prized exchanges with the United States, threatened to produce its own form for studying in the United States, forcing the conservative prime minister, Li Peng, to agree that the SEDC restrictions on studying in the United States would not apply to scholars sponsored by the SSTC.

Still, the tightening intensified. Visits by spouses were stopped.[47] Government-funded students in the United States suddenly had only five years to complete their degree, and if they did not return on time their families would be fined.[48] Those already abroad for five years would receive a one-year extension on their passports, which would be revoked if they failed to return, making them stateless.

Again Chinese students in the United States spoke out. Their new letter to the CCP challenged the five-year limit.[49] They also evaded the restrictions on going to the United States by enrolling first in schools in other countries and then transferring to the United States; or they applied to the United States as visiting scholars but entered graduate school once in America. In the end, the restrictions failed because students wanted to attend American universities which, along with various U.S. foundations, were providing U.S.$100 million a year in scholarships to Chinese students.

To impose further constraints, in 1988 the SEDC encouraged university lecturers going abroad to the United States for Ph.D.s to apply for the more restrictive J-1 student visa, rather than the more flexible F-1 visa.[50] According to U.S. law, people on J-1 visas must return to their country of origin after graduation, and cannot apply for H-1 employment visas while in the United States; F-1 visas could be extended almost indefinitely. To encourage acquiescence to these restrictions, the jobs, apartments, and salaries in China of J-1 visa holders were protected until they returned, while all links were severed with those going out on F-1 visas. Many accepted the SEDC's offer, as it allowed their spouses and children to live comfortably on campus in China while they studied abroad.

Zhao Fails to Liberalize the Policy

In September 1988, Zhao Ziyang, who replaced Hu Yaobang as general secretary of the CCP, tried to allay concerns about the brain drain, and return to a more moderate policy, when he reportedly convened a top-level meeting to discuss the problem.[51] Apparently, at the meeting the SEDC insisted that, due to the brain drain, all overseas students must return immediately, while the SSTC understood that the longer people stayed abroad, the more likely they were to gain access to U.S. high-tech facilities, which would benefit China's S&T sector. The Overseas Affairs Office of the State Council hoped some students could become American citizens and promote the PRC's influence in overseas Chinese communities. Finally, the Personnel Ministry, which had difficulty finding good jobs for returnees, saw too many of them as problematic.[52] Zhao, putting a positive spin on the problem, called it "storing talent (or brain power) abroad," reflecting a prescient perspective similar to Saxenian's "brain circulation."[53] Nevertheless, education officials in the Washington embassy rejected Zhao's view, and in March 1989, Chinese embassies circulated a critical speech on overseas policy, defeating Zhao's effort to moderate the policy.[54]

Tightening Up after June 4

June 4, 1989, and the assault by the Chinese army on thousands of protestors in Beijing, deepened the rift between the CCP and Chinese students worldwide. Conservatives within the CCP intensified the dilemma by arguing that China had allowed returned academics to inculcate Western values into their university's curriculum during the 1980s as new courses were not scrutinized.[55] Chinese students wanted out. Self-funded applications jumped; the numbers taking TOEFL rose from 36,000 in 1989 to 60,000 in 1990; and the number of government-funded students staying abroad became "a serious problem."[56] A new diaspora composed of Mainlanders who feared, if not opposed, the CCP and the Chinese state suddenly emerged (figure 11-1).

The state also imposed new controls on overseas study. Older scholars were favored over younger ones; more visiting scholars were to be funded for short-term tours; and fewer degree candidates were permitted to study abroad and only in fields in which China had a shortage of talent. "Hotbeds," such as the United States, were to be avoided. New graduates would have to work for five years before going abroad, and limits were set on the numbers going to study social sciences and humanities.[57] Finally, the right of approval was transferred from the workplace to provincial education commissions, tightening the state's oversight. The result was a 13 percent drop in

FIGURE 11-1. Number of Non-U.S. Citizens Awarded Doctorates in Science and Engineering: PRC, Taiwan, and India, 1985–2001

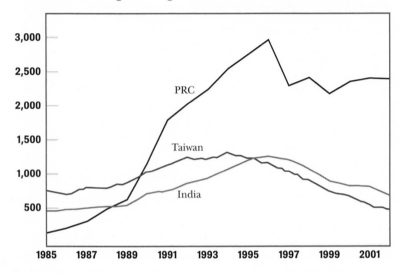

Source: Science and Engineering Doctorate Awards, 2002 (SRS home page, October 2003).

1990–91 over 1989–90 in the number of self-paying students.[58] The decrease continued through 1992, while the number of returnees almost halved between 1988 and 1989, dropping again in 1990.

President Bush's Executive Order of April 1990, which allowed 50,000 Chinese in the United States to apply for permanent residence, and all J-1 visa holders to shift to F-1 student visas,[59] as well as similar policies in Canada and Australia, granted over 80,000 Chinese students the legal right to stay abroad. In response, a secret document sent to Chinese embassies worldwide declared that "PRC policy on overseas students must be raised to the high plane of international struggle and competition for our talented personnel. The personnel stationed abroad on the front lines are now engaged in a very hard struggle that will affect our destiny."[60]

In October 1989, the CCP committee in the SEDC apologized to the Central Committee's General Office for underestimating the efforts by foreign forces to turn overseas Chinese students against the state.[61] Their mea culpa included an admission that they had not been sufficiently concerned about the "political quality" of the state-financed students they had selected. They called for a major cutback in the number of state-funded people going out for degrees, and insisted that those who went could do so only with the permission of the SEDC. The following year, prospective visiting scholars had to undergo an interview with their unit's party committee, while the unit's CCP secretary had to sign a document "taking responsibility for them."[62]

Deng to the Rescue, 1992–93

By staying abroad, students and scholars threatened Deng's goal of modernizing China through overseas study. But before they would begin to return, they demanded the freedom of movement, both at home and abroad. They also worried that they would be punished for having participated overseas in anti-government activity after June 4. Thus during his "Southern Tour" of January 1992, Deng replaced the class-struggle rhetoric, that had emanated from the SEDC after June 4, with conciliatory language. In Shenzhen, he promised a warm reception for all students who returned, as long as they ceased anti-government activities.

The external pressure and Deng's intervention succeeded. In March 1992, Prime Minister Li Peng publicly guaranteed overseas students and scholars the right to "come and go freely." In August 1992, a government document announced that publicly funded scholars could extend their expired passports at consulates without returning to China.[63] Students who had gone abroad on public passports could switch to private ones. And even if students owed their home unit money, these disputes could not hold up the resolution of the passport issue.

Suddenly, people returning did not need to go back to their original unit, loosening the domestic talent market nationwide. Relatives of publicly sponsored scholars were again allowed to visit them overseas, while the Public Security Bureau announced that when family members of publicly funded scholars went to visit, the unit that had originally sponsored the scholar could not hold up the visit to pressure for the resolution of any financial claims.

In March 1992, the Ministry of Personnel announced the strategy of "improving services for returned students."[64] The new policy included,

1. Job introduction centers for returned students in Shenzhen, Shanghai, and Fujian;
2. Preferential policies for returnees, including
   a. more living space and more chances to receive higher professional titles.
   b. letting family members move to new cities where the returnees had found jobs.
   c. permitting students who had signed two- or three-year contracts with their research centers to switch jobs once their agreements expired.
3. The founding of a national association of returned students; and
4. Provisions for greater support for scientific research.

In March 1993, at the 8th Session of the National People's Congress (NPC), Prime Minister Li Peng announced that returnees were "free to come and go." The following month, the Conference on the Work of Sending Personnel to Study Abroad admitted that policies since 1989 had been "too political."[65] New rules permitted schools and units to establish their own standards for approving study abroad candidates. Then the Third Plenum of the 14th Party Congress in 1993 formally announced the "12-character slogan"—"Support overseas study, encourage returnees, allow them to come and go freely"— that guided policy for over twenty years.

Jiang Zemin's Market View of China's Global Talent

Jiang Zemin transformed policy toward overseas students and scholars. First, he accepted the notion that Chinese intellectuals were part of a global talent pool who needed to go abroad to increase their human capital; China, therefore, had to improve its policies to compete internationally for its own citizens. Prime Minister Zhu Rongji concurred, announcing that henceforth "China would change the emphasis of the open policy from attracting foreign capital to attracting human talent and technology."[66]

Second, in May 1998, Jiang announced his policy to create "world class universities." Under this "985 Program," nine leading universities received hundreds of millions of RMB of which 20 percent was to be used to pay high salaries for attracting overseas scholars (table 11-1). CAS had earlier (1995) introduced its Hundred Talents Program, which gave returned scientists who met its criteria 2.2 million RMB, while the MOE announced its "Changjiang Scholars Program" funded with the support of Hong Kong tycoon Li Ka-hsing. These programs gave returnees wage subsidies and a host of privileges. In 2002, the Natural Science Foundation's Distinguished Young Scholars Program offered returnees doing scientific experiments one million RMB, while those engaged in theoretical research received 800,000 RMB.[67]

To encourage China's private entrepreneurs to return from abroad, Jiang revised China's Constitution, making the private sector "a core part of the national economy," while the SSTC significantly expanded the number of incubators in high-tech zones around the country where returnees could establish start-up companies. In 2002, Jiang also proposed that China adopt the strategy of "strengthening the country through talent."[68]

To utilize the knowhow of Mainlanders who remained abroad, China under Jiang introduced its version of the "Diaspora Option,"[69] labeling it "Serving the Nation." While some officials viewed non-returnees as traitors, particularly if they had received state funding to go abroad, this new policy encouraged them to help national self-strengthening. In 2001, the new policy document, composed by many interested ministries, called on Mainlanders overseas to "serve the nation" (*wei guo fuwu*), even if they did not "return to the nation" (*hui guo fuwu*). Methods included (1) holding concurrent positions in China and overseas; (2) engaging in cooperative research in China and abroad; (3) teaching and conducting academic and technical exchanges in China; (4) setting up businesses in China; (5) conducting inspections and consultations; and (6) engaging in intermediary services, such as running conferences, importing technology or foreign funds, or helping Chinese firms find export markets.[70]

TABLE 11-1. Funding for Universities under
the "985" Plan, in RMB, 1998

Peking University (1.8 billion)	Wuhan University (800 million)
Tsinghua University (1.8 billion)	Jilin University (700 million)
Fudan University (1.2 billion)	Tongji University (600 million)
Harbin Institute of Technology (1 billion)	Northwest Polytech Univ. (900 million)
Nanjing University (1.2 billion)	Nankai University (700 million)
Shanghai Jiao Tong (1.2 billion)	Xiamen University (800 million)
Xi'an Jiao Tong (900 million)	East China Normal (600 million)
Zhejiang University (1.4 billion)	Southeast University (600 million)
Beijing Institute of Technology (1 billion)	Shandong University (1.2 million)
Beijing Normal (1.2 billion)	Sichuan University (720 million)
Beihang University (900 million)	Tianjin University (700 million)
Huazhong University of Science and Technology (600 million)	University of Science and Technology in China (900 million)

Source: Ministry of Education.

Given the enormous interest among overseas Mainlanders to benefit from China's economic boom, the Chinese government's encouragement to academics, scientists, and businessmen overseas to engage with China was well timed. In 2003, Chen estimated that

25 percent of overseas Mainlanders were "serving the country" in some form.[71]

Zeng Qinghong Brings the Party Back In

Near the end of the Jiang era, the CCP ratcheted up its policy on talent. In May 2002, the Central Committee and the State Council jointly promulgated the "2002–2005 Outline for Building the Ranks of Nationwide Talent," with its "strategy of strengthening the country through human talent."[72] The guiding principle for returnees was to accord them "complete trust," select "highly talented returnees to take up leadership positions," and promote them rapidly.[73]

Even after Jiang stepped down, the CCP intensified its focus on returnees. The CCP had always been responsible for developing internal talent under its portfolio of "managing cadres." But at the end of 2002, Zeng Qinghong, the Politburo Standing Committee member responsible for personnel and the head of the CCP's Organization Department, announced that the CCP should also "manage talent." A Central Leadership Small Group to Coordinate the Work on Talent (LSGT) was approved by the Politburo in May 2003 to coordinate the work of more than twenty ministries and commissions. On December 26, 2003, a document from the Central Committee and the State Council emphasized that the CCP had to import "high quality talent," which is in "short supply."

However, the CCP could not liberalize the environment inside academic and research organizations around China, which stopped people from returning. A survey in 2004 of 3,000 respondents found that the most important force holding people back from returning was "the complicated role of human relations in Chinese society,"[74] a code for bureaucratic interference, invisible networks, and the constraints imposed on returnees by Chinese culture. A later survey in 2007 found that, when calculating whether to return or not, Chinese expatriates preferred a "systematic reform of China's environment on human talent," rather than "special privileges."[75] In 2007, explosive new data showed that among Chinese who received doctorates in the United States in 2002, 92 percent remained in the United States five years after graduation. China's rate was the highest in the world;

India's staying rate was 81 percent, Canada's 55 percent, Taiwan's 43 percent, South Korea's 41 percent, while Japan's and Mexico's were 33 percent and 32 percent, respectively. Another report from the U.S. National Science Foundation found that as of 2007, 90.2 percent of Chinese Ph.D.s in Science and Engineering were planning to stay in the United States.[76] Reflecting these problems, the director of a CAS institute in China's Northeast told the author in 2004 that he could not attract the top 20 percent of Mainland scientists living abroad. Li Jin, a returnee who had become dean of life sciences at Fudan University, commented in 2006, "The returnees so far . . . are not superstars. Few are from first-tier universities and/or doing first-rate work."[77]

Li Yuanchao and the Thousand Talents Plan

In fall 2007, Li Yuanchao became head of the Organization Department and head of the LSGT. Li was tailor made for this portfolio. While party secretary of Jiangsu Province he had created the "530 Plan," under which Wuxi Municipality's government funded half of the costs of start-up firms run by returnees.

Once in Beijing, Li targeted that top 20 percent who refused to come home by directly addressing the environment within institutions. Speaking to the LSGT in December 2008, he called for creating a welcoming environment that would be "relaxed, tolerant, and lenient."[78] He called on executives of organizations seeking to attract returnees to appeal to their "love of country," but also to their "love of their careers" and their "heartfelt need for self-esteem."

In fall 2009, he galvanized cities around China to create their own Thousand Talents Program. Each municipality had to devise a plan for restructuring their economy, determine how many talented people they would need from abroad to complete this job, and then recruit that talent from overseas.[79]

However, the policy ran into problems.[80] While the goal of the policy had been to get the very best people to return full-time, or for a minimum of six months/year, by 2011, 73.5 percent of scientific and academic returnees, many of whom had good jobs overseas precisely because they were world class, decided not to give up their tenured positions overseas. Their hesitancy forced Li to introduce a short-term, two- to three-month platform, which most of them chose. Local governments also granted the award to people who had already returned as a way to fulfill the commitments they had made to the Organization Department. As of 2011, approximately 50 percent of the initial 1,500 awardees under the program had actually returned to China before 2008, when the program began.

The problematic intellectual and scientific climate within China's academic and research institutions remains. A survey carried out on behalf of the Organization Department in 2011 found that among the 394 interviewees who had received a Thousand Talents Award, 49 percent reported that "the research atmosphere was not good, and too much time was spent in 'public activities' that were non-academic."[81] A further 45.9 percent complained that research applications were not transparent and involved building connections and using the back door," while 40.1 percent reflected that in the realm of scientific research in China, "personal relationships are too complicated and one must spend a great deal of time handling them." The survey also included leaders of 1,508 units that employed high-quality re-turnees and 2,156 domestically trained, talented people. Among unit leaders, 64.9 percent said the biggest problem facing the domestic research environment was that "personal relations were too com-plicated," while 55.6 percent of the domestic trained talents felt the same.[82]

THE SOURCE OF ADMINISTRATIVE RESISTANCE
TO THE THOUSAND TALENTS PLAN

The source of resistance to the Thousand Talents Plan was evident in June 2012. At a meeting in Shenzhen with Li Yuanchao, then Director of the Organization Department, the president of Dalian Polytechnic University, which is funded under the "985 world-class university program," criticized the program's large salaries, bonuses, and what he saw as unfair privileges given to these high-flying re-turnees, which he said harmed the enthusiasm of locally trained scholars. He, and the director of a CAS institute in Beijing who was sitting beside him at the meeting, both of whom had been visiting scholars overseas, preferred more equality and less income and status differentiation. No doubt, they also liked the fact that most research money flowed through their hands, rather than through competitive grants under the Natural Science Foundation of China, helping them maintain their own network. Li took great exception to their views, declaring that the goal of the policy was to promote "development" not "equality," and by the end of the summer, the president of this university was out of a job.[83]

That meeting suggested an administrative source of resistance to this policy: the presidents of universities and the directors of research centers under CAS. Thus I hypothesized that (1) *academic and scientific administrators who do not have an overseas Ph.D. are less likely to encourage overseas scholars with Ph.D.s to join their institutions.* I assume that while these administrators may have benefited from their time abroad, visiting scholars were not subject to the rigors of a Ph.D. program.[84] As a result, they may not appreciate the intense academic training offered by top academic institutions abroad. Second, the internal promotion system for university presidents fosters leaders who represent the interests of the whole university.[85] Therefore, one might also hypothesize that (2) *presidents who have risen through the ranks of the university of which they are the president are less likely to bring in overseas Ph.Ds.* These presidents worry that outsiders with strong academic training can challenge the faculty trained within their own school. Also, internally promoted presidents are likely to have created their own circle of supporters in the university. The final section of the paper explores these two hypotheses.

Figure 11-2 shows the experiences of presidents and CCP secretaries in the top thirty-eight universities in China. In 1999, over 40 percent of university presidents had been visiting scholars, while less than 25 percent had overseas Ph.D.s. And while in 2000–2005, the number of presidents with overseas Ph.D.s jumped from 20 percent to 50 percent, so that as of 2004–05, foreign Ph.D. holders surpassed visiting scholars, the proportion shifted after 2007, as presidents with the more limited overseas training again took over many universities.

Another proxy for resistance could be the number of years since these administrators spent any extended time overseas. Presidents

FIGURE 11-2. Share of Presidents and CCP Secretaries with Overseas Experience in China's Top Universities, 1999–2013

Percent

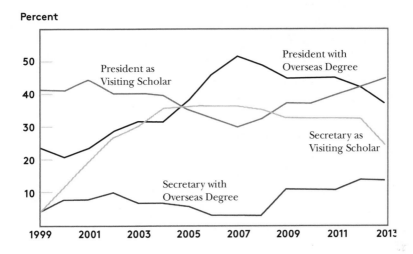

Source: Kang Siqin's calculations. N = 38.

who have been back in China for a long time are less likely than more recent Ph.D.s to have maintained strong academic credentials and strong links to international scholarship. Therefore, much like the president of Dalian Institute of Technology, they are likely to resent the "superstars" recruited after 2008 under the Thousand Talents Plan. Our data show that, while in 1999, the average length of time that had elapsed since the presidents of these thirty-eight universities had returned from overseas study was fifteen years—many had been visiting scholars in the late 1970s and early-to-mid 1980s—by 2013, the average length of time since they had returned from their stint abroad had increased to 22.6 years.[86]

The data on the international academic experiences of the directors of CAS institutes (table 11-2) show a slightly different pattern. Between 2002 and 2013, the percent of former visiting scholars rose from 41.9 percent to 45.5 percent, while the share of institute directors with overseas Ph.D.s also increased from 18.9 percent at the turn of the century to 26.8 percent by 2013. But visiting scholars still dominated. And with 27.7 percent of directors with no overseas

TABLE 11-2. Percentage of International Experience of
Institute Directors under CAS, 2002 and 2013

Year	Visiting scholars	Overseas Ph.D.	No overseas experience
2002	41.9	18.9	39.2
2013	45.5	26.8	27.7

TABLE 11-3. Summary Statistics of Variables

	N^a	Mean	Standard deviation	Min	Max
Returnees to university each year	376	3.04	3.03	0	17
Internal promotion	376	.609	.489	0	1
Current president was a visiting scholar	376	.346	.476	0	1
Current president holds an overseas Ph.D.	376	.383	.487	0	1
Years in post	376	5.09	2.91	1	17

a. N = total number of observations in 27 universities over 14 years.

experience at all, it is not surprising that returnees felt a great deal of bias within CAS institutes.[87]

To test the above two hypotheses, we constructed a data set of the sixty-three presidents who had run twenty-seven universities between 1999 and 2012.[88] We also collected data on the returnees recruited to these universities under either the Changjiang Scholars or the Thousand Talents Programs. These two programs incorporate the best talent that is recruited back to China and the data for each university is available on their websites, as the number of returnees they recruit under these programs demonstrates the achievements and quality of the school. (Descriptive statistics are in table 11-3.)

Dependent Variable:

Our dependent variable is the number of returned scholars recruited under the Thousand Talents or the Changjiang Scholars Programs to that university each year.

Independent Variables:

Promoted internally. A university president who climbed the administrative ladder through the incumbent university is considered "internally promoted." Our measure of "internally promoted" is if they served as dean of a school in that university. If they held only the position of vice president for a period of time, they are coded as "externally promoted."

Overseas Experience. Our analysis differentiates among presidents holding an Overseas Ph.D.,[89] visiting scholars (those with at least two continuous years overseas, either as a visiting scholar or a post-doc), or no overseas experience.

OVERSEAS EXPERIENCE AND THE RECRUITMENT OF RETURNEES: THE EVIDENCE

Table 11-4 reports our results, which confirm *hypothesis 1.* According to our Baseline Model (column 1), which compares presidents with overseas Ph.D.s to presidents with no overseas experience at all, we find that presidents with an overseas Ph.D. bring in 1.95 more top-ranked returnees each year, a finding which is statistically significant at the 0.01 level. This finding is also 64.1 percent more than the average number of returnees to all these universities each year (table 11-3), which was 3.04, reflecting a large practical difference. On the other hand, having a president who has been a visiting scholar has no statistically significant effect on the number of returnees recruited when compared to those who have had no overseas experience. Thus spending two years abroad has the same impact on recruitment of top talent as having spent no time abroad. This finding sheds light on the confrontation between Li Yuanchao and the two administrators.

TABLE 11-4. Regression on University Presidents and Number of High-End Returnees[a]

Independent variables[b]	Baseline model[c]	Internal promotion	Robustness— age	Visiting scholar as baseline[d]	Visiting scholar robustness
	(1)	(2)	(3)	(4)	(5)
Overseas Ph.D.	1.95*** (.694)	1.52** (.667)	1.46** (.689)	1.43** (.670)	1.47** (.687)
Visiting scholar	1.25 (.787)	.916 (.627)	.815 (.691)		
Promoted internally[e]		-1.15** (.443)	-1.14** (.431)	-.946* (.546)	-.981* (.528)
University fixed effect	Yes	Yes	Yes	Yes	Yes
Year fixed effect	Yes	Yes	Yes	Yes	Yes
Observations	376	376	376	265	265

a. We use a Fixed Effects Model based on combining all the university presidents. University Fixed Effects controls for unique qualities in the data that may result because some universities, such as Peking or Tsinghua universities, recruit many more returnees. Similarly, Year Fixed Effects limits the impact of shifts in the flows that may be due to unique historical events. To allow for heterogeneity across different universities, we estimate the result with the robust standard error clustered by universities.

b. The dependent variable is the number of returnees under national talent programs entering the university that year.

c. The baseline model for this column is presidents with no overseas experience at all.

d. For this column, we drop the cases of all presidents who never went abroad and compare only overseas Ph.D.s and Visiting Scholars, with the baseline being Visiting Scholars.

e. The baseline for this variable is presidents who were externally promoted.

Note: *p<0.1 **p<0.05 ***p<0.01

Second, we analyze *hypothesis 2*, career trajectory, in our second model (column 2) and find that whether or not a president is internally promoted, as compared to being brought in from the outside (externally promoted), affects whether the university recruits overseas returnees from the two programs. Universities whose president was internally promoted recruited 1.15 *fewer* high-quality returnees than universities with externally promoted presidents. Also, in this second model, we still find that universities with a president with an overseas Ph.D. are 50 percent more likely to hire a returnee and overall hire 1.52 more returnees each year. The decreased impact of the overseas Ph.D. degree, from .667 to .443, is because presidents who are overseas Ph.D.s are much more likely to be externally promoted.

Finally, the model in column 4 directly compares the difference between having an overseas Ph.D. and being a visiting scholar. We find that having an overseas Ph.D. remains statistically significant ($p < .05$), and that universities with a president who had an overseas Ph.D. are likely to recruit 1.43 more returnees per year than universities whose president had been a visiting scholar. However, because of the decrease in the number of observations to 265, and the increase in the standard deviation for each case, the level of significance of internal promotion drops to 0.1. Nevertheless, we argue that having a president with an overseas Ph.D., as compared to having a president with no overseas experience or experience only as a visiting scholar, means that the university is more likely to recruit world-class scholars from abroad.

WHERE DO WE STAND TODAY?

China's relatively successful reverse migration is due in no small part to its top leaders who, wielding the power of the party / state and its purse, have introduced a plethora of mechanisms to attract China's overseas talent. Their ability to maintain momentum within this issue area has been remarkable.

Xi Jinping is no different. But time will tell whether his influence will be positive or negative. In a major policy address in October 2013, to celebrate the one hundredth anniversary of the Western Returned Scholars Association (*Ou Mei tongxuehui*—hereafter WRSA), Xi supplemented the "12-character slogan" ("send people abroad, encourage returning, freedom to come and go"), established as the core policy position in 1993, with a new phrase that emphasized helping returnees "manifest their usefulness" (*fahui zuoyong*).[90]

His speech applauded the contributions of returnees to China's development, but also raised traditional themes that had become somewhat dormant since the 1990s, such as the role of patriotism as a motivating force for Chinese who studied abroad. Managing returnees was now seconded under a "united front" strategy whereby local CCP committees would establish local WRSAs; overseas educated Chinese were also encouraged to speak well of China and enhance China's soft power.[91] The new emphasis on "utilizing talent" implied that China should maximize the talent that had already returned more than attract those who remained abroad, a policy line that echoes Xi's emerging anti-Western policy and his fear of Western efforts to infiltrate China and change China's "color."

Xi's views took on new meaning in light of the decision in 2015 to constrain NGOs tightly and place civil society groups under CCP leadership. In August 2016, a policy directive from the General Office of the Central Committee, entitled "Some ideas on strengthening the building of the Western Returnees Scholars Association," advocated turning the WRSA into a mass organization under the United Front Work Department (UFWD) of the CCP, which would "manage" or supervise it on behalf of the Secretariat of the Central Committee.[92] Mirroring the "corporatist" or syndicalist nature of many authoritarian regimes, whereby professional associations come under tight state control, the document set as its main task to establish a "sound organizational system," with branches in most provinces, large municipalities and organizations, such as universities, research institutes, development zones and large companies, to be led by the CCP committee at the same level. No doubt, active leadership would come from the territorial UFWD. Another goal was to pull in more members, and strengthen the leadership of the WRSA branches through training sessions, careful leadership selection, regular evaluations and monitoring, and to insure that local leaders of the WRSA were closely tied to the CCP. But politicizing the WRSA's local leadership—it called on them to pay greater attention to politics—could attract left-leaning returnees who will insure that the WRSA does not become an autonomous voice for the interests of cosmopolitan Chinese who want close ties to the global community. Instead the WRSA could become another channel for pro-CCP forces to advance their own political careers and could reinforce concerns of those currently abroad who fear that returning will place them under the control of China's academic and scientific bureaucracy. As the CCP continues to prioritize its security and tighten its control over Chinese society, the reverse migration of the best Chinese overseas researchers could slow, undermining China's scientific modernization.[93]

APPENDIX A **UNIVERSITIES**

Beijing:	Peking University, Tsinghua University, China Agriculture University, Beijing Normal University, Renmin University of China
Chongqing	Chongqing University
Nanjing	Southeast University, Nanjing University
Shanghai	Fudan University, Shanghai Jiaotong University, East China Normal University, Tongji University, East China University of Technology
Harbin	Harbin University of Industry
Wuhan	Huazhong University of Science and Technology
Chengdu	Sichuan University, Southwest Jiaotong University
Tianjin	Tianjin University, Nankai University
Wuhan	Wuhan University
Xi'an	Xi'an Jiaotong University
Xiamen	Xiamen University
Hangzhou	Zhejiang University
Changsha	Zhongnan University
Guangzhou	Sun Yat Sen University
Hefei	Chinese University of Science and Technology
Dalian	Dalian Institute of Technology

APPENDIX B **ON DATA FOR THE REGRESSION**

To collect the data on all top returnees to universities is nigh to impossible. Nowadays, hundreds of overseas Ph.D.s return each year. Also, not all are "high quality returnees," meeting the standards of the national programs. So, we chose to find awardees under the national talent programs. While dozens of programs recruit and support high-end returnees, the Changjiang Scholars Plan and the Thousand Talents Plan are the most prestigious. Applicants are reviewed by an overseas panel to guarantee a fair selection process.

However, not all people enrolled in these two programs are suitable for our study, particularly as a considerable number of Changjiang scholars had only one year of continuous overseas experience. Many awardees under this program had only been "visiting" in one-year training programs. So our visiting scholars had to have had at least two years of overseas experience, either as a post-doc or as a visiting scholar. This rule differentiates real returnees from people with on-job training.

NOTES

A version of this paper, entitled " 'Crossing the River by Feeling the Stones': China's Flexible Diaspora Strategy," was first presented at the Conference on "The Diaspora Strategies' of Migrant-Sending Counties: Migration-As-Development Reinvented," Asia Research Institute, National University of Singapore, November 2012.

Many thanks to Kang Siqin for his research assistance and to both the Chang Tseng-Hsi Foundation and the Research Grants Council of Hong Kong's Prestigious Fellowship Award (2013–14) for financial support.

1. Valerie Bunce, *Do New Leaders Make a Difference? Executive Succession and Public Policy Under Capitalism and Socialism* (Princeton University Press, 1981).

2. J. Mason and S. Holland, "Obama to Use Executive Actions to Advance Immigration Reform," Reuters, June 30, 2014.

3. Robert Hutton, "Farage Vows UKIP 'Earthquake' in May Vote as Immigration Soars," *Bloomberg News*, February 28, 2014.

4. Matthew Weaver, "Angela Merkel: German Multiculturalism Has 'Utterly Failed,'" *The Guardian*, October 17, 2010.

5. Herbert Brücker et. al., eds., *Brain Drain and Brain Gain: The Global Competition to Attract High-Skilled Migrants* (Oxford University Press, 2012),

and Wang Huiyao, *Rencai zhanzheng: quan qiu zui xique ziyuan de zhengduo zhan* [Talent war: The fierce competition over the world's most scarce resource] (Beijing: China Citic Press, 2009).

6. S. Y. Bang, "Reverse Brain Drain in South Korea State Led Model," *Studies in Comparative International Development* 27, no. 1 (1992), pp. 4–26.

7. Jean-Pierre Cassarino, "Theorising Return Migration: The Conceptual Approach to Return Migrants Revisited," *International Journal on Multicultural Societies* 6, no. 2 (2004), pp. 253–79.

8. Nancy Gore Saravia and Juan Francisco Miranda, "Plumbing the Brain Drain," *Bulletin of the World Health Organization*, no. 82 (2004), pp. 608–15.

9. Ibid.

10. Kathleen Newland, *Circular Migration and Human Development*, Human Development Research Paper, no. 42 (New York: United Nations Development Programme, 2009).

11. Donald D. H. Lien, "Asymmetric Information and the Brain Drain," *Journal of Population Economics*, no. 6 (1992), pp. 169–80.

12. David Zweig, *"Hui dao Zhongguo Kexueyuan: Xique, huanjing yu jili"* [Returning to the Chinese Academy of Sciences: Shortage, environment and incentives], in *Zhongguo haigui fazhan baogao* [Report on the development of China's returnees], edited by Wang Huiyao and Miao Lv (Social Sciences Press), no. 2 (2013), pp. 133–65.

13. Lauren M. McLaren, "Anti-Immigrant Prejudice in Europe: Contact, Threat Perception, and Preference for the Exclusion of Migrants," *Social Forces* 81, no. 3 (2003), 909–36.

14. B. McCormick and J. Wahba, "Return International Migration and Geographical Inequality: The Case of Egypt," *Journal of African Economies* 12, no. 4 (2003) 500–32.

15. Devesh Kapur, *Diasporas, Development, and Democracy* (Princeton University Press, 2010), p. 16.

16. F. P. Cerase, "Expectations and Reality: A Case Study of Return Migration from the United States to Southern Italy," *International Migration Review* 8, no. 2 (1974), pp. 245–62.

17. Ibid.

18. Etel Solingnen, "Of Dominoes and Firewalls: The Domestic, Regional, and Global Politics of International Diffusion," *International Studies Quarterly* 56 (2012), pp. 631–44.

19. David Zweig and Feng Yang, "Overseas Students, Returnees and the Diffusion of International Norms into Post-Mao China," *International Studies Review* 16 (Fall 2014), pp. 252–63.

20. Kapur, *Diasporas, Development, and Democracy*, p. 16.

21. David Zweig, Changgui Chen, and Stanley Rosen, "Globalization and Transnational Human Capital: Overseas and Returnee Scholars to China," *China Quarterly* 179 (September 2004), pp. 735–57.

22. Albert O. Hirschman, *Exit, Voice, and Loyalty: Responses to Declines in Firms, Organizations, and States* (Harvard University Press, 1970).

23. Shu-Yun Ma, "The Exit, Voice, and Struggle to Return of Chinese Political Exiles," *Pacific Affairs* 66, no. 3 (Autumn 1993), pp. 368–85.

24. David Zweig and Huiyao Wang, "Can China Bring Back the Best? The Communist Party Organizes China's Search for Talent," *China Quarterly*, no. 215 (September 2014), pp. 590–615.

25. David Zweig, Chung Siu-Fung and Han Donglin, "Redefining the 'Brain Drain': China's Diaspora Option," *Science, Technology and Society* 13, no.1 (2008), pp. 1–33.

26. John King Fairbank, *Trade and Diplomacy on the China Coast: The Opening of the Treaty Ports, 1842–1854* (Harvard University Press, 1964).

27. Thomas E. LaFargue, *China's First Hundred: Educational Mission Students in the United States, 1872–1881* (Washington State University Press, 1987).

28. Jude Howell, *China Opens Its Door: The Politics of Economic Transition* (Boulder, CO: Lynne Reinner Publishers, 1993); and David Zweig, *Internationalizing China: Domestic Interests and Global Linkages* (Cornell University Press, 2002).

29. Kan Da, " '*Hai gui*' '*tu bie*' *wowo shou*" [Sea turtles' and 'ground beetles' (land turtles) should shake hands], *Zhongguo daxue sheng* [China Campus], no. 3 (2002), 17; also available at *Chinese Education and Society* 37, no. 2 (2004), pp. 12–14.

30. David Zweig, Chen Changgui and Stanley Rosen, "Transnational Human Capital: Returnees to China," in *Globalization and China's Reforms*, edited by David Zweig and Chen Zhimin (London: Routledge, 2007), pp. 204–22.

31. Zweig, "Returning to the Chinese Academy of Sciences." All findings significant at the .05 level.

32. Wang, *Talent War*, p. 279.

33. Kenneth Lieberthal, *Governing China* (New York: W. W. Norton, 2005).

34. Data on academic publications by CAS returnees that we have collected show that in 2011–12, and previous to 2009, the research quality of CAS returnees under its Hundred Talents Plan is much less than the quality of people joining universities under the Ministry of Education's Changjiang Program or people being awarded the Thousand Talents Award by the Organization Department of the CCP.

35. Zweig and Wang, "Can China Bring Back the Best?"

36. "SOE Job Fair Lures Talent," *China Daily*, December 22, 2004, p. 9.

37. *"Wei liuxue renyuan fuwu, wei liuxue gongzuo fuwu—fang zhongguo liuxue fuwu zhongxin zhuren, Bai Zhande"* [Serve overseas students, serve overseas study work—An interview with the director of the Chinese Overseas Students Service Center, Bai Zhangde], *Shenzou xueren* [China Scholars Abroad], no. 230 (April 20, 2009).

38. Guozheng Jiao, *"Pengbo fazhan de chuguo liuxue gongzuo"* [Flourishing development of the work of sending out overseas students], *Zhongguo gaodeng jiaoyu* [Higher Education in China, Beijing], no. 12 (1998), pp. 6–8.

39. Shiqi Huang, "Contemporary Educational Relations with the Industrialized World: A Chinese View," in *China's Education and the Industrialized World: Studies in Cultural Transfer*, edited by Ruth Hayhoe and Marianne Bastid (Armonk, N.Y.: M. E. Sharpe, 1987), pp. 227–28.

40. Paul Engelsberg, "Reversing China's Brain Drain: The Study Abroad Policy, 1978–1993," in *Great Policies: Strategic Innovations in Asia and the Pacific Basin*, edited by John D. Montgomery and Dennis A. Rondinelli (Westport, Conn.: Praeger, 1995), p. 102.

41. Ruiming Yang, "Pointing the Way to Reforming the Education System," *Liaowang* 23 (June 1985), 9–12, in *Foreign Broadcast Information Service-CHI*, June 26, 1985, pp. K11–17.

42. Engelsberg, "Reversing China's Brain Drain."

43. "Decision of the CC-CCP on Reform of the Educational System, 27 May 1985," *Foreign Broadcast Information Service-CHI*, May 30, 1985, pp. K1–11.

44. Leo A. Orleans, *Chinese Students in America: Policies, Issues, and Numbers* (Washington, D.C.: National Academy Press, 1988).

45. *Zhong Bao*, January 21, 1987, cited in Tom P. Bernstein, "China: Growth without Political Liberalization," in *Driven by Growth: Political Change in the Asia-Pacific Region, Revised Edition*, edited by James W. Morley (Armonk, N.Y.: M. E. Sharpe, 1999), p. 111.

46. Interview with former official in the State Education Commission, Cambridge, Mass., December 1989.

47. Ibid.

48. Dennis Harvest, "China Policy Shift on Study Overseas," *New York Times*, April 4, 1988.

49. Interview with a former official in the State Education Commission, Cambridge, Mass., December 1989.

50. Interview with a Wuhan education official, Hubei, China, 1991.

51. Interview with a former official in the State Education Commission, Cambridge, Mass., December 1989.

52. Xu Lin, lecture in Fairbank Center, Harvard University, December 1989.

53. AnnaLee Saxenian, *Silicon Valley's New Immigrant Entrepreneurs* (San Francisco, CA: Public Policy Institute of California, 1999).

54. This point is based on a conversation at the time between the author and a senior official in the Chinese embassy in Washington.

55. Wang, Renzhi, "On Opposing Bourgeois Liberalization," *Qiushi*, no. 3 (February 15, 1990); reprinted in *Foreign Broadcast Information Service*, February 23, 1990, pp. 12–23.

56. Guozheng Jiao, *"Pengbo fazhan de chuguo liuxue gongzuo"* [Flourishing development of the work of sending out overseas students].

57. Sheryl WuDunn, "China Weighs New Restrictions on Study Abroad," *New York Times*. October 18, 1989.

58. "Decline in Students Abroad," *China Daily*. February 20, 1991.

59. David Zweig and Chen Changgui, with Stanley Rosen, *China's Brain Drain to the United States: Views of Overseas Chinese Students and Scholars in the 1990s*, China Research Monograph Series (Berkeley, Calif.: Institute for East Asian Studies, 1995).

60. JPRS, "Internal Document on Overseas Student Policy," *Joint Publication Research Service, China,* August 31, 1990, pp. 17–23.

61. Danguo Miao, *Chuguo liuxue liushi nian* [Sixty years of overseas study] (Beijing: Zhongyang wenxian chubanshe, 2010), pp. 234–35.

62. Ibid., pp. 235–36.

63. Ibid., pp. 306–7.

64. Xinhua General News Service, "China to Improve Service for Returned Students," March 13, 1992.

65. "SEC Holds Work Conference, Decides to Relax Policies for Overseas Study," *Xinwen ziyou daobao* [Press Freedom Guardian], April 16, 1993, p. 1.

66. Miao, *Sixty Years*, p. 888.

67. Denis Fred Simon and Cong Cao, *China's Emerging Technological Edge: Assessing the Role of High-End Talent* (Cambridge University Press, 2010), p. 51.

68. Miao, *Sixty Years*, p. 425.

69. Jean-Baptiste Meyer et. al., "Turning Brain Drain into Brain Gain: The Colombian Experience of the Diaspora Option," *Science, Technology and Society* 2, no. 2 (1997).

70. "A Number of Opinions on Encouraging Overseas Students to Provide China with Many Different Forms of Service," *Renfa*, no. 49 (2001); reprinted in *Chinese Education and Society* 36, no. 2 (March–April 2003), pp. 6–11.

71. Xuefei Chen et. al., *Liuxue jiaoyu de chengben yu xiaoyi: Wo guo gaige kaifang yilai gong pai liuxue xiaoyi yanjiu* [The cost and efficiency of overseas study: Research on the efficiency of publicly sponsored overseas study since the opening of our country] (Beijing: Jiaoyu kexue chubanshe, 2003).

72. Miao, *Sixty Years*, p. 434.

73. Ibid., pp. 889–90.

74. Ibid., p. 897.

75. Ibid., p. 897.

76. National Science Foundation, Division of Science Resources Statistics, *Science and Engineering Indicators 2010*, appendix table 2-31 (http://www.nsf.gov/statistics/seind10/appendix.htm).

77. Dennis Normile, "Scientific Workforce: Many Overseas Chinese Researchers Find Coming Home a Revelation." *Science* 313, no. 5794 (2006), p. 1722.

78. Miao, *Sixty Years*, pp. 442–43.

79. China Economic Net, "Shanghai to Recruit Overseas Financial Talents" (http://en.ce.cn/National/Local/200912/05/t20091205_20562105.shtml).

80. Zweig and Wang, "Can China Bring Back the Best?"

81. *Zhongyang zuzhibu rencai gongzuo ju* [Central Organization Department's Bureau for the Work on Human Talent], "*Qian ren ji hua shishi zhuangkuang wenjuan diaocha zongshu*" [A summary of a survey on the implementation of the Thousand Talents Plan], *Zhongguo rencai* [China's Human Talent), October 2011, pp. 16–18.

82. Ibid., p. 18.

83. At that meeting, the author made his own presentation to Li Yuanchao on the Thousand Talents Plan and so observed these events. On the bus to the meeting, the author had already discussed with Li's two antagonists their concerns about the program.

84. E-mail from Stanley Rosen to the author, August 18, 2004.

85. Wang, *Talent War*, 2009.

86. These data were collected and analyzed by Kang Siqin, my RA at HKUST. Thanks, too, to the Chang Tseng-Hsi Foundation, as well as the Research Grants Council of Hong Kong's Prestigious Fellowship Award (2013–14), for financial support.

87. Zweig, "Returning to the Chinese Academy of Sciences."

88. There are thirty-one vice-ministry level universities under the Ministry of Education, but four of them are too specialized to have many returnees. So, we excluded them. The names of the universities in our sample are in Appendix 1.

89. Here overseas Ph.D. only includes those with at least four years overseas in a Ph.D. program. Joint programs that may include only one year of overseas study are excluded, as are honorific Ph.D. degrees granted by overseas universities.

90. Xinhua Wang (Xinhua website), *Xi Jinping zai Ou Mei Tonxue Hui chengli 100 zhou nian qingzhu dahui shang jianghua* [Xi Jinping's speech at the meeting to celebrate the 100th anniversary of the founding of the Western

Returnees Scholars Association], *China News,* October 23, 2013 (http://www.chinanews.com/gn/2013/10-21/5406110.shtml).

91. *"Guanyu renzhen xuexi xuanchuan guanche Xi Jinping Zongshuji zai Oumei Tongxue hui chengli 100 nian qingzhu dahui shang de zhongyao jianghua de tong-zhi"* [The notification concerning enthusiastically studying, propagandizing and carrying out the important speech by General Secretary Xi Jinping on the 100th anniversary of the WRSA] (http://www.wrsa.net, 2013-11-14).

92. Xinhuashe [Xinhua News Service], *"Zhonggong zhongyang bangongting yinfa, Guanyu jiaqiang Oumei Tongxue Hui (Liuxue renyuan lianyihui) jianshe de yijian"* [A publication of the views of the Central Committee Office on strengthening the construction of the Western Returned Students Association (WRSA)], August 3, 2016.

93. Still, some moderate voices working in the area of returnees say that some entrepreneurs see the CCP's efforts to work closely with the WRSA in a positive light, as it improves their status and means that more money will be spent to support them.

TWELVE

The Chinese Dream in Popular Culture

*China as Producer and Consumer of Films
at Home and Abroad*

STANLEY ROSEN

 A rising China, manifested most clearly in its steadily increasing role in the world economy, has begun to challenge the undisputed leadership of the United States in key arenas of world affairs. To take one example, despite direct pleas from the Obama administration, Europe's biggest economies and some of the key allies of the United States in Asia became founding members of a Chinese investment bank—the Asian Infrastructure Investment Bank (AIIB)—which, from the American point of view, poses a direct challenge to the World Bank and other American-led institutions that have exercised global economic dominance going back to the Bretton Woods conference in 1944.[1] China's ascent to become the world's second-largest economy is just one arena in which the emerging Asian giant has risen to second place. China's film market as well, growing around 35 percent a year, is now also the second largest, with expectations that it will surpass the flat North American market (the United

States and Canada) in 2017 or 2018. Indeed, in February 2015, during the lucrative Lunar New Year holiday when Hollywood and other foreign films are routinely barred from distribution, China's monthly box office earnings for the first time surpassed those of the United States.[2] Moreover, new milestones continue to be set. For example, *Fast and Furious 7*, which taps into middle-class obsessions with owning a car, took in 391 million renminbi (RMB) ($63.1 million) on its opening day on April 12, 2015, almost doubling the previous record of *Transformers 4: Age of Extinction*, which took in 194.8 million RMB on June 27, 2014.[3] *Furious 7* finished its run at $390 million, breaking the record of $320 million set by *Transformers 4* in 2014, although even that record has now been surpassed in 2016 by Stephen Chow's *The Mermaid (Meiren yu)*, which took in a staggering $526.8 million.[4]

Hollywood has achieved its success even with the obvious market manipulation intended to limit foreign film penetration and ensure that Chinese films generate over 50 percent of the domestic box office each year, in effect recognition that China's cultural products are less attractive than their foreign counterparts. Thus, just as a rising China has been frustrated by the continued monopolization of leadership roles by the West and Japan within established economic institutions, in the culture and media fields as well, highlighted by Hollywood's success in China and China's failure in overseas film markets, China has sought to devise strategies that will make their cultural productions more attractive to Western consumers, while at the same time limiting their own consumption of foreign culture.

Given China's global ambitions and the growing importance of the domestic Chinese market for their product, Hollywood studios have been virtually compelled to partner more closely with their Chinese counterparts; indeed, major Hollywood players, including both television and movie production units, have been signing deals and setting up joint ventures and co-financing projects with China at a record pace. Rather than continuing the current one-way street, in which Hollywood film, Western and Korean television series, and other foreign cultural products succeed in the Chinese market while Chinese cultural products are almost invisible abroad, Chinese media executives have been very clear on their goals. For example, Ren Zhonglun, president of the state-run Shanghai Film Group, told a Western reporter, "We want to learn how to make movies that appeal to a global audience," an aspiration often repeated by other Chinese film executives.[5]

This relationship between Hollywood and China, marked primarily by competition within China's domestic market, but increasingly revealing patterns of cooperation both domestically and internationally, is part of a wider competition that has become increasingly clear since late 2012, between the then newly minted "Chinese dream" and the long-established "American dream." While the Chinese dream, as is true of the American dream, is intended to appeal both to domestic and international constituencies, at present the competition has been manifested most directly *within* the Chinese domestic market, with the primary target audience Chinese youth—the so-called post-'80s and post-'90s generations—as well as the ever-expanding middle class, and their newly disposable income. As suggested above, the competition between the two dreams is most pronounced within the cultural field, particularly entertainment, as China has sought to expand to become a major content producer and not just a consumer of cultural products from abroad. Their efforts have to date been far more successful in their domestic market than overseas, but such success has required certain compromises with state-sanctioned values and, arguably, represents an acknowledgment of the power and seductiveness of the American dream, and foreign culture more generally.

Given the arguments to follow, it is important to note at the outset that a comparison between the Chinese and American dreams requires a disaggregation of the two dreams. For example, it should be clear that there is widespread support within China for China's rise and its foreign policy initiatives—indeed, for the pursuit of China's "national interest"—and widespread criticism of American foreign policy initiatives. At the same time, however, the American dream to this point appears to be more attractive to Chinese youth than its Chinese counterpart, with Chinese propaganda officials and China's leadership actively seeking to counter the enticements offered by the West. What this means in effect is that for Chinese youth there are *two* Chinas and *two* Americas, with Chinese youth strongly supporting China while sharply criticizing America on the international stage, but favoring America over China when it comes to cultural issues, particularly popular culture, and other aspects of domestic society including, based on compelling internal survey data from Chinese social scientists, the American political system.[6] Film box office and TV series viewership, as well as other documentary materials, some of which are discussed below, also support this conclusion.

In the course of the chapter I demonstrate a number of ironies and contradictions that mark this competition. First, as suggested above, despite the fact that the present and future rise of China to superpower status has been widely documented in public opinion studies, and American power appears to be declining, major aspects of the American dream still resonate with Chinese youth; indeed, the rise of the American dream in China has occurred precisely when the failures of the dream for American youth have been widely acknowledged. Second, and related to the first point, those promoting the Chinese dream and Chinese exceptionalism more broadly often begin with the superiority of Chinese culture, yet China has been losing the cultural war to the United States, not only internationally in terms of soft power projection, but also to a surprising extent domestically, an outcome that is particularly galling to those responsible for promoting Chinese culture. Third, as I note below, one major reason for the lack of Chinese success is a basic contradiction in Chinese cultural policy, which has multiple aims, including the production of culture that is consistent with "socialist values" and the Chinese dream, unlike the high-concept Hollywood films and other Western cultural products that are aimed to appeal universally, across all cultures, and simply to turn a profit. Moreover, in its efforts to "prove" that a China that has risen to superpower status will not imitate American hegemonist policies, China has attempted to demonstrate the country's *uniqueness*, which not surprisingly has limited its appeal outside the country;[7] ironically, this approach has also limited its appeal *within* China as well.

COMPARING DREAMS

Despite some quite obvious differences in content, the Chinese and American dreams are linked together in a number of important ways and are very much in competition for the affections of Chinese youth. Moreover, Chinese authorities have indirectly acknowledged the existence of this competition and have issued consistent warnings against the seductiveness of Western, primarily American, culture and values.[8] Indeed, there is some evidence that even the Chinese dream concept and discourse was stimulated in part by an article by *New York Times* columnist Thomas Friedman, who suggested in a column prior to the 18th Party Congress held in November 2012 that Xi Jinping needed to have a Chinese dream that was different from the American dream.[9] China's biggest circulation newspaper, *Reference News*, published a translation and, according to Xinhua, the Chinese dream "suddenly became a hot topic . . . at home and abroad."[10] After Xi began to use the phrase, a magazine published by Xinhua called Xi's idea "the best response to Friedman."[11]

Discussions of the American dream are long-standing in the literature on American history and culture, and are often linked with American exceptionalism. While there are variations and the meaning has changed over time, the dream generally has included such aspects as freedom, upward mobility, equality, and home ownership, although perhaps James Truslow Adams, the "godfather" of the American dream discourse, put it best when he wrote "the *American Dream*, that dream of a land in which life should be better and richer and fuller for everyone, with opportunity for each according to ability or achievement . . . regardless of the fortuitous circumstances of birth or position."[12]

In contrast to the American dream, the Chinese dream, at least in its current form, is a new initiative, although the themes of building a rich and powerful China have been a part of various reform movements for over one hundred years. Its most recent iteration and current meaning can be traced to the visit by Xi and six other members of the standing committee of the Politburo to the Revolutionary History Museum to view "The Road toward Renewal" exhibition on November 29, 2012. In Xi's speech introducing the Chinese dream he spoke of "the great rejuvenation of the Chinese nation" and emphasized how the humiliations suffered by China since the nineteenth century due to weakness and backwardness would soon be over, that China was "now closer than ever to the goal of . . . national revival."[13] Right from the start, therefore, unlike the American dream, the Chinese dream has been more about the nation than about the individual. To be sure, everyone is also encouraged to have his or her own dream,[14] and it is instructive to examine through the available survey data whether these individual dreams fit within the larger narrative of a collective dream for China. However, commentaries in the official media make it clear that the Chinese dream is about patriotism and collectivism more than personal struggles, and that its realization relies on Party leadership.[15]

Not surprisingly, the Chinese media has sought to distinguish the two dreams, and has been quite consistent in pointing out the differences. One of the most useful comparisons, published in a restricted circulation journal by Shi Yuzhi, a Chinese academic in Singapore, points out seven differences between the Chinese and American dreams, with the clear message that the two dreams are based on very different geographical and historical experiences, and while the American dream is based on individual efforts and individual success, the Chinese dream unites the individual and the state in an indivisible whole.[16] For example, he notes that since ancient times China has always had the concept of the country as a family (*jiaguo*), with a strong collective consciousness so that happiness can only be shared together (*gongxiang*), both for the family and the state. On the other hand, European and American culture stresses individualism and the pursuit of individual freedom and success. In addition, since the Opium War, China and its people have struggled and paid a heavy price in dealing with adversity, while America has not felt this kind of pain. Therefore the Chinese dream must be for the glory of the nation (*minzu*) while the American dream stresses individual prosperity, success and a rise in social status. As Shi concludes, this means that the Chinese dream cannot separate the individual from the nation; they are like two feet on the same body.

Although he does not state it directly, his analysis makes it clear that whereas the Chinese dream calls for a great deal of self-sacrifice for the interests of the nation, the American dream offers an individual success without reference to the nation or any collective force beyond his or her own efforts. Survey and public opinion research reveal how individual values currently prevalent in China make the state-sanctioned values highlighted in the Chinese dream such a hard sell when juxtaposed against American or Western values. For example, a global survey conducted by the French public opinion firm Ipsos, published in December 2013, found that happiness is more tied to material possession in China than anywhere else. Globally, 34 percent of 16,000 people across twenty countries said they measured their success by the things they owned; in China the percentage was more than double the global average, reaching as high as 71 percent. In addition, two out of three Chinese respondents noted they felt "under a lot of pressure to be successful and make money," more than in any other surveyed country.[17] *Shanghai Daily* ran a weekly series asking respondents from different generations to discuss their own dreams.[18] For the youngest generations, the results likewise showed the importance of materialism and individual goals. One interviewee from each generation was highlighted. The youngest participant, a six-year-old, said, "My dream is to study in America, to play piano better than Lang Lang and give concerts all over the world." Those born in the 1980s and 1990s expressed a similar emphasis on material success. For example, the representative of twenty-something Chinese noted, "My dream is to find a good husband who is honest, economically stable, owns a downtown apartment and has a car."

CHINA AS A FILM PRODUCER AND CONSUMER IN THE DOMESTIC MARKET

The detailed discussion above comparing the Chinese and American dreams and the importance of materialism for a younger generation, which, in contrast to their elders, has been raised in an era of relative prosperity, is meant to provide some context to the decisions Chinese film and political authorities have made with regard to the promotion of the film industry. In the intense competition with

Hollywood for market share, the local films that have done best have generally been broad or romantic comedies in which material success is highlighted, or action films with impressive special effects, a well-known feature of Hollywood films. At the same time, there has been an attempt to balance the pure entertainment by producing "main melody films" (*zhu xuan lv*), focusing on the Party's revolutionary history and political icons, albeit with very limited success. Faced with a choice between using film to foster state-sanctioned "socialist core values," to use the terminology of film bureaucrats, or winning the box office battle with Hollywood, the latter goal has proven far more compelling than the former.

The growth of China's domestic film market has been a remarkable success story, as figure 12-1 demonstrates. Hollywood was invited to enter China's theatrical film market in 1994 with the Warner Brothers film *The Fugitive* at a time when the Chinese domestic box office had reached its nadir and needed to be "rescued," but Hollywood's success was at first limited, primarily by a quota system that permitted only ten foreign-language films a year, but also by issues of censorship, including a ban on three major Hollywood studios in 1997 because of "anti-China bias" in specific films never intended for distribution in China. In addition, Hollywood had to accept a revenue-sharing system that limited their box office share to 10–13 percent of box office receipts, far less than in other markets. By 2000, despite a massive effort, the annual return from China was only about $20 million, roughly the size of the return from Peru, and less than returns from Singapore, Malaysia, Thailand, or the Philippines.[19] By contrast, given the market today, no Hollywood studio can afford to make a major film without first considering the reception in China, and it has become common for blockbuster films to add "China-friendly" components to help ensure success in that market. *Transformers 4: Age of Extinction* which, although since surpassed, became the most successful film of all time in China after its release in 2014, used Hong Kong locations, Chinese actors, and the product placement of Chinese brands as part of its appeal.

Moreover, as noted in figure 12-2, by 2017 or 2018 China is likely to replace North America as the largest film market in the world. These trends have had an enormous influence on Hollywood's rela-

FIGURE 12-1. China's Domestic Box Office Share of
Worldwide Box Office, 2005–20 (estimate)

Percent

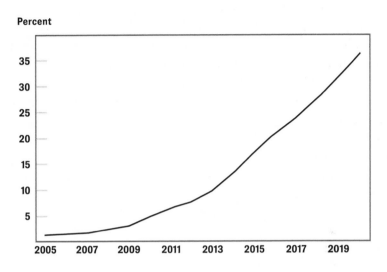

Source: Rob Cain, "Faster and Furiouser: China's Q1 Box Office Review," April 8, 2015 (chinafilmbiz.com).

tionship with China, as well as China's overall film market strategy. Given the success of Chinese films at home and their lack of success outside China—to be discussed below—it might be expected that film authorities would be willing to forego the overseas market and simply concentrate on the competition with Hollywood in China's domestic market. Indeed, no film industry has been able to compete with Hollywood on the world market, much less within North America's own market. However, Chinese ambitions are not simply based on box office results in film markets, but include a strong desire to project a positive image of China abroad and to demonstrate that depictions of Chinese culture have an appeal beyond the country's borders.

In order to combat the Hollywood juggernaut within China, a number of strategies have been adopted, ranging from the quota system mentioned above, which has now been raised to thirty-four foreign-language films, most of which are from Hollywood, with fourteen of the thirty-four reserved for IMAX or 3-D films; blackout dates to reserve the busiest times of the year for domestic productions;

FIGURE 12-2. Projected Annual Box Office,
China versus North America, 2014–20

Billions of U.S. Dollars

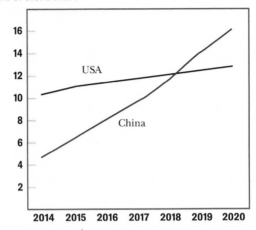

Source: Rob Cain, "Faster and Furiouser: China's Q1 Box Office Review," April 8, 2015 (chinafilmbiz.com).

the release of two Hollywood blockbusters on the same date, or a delay in the release of a blockbuster until after its appearance in other markets; an often "benign neglect" to the problem of illegal downloading or piracy; the removal of Hollywood films while they were still successfully generating income; and manipulating box office receipts in favor of domestic films, particularly "patriotic" films that cannot succeed based simply on consumer demand. The goal of keeping Hollywood's market share below 50 percent each year has been successful, as table 12-1 makes clear. However, the table does not fully reveal the relative success of Hollywood films in China. China produced 638 theatrical feature films in 2013,[20] 618 in 2014, and 686 in 2015, although many of these never make it into first-run theaters. In 2013, for example, only 250 feature films, including imports, coproductions, and Hong Kong and Taiwan films actually made it into a theater that was part of a theater chain, although the number of domestic films shown in such venues increased to 259 in 2014 and 320 in 2015.[21] By contrast, in 2014 the foreign titles that made up the thirty-four-film quota—virtually all of which were

TABLE 12-1. Box Office Comparison between Domestic and Imported Films from 2007–15

Year	Domestic films, U.S. dollars	Market percentage	Imported films, U.S. dollars	Market percentage
2007	291 million	52.5	263 million	47.5
2008	421 million	60.0	280 million	40.0
2009	566 million	56.5	436 million	43.5
2010	926 million	56.4	717 million	43.6
2011	1.135 billion	53.6	982 million	46.4
2012	1.336 billion	48.5	1.421 billion	51.5
2013	2.061 billion	58.6	1.454 billion	41.4
2014	2.65 billion	54.5	2.17 billion	45.5
2015[a]	4.17 billion	61.6	2.61 billion	38.4

Box office above 100 million yuan

Domestic films	Imported films
3	4
9	3
12	8
17	10
20	18
22	21
32	28
36	30
48	33

Sources: For regular domestic and imported films, 2007–13: *China Film Industry Report 2013-2014* (Shared version), EntGroup Inc., January 2014, p. 8 (online). For films that brought in more than 100 million yuan, 2007–12: *2012-2013 nian Zhongguo dianying chanye yanjiu baogao* [China Film Industry Research Report 2012–2013], Yi en zixun [EntGroup Inc.], March 2013, p. 36 (online). Remaining data, except for 2015, are from *Zhongguo dianying chanye yanjiu baogao, 2014* [The Research Report on China Film Industry, 2014] (Beijing: Zhongguo dianying chubanshe, 2014), pp. 239-246; Clifford Coonan, "China's Box Office Surges 36 percent in 2014 to $4.76 Billion," *The Hollywood Reporter*, January 1, 2015 (online). All data from 2015 are from *Zhongguo dianying chanye yanjiu baogao, 2016* [The Research Report on China Film Industry, 2016] (Beijing: Zhongguo dianying chubanshe, 2016), p. 32; *Variety*, December 31, 2015 (online); the 4.76 billion reported in 2015 was adjusted to 4.82 billion in this report.

a. For 2015 the top twenty-eight imported films were all IMAX and/or 3-D, which was true for ten of the top fourteen domestic films.

TABLE 12-2. China Yearly Box Office, 2016, as of August[a]

Rank	Movie title	Gross	Release
1	*The Mermaid*	$526,848,189	2/8
2	***Zootopia***	$235,591,000	3/4
3	***Warcraft***	$220,841,090	6/8
4	***Captain America: Civil War***	$190,429,000	5/6
5	*The Monkey King 2 in 3D*	$185,402,420	2/8
6	*From Vegas to Macau 3*	$172,104,369	2/8
7	***Kung Fu Panda 3***	$154,304,371	1/29
8	***The Jungle Book***	$150,140,000	4/15
9	*Skiptrace*	$133,103,621	7/21
10	*Time Raiders*	$127,034,013	8/5
11	***Star Wars: The Force Awakens***	$124,159,138	1/9
12	*Ip Man 3*	$124,101,198	3/4
13	***X-Men: Apocalypse***	$120,765,095	6/3

Source: www.boxofficemojo.com.

a. Hollywood films are shown in bold type; *Kung Fu Panda* was a coproduction between DreamWorks Animation, its Chinese unit Oriental DreamWorks, and their Chinese partners, which include China Media Capital, Shanghai Media Group, and Shanghai Alliance.

Hollywood films—grossed $1.81 billion, around 38 percent of the total.[22] Table 12-2, which lists the top thirteen box office hits for 2016 (as of August), with Hollywood films in bold, provides a good indication of the latter's appeal. Indeed, when the Chinese box office suffered a 4.6 percent drop in the second quarter of 2016, the first full quarter drop in over half a decade, the government took the unprecedented step of letting a few Hollywood movies into the market in July, a period usually reserved for local productions, although that did not prevent a further 18 percent drop in the film market in July, compared to the year before.[23]

The competition in the film industry for the domestic market is part of a larger competition China confronts as it seeks to temper and control the dissemination of Western culture, which has become particularly popular among university students and the rising middle class. Wang Zhonglei, the cofounder of Huayi Brothers, one of China's leading film production companies, noted that 44 percent of the film audience in China can be found among those between the ages of eighteen and twenty-four, while another 7 percent is made up of those between the ages of thirteen and seventeen.[24] One recent survey that has received a considerable amount of attention within China focused on those Chinese who have already become "internationalized," the so-called Generation of International Floaters (*Guojipiao yidai*).[25] Conducted in 2013 and covering 4,900 people in sixty-two cities, the study found that the post-1980s generation constituted 59.3 percent of these "floaters," while the post-1990s generation made up 18.6 percent. By comparison, those from the post-1970s generation made up 13.8 percent, with earlier generations making up only 8.1 percent. It is not surprising that almost 80 percent of this new group consists of young people since educational attainment is an important criterion, with the large majority either having already studied abroad or with future plans to do so. Among this group, 29.9 percent plan to go abroad for a vacation each year. As many as 53.3 percent like to watch English-language films *without* Chinese subtitles and to use foreign websites such as Facebook and Twitter, which are banned in China. They favor international brand-name products because of their high quality and durability, and prefer to drink Starbucks and Chivas Regal and to drive Volkswagens, Audis, and Fords. Recognizing the attractiveness of the foreign, Chinese entrepreneurs have built hotels in China with names like Marvelot (using the same Chinese characters as the Marriott), Haiyatt, and Peninsula.[26]

In terms of popular culture, as many as 67.4 percent prefer English and American TV series, with only 20.8 percent choosing Chinese domestic shows. American shows that were particularly popular included *The Big Bang Theory* (likely the most popular show since it has reportedly been streamed more than 1.3 billion times over the past five years), *The Vampire Diaries*, and *2 Broke Girls*. Other recent popular shows include *House of Cards*, the British show *Sherlock*, and *Masters of Sex*. It is important to note that many of the most popular shows have been legally licensed and shown on streaming sites, which have been less subject to censorship than regular TV. According to the

Chinese entertainment research firm EntGroup, in 2012 Sohu had 144 American and British TV shows available for streaming, Tencent had 123 shows and Youku Tudou had 109, suggesting that the influence of these channels of distribution are even more important in introducing Western culture to China than regular TV or theatrical films. This "loophole" in the censorship system had allowed Chinese viewers to watch shows with the type of violence, scandal, superstition, or other sensitive themes that would not otherwise be approved. However, this loophole has now been closed since new rules announced in September 2014 and implemented in April 2015 require video sites such as Sohu.com and Baidu's iQiyi, previously left to police themselves, to submit episodes to censors for approval only once the full seasons have aired. Seasons beginning in September and ending in May in the United States won't be legally available to Chinese Internet users until June at the earliest, and then only after censorship. The restrictions are a setback for foreign media companies such as 21st Century Fox and CBS, which have struck licensing deals with Sohu, iQiyi, and Youku Tudou, and will likely stimulate a revival of piracy through illegal downloading and illicit DVD sales.[27]

Perhaps equally telling is the impact of globalization on even the most popular Chinese TV programs among post-1980s youth and other international floaters. Five of the top ten TV shows revealed by the survey, including the top three, were Chinese versions of foreign programs, often with copyrights, which have been purchased. And even some of the "pure" Chinese programs on the list have foreign components, for example a South Korean host, a program introducing foreign culture, or an obvious rip-off of a foreign show that did not receive copyright approval. Nor are the foreign influences in Chinese popular culture solely Western. By far the most popular program—chosen by over 40 percent of respondents, with 75 million viewers per episode and a number one national ranking—was the Hunan Provincial TV reality travel show *Where Are We Going, Dad?*, a Chinese remake of a Korean show. In addition, the enormous popularity of the South Korean drama *My Love from the Star* (*Laizi xingxing de ni*) which, although never broadcast on a major network, had over three billion viewers on major Internet sites, and sparked a craze in China for Korean-style fried chicken served with beer, after the female star was repeatedly shown eating the meal in the show.

Well aware of the craze the drama has created in China, one member of the Chinese People's Political Consultative Committee (CPPCC) complained that, "It is more than just a Korean soap opera. It hurts our cultural dignity," openly wondering why China could not make a show as good or as big of a hit.[28] The number two show was the Zhejiang Provincial TV program *The Voice of China*, a reality talent show based on the Dutch program *The Voice of Holland*. When released in February 2016, *Descendants of the Sun* (*Taiyang de houyi*) was equally popular, with even more direct warnings from the Ministry of Public Security on the dangers of watching Korean dramas.[29]

However, even these impressive figures do not reveal the full impact of globalization on the Chinese film and TV markets. For example, the eighth-largest hit in 2014 was the Chinese film version of the TV show *Where Are We Going, Dad?* In addition, among the top ten Chinese films in 2013 were *Finding Mr. Right*, loosely based on *Sleepless in Seattle*, in which the leading characters successfully pursue the American dream by leaving China for Seattle; *Tiny Times*, which has been compared to a Chinese version of *Sex and the City*, without the sex; and *American Dreams in China*, which is based on the true story of a successful Beijing school set up to teach English to Chinese who wanted to study in the United States. Despite—or perhaps because of—their popularity, the government has begun to crack down on some of the most popular TV shows. For example, new regulations issued in 2016 stipulated that children, especially children of celebrities, could no longer be featured on Chinese reality television, ostensibly to protect children from the pitfalls of overnight fame. This restriction seemed particularly aimed at the aforementioned *Where Are We Going, Dad?* and Zhejiang TV's similar *Dad Is Back*, both of which featured children of celebrities.[30]

CHINA AS A FILM PRODUCER FOR THE OVERSEAS MARKET

As suggested above, the competition with Hollywood for China's domestic market has been a major story, both in China and the United States. Less often discussed is the competition overseas, including the lucrative North American market.[31] If the issue were only box office results, a strong case could be made that pursuing overseas success, particularly in the highly developed North American and European markets, could not yield a winning strategy.[32] However, the rise of China internationally is considered incomplete without the strong promotion of Chinese cultural products outside the country's borders, in part because of the leadership's concern that China's image is being distorted by Western media and that the delivery of China's message can only be entrusted to Chinese media.

There was a time when there was considerable optimism over the prospects for Chinese-language films in North America and Europe, particularly in the wake of the success of *Crouching Tiger, Hidden Dragon*, which brought in $128 million at the box office in the United States and Canada, still more than twice as much as any foreign-language film has ever made in that market. This was followed by the box office success of such films as *Hero, Fearless, Kung Fu Hustle, Iron Monkey*, and *House of Flying Daggers*, all still among the top twenty-five foreign-language films ever marketed in North America. At the time the last of these successes was being released, around ten years ago, it appeared that martial arts films in Chinese were China's best hope to penetrate the North American and other Western markets. However, China has not had any notable successes in this market after 2006. Indeed, with rare exceptions, no recent foreign-language films have been box office successes.

This has required the search for new strategies to try and find a genre or formula that might succeed. One approach, adopted by Zhang Yimou and Feng Xiaogang, generally considered to be China's most successful directors, is the use of prominent Hollywood actors such as Christian Bale, Donald Sutherland, Adrien Brody, and Tim Robbins in their films, albeit still without positive results.[33] A second strategy, applied by Western distributors rather than Chinese film companies themselves, has been to take an action or martial arts film that has been successful in China and parts of Asia and reconfigure it—in effect to "dumb it down"—for Western audiences unfamiliar with Chinese history, culture, and Chinese film aesthetics. A classic example was *Red Cliff* (*Chi bi*), a five-hour film on the Three Kingdoms period that was released separately in two parts and had been a big hit not only in China, but also in Japan and

South Korea. For the American version the distributor released a highly truncated single film with a running time of 148 minutes, primarily focused on the thrilling naval battle that occurs in Part 2, leaving out the long back story in Part 1 on the complex interrelationships among the major historical players. Despite the fact that the well-known John Woo, who has directed such American blockbusters as *Mission Impossible II* and *Face/Off*, directed it, the film made only $627,047 in North America.

This strategy is most closely associated with producer Harvey Weinstein, who has had previous success in bringing Chinese films to North America and promoting them with extensive advertising in print and broadcast media. Nicknamed "Harvey Scissorhands," the list of films he has altered in an effort to expand their market, and his feuds with the original creators of these films, have become legendary.[34] His most recent attempt featured Hong Kong auteur Wong Kar Wai's *The Grandmaster* (*Yidai zongshi*), one of many films about Ip Man, best known as the martial arts teacher of Bruce Lee. In a familiar pattern, for its North American release Weinstein had the film reedited to cut out twenty-two minutes, used intertitles to explain Chinese history, had an on-screen identification of characters, and a voiceover by lead actor Tony Leung. *The Grandmaster* did prove to be the most successful Chinese film marketed in North America since 2006, bringing in $6.5 million at the box office, ranking number forty-six among all foreign-language films since 1980. Moreover, unlike other Chinese-language films marketed in North America in recent years, which generally are shown only in Chinese communities in large cities and play on fewer than thirty screens during their theatrical run, *The Grandmaster* played on 804 screens, including those in communities with few Chinese residents. But very few, if any, Chinese films can afford the advertising budget allocated to Wong's film; indeed, the majority of the films from China are released by the Chinese distributor China Lion, which chooses Chinese blockbusters that have been highly successful in China and limits their distribution to Chinese communities. It is therefore not surprising that, *Grandmaster* aside, even the most successful Chinese blockbusters, with a few rare exceptions, bring in less than $1.5 million, often much less.[35]

The reception of the *Detective Dee* films are a good indication of the changes in the last decade for Chinese action and martial arts films. Receiving outstanding reviews in such prestigious publications as the *New York Times*, the first *Detective Dee* film opened in September 2011, played on forty-eight screens, and brought in about $460,000 at the box office. The second film in the series, which opened two years later in September 2013, played on thirty-five screens but brought in less than $88,000. In his review of the first film, A. O. Scott suggested one of the crucial obstacles faced by any foreign-language film in this market, when he noted: "In a utopian, borderless world without subtitles, the arrival of *Detective Dee and the Mystery of the Phantom Flame* would be a global, multiplex event, and the work of its director, Tsui Hark, would be at least as well known among American seekers of cinematic thrills as that of Jerry Bruckheimer and Michael Bay."[36] The problem, of course, is that we don't live in such a world, and distributors and theater owners, whether it is a martial arts film or a broad comedy, view any subtitled film as an art-house film. This situation is not new; when the production manager for Feng Xiaogang's film *Be There or Be Square (Bujian busan)*, which was shot in Los Angeles, made the rounds in Hollywood to seek American distribution, he was told that, at best, it could only be marketed as an art-house film. When he protested that the film was directed by China's most popular director and starred two very famous actors, and was a cross-cultural comedy that would have broad appeal, he was again asked the language of the film. He reiterated that it was in Chinese, and that ended the conversation.[37] It is this perception of Chinese films, and foreign-language films more generally, that is so prevalent today that makes the earlier success of Chinese martial arts films from 2000 to 2006 all the more striking.

The current strategy that is favored by Chinese film officials and indeed has had the most success in promoting Chinese films in overseas markets is an emphasis on coproductions. For example, in 2013, the top seven films and nine of the top ten Chinese films in overseas markets were coproductions.[38] In examining those coproductions that made at least 100 million Chinese yuan at the box office, 70 percent have been action films, which translate best in world markets, while no other genre makes up more than 20 percent.[39] China's promotion of coproductions was clearly seen in the choice of *The Nightingale* as its foreign-language Oscar submission in 2014. While many had expected Zhang Yimou's *Coming Home* or Diao Yinan's Golden Bear winner at Berlin, *Black Coal, Thin Ice*, to be the choice, the small-budget remake by French director Philippe Muyl of one of his earlier films surprised even the filmmaker who, when asked about the decision at a preview screening in Los Angeles, had no idea why his film was chosen, other than the fact that it was a coproduction.[40] By contrast, a very small number of films do lend themselves particularly well to coproductions and are virtually guaranteed a successful box office in China and overseas. The most prominent example, as will be noted below, is *Kungfu Panda 3*, which was awarded coproduction status on January 15, 2015.[41]

There are, however, reasons to be cautious in noting the limits on the success of coproductions where the coproduction partner is not within "Greater China." First, from 2002 to 2012, 68.5 percent (293 films) of coproductions have been partnered with Hong Kong, while another 11.7 percent were with Taiwan, making up over 80 percent of all coproductions. The United States followed with 8.6 percent, although as will be noted below, even that relatively low figure is a bit misleading. The trend continued in 2013, when eight of the top ten films were coproductions with Hong Kong.[42] For 2015, thirty-eight of the sixty-one coproductions (62.3 percent) approved for release were with Hong Kong, with an additional five having a partner from Taiwan.[43] Second, as figure 12-3 reveals, the high tide for coproductions took place earlier, between 2008 and 2010, with steep declines in 2011 (42.5 percent) and 2012 (47.5 percent), before an upward trajectory for 2013, 2014, and 2015, which still left the results well short of the figure for 2010, when Chinese films abroad made more than 3.5 billion yuan ($500 million).[44] The clear reason for the decline was the lack of coproductions with Hollywood. The earlier successes were largely due to a single film each year. For example, *Mummy 3* (2009) made 1.15 billion yuan overseas, which accounted for 41 percent of the box office for all Chinese films abroad that year. *Red Cliff 2* was a distant second at 650 million yuan. *Karate Kid* (2010) made more than 2.36 billion yuan overseas, making up 67.9 percent of the box office of all Chinese films overseas that year; in second place was *Ip Man 2*,

FIGURE 12-3. Changes in the Overseas Box Office
Revenues of Chinese Films, 2006–15

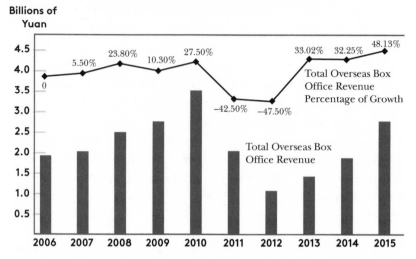

Sources: For 2006–12, Yi en zixun, *2012–2013 nian zhongguo dianying chanye yanjiu baogao* [EntGroup Consulting, Chinese Film Industry Research Report 2012–2013], p. 200; for 2013, *Zhongguo dianying chanye yanjiu baogao, 2014* [The Research Report on the Chinese Film Industry, 2014], p. 32; for 2014, *2014 Zhongguo dianying ying-xiaofei 36 yi, 19–40 sui guanzhong gongxian 87% piaofang* [Sohu Entertainment, Chinese Film Marketing Fees in 2014 Are 3.6 Billion Yuan; 19–40 Year Olds Make up 87% of the Box Office], January 6, 2015 (online); for 2015, *Zhongguo dianying chanye yanjiu baogao, 2015* [The Research Report on the Chinese Film Industry, 2016], p. 47.

with only 218 million yuan. However, one could argue that *Mummy 3* and *Karate Kid* were really Hollywood films disguised as Chinese co-productions, and indeed Chinese microblogs contained many criticisms of these two films for presenting a poor image of the country to foreigners. Moreover, the Chinese in *Karate Kid* were far more benign in the version shown only in China, reflecting the problems with coproductions that have to meet the demands of multiple markets.

This dilemma has openly surfaced on a number of occasions, particularly with the introduction of politically correct requirements in a manner virtually guaranteed to produce a result counterproductive to state intentions. In discussing the film industry, which Chinese officials have openly stated is facing a war with Hollywood,[45]

Politburo member and Director of the Propaganda (Publicity) Department of the Central Committee of the CCP, Liu Qibao, has praised the success of Chinese films in the domestic market and noted that China should also become an international movie power, but at the same time he has called for the country's films to take "socialist core values as a guide" and "contain more elements of the Chinese dream."[46] Liu's comments may appeal to Xi Jinping and his colleagues on the Politburo, but they reflect a lack of knowledge of audience preferences. When political considerations have trumped audience demands, the result has been embarrassing, whether it is the removal of *Avatar* from Chinese theaters early to accommodate the patriotic film *Confucius*, or the release of three Lei Feng films in 2013 to commemorate Lei Feng Day on March 5. The decision to promote *Confucius* was even ridiculed in the official press while theater owners made it widely known that they couldn't sell a single ticket for the Lei Feng films.[47] Clearly, such a policy has even less hope of succeeding on the highly competitive international market.

CONCLUSION

Chinese leaders are well aware of the success of the American dream, so successfully propagated by Hollywood films, and Western ideas more generally among Chinese youth, and there have been repeated warnings about the dangers of the West's assault on Chinese culture and ideology; the problem has been to devise a strategy to counteract such influence. One plank in the strategy has been to assert repeatedly that the concept of the "two Americas" is a myth, that Hollywood works closely in concert with the American government to infiltrate subversive ideas into China and undermine the Chinese political system through what in earlier political campaigns in the Dengist era had been called "peaceful evolution" (*heping yanbian*). Their best opportunity occurred in May 1999 when NATO forces, led by the United States, bombed the Chinese Embassy in Belgrade, Yugoslavia, during the war in Kosovo, killing three Chinese citizens. The Chinese media went into overdrive trying to link the hegemonist United States with the cultural United States, asserting that everything from American blockbuster films to the promotion of human rights and globalization, as well as Western civilization more generally, was part of a deliberate conspiracy by America to control the world. While this analysis had an immediate impact in the aftermath of the bombing, with busloads of university students driven to the American Embassy in Beijing to throw rocks, student calls to boycott McDonald's and KFC, and students publicly tearing up their admission letters to American universities, surveys done not long afterward revealed that while the anger at the hegemonist United States continued, the spillover effect into cultural issues was short-lived, that the concept of what the surveyors called "the two Americas," was still applicable.[48]

Many of the obstacles China faces in combating Western influence are so embedded within the Chinese political system and traditional culture that they will be difficult to overcome, and are indeed reflected in the respective dreams discussed above. The clearest example of this is the Chinese emphasis on the collective over the individual, which was strikingly evident in the response within China to Chinese writer Mo Yan's success in winning the 2012 Nobel Prize for Literature. As the first "mainstream" Chinese writer to be accorded such an honor, which has also eluded scientists who are citizens of the PRC, it was not surprising that Mo Yan's victory was front-page news within China. However, while Mo Yan noted that it was an individual prize and suggested that it was unlikely to have a lasting impact on Chinese literature or even the popularity of his own works,[49] local officials in his hometown of Gaomi in eastern Shandong province emphasized the value of the prize for the larger community. Within a week they announced plans to spend 670 million RMB ($107 million) to transform Mo Yan's home village into a "Red Sorghum Culture and Experience Zone," and have local residents cultivate the red sorghum that had already been proven to be unprofitable. As a local official noted to Mo's ninety-year-old father, "Your son is no longer your son, and the house is no longer your house" since your son is now the pride of China. "It does not really matter if you agree or not."[50] An official from the local tourism bureau explained that provincial authorities ordered Gaomi to execute the tourism program regardless of how Mo Yan and his family felt about it.[51] This same issue explains why a Chinese sports superstar such as Li Na could only become successful internationally once she left the Chinese national team and left the country, and how there is still a love-hate relationship between her and Chinese tennis officials.[52]

Despite the obstacles noted above, there are a number of countervailing trends that suggest some optimism for the Chinese film industry. First and most obvious, in comparison to almost any market outside of India, China has done an excellent job in competing with Hollywood domestically, albeit succeeding in part through the use of non-market administrative mechanisms. Second, even in the overseas market, recent initiatives suggest at least the possibility of greater success. Most prominently, Zhang Yimou's decision to make a blockbuster action film in English—a language he does not speak—offers one possible solution to the lack of success of Chinese films overseas. However, assuming that Zhang's film does well in world markets, it is worth asking whether this should be seen as victory for the Chinese film industry or, rather, an admission of defeat. When Zhang was attached to an earlier English-language project—*Quasimodo*, based on *The Hunchback of Notre Dame*—one could certainly argue that directing a film in the English language taken from a very famous Western novel with top American stars was not a step forward for the Chinese film industry, despite the individual success it would bring Zhang himself. He would simply join many foreign directors who were seduced by Hollywood. However, his new project, budgeted at $150 million and entitled *The Great Wall*, despite the sci-fi components and A-list Hollywood stars, should contain the appropriate Chinese cultural content that can enhance the positive image that the Chinese government has tried so assiduously to promote. At the same time, apart from Ang Lee and probably John Woo, there are no other Chinese directors that would be entrusted with such a large project, so it again appears to be an individual achievement rather than a long-term strategy for Chinese film abroad.

Third, China's best chance for overseas success may be in animation since films for young audiences with cartoon characters will be dubbed into local languages and face fewer issues of censorship than more adult fare. DreamWorks Animation, with an investment of $330 million to set up the joint venture Oriental DreamWorks in Shanghai in 2012, is a pioneer in this regard. *Kung Fu Panda 3*, budgeted around $140 million, opened as a coproduction over the coveted Chinese New Year holiday in 2016, a period usually reserved for domestic films, and went on to gross $154 million in China, $144 million in North America, with a worldwide total of $520 million. Significantly, there were separate scripts in Mandarin and English, with the former shown only in China, which is also be the case for two additional animated films currently under preparation at the company.[53]

Finally, as indicated in the DreamWorks model above, the relationship between Hollywood and China is becoming far more complex and intertwined, which suggests that new models for promoting Chinese films abroad are just in their early stages. For example, the prominent Taiwan-born American director Justin Lin was listed as one of the coproducers and co-screenwriters of a film set in Los Angeles entitled *Hollywood Adventures*, with prominent Chinese stars as well as lesser-known American actors. Budgeted at $30 million, it was the largest Chinese language movie to film in Southern California and is part of the strategy of producer Bruno Wu and his partners to make Chinese films that look like Hollywood films, with local American crews and American directors.[54] However, aside from China, the film played theatrically in only a few Asian markets, with no American release, making $51.6 million in China, only ranking forty-fourth among all releases in China in 2015.[55] Another development worth watching is the entry of Alibaba Pictures into the filmmaking business, with the company's first film—*The Ferryman* (*Bai du ren*) as of mid-2016 still in postproduction—a comedy produced and co-written by Wong Kar Wai and best-selling author Zhang Jiajia (also a first-time director), and starring Tony Leung and a prominent Asian cast.[56] Alibaba founder Jack Ma has noted in interviews how he appreciates the difference between American and Chinese heroes, indirectly suggesting that his company could potentially produce films emulating the successful American model.[57] Perhaps *Furious 7*, cited at the beginning of this paper, is the best example of the new complex relationship between China and Hollywood. On the one hand, Chinese regulators monitored its enormous success, concerned that it could skew the box office too strongly in favor of foreign films and, indeed, there is evidence of box office deceit in attempts to promote Chinese films over their Hollywood competition.[58] On the other hand, the state-owned China Film Group had a stake reported at around 10 percent in this film and, since they control distribution within China, ensured a strong screen presence for the film—reaching more than 70 percent of all screens in its first week—and therefore benefited financially when the film broke all previous box office records, showing yet again the contradictions that mark the Chinese film industry.[59]

NOTES

1. Andrew Higgins and David E. Sanger, "3 European Powers Say They Will Join China-Led Bank," *New York Times*, March 18, 2015, p. A4; "U.S. Allies, Lured by China's Bank" (editorial), *New York Times*, March 20, 2015, p. A26. Other American allies, including Australia and South Korea, were expected to follow.

2. "China Tops U.S. At the Box Office," *New York Times*, March 3, 2015, p. C3. China's box office revenue that month totaled $650 million, while the U.S. revenue totaled $640 million.

3. Rob Cain, chinafilmbiz.com, April 13, 2015.

4. Box Office Mojo (www.boxofficemojo.com/intl/china/yearly/?yr =2016&p=.htm). Although there had been claims that the 2015 Chinese film *Monster Hunt* (*Zhuo yao ji*) had already (barely) broken the record, subsequent data questioned the earlier totals for both *Furious 7* (under reported) and *Monster Hunt*.

5. David Barboza, "Hollywood East. Far East," *New York Times*, April 6, 2015, pp. B1, 7.

6. Chen Shengluo, "Survey Study on Chinese University Students' Perceptions of the Political Systems of China and the United States"; reprinted in Stanley Rosen and Chen Shengluo, eds., "Attitudes and Behavior of Contemporary Chinese Youth: Nationalism, Materialism, and Internationalism," *Chinese Education and Society* 44, nos. 2–3 (March–April / May–June 2011), pp. 13–57.

7. David Shambaugh, *China Goes Global: The Partial Power* (Oxford University Press, 2013), p. 212.

8. Stanley Rosen, "China's Post-1980's Generation, between the Nation and the World," *World Politics Review*, July 15, 2014, pp. 15–19. For example, then General Secretary Hu Jintao gave an internal speech in October 2011 warning against the West's assault on China's culture and ideology, which carried "the strategic plot of westernizing and dividing China." When his

speech was openly published in a leading Chinese ideological journal early in 2012, it signaled a major policy initiative to promote Chinese soft power at home and abroad to combat "long-term infiltration" from the West. This initiative has continued under Xi Jinping. In an internal memo known as Document No. 9, which was distributed to Party officials throughout the country in 2013, "seven perils" were noted that if left unchecked could result in the downfall of the Communist Party. Among the perils were Western constitutional democracy, the promotion of "universal values" such as human rights, Western-inspired notions of media independence and civic participation, and ardently pro-market "neoliberalism." In early 2014, a People's Liberation Army colonel noted that the recently established National Security Committee would plan responses to "extremists, online agitators and the West's cultural influence," again suggesting the importance of the threat from Western culture.

9. Thomas Friedman, "China Needs Its Own Dream," *New York Times*, October 3, 2012, p. A27. It should be noted, however, that the term was also used by a retired PLA colonel in a book originally published in Chinese in 2010. See Liu Mingfu, *The China Dream: Great Power Thinking and Strategic Posture in the Post-American Era* (New York: CN Times Books, 2015).

10. "Chasing the Chinese Dream," *The Economist*, May 4, 2013.

11. Ibid., citing *Globe* magazine.

12. James Truslow Adams, *The Epic of America* (Boston: Little, Brown, 1931), p. 405. I have addressed this issue in far more detail in Stanley Rosen, "Comparing Exceptionalisms and Dreams: The Relevance of the Chinese and American 'Models' for Post-80's and Post-90's Chinese Youth," paper presented at the conference on "Chinese Exceptionalism: Imagined or Historically-Grounded?" at the University of Nottingham.

13. Zhang Baohui, "Xi Jinping, 'Pragmatic' Offensive Realism and China's Rise," *Global Asia* 9, no. 2 (Summer 2014), p. 72; more generally, see Joseph Fewsmith, "Xi Jinping's Fast Start," *China Leadership Monitor* 41 (Spring 2013).

14. For example, the *Shanghai Daily* ran a weekly series that encouraged readers to share their individual dreams (http://coverage.shanghaidaily.com/ChineseDream/). Also see, inter alia, the cover story, survey, and series of articles entitled "*Xifang jiating chengjiu zhongguo meng*" [The Chinese dream is a happy family], *Liaowang zhoukan* [Outlook Weekly], no. 2 (January 13, 2014), pp. 20–31, and Meng Jian and Sun Xiangfei, "*'Zhongguo meng' de huayu chanshi yu minjian xiangxiang: jiyu xinlang weibo 16wanyu tiao yuanchuang bowen de shuju fenxi*" [Discourse interpretation and popular imagination of the "Chinese dream": Data analysis based on more than 160,000

original posts on Sina Weibo], *Xinwen yu chuanbo yanjiu* [Research on Journalism and Communications], no. 11 (November 2013), pp. 27–43.

15. Xinhua Reporter, "*Zai shixian zhongguo meng zhengtushang angyang fendou*" [The Journey to the realization of the Chinese dream is a high-spirited struggle], *Zhongguo qingnian bao* [China Youth Daily], January 10, 2014, pp. 1, 3; Lin Yahua, "*Zhongguo meng de shehui zhuyi jiazhi lixiang*" [The Socialist value ideals of the Chinese dream], *Zhonggong zhongyang dangxiao xuebao* [Journal of the Party School of the Central Committee of the CCP] 18, no. 2, (April 2014), pp. 16–19; Fewsmith, "Xi Jinping's Fast Start."

16. Shi Yuzhi, "*Zhongguo meng yu meiguo meng de qi da qubie*" [The seven great differences between the Chinese and American dreams], *Gaige neican: Wenzhai* [Internal Reference on Reform: Digest], no. 10, 2013, pp. 36–37. Professor Shi teaches at the National University of Singapore.

17. Patrick Boehler, "The Chinese Dream in Surveys: A Happy Middle Class," *South China Morning Post*, December 18, 2013.

18. "The Chinese Dream," *Shanghai Daily*, July 30, 2013.

19. Stanley Rosen, "The Wolf at the Door: Hollywood and the Film Market in China," in *Southern California and the World*, edited by Eric J. Heikkila and Rafael Pizarro (Westport, Conn., 2002), pp. 49–77. The banned studios were MGM (for *Red Corner*), Touchstone / Disney (for *Kundun*), and Sony / Columbia Tristar (for *Seven Years in Tibet*).

20. If films made for television were included, the number produced would be 730.

21. For 2013, see *Zhongguo dianying chanye yanjiu baogao, 2014* [The research report on China film industry, 2014] (Beijing: Zhongguo dianying chubanshe, 2014), p. 7; for 2014 and 2015 data, see *Zhongguo dianying chubanshe, 2016* [The research report on the China film industry, 2016] (Beijing: Zhongguo dianying chubanshe, 2016), p. 14.

22. Clifford Coonan, "China's Box Office Surges 36 percent in 2014 to $4.76 Billion," *Hollywood Reporter*, January 1, 2015.

23. Patrick Brzeski, "China Box Office Slumps 18 Percent in July," *Hollywood Reporter*, August 12, 2016. Among other reasons, the decline was associated with a weaker crop of local and imported films, fewer discounts on movie tickets, changing demographics in the market, and a consumer slowdown in the broader Chinese economy. For additional details, see Brzeski, "What's Behind China's Sudden Box-Office Slump," *Hollywood Reporter*, July 20, 2016.

24. These comments were made during a Q and A session at the University of Southern California on April 8, 2015.

25. The next four paragraphs, in particular the analysis of this survey, draw from Stanley Rosen, "China's Post-1980's Generation, Between the Nation

and the World," *World Politics Review*, July 15, 2014. For Chinese reporting on the survey see, inter alia, *"Zhongguode, ye shi shijiede; 2013 guojiren diaocha yanjiu baogao"* [China's is also the world's: The 2013 investigative research report on those who are internationals], *Waitan huabao* [Bund Pictorial], no. 12 (December 2013).

26. Julie Weed, "Welcome to the Haiyatt: In China, It's Not the Hotel It Sounds Like," *New York Times*, April 29, 2014, pp. B1, 8.

27. Lulu Yilun Chen, "China's Streaming Fans Face a Long Wait," *Bloomberg News*, January 22, 2015.

28. William Wan, "Chinese Officials Debate Why China Can't Make a Soap Opera as Good as South Korea's," *Washington Post*, March 7, 2014.

29. CNBC, March 16, 2016. The agreement between the U.S. and South Korea in July 2016 to deploy the THAAD anti-missile system gave China the pretext to begin to ban South Korean dramas and Korean stars in China.

30. Amy Qin, "China Cracking Down on Children on Reality TV," *New York Times*, April 18, 2016. When I complimented a leading Chinese film official for allowing the release of *Finding Mr. Right*, with its promotion of the American dream over the Chinese Dream, his response was: "That's why we won't approve such a film again!" (Los Angeles, US-China Film Summit, November 7, 2014).

31. Stanley Rosen, "Can China Devise a Strategy to Promote Its Films Abroad? Obstacles and Suggestions," in *Zhongguo dianying lishi quanjing guanzhao* [A Panoramic view of Chinese film history], edited by Zhou Xing and Zhang Yan (Beijing: Zhongguo dianying chubanshe, 2015), pp. 259–79.

32. Stanley Rosen, "Chinese Cinema's International Market," in *Art, Politics and Commerce in Chinese Cinema*, edited by Ying Zhu and Stanley Rosen (Hong Kong University Press, 2010), pp. 35–54.

33. The evolution of Zhang Yimou's career and his box office performance in North America is discussed in Rosen, "Can China Devise a Strategy to Promote Its Films Abroad?"

34. The films include *Shaolin Soccer, Hero, Princess Mononoke,* and *Snowpiercer.* He defends himself by noting, "I'm not cutting for fun. . . . I'm cutting for the shit to work." Ben Child, "Snowpiercer Director Reportedly Furious about Weinstein English-version Cuts," *The Guardian*, October 8, 2013.

35. Rosen, "Can China Devise a Strategy to Promote Its Films Abroad?"; boxofficemojo.com. It should be noted that Ang Lee's *Lust, Caution* made $4.6 million in 2007. One of the rare exceptions was *The Mermaid*, which was released in North America on February 19, 2016, was shown on 106 screens in its widest release, and made $3.2 million. However, as the most successful film of all time in China, with a box office of $526.8 million (and $554 million in all markets outside North America), the $3.2 million made

up only 0.6 percent of its total box office. Sony / Columbia, because of the usual low expectations for Chinese-language films in North America, did little to promote it (www.boxofficemojo.com/movies/?id=mermaid2016 .htm; accessed on October 27, 2016).

36. A. O. Scott review in *New York Times*, September 2, 2011.

37. Interview with the production manager, 1998, in Los Angeles.

38. *Zhongguo dianying chanye yanjiu baogao, 2014* [The research report on the Chinese film industry, 2014], p. 32.

39. *China International Film Co-Production Handbook* (Motion Picture Association and China Film Co-Production Corporation, 2014), p. 52. Note that the total figures in the table would add up to 183 percent since many films cover more than one genre.

40. Q and A at the MPA Preview Screening at AMC Theaters, Century City, Los Angeles, November 7, 2014, in conjunction with the U.S.-China Film Summit.

41. Clifford Coonan, " 'Kung Fu Panda 3' Gets Co-Production Status in China," *Hollywood Reporter*, January 23, 2015.

42. See *China International Film Co-Production Handbook*, pp. 32 and 53.

43. *Zhongguo dianying chanye yanjiu baogao, 2016* [The research report on the Chinese film industry, 2016], pp. 18–19.

44. This draws from Stanley Rosen, "Cross-Cultural Dramas Fraught with Difficulty," *China Daily* (USA), June 5, 2014, p. 10. In addition, see *Zhongguo dianying chanye yanjiu baogao, 2014*, p. 32, for data on 2013 and 2014; *"Zhongguo dianying yingxiaofei 36yi: 19–40 sui guanzhong gongxian 87% piaofang"* [Chinese film marketing fees in 2014 are 3.6 billion yuan; 19–40 year olds make up 87% of the box office], *Sohu yule* [Sohu Entertainment], January 6, 2015. There were a few relatively successful films overseas in 2015, for example *Wolf Totem*, which did particularly well in France ($8.8 million), and had some success in Italy ($3.5 million) and Spain ($1.5 million), no doubt in part because a well-known French director, Jean-Jacques Annaud, was behind the camera.

45. Clifford Coonan, "China Film Bureau Boss Urges Local Industry to 'Prepare for War with Hollywood,' " *Hollywood Reporter*, June 27, 2014.

46. Clifford Coonan, "Communist Propaganda Czar Wants China to Become a Movie Power," *Hollywood Reporter*, July 9, 2014.

47. On *Confucius*, see " '*Kongzi*', *ping shenme rang 'Afanda' rang dao*" ["Confucius," why do you want "Avatar" to Yield to Make Way for You?] *Shanxi wanbao* [Shanxi Evening News], January 21, 2010; Raymond Zhou, "Confucius Loses His Way," *China Daily*, January 29, 2010, which also includes a cartoon by Li Min showing middle-school students sleeping during a classroom showing of *Confucius*." On the Lei Feng films, see *Hollywood Reporter*, March 5,

2013 and the SARFT website of that same date for the directive encouraging the issuing of group or special price tickets for those films.

48. Rosen, "China's Post-1980's Generation, between the Nation and the World," p. 18.

49. Fiona Tam, "It is Hard to be Happy Even in Joy, Mo Yan Says," *South China Morning Post*, October 16, 2012, p. 7.

50. *"Mo Yan jiaxiang yi tou 6.7yi hengyang hong gaoliang wenhua; guanmin jun kangfen"* [Mo Yan's home village will rely on an investment of 6.7 million RMB to promote Red Sorghum culture: Officials are all very excited], *Xin Jing Bao* [New Beijing News], October 18, 2012 (online); Malcolm Moore, "China to Spend 70 Million Pounds Sprucing Up Nobel Prize Winner's Hometown," *The Telegraph*, October 18, 2012; Perry Link, "Does This Writer Deserve the Prize?" *New York Review of Books*, December 6, 2012.

51. Raymond Li, "Mo Yan's Hometown Is Looking to Cash In," *South China Morning Post*, October 19, 2012, p. 7.

52. "Free Spirit: A Tennis Star Gives Officials the Cold Shoulder," *The Economist* (online), February 1, 2014; Cao Jing, *"Li Na zai duoguan daobi zhongguo tiyu gaige"* [Another championship by Li Na compels a reform in Chinese sports], *Zhongguo qingnian bao* [China Youth Daily], January 26, 2014, p. 1.

53. Julie Makinen and Richard Verrier, "A Studio's Big Bet on China," *Los Angeles Times*, June 9, 2015, pp. C1, 5.

54. Richard Verrier, "Chinese Stars and Crew of 75 Filming in L.A.," *Los Angeles Times*, November 12, 2014, pp. B1, 3.

55. Box Office Mojo (www.boxofficemojo.com).

56. Julie Makinen, "Alibaba Pictures Says Its First Film Will Be Comedy," *Los Angeles Times*, January 13, 2015, p. C3; "Why Alibaba's First Movie *Bai Du Ren* Is a Must Watch," *GrateNews*, January 13, 2015; Internet Movie Database (imdb.com, an online database of information related to films, television programs and video games).

57. George Szalai, "Jack Ma on Alibaba's Hollywood Ambitions, Growth Outlook," *Hollywood Reporter*, January 23, 2015.

58. Charles Liu, "China Artificially Inflating Box Office Figures, But Vows a Crackdown," May 27, 2016 (www.news.cn, part of the Xinhua News Agency).

59. Clifford Coonan, "China Box Office: 'Furious 7' on Track to Beat 'Transformers' Record," *Hollywood Reporter*, April 21, 2015; Robert Cain, "Why Is China So 'Furious'?" chinafilmbiz.com, April 22, 2015.

THIRTEEN

Chinese Culture in a Global Context

The Confucius Institute as a Geo-Cultural Force

RANDY KLUVER

 As China's economy and geopolitical weight has grown since the late 1980s, the nation has also sought to have a corresponding cultural impact. Whether expressed through the framework of "soft power," "cultural power," or another term, there is little doubt that the Chinese government seeks to develop a global cultural influence that is at least as powerful as its growing economic, military, and political influence. The Confucius Institute (CI) project reflects a deep anxiety on the part of China's leadership, and much of the population, about China's relatively ineffectual impact on global trends in values, goals, and aspirations; and seeks to create a "place at the table," as it were, for Chinese history, philosophy, and culture to enter a global cultural conversation.

Although the concept of "soft power" has received numerous critiques as an analytical framework, it remains a highly popular term among journalists, political leaders, and even a number of academics.

China's leadership clearly likes the term, and appropriates it freely to argue that China needs more of it. Likewise, critics of China in general, and of the Confucius Institute project in particular, use the term freely to argue that China's growing clout in geopolitics should be checked, or at least acknowledged, and that Chinese culture and politics are deeply intertwined. Certainly, culture (from an anthropological perspective) embodies political principles, values, and goals. But as I argue in this essay, to freely equate cultural influence with political or geopolitical power is deeply reductionist, and this reductionism serves to obscure the deeper implications of the Confucius Institute project.

My goal in this essay is, first, to position the Confucius Institute project as primarily an attempt to influence global cultural discourse, rather than as a "political" project concerned with forcing Chinese political doctrine upon the rest of the world. The "propaganda" model of the Confucius Institute is far too narrow, and as I argue, misses the real potential of Chinese culture to contribute to global cultural discourse. I also seek to redirect the discussion from a grounding solely in the geopolitical context, and instead argue that any discussion of the Confucius Institute should properly be grounded upon a "geo-cultural" foundation, one that recognizes that larger global trends are driven not just by near-term political agendas and activities, but upon the assumptions, beliefs, and values that emerge in a context of global cultural flows.[1]

To be clear, I am not denying that the Chinese government has both internal political goals as well as geopolitical goals for the Confucius Institute. Few governmental initiatives in China have no political rationale, goals, or impact, and there is little doubt that China intends for the Confucius Institute to enhance its global political standing, and indeed its "soft power." The presence of Vice Premier Liu Yandong as chair of the executive council of the CI, as well as the active engagement of former propaganda chief Li Changchun in the overall project, makes this abundantly clear. However, I argue that understanding the CI project from only, or even primarily, from that perspective is overly restrictive, and blinds us to the far more long-term, and consequential, impact of the project. Likewise, there can be little doubt that the Fulbright program funded by the U.S. government has political rationale and implications. But to restrict our understanding of that program to just that aspect would blind us to the long-term cultural, scientific, and educational impact of the program.

Although the term "geo-cultural" is not a new one, I mean to reposition the term away from its normal anthropological sense (of the influence of geography on culture) and toward the idea of a cultural counterforce to "geopolitics." Whereas geopolitics refers to the power relations and dynamics between nation-states, normally upon the stage of political institutions, I define "geo-cultural influence" as a nation's ability to influence larger cultural trends, values, habits, and customs. Geo-cultural influence isn't enacted in political engagements, but rather in the habits, beliefs, and values that are adopted as part of the normal course of life of social development. Geo-cultural influence is made manifest in the cultural and symbolic flows manifested in media, the arts, popular culture, and other cultural forms, which clearly do not abide by political boundaries.

This distinction between geo-cultural influence and geopolitical influence helps to bring more nuance to the analytical imprecision of the term "soft power." Joseph Nye's original articulation of soft power doesn't discriminate between the two arenas of influence, and in fact conflates them. For example, Nye's bumper-sticker definition of soft power, "getting others to want the outcomes that you want," conflates these by arguing that cultural influence is more or less the same as obtaining desired political outcomes.[2] In fact, Nye clearly argues that soft power is "not the same as influence," and is only manifested by the presence of clearly identified political outcomes. In a later work, Nye includes a number of examples of effective soft power, including U.S. education abroad, positive foreign media coverage of Barack Obama's election, and others, but uses political efficacy as a measure of the impact of this soft power, demonstrating again the conflation of the geo-cultural and geopolitical domains.[3] However, by distinguishing between the two, it becomes easier to understand the longer-term impact of the Confucius Institute globally.

My second goal here is to review the ways in which Confucius Institutes seek to fulfill this larger goal, with a foundation in language teaching, but including a large number of cultural elements. Around the world, these institutes seek to embody Chinese cultural traditions in local contexts, but not always effectively. I will use four case studies of Confucius Institutes to illustrate the way in which CIs seek to articulate and embody Chinese culture in very different national and cultural contexts.

Finally, I seek to explore the likelihood of China achieving these larger geo-cultural goals, and the distortions to both Chinese culture and the way the Chinese state symbolizes "Chineseness" through the Confucius Institute. I examine in particular the model of cultural influence embodied in the Confucius Institute, and assess that model within the context of globalization. I also seek to move the discussion of the Confucius Institutes within the context of Western academic institutions to a larger global context, and argue that an overemphasis on the meaning of the presence of a CI at an institution like the University of Chicago or Penn State seriously distorts our understanding of the larger geo-cultural and geopolitical impact the CI might achieve.

I draw upon a number of sources to make this argument, including nine years of direct experience in starting up, and subsequently running a Confucius Institute, interaction in multiple contexts with Confucius Institutes and their staffs globally, the internal rules and guidelines documents that govern and guide the institutes, as well as material prepared for public distribution. I also draw upon public comments and communications of the leadership of the Confucius Institute headquarters, particularly its Director General, Xu Lin, as well as other Chinese leaders involved in the project. But prior to beginning this overview, it is necessary to address briefly the numerous charges that the Confucius Institutes are primarily an instrument of Chinese propaganda that have recently gained attention. My argument is that the CI is best understood as a geo-cultural strategy, rather than a geopolitical one; nevertheless, any discussion of the CIs must take into account the charged political atmosphere surrounding the institutes and their sponsor, Hanban.

THE GLOBAL CONTROVERSY OVER
CONFUCIUS INSTITUTES

The Confucius Institute project began in 2004, with a goal of developing a network of institutes around the world that would provide resources for Chinese-language instruction and cultural outreach. The project is officially under the supervision of Hanban, or the Office of Chinese Language International, which is in turn supervised by and receives funding from the Ministry of Education of the People's Republic of China. The project began with a fairly simple premise, that there would be great value in deploying Chinese-language teachers, educated in China, to teach Chinese to a growing population of interested learners. The project grew quickly, however, both in scope and in the mechanisms of its implication. At the end of 2015, there were approximately five hundred institutes in 126 nations, with another thousand Confucius Classrooms (local school programs, typically outreach efforts of CIs). This was halfway to the goal articulated in the 2010–12 development plan, which called for the establishment of one thousand institutes globally.[4]

Particularly in the United States and Canada, and Western Europe, there has been concern over the "propaganda" role of the Confucius Institutes. This concern primarily arises from a fear that the CIs are subject to undue pressure from Hanban, both in receiving money for the institute activities as well as receiving staff employed at Chinese institutions, but sent by Hanban. Because of these two sources of influence (money and staff), it is argued, academic integrity is undermined, and the government of the PRC gains an undue influence over academic programming about China, its culture, and its politics. Although this debate has been most prominent in the Western world, many of the same questions have been raised globally, including in the developing world, where the Confucius Institutes can have an outsized role in local curriculums, due to the significant funding that comes from Hanban.

Although this argument at times became extreme, including accusations that visiting scholars sent by Hanban are engaged in espionage; more typically, these concerns were raised about whether a host university or organization abdicated its ability to engage in critical discussion of Chinese politics, foreign policy, or human rights.[5] In the United States, this issue gained a particular ferocity over the case of the CI at the University of Chicago, when an emeritus law professor, Marshall Sahlins, publicly questioned the role of the Confucius Institute in the university's programs, and over one hundred faculty members signed a letter calling on the university to close the CI. Largely due to this concern, and relying heavily on Sahlins's accusations, the American Association of University Professors (AAUP) issued a statement calling on universities to suspend CIs unless academic freedom, including the open and free exchange of criticism of China's policies, was guaranteed.[6]

Soon thereafter, the University of Chicago suspended negotiations to renew the CI Memorandum of Agreement with Hanban due to an article published in a Chinese news outlet that seemed to undermine the autonomy of the university, and later decided not to renew the CI agreement with Hanban. This was not due to concerns over accusations of political influence, although the university took them seriously, but primarily because the faculty member at the university who had begun the institute had moved to a different role, and no other faculty member was willing to take on the responsibility associated with running the institute.[7] Not long afterward, Pennsylvania State University shut down its Confucius Institute, with a statement that the university's goals were "not consistent" with those of Hanban, but with no further detail provided.[8]

Consequently, a robust debate about the academic value of the institutes in light of these concerns arose, a debate to which I have previously contributed. The most high-profile challenge to the CIs occurred in December of 2014, when Representative Christopher Smith from New Jersey convened a panel for the House Committee on Foreign Affairs Subcommittee on Africa, Global Health, Global Human Rights, and International Organizations, focused on the subject of China's influence on U.S. universities. Although a number of questions were addressed in the panel, including U.S. satellite campuses in China and exchange programs, the focus was clearly on whether U.S. universities were "outsourcing" critical curriculum issues to China through the Confucius Institute mechanism, and thereby stifling critical inquiry on China. Representative Smith himself asked the question, "Are U.S. colleges and universities undermining the principle of academic freedom—and, in the process, their credibility—in exchange for China's education dollars?"[9]

Although Smith's charges were placed in the context of U.S. concerns, the issue of Chinese governmental control has been shared in other nations. Earlier in 2014, the Toronto (Ont.) District School Board voted to sever ties with Hanban to end months of controversy over the role of CIs in elementary curriculum. European concerns about the political control of the CIs were exacerbated by an incident at the European Association for Chinese Studies meeting in July of 2014, when Xu Lin, director-general of Hanban, demanded that pages from the conference program be removed because of an ad in the program placed by the Chiang Ching-Kuo Foundation ("Report: The Deletion of Pages from EACS Conference materials in Braga [July 2014]," 2014).[10] In lesser-developed contexts, such as parts of Asia and Africa, the Confucius Institutes have been interpreted as neocolonial enterprises, meant to leapfrog Chinese influence in the regions, and especially in Asian countries where China has long had a hegemonic influence, critics have loudly called for elimination of the institutes.

Without dismissing the importance of these concerns, it is important to note that there are few, if any, actual instances of political intrusion on academic programming. Most university staff associated with Confucius Institutes strenuously deny any such attempt to influence either curricula or other types of programming, but this has done little to quell the suspicion. I have addressed those charges elsewhere,[11] so will not seek to do that here.

THE CONFUCIUS INSTITUTES AND GEO-CULTURAL INFLUENCE

With this background, then, it is helpful to propose an alternative understanding of the Confucius Institutes, not as a form of geopolitical power, but rather of geo-cultural influence. I have argued elsewhere that the best way of understanding Chinese intentions regarding the CIs is through a framework that focuses on cultural influence, rather than political. To briefly review, Castell's theory of "Communication Power" is helpful in articulating an understanding of global influence as due to one's role in both maintaining a central hub status in global information networks, and in the ability to program those networks with values, assumptions, expectations, and norms.[12] Further, I argue that the Confucius Institute, regardless of the express cultural intent of the project, ultimately rested upon its ability to develop a global audience linguistically capable of accessing China's literary, philosophical, and cultural heritage through the accumulation of Chinese-language skills. It is possible to gain some understanding of China's cultural tradition through translated materials, although that is a poor substitute for the understanding that comes when one can access cultural resources in their original language. Building upon that foundation, I will briefly explore what role this might have in geo-cultural power, and how the Confucius Institute best exemplifies that framework.

For much of the twentieth century, there has been a vibrant debate regarding the role of cultural influence across national borders. There remains little doubt that cultural products, in the form of media, music, educational systems, and the like, can have a marked impact when transplanted to a new nation, although there remains considerable debate regarding the nature of that impact. Although a number of scholars remain who argue that the forces of globalization undermine local cultures (and cultural diversity) in favor of mass-produced consumeristic cultures from the West, a rising number of voices argue that this is an oversimplistic model of cultural influence, and that the capacity of local cultures to resist global cultural trends is remarkably resilient.

One useful perspective that emerges from the academic literature on cultural globalization is that of Marwan Kraidy, who argues that most, if not all, transnational cultural trends reflect not a mindless reiteration of the original cultural context, but rather a process of "hybridization," in which foreign influences are reinterpreted into local contexts, creating a fusion of meaning and form that is unique to that context.[13] Kraidy's emphasis is more on the reading of cultural texts (television, novels, or the like), but this insight might provide some clues as to the institutional forms and meanings that Confucius Institutes take globally, and would predict that there is no unified meaning to Confucius Institutes, but rather, that the larger geo-cultural meaning of the project as a whole might be undermined by the local meanings, which might carry little salience beyond that context.

A more recent contribution to this debate is that of Pippa Norris and Ron Inglehart, who propose a "firewall" model of "cosmopolitan communication," in which the impact of global cultural products, especially media, can be significantly hindered by a number of individual, social, legal, and cultural constraints.[14] This theory of conditional effects posits that there are a host of factors that might inhibit or contribute to both the speed and direction of cultural change of a given nation. Norris and Inglehart's model is particularly salient in the context of the Confucius Institutes, as one of the express aims of the Confucius Institutes is to bridge cultural divides, serve as a platform for cultural exchange, and convey "Chinese culture" to nations around the world. Their model would predict, among other things, that the impact of any single Confucius Institute, and hence China's global cultural impact, would differ dramatically based on local cultural traditions, legal and political structures, and perhaps most importantly, individual attitudes toward Chinese history, language, and culture. Moreover, as noted, accessing China's cultural tradition is difficult without Chinese-language skills, and although Norris and Inglehart didn't expressly note this in their model, it seems obvious that linguistic ability would have a marked impact on one's capacity to absorb foreign cultural values and ideas.

The context of modern society is one in which it is possible to clearly identify a "globalized world," although there remain sharp disagreements as to the exact nature of that globalization. The question is really not whether or not globalization is happening, but to what extent globalization is imbued with American presumptions and values. With this background then, I will turn to an examination of the express goals of the Chinese leadership regarding the Confucius Institute, and the salience of those goals in understanding the ultimate impact of the CI project.

THE GEO-CULTURAL GOALS OF THE CONFUCIUS INSTITUTE PROJECT

The Confucius Institute was originally conceived as primarily a language teaching enterprise, and this remains the main focus, although since the founding, the goals and activities of CIs (especially those supported financially by Hanban) have grown significantly. The original agreement template between host institutions and Hanban referred solely to the goal of strengthening educational cooperation, promoting the development of Chinese-language education, and "increasing mutual understanding." Initially, Hanban staff were uncomfortable with the idea of the CI as a form of diplomacy of any sort, particularly in the context of soft power. I asked a senior-level administrator for Hanban in 2009 if the organization saw the CI as an element of public diplomacy, and with visible discomfort, that administrator said that "diplomacy is the role of the Ministry of Foreign Affairs. The Confucius Institute is only about teaching Chinese language." Within a couple of years, however, the leadership of Hanban recognized the obvious public diplomacy aspect of the CIs and began to encourage CIs to think more broadly about cultural outreach, academic research, and other forms of cultural exchange. By 2012, CIs were encouraged to submit budget propsals that included a greater variety of cultural outreach activities as well as to develop more individualized portfolios of programs, such as those in Chinese business, or traditional Chinese medicine.

Although the actual cause of this growing acceptance of a role in cultural diplomacy is not transparent, it seems that much of it must be due to the explicit goals of Xi Jinping and other senior leaders to accelerate China's cultural influence around the world. In December of 2013, for example, Xi gave a speech to the Politburo of the 18th Central Committee, in which he argued that among other goals, the party needed to "showcase the unique charms of Chinese culture," which had developed over 5,000 years. Xi argued that "we should disseminate Chinese culture in a popular way . . . we should popularize our cultural spirit across countries as well as across time and space . . . we should tell the rest of the world about the new achievements of modern Chinese culture." In a note acknowledging the tenth anniversary of the movement, Xi later said that "Confucius Institutes belong to China, and they also belong to the world."[15]

Obviously and unambiguously, Xi argues that the cultural impact of the CIs will result in a positive geopolitical role for China. He further urged the leadership that cultural outreach was essential, and ought to be reinforced by intensifying China's "international right of speech," or its capacities in international communication, and in developing a system for communicating to the globe the achievements of Chinese society. Only with these efforts, Xi declared, would China achieve its soft power goals; namely, enhancing the nation's creativity, influence, and public trust. It is important to note, however, that Xi's articulation of such goals focuses not on short-term political goals (such as support for China's claims in the South China Sea), but rather on long-term cultural influence around the globe.

Other senior leaders have also endorsed the Confucius Institute project, and commented directly upon the role of cultural exchange in enhancing China's image and reputation abroad. CPC Central Committee member and chair of the Ideology and Propaganda Small Group of the Central Committee, Li Changchun, has been engaged with the Confucius Institute project from its beginning, and is closely associated with the project. He has frequently spoken about the soft power side of the Confucius Institute, and recently noted that the project plays an important role in the enhancement of China's soft power and has become a "brand" of Chinese culture. Li's association and endorsement of the project, of course, gives greater strength to the arguments that the CI's play a propaganda role.

Finally, Vice Premier and Chair of the Confucius Institute Council Liu Yandong often addresses representatives of the CIs, and gave a speech at the international directors meeting in Xiamen in December 2014, in which she also drew upon the idea of the Confucius Institute as a brand. She argued that the CI project had been successful beyond initial expectations, primarily because it was a proactive response to a rising trend of "multi-polarization and globalization." She argued that the CIs are not only important language-teaching platforms, but also "key carriers of people-to-people exchange and mutual learning between different civilizations."[16] Liu's comments directly position China as an alternative (primarily to the United

States) source of global cultural influence through her "multi-polarization" model.

Taiwan's leaders have watched the growth of the Confucius Institute and noted the likely impact of these efforts in displacing Taiwan. In fact, Taiwan's displacement as the "symbol" of Chinese culture happened at least one decade earlier, but the Confucius Institute project threatens to remove Taiwan's visibility even further, as the Confucius Institute takes on the responsibility for defining China's history and culture. In response, in 2011, the Ministry of Culture in Taiwan announced a project called the Taiwan Academy, with a specific mandate for cultural diplomacy. Although the academy effort did not include a Chinese-language component, as did the Confucius Institutes, the effort did focus on academic research and exchange. The Taiwan Academy project did not entail host institutions' making formal commitments, but merely willing to participate in academy-oriented funding projects. The goal of the project was to promote cultural exchange and "cultivate a greater interest in and appreciation of Taiwan's culture in the international community," and of course, to develop alternatives to the CI scholarship program, and keep students and researchers engaged with Taiwan. In the United States, these academies are managed out of the Taiwan Economic and Cultural Offices in New York, Los Angeles, and Houston. Universities that agreed to host the Taiwan Academy projects were eligible for project-specific funding of up to $20,000 for projects that would engage students or researchers in projects focused on Taiwan, including visual or performing arts, exhibitions, and industrial collaborations. The call for proposals issued by the project also called for comprehensive "Taiwan Week / Taiwan Month" programs that would focus attention on Taiwanese society and culture for a period of time. Take-up of this effort was limited, with just twelve institutions being awarded funding in 2013, including UCLA, the University of Texas at Austin, the University of Heidelberg, and Nanyang Technological University in Singapore. It is worth noting that approximately half of the institutions awarded Taiwan Spotlight Awards in 2013 through the project also hosted Confucius Institutes, with no seeming dissonance between the two sources of funding.[17]

As has been noted before, Confucius himself has little relevance to most of the programming of the Confucius Institutes.[18] The teachings of the sage rarely appear in any of the curriculum, and the name was chosen primarily as an easily recognizable brand name for the project, as Confucius is probably the single Chinese individual, past or present, with the strongest name recognition outside of China. Individual institutes do use the image of Confucius frequently, and occasionally, the Chinese government will bestow a statue of Confucius on a host institution or city. But beyond this brand-name recognition, Confucius Institutes rarely appropriate the teachings or philosophy of the fifth century BCE philosopher.

This discussion highlights the explicit cultural goals of the CI project, but also demonstrates the difficulty in considering these cultural goals apart from China's desire for enhanced global prestige as well. Clearly, China's leadership, as do many of its citizens, believes that the CI is a direct strategy to develop China's soft power, in Nye's sense. But my argument is that regardless of the intentions of China's leaders, in practice, the CI's enact *local* agendas that certainly enhance China's role, but at a cultural rather than political level. So far, I have argued that the primary lens by which we should interpret the impact of the Confucius Institute is geo-cultural, rather than geopolitical. To provide more depth to this argument, I would like to look more closely at a number of individual institutes, each of which embodies a slightly different approach to cultural outreach.

CONFUCIUS INSTITUTES IN LOCAL CONTEXTS

I am hesitant to ascribe much predictive power to the data represented by only four samples, but any discussion as to the impact of the Confucius Institute project globally does need to be grounded in real data, rather than conjecture. As table 13-1 indicates, these examples are but a fraction of the hundreds of institutes around the world. Each of the examples I discuss below could be discontinued in a matter of days, and new institutes could arise to take their place. Each of these also represents an "elite" institution, albeit from different national contexts, in that two of the four are largely ranked in

TABLE 13-1. Global Distribution of Confucius Institutes

	Confucius institutes	Confucius classrooms
Africa	46	23
Americas	157	544
Asia	110	90
Europe	169	257
Oceania	18	86
Total	**500**	**1000**

Source: Hanban, August 2016 (http://english.hanban.org/node_10971.htm).

the top tiers of global universities, and three of the four rank within the top two hundred. Nevertheless, I have chosen these four as examples of what the Confucius Institute looks like in four separate locations to demonstrate the flexibility of its programs within a larger framework of language instruction and cultural exchange, and to represent the cultural milieu in which each exists and seeks to have an impact. Out of the almost five hundred institutes that currently exist, it is fair to say that the programs and operations of all are different from one another, depending on the host institution, the local needs, and the resource base, including the strengths of leadership and personnel. But within those areas of variance, each seeks to implement a vision of Chinese-language and cultural outreach.

The Confucius Institute at Ca' Foscari University in Venice, Italy, was approved in 2007 and began operations in 2008. The host institution, although originally founded as primarily a school of business and diplomacy, has approximately 19,000 students, and has a robust program in international studies and modern languages. The university boasts one of the largest Chinese-language programs in Europe, if not the world, with close to 1,500 Chinese-language majors. Although the CI is headed by a full-time faculty member, the visiting scholars and faculty do not contribute to the credit-based language program.

Venice, of course, has a history of well over thirteen hundred years as a major cultural capital. Venetian merchants, diplomats, and traders built a global trading empire that dominated trade from the Silk Road of Asia for hundreds of years, which finally began to break down with the advent of transatlantic trade in the sixteenth century. Perhaps the most famous Venetian of all, Marco Polo, is primarily known for his travels in Asia, including China, and the institute appeals to this history to position itself as a center for cultural exchange between China and the Western world. After Venice lost its independence to Napoleon in the seventeenth century, the city became identified as a cultural hub, and by the nineteenth century had become a requisite stop in the so-called grand tour of European elites.

Although Venice's importance as a commercial center has long been transcended by other financial and commercial cities, the city remains an incredibly important global city, and is one of the top tourist destinations in the world. Although the city only has a permanent population of just over 53,000 in the city itself, it receives approximately 60,000 visitors per day, effectively doubling its population each day. The tourists come from all over the world, of course, with an increasing number of Chinese. The city, therefore, hardly needs more cultural input, as it is already one of the most global cities in the world, as well as a city with a wealth of historical and cultural resources.

The CI at Ca' Foscari builds upon Venice's cultural heritage and historical positioning to position itself as a bridge between Italy and China, and focuses much of its efforts on "high culture" activities, such as art exhibitions, performances of Chinese music and opera, and talks by Chinese novelists and artists. The institute contributes to Venice's famed Bienniale, hosting film screenings and other artistic exchanges from China. Recent programming included photographic exhibitions of Chinese cities, Chinese-language testing, and essay contests on Chinese literature.

A second model of cultural exchange is illustrated by the CI at Nanyang Technological University (NTU) in Singapore. Singapore, of course, has the world's highest percentage of ethnic Chinese in its population, outside of Taiwan and the PRC. Singapore's government has been focused on strengthening Chinese-language programming for at least two decades as part of the "Mother Tongue" program, and the CI is positioned to enhance this strong commitment to Chinese-language education.

Like Venice, Singapore is also a cultural hub, with strong international tourism and worldwide recognition, and a city that is seeking to remain relevant in the new global future. In a number of studies during the 2000s, the city-state consistently ranked among the "most globalized" nations, according to numerous rankings. The city is widely acknowledged as both one of the most globalized cities in the world and as the most globalized nation in Asia, as measured by the amount of cultural flows (import / export of cultural products, such as print or other types of media).[19]

Unlike Venice, however, Singapore lacks the historical legacy or reputation for high culture, such as literature and the arts. The CI at NTU, therefore, takes a very different approach to ties with China, with an emphasis on the practical, including enhanced language education, business, and economic programs, and cultural programs that focus more on traditional Chinese practices and arts, such as traditional Chinese medicine, calligraphy, and painting.

Although Mandarin is one of the four official languages of Singapore, there has of late been little prestige associated with the language. Rather, since its independence in 1965, the leaders of the city-state have sought to make the nation relevant to the English-speaking world, in order to guarantee the sustainability of the nation. The percentage of children in Singapore from primarily English-speaking homes rose from 36 percent in 1994 to 50 percent in 1998.[20] These effects of globalization ultimately weakened the sense of belonging for many younger Singaporeans, and led to a penetrating national debate over national identity and loyalty.[21] Moreover, such globalization contributed to a sense of cultural isolation from China itself, as English was and remains the primary language of government, education, and commerce, and hence is considered a more opportunistic language than Mandarin. In order to capitalize on China's economic and geopolitical clout, however, Singapore's government later sought to reemphasize Mandarin, and introduced a mother-tongue policy in 1966 that required all students to become fully bilingual in English and either Chinese, Malay, or Tamil, depending on one's ethnicity. For the approximately 70 percent of Singapore's population that is ethnic Chinese, this means Mandarin, rather than the regional dialects that were often spoken in the home, such as Hokkien, Cantonese, Teochew, or Hainanese. Even Minister Mentor Lee Kuan Yew contributed to a book designed both to spur on Singaporeans' efforts to learn the language and to provide helpful encouragement from the Minister Mentor concerning language learning.[22]

To meet these goals, the nation introduced changes to its governing policies regarding language instruction in 2004, and the next year, the CI at NTU was founded. The CI at NTU also periodically hosts artists and writers, but doesn't have the same high-culture focus as the CI at Ca' Foscari. Rather, the clear focus is creating programs for Chinese-language learning directed to ethnic Chinese in Singapore, especially children and youth. One hoped-for outcome is the development of a fully bilingual and bicultural elite who would be able to navigate both the Western world—which has provided the fuel, as it were, for Singapore's growth into a modern city-state—and China, where the government senses its future lies.

Yet another CI with a very different focus is based at the University of California at Davis. UC Davis is widely recognized as one of the top universities in the world, and as a land-grant institution, is well known for its emphasis in practical arts and sciences, including agriculture.[23] The CI at Davis was founded in 2013, and unlike most CIs, offers no language classes at all. Rather, the focus is on understanding and appreciating Chinese culture, particularly through the media of food and wine. The university, already well-known for its strong emphasis on agricultural and food sciences, developed a reputation in viticulture and enology, and the institute often conducts is programs in partnership with the Robert Mondavi Institute for Wine and Food Science. Programs offered by the CT at Davis consist of seminars, wine tastings, tea, and other programs related to food production and consumption. The only language offering is a regular seminar on Chinese calligraphy, but this is clearly incidental to the key programs of the institute.

Unlike Venice or Singapore, Davis is not typically considered a global city, with negligible numbers of tourists. But the university is considered a "node," in Castell's language, in global research and education, and thus a CI positioned at the university makes some strategic sense. Although it might be argued that a Confucius Institute focused on wine is trivial, I think this is a misreading of the potential impact of the institute. Rather, the CI is positioned to capitalize on the university's core strength in agriculture, food science, and wine, and tie it to Chinese culture, particularly its burgeoning food and wine industries. Again, unlike CIs at many universities, which are led by language instructors or literary experts, the CI at UCD is led by a professor of food science, in keeping with the institute's profile.

A final example is the Confucius Institute at Prairie View A&M University, a historically black university located in Texas, with an enrollment of over 90 percent African American. PVAMU's CI opened only in 2014, and is the third to be located at a historically black college / university (HBCU). Unlike the other institutions noted thus far, PVAMU is not considered an elite global university, but has developed its CI as one element of a strategy to develop an elite and globally sophisticated African American cohort of diplomats, engineers, and doctors. Like many CIs, the PVAMU CI offers Chinese-language classes and cultural outreach to a broad campus constituency, but the primary audience is the honors students of the university.

Administrators at PVAMU have developed two critical language programs (Chinese and Arabic) to provide a competitive edge to their students, many of whom go on to graduate degrees at Ivy League universities, and careers in law, politics, medicine, diplomacy, and other career tracks. The Chinese-language skills, and short-term stays in China, offered by the CI provide an additional competitive factor for these students, but the program is focused not just on that competitive advantage, but in developing a global sophistication among the honors students at the university. As an institution with a student population that is typically much more concerned with Africa than with China, administrators hope that the CI will give these students expertise in China that will also work to the benefit of Africa, given the unequal relationship that is developing between African nations and China.[24]

Because the CI at PVAMU is relatively new, its programming has not yet matured to demonstrate a trajectory of programming, but early initiatives and programs are consistent with the programs of most CIs, with Chinese-language courses and cultural outreach. This CI spends a significant amount of effort in programs to engage a student population with little to no initial interest in or knowledge of China, with the goal of creating a pool of students who see Chinese-language skills and cultural competency as an indispensable set of skills for a future of leadership. The CI also sponsors talks by faculty experts and visiting scholars, linking Chinese culture and language to subjects of interest to the student body on Chinese culture and society, but also subjects such as the influence of hip-hop music in China or the "misspellings" that occur in Chinese-language tattoos, which link U.S. pop culture to China.

These four examples, drawn from four different cultural and national contexts, provide some foundation for considering the role of the CI as a type of geo-cultural influence. I have oversampled CIs from the United States, but this this is because Hanban has put more CIs in the United States than any other country; in fact, almost four times as many as the next-largest host nation, the UK. The greatest concentration of CIs worldwide (as of November, 2016) are as follows:

United States	109
United Kingdom	29
Republic of Korea (South Korea)	22
Russia	17
Germany	17
France	17

The four CI institutes I've described illustrate how the Confucius Institute project represents less a geopolitical impulse, and more of an attempt to capitalize on global cultural trends and influences. Each seeks to build upon and reinforce the national economic and cultural goals of their hosts; Ca' Foscari by building upon and reinforcing Venice's legacy as a cultural hub, NTU by reinforcing Singapore's goal to create a bilingual elite, UC Davis by enhancing the university's status as a global leader in food and agricultural sciences, Prairie View A&M by building up a cadre of globally and linguistically competent African American students.

These examples might seem atypical, in that each aligns closely with the histories and global focus of their host institutions, but my argument is that that is very typical. The majority of Confucius Institutes are more similar than dissimilar, and focus on a few key programs. Almost all offer some type of Chinese-language instruction and some form of cultural outreach activity (such as hosting lunar New Year celebrations); they also administer HSK (Chinese language competency) exams and Chinese speech competitions, as well as scholarship programs for students to study in China. Many are not located in politically or economically sensitive locations, but especially in the United States, they are often situated in more rural areas.

But I would argue that these institutions, although some are focused to a greater degree than others, illustrate a general principle of the CIs, which is that each is designed not to fulfill China's soft power goals, but rather to enable their own students' access and expertise that will strengthen their own global influence. Other examples include the recently opened CI at Moi University in Kenya, which is expected to "boost Kenya-China textile ties," by linking two universities with strong interests in textile science to one another, leading to both trade deals and possibly technology transfer from China to Kenya, the CI at London South Bank University, which focuses solely on traditional Chinese medicine (TCM), or the CI at Purdue University, which focuses primarily on language learning within the engineering and business contexts.

When we consider these four examples of localized Confucius Institutes within the context of the academic literature on globalization, it seems clear that in many ways, these institutes are "glocalized," or in Kraidy's term, hybrid forms of culture, that draw upon Chinese cultural traditions and forms, but reinterpret them within the context of local institutional imperatives and goals. None of these particular examples (less than 1 percent of all Confucius Institutes globally, by the way) would indicate that Confucius Institutes represent a new Chinese hegemony meant to counter U.S. or other Western influence on global culture, but rather that some components of Chinese culture (whether literature, language, or wine) are appropriated and used for local goals. UC Davis, for example, doesn't use its Confucius Institute to "promote" Chinese language and culture as much as it does to promote UC Davis's reputation as a globally important university in food and wine production. Prairie View A&M likewise uses its Confucius Institute to promote its identity as an elite institution for African Americans. The "firewalls" that Norris and Inglehart identify would include not just local values and global engagement, but also help to reinterpret the matériel of Chinese culture into local goals.

It is entirely possible, indeed probably likely, that all of these lofty cultural linkage goals won't be met, but this does provide some context as to how to assess the likely impact of Confucius Institutes. If, as I have argued, the CI should properly be examined as an attempt at geo-cultural rather than geopolitical power, these examples provide something to assess in asking, to what extent can the CI project fulfill this goal of impacting global cultural flows, and hence ideas, values, and beliefs that constitute "culture"? It is to that question that I will turn in the next section of this essay.

THE CONFUCIUS INSTITUTE AND THE REPRESENTATION OF CHINESE CULTURE

Given my argument so far that the CI project is best understood as a geo-cultural influence, what might be the long-term cultural impact of this project around the world? I will attempt to answer this from within the framework that I established earlier, that the CI is best understood as an attempt at geo-cultural, rather than geopolitical, influence. The academic literature on globalization, of course, is highly varied, and there are multiple understandings of the future of global culture. But the goal of establishing Chinese as a global language network is an important one, and in many ways serves as the foundation for China to enter the global cultural sphere.

That task, of course, is not easy. The examples given here demonstrate some of the complexities of the task, in that through the Confucius Institute project, China is essentially "outsourcing" its language-teaching tasks. Although much of the teaching is actually done by volunteers provided by Hanban, clearly, the audiences, contexts, venues, and requirements for these classes, seminars, workshops, and events are being generated by local staff, in line with their own institutional objectives. As these examples illustrate, each has attempted to develop programming that enhances the reputation and goals of the host institution, rather than those of Hanban (and I would argue these attempts have been largely successful).

If we examine more closely Hanban's own metrics, which largely rely on numerical measures of impact, it is easy to see that the achievements of the Confucius Institutes are modest. In September of 2014, CCTV, drawing upon Hanban's data, claimed that in the ten years of the Confucius Institute to date, some 1 million people had received some type of language instruction or cultural outreach, and claimed that the Confucius Institute website had over 1 million visitors. It must be remembered, though, that the 1 million figure most certainly includes people who merely attended an event, such as a lunar New Year celebration, and does not mean that they are actively engaged, or ever were, with actual Chinese-language study. Hanban, in its 2013 annual report, set a goal of 1.5 million students by 2015.

In terms of its website, Hanban's 1 million visitors compares quite poorly with its aspirant institutions. In April of 2015, Alexa (a prominent Web traffic analysis service) estimated that Hanban's Alexa Rank (a global ranking of influence, based on Web traffic) was approximately 240,000, compared to the UK's British Council, which ranked approximately 5,363, but ahead of that of the Alliance Francais, and far behind the *New York Times* rank of 98 in terms of global website traffic. In fact, my own institution's (Texas A&M) Alexa Rank is 4,013, ranking above Hanban's by over 200,000 places. The much-heralded "Confucius Institute Online" resource ranked 237,929, surely far below China's hopes.

When considering these goals against expenditures, it isn't clear that Hanban is at all efficient in its efforts. Its 2013 budget expenditures provided by China on the CI project totaled over U.S.$278 million, or approximately U.S.$270 per Chinese-language student. But of course, much of that spending is on administrative overhead, cultural outreach, and personnel. That figure was up 43 percent from the previous year's budget, by the way, demonstrating the Chinese government's trust in the effort. This funding contributed to over 20,000 cultural activities, including lectures that drew over 9 million participants, and for over 1,500 educators and 10,500 students to visit China.

There are, however, at least three key consequences of the Confucius Institute that need to be considered in any analysis of the long-term impact of the institute. The first is the rise of Mandarin as a "global language," in which Chinese-language conversations enter global cultural discourse. The second is the displacement of Taiwan as the most visible symbol of "China" in global discourse, and finally, the collapse of multiple Chinese cultures into a highly generic and commodified Chinese culture.

As I have argued elsewhere, outside of China, there are few cultural elites who actually have the linguistic skills to access the deep reservoirs of Chinese philosophy, literature, and art.[25] Thus, the extent to which the CI project actually builds a global community of cultural elites who can access those reservoirs and bring them into the ongoing global cultural dialogue is one key indicator of China's success. A recent study that analyzed global language networks and their role in transmitting ideas and values identified four "global language networks," including English, Spanish, French, and German. This study, which analyzed translation rates of various media, found that content published in these languages was far more likely to be translated into, and impact, other languages and cultures. Chinese, Arabic, and Hindi, although popular languages (in the overall number of speakers), were much less likely to generate content that would ever find its way into translation, and subsequently to have global impact.[26]

Developing linguistic competency around the world, of course, is a multi-decade, perhaps multigenerational, effort, and it is hardly surprising that the efforts of Hanban couldn't generate that kind of impact in the one decade that the project has existed. But, by creating a value to learning Chinese, and developing cultural interest, China has taken an important first step toward generating a pool of Chinese speakers who are able to draw upon the resources of Chinese cultural traditions.

A scene in the movie *Looper* illustrates this point. The time-traveling action movie features a character from the future talking to a young assassin, who insists on learning French so that he can travel to

France. The time-traveling character, portrayed by Jeff Daniels, asks the assassin if he is studying his Mandarin, and when told he is studying French instead, so that he can travel to France, argues, "I am from the future, you should go to China." Although perhaps trivial, the quote illustrates an important change in perception that is occurring. Whereas Hollywood movies, for example, in the 1980s would feature Japanese as the important language of the future (as in, for example, *Blade Runner*), Chinese is now increasingly seen as the "important" language. Likewise, the Joss Whedon–produced television series *Firefly* portrayed its characters (also from the future) frequently using Chinese phrases, and made extensive use of Chinese written characters in each episode. It is this sense of the importance of China to the future that helps create the longer-term interest in Chinese language.

It isn't just popular culture in which this is happening, but rather, a larger reorientation toward China, and Chinese, that is occurring in many educational contexts. The increasing number of nations that trade with China is the most obvious evidence of this importance. An Asia Society report in 2010 asked the question, "Chinese: The Language of the Future?," reporting that yes, it is. Likewise, the VOA reported a statistic from Rosetta Stone, Inc., indicating that sales of its Chinese-language software increased over 700 percent from 2008 to 2009. Obviously, this larger cultural interest in China, or what Chinese leaders like to call "China fever," is not due to the efforts of the Confucius Institutes around the world, but rather the CIs are a response to this interest. In spite of the negative publicity associated with the shutdown of the CIs at Chicago and Penn State, new CIs open in the United States and around the world on a regular basis with little outright controversy.

A second likely consequence of the Confucius Institute is the potential recentering of global perceptions of Chinese culture toward that of mainland China, and away from Taiwan. Since Western ties with China were largely severed after 1949, the Republic of China on Taiwan (and to some extent, Hong Kong) became the de facto representative of Chinese tradition, art, philosophy, and literature. The Taiwan Economic and Commercial Office in the United States operates a "Chinese Culture Center" project, which is not altogether different from the kinds of resources provided by CIs. Obviously, Taiwan was able to draw upon a long history that included all of China's tradition, and used this to maximize its own geopolitical influence.

The reaction of the Taiwanese government to the Confucius Institute project is telling. As noted earlier, Taiwan has largely created shadow versions of the Confucius Institute project, although with less local commitment than Hanban demands. The Taiwan Academy project has generated none of the negative backlash against the project that the Confucius Institute project has, but neither has it begun to impact institutions the way that the CIs have.

One final potential consequence of the rise of the Confucius Institute as a "brand," as Li Changchun, Liu Yandong, and others have argued, is the potential collapse of distinct regional variations into one relatively homogenized "Chinese culture," represented by elements such as tea, paper-cutting, calligraphy, and traditional opera. What is remarkable about this project is the distillation of Chinese culture into just a few easily recognizable elements, and it certainly doesn't reflect the elements of "advanced Chinese culture" that Xi Jinping indicated were the keys to China's soft power; namely, a developed economy, social stability, a unified people, and socialism with Chinese characteristics. In numerous ways, the various Confucius Institutes around the world do a better job than Hanban itself of articulating Chinese culture, as they are not bound by this overly narrow (and it should be noted, relatively noncontroversial) definition of Chinese culture.

CONCLUSION

My argument in this essay has been that although the Chinese government, as well as Western critics, see the Confucius Institute as part of a geopolitical strategy, the project offers its greatest potential as a geo-cultural initiative, an attempt to insert Chinese language, cultural traditions, and resources into the main currents of global cultural evolution. Based on the programs offered by Confucius Institutes worldwide, there is little direct evidence that CIs are ever used to push Chinese political stances, or that they would be effective if they tried. Rather, Confucius Institutes reflect the priorities of their own institutions quite well, and often do a remarkable job of leveraging their own role in the global cultural sphere to introduce Chinese cultural ideals and practices into that sphere.

When we consider the Confucius Institute not as a geopolitical project by the Chinese state, but rather as a phenomenon of cultural globalization, it undermines some of the concerns about the political importance of the institutes. Any given Confucius Institute is localized, or hybridized, in Kraidy's terms, and creates something that is neither entirely Chinese nor entirely local. UC Davis is known for its academic and scientific programs in food and wine production, obviously, but by introducing Chinese industries, traditions, and products, it goes beyond its primarily local identity and reinforces its role as a "global" arbiter of food and wine quality, thereby enhancing its own reputation, but also introducing Chinese food culture into a larger geo-cultural conversation in which the university has an inordinately large role.

Of course, the obvious objection is that it is difficult, if not impossible, to separate cultural values and norms from politics, and this is obviously true. China's long tradition of hierarchy, central control, and desire for political unity spring from the deep reserves of Chinese cultural values, and as many have argued, there is actually great continuity between the prerevolutionary political organization and the current role and activities of the Chinese Communist Party. But there is a clear and discernible difference between current geopolitical issues and policies, such as China's role in the South China Sea, the continuing dominance of the CCP, or its policy toward Tibet and the global cultural sphere, in which global popular culture is overwhelmingly influenced by Western standards and tastes.

The Confucius Institute is better understood as a response to, rather than a cause of, China's emerging political and economic status. Certainly, the growing importance of trade with China; of Chinese construction companies building transportation, media, and other types of infrastructure in Africa and elsewhere; as well as China's growing military strength, gives nations around the world an understandable interest in Chinese language and culture, and this creates a bit of a self-reinforcing trend. The rapid growth of

Confucius Institutes, and the publicity generated by Hanban to illustrate that growth, contributes to the larger sense that China is growing in geo-cultural influence, thereby contributing to its geopolitical positioning as well.

NOTES

1. Joshua Kurlantzick, *Charm Offensive: How China's Soft Power Is Transforming the World* (Yale University Press, 2007).

2. Joseph S. Nye Jr., *Soft Power: The Means to Success in World Politics* (New York: Public Affairs, 2004), p. 6.

3. Joseph S. Nye Jr., *The Future of Power* (New York: Public Affairs, 2011).

4. *Confucius Institute Annual Development Report* (Beijing: Confucius Institute Headquarters, 2014), p. 3.

5. For an example of the former charge, see Omid Ghoreishi, "Beijing Uses Confucius Institutes for Espionage, says Canadian Intelligence Veteran. *Epoch Times,* October 14, 2014 (http://www.theepochtimes.com/n3/1018292 -hosting-confucius-institute-a-bad-idea-says-intelligence-veteran/). The more common latter argument can be seen in a number of the responses to the online discussion on CIs hosted by the Asia Society during the summer of 2014. "The Debate Over Confucius Institutes: A ChinaFile Conversation," *ChinaFile,* June 23, 2014 (http://www.chinafile.com/conversation/debate -over-confucius-institutes), and "The Debate Over Confucius Institutes, Part II," *ChinaFile,* July 1, 2014 (http://www.chinafile.com/conversation/debate -over-confucius-institutes-part-ii).

6. American Association of University Professors, *On Partnerships with Foreign Governments: the Case of Confucius Institutes,* June 2014 (http://www .aaup.org/report/confucius-institutes).

7. Personal communication with University of Chicago, December 2014.

8. "Confucius Institute Update," Pennsylvania State University, College of Liberal Arts, 2014 (http://www.la.psu.edu/news/confucius-institute -update).

9. C. Smith, "Hearing Probes China's Influence on U.S. Universities," 2014 (http://chrissmith.house.gov/news/documentsingle.aspx?DocumentID =397762).

10. For coverage of these events, see Karen Howlett and Caroline Alphonso, "TDSB Votes to Officially Cut Ties with Confucius Institutes," *Globe and Mail,* October 29, 2014, as well as the report from the European Association for Asian Studies, "Report: The Deletion of Pages from EACS Conference

Materials in Braga" (July 2014) (http://www.chinesestudies.eu/index.php
/432-report-the-deletion-of-pages-from-eacs-conference-materials-in-braga
-july-2014).

11. Kluver, "The Debate Over Confucius Institutes, Part II.

12. Manuel Castells, *Communication Power* (Oxford University Press,
2009). See also R. Kluver, "The Sage as Strategy: Nodes, Networks and the
Quest for Geopolitical Power in the Confucius Institute," *Communication,
Culture, and Critique* 7, no. 2 (2014), pp. 192–209.

13. Marwan Kraidy, *Hybridity, or the Cultural Logic of Globalization* (Temple
University Press, 2005).

14. Pippa Norris and Ronald Inglehart, *Cosmopolitan Communications: Cultural Diversity in the Globalized World* (Cambridge University Press, 2009).

15. Xi Jinping, *Enhance China's Cultural Soft Power* (Beijing: Foreign Language Press, 2013). See also Xi's congratulatory letter in the Confucius Institute Annual Report 2014.

16. Liu Yandong, "Towards a New decade of Confucius Institutes: Keynote Speech at the Opening of the 9th Confucius Institute Conference"
(Xiamen, Fujian, China, December 7, 2014).

17. "Spotlight Taiwan Awards," Ministry of Culture (https://english.moc
.gov.tw/article/index.php?sn=1357).

18. See Kluver, "The Sage as Strategy."

19. R. Kluver and W. Fu, "Measuring Cultural Globalization in Southeast
Asia", in *Globalization and Its Counter-Forces in Southeast Asia* (Singapore: Institute of Southeast Asian Studies, 2008).

20. C. Tan, "Change and Continuity: Chinese Language Policy in Singapore," *Language Policy* 5, no. 1 (2006), pp. 41–62.

21. See R. Kluver and I. Weber, "Patriotism and the limits of globalization: The renegotiation of citizenship in Singapore." *Journal of Communication Inquiry* 27, no. 4 (2003), pp. 371–88.

22. C. C. Lay, *Keeping My Mandarin Alive: Lee Kuan Yew's Language Learning Experience* (Singapore: World Scientific Press, 2005).

23. Land-grant institutions are colleges and universities in the U.S. designated to receive the benefits of the Morrill Acts of 1862 and 1890, primarily
by focusing their efforts on practical areas of study, such as agriculture,
engineering, and science, rather than a classical liberal arts approach to
education.

24. Personal communication with administrators at PVAMU, April, 2015.

25. Kluver, "The Sage as Strategy."

26. S. Ronen and others, "Links That Speak: The Global Language Network and Its Association with Gobal Fame," *Proceedings of the National Academy of Science* 111, no. 52 (December 2014), pp. E5616–22.

CONTRIBUTORS

ALLEN CARLSON, associate professor of government, Cornell University

GREGORY T. CHIN, associate professor of political science, and faculty of graduate studies, York University (Canada)

DANIEL C. K. CHOW, Joseph S. Platt-Porter Wright Morris & Arthur Professor of Law, Ohio State University

JACQUES DELISLE, Stephen A. Cozen Professor of Law, and deputy director of the Center for the Study of Contemporary China, University of Pennsylvania

AVERY GOLDSTEIN, David M. Knott Professor of Global Politics and International Relations, Political Science Department, and director of the Center for the Study of Contemporary China, University of Pennsylvania

RANDY KLUVER, associate professor in the Department of Communication, and executive director of global partnerships in the Office of the Provost, Texas A&M University

JONATHAN D. POLLACK, Interim SK-Korea Foundation Chair in Korea Studies, Center for East Asia Policy Studies and senior fellow, John L. Thornton China Center, The Brookings Institution

PITTMAN B. POTTER, professor of law, and HSBC Chair in Asian Research at the Institute of Asian Research, University of British Columbia

STANLEY ROSEN, professor of political science, University of Southern California

ROBERT S. ROSS, professor of political science, Boston College, and associate, John King Fairbank Center for Chinese Studies, Harvard University

EDWARD S. STEINFELD, professor of political science, and Howard Swearer Director, Thomas J. Watson Jr. Institute for International & Public Affairs, Brown University

CYNTHIA A. WATSON, professor of security, National War College

DAVID ZWEIG, chair professor of social science, and director of the Center on China's Transnational Relations, Hong Kong University of Science & Technology

INDEX

Abe Shinzo, 240
Adams, James Truslow, 363
Afghanistan: China's security on
  borders with, 212; U.S. military
  in, 12, 13
Agreement on Trade Related
  Intellectual Property Rights
  (TRIPS), 70
AIIB. *See* Asian Infrastructure
  Investment Bank
Air Defense Identification Zone
  (ADIZ), 238, 239, 243, 253, 269
American Dreams in China, 373
Andean Common Market, 132
Anti-Monopoly Law, 67, 71, 75,
  76–80
Anti-Unfair Competition Law, 67
Apple-Foxconn relationship, 110
Applied Materials, 104–05, 114, 116
Areva, 106
Argentina: China's economic
  engagement in, 131, 133, 135,
  139–41, 148–49; China's human

rights policy stance of, 302; debt
  of, 131; economic nationalism in,
  127; global monetary system
  reform stance of, 51; Kirchner
  presidencies in, 139, 140–41, 148;
  Macri presidency in, 141, 148–49;
  Menem presidency in, 139–40;
  Peron presidency in, 127, 139
Art and popular culture, twenty-
  first century opening of, 19–20.
  See also Film and television
  industry
ASEAN (Association of Southeast
  Asian Nations), 239
Asia Development Bank, 10
Asian Infrastructure Investment
  Bank (AIIB): China's leadership
  in, 10, 11, 85–86, 163, 359; Latin
  American memberships in, 144;
  RMB currency in, 47
Asia-Pacific security, 155–82;
  China's national security
  considerations with, 169–71,

Asia-Pacific security (cont.)
172–73, 174, 176; China's
strategic periphery in, 169–76;
Chinese-U.S. rivalry over, 12–13,
155–78; economic engagement
and international trade
impacted by, 155–78; future
and prospective developments
in, 176–78; inherited and
prospective architectures for,
155–56, 161–69; international
order in, 157–61, 170–71;
maritime region, 159, 161–63,
166, 169, 171–72; military power
in relation to, 156, 159–60,
161–62, 164–65, 169, 173–74,
175–76, 177; "One Belt, One
Road" initiative in relation to,
163, 167–68; overview of, 25,
155–57; post-9/11 changes in,
159, 160–61; RCEP impacting,
163; TPP impacting, 163–64;
U.S. alliances influencing, 163,
167–68, 170–76
Association of Southeast Asian
Nations (ASEAN), 239
Audi, 79
Australia: BITs and FTAs with, 163;
China's human rights policy
stance of, 302; dollar of, in global
monetary system, 47; reverse
migration from, 336; U.S. naval
power in, 219–20
Austria, China's human rights
policy stance of, 302
Automobiles, Chinese commercial
innovation in, 99

Bangkok Declaration on Human
Rights, 297
Bank for International Settlements
(BIS), 48–49, 50
Bank of England, 53
Be There or Be Square (Bujian busan),
376

Bhutan, China's security on borders
with, 213
Bilateral investment treaties (BITs),
71, 83–84, 163
Boeing, 111
Bolívar, Simón, 141
Bolivia, China's economic
engagement in, 134, 141
Bosch, 53
Brazil: AIIB membership of, 144;
China's economic engagement
in, 123, 131, 133–34, 135, 143–44,
147, 149; China's human rights
policy stance of, 302; debt of, 131;
economic nationalism in, 127;
global monetary system reform
stance of, 46, 51. *See also* BRICS
Bribery, investment trade
regulation on, 68, 69, 71, 75,
80–82, 84–85, 87
BRICS (Brazil, Russia, India,
China, and South Africa):
China's leadership in, 11; global
monetary system reform goals
presented to leaders of, 39; New
Development Bank of, 47. *See also
specific countries*
Burma. *See* Myanmar
Bush, George H. W., 131, 139
Bush, George W., 58, 132–33, 140,
160, 336

Cameron, David, 52
Canada: China's human rights policy
stance of, 302; Confucius Institute
concerns of, 393, 395; dollar of,
in global monetary system, 47;
film and TV industry in, 360, 374;
global monetary system reform
stance of, 46; reverse migration
from and to, 336, 342
CCTV network, 18, 141
Censorship: in film industry, 19, 20,
366, 371–72, 373, 381; of human
rights issues, 302

Central American Common Market, 132

Challenges of global engagement, 1–33; book chapters detailing, 22–30; China's changing role in global society as, 15–30; Cold War era changes as background for, 4–6; economic engagement as, 8–11; geo-cultural impacts as, 15–22; human rights considerations as, 20–22; military-security concerns as, 11–14; overview of, 1–2; post–Cold War reforms as background for, 6–8; regional to global transition as, 2–4

Changjiang Scholars Program, 339, 352

Chávez Frías, Hugo, 141–42, 148

Chen Yuan, 46

Chen Zhimin, 199

Chile: AIIB interest of, 144; Andean Common Market with, 132; China's economic engagement in, 130, 133, 134, 135, 138, 144, 146; economic nationalism in, 127; global monetary system reform stance of, 51

China, People's Republic of: Communist Party in (*see* Chinese Communist Party); global engagement of (*see* China's global engagement); Hong Kong in (*see* Hong Kong); Taiwan in (*see* Taiwan)

China Construction Bank (CCB) (London), 53

China Development Bank, 142

China Film Group, 383

China Guangdong Nuclear Power Holding Company, 106

China National Knowledge Infrastructure, 186

China Nuclear Power Technology Research Institute, 106

China's global engagement: in Asia-Pacific security (*see* Asia-Pacific security); challenges of (*see* Challenges of global engagement); Confucius Institutes for (*see* Confucius Institutes); in film industry (*see* Film and television industry); geo-cultural impacts of (*see* Geo-cultural impacts); in global monetary system (*see* Global monetary system); human rights policies and (*see* Human rights policies); international commerce and trade as (*see* International commerce and trade); international law in relation to (*see* International law); in interventions (*see* Interventions); investment trade regulation and (*see* Investment trade regulation); in Latin America (*see* Latin American economic engagement); leadership in (*see* Leaders); naval power as (*see* Naval power); reverse migration and (*see* Reverse migration policies); South and East China Seas disputes with (*see* South and East China Seas disputes); in sustainable energy technologies (*see* Sustainable energy technology development)

Chinese Academy of Sciences (CAS), 330, 331, 332, 339, 343–44, 345–46

Chinese Communist Party (CCP): bribes to officials of, 80–81, 82; challenges to regime legitimacy of, 305–08; Chinese dream relying on, 364; economic development imperative of, 297–98; geo-cultural reforms and restrictions by, 15, 19; global monetary

Chinese Communist Party (CCP) (cont.)
system reform goals of, 37, 41, 58; human rights subordination to authority of, 291, 292–98, 302, 303, 304; investment trade positions of, 72, 77, 87; Latin American economic engagement under, 133, 141; naval power under, 208; Party leadership, 291, 292–96, 302, 303, 304, 364; Party organs established by, 294; regime established by, 4; reverse migration policies of, 326, 329–51; South and East China Seas disputes stance of, 242

Chinese Securities Journal, 43

Chrysler, 79

Chunxiao/Shirakaba Joint Development Agreement, 257, 273

Climate change: fishing impacts of, 236; sustainable energy technology development to address, 91–92, 95

Clinton, Hillary, 192, 238

Clinton, William "Bill," 131, 139

Coca-Cola/Huiyuan Juice acquisition, 78

Cold War: changes in China during, 4–6; global impacts of end of, 158; post–Cold War approach to intervention, 185–87; post–Cold War reforms, 6–8, 128, 131

Colombia: AIIB interest of, 144; Andean Common Market with, 132; China's economic engagement in, 137–39, 144, 146; Panama Canal replacement in, 137–38

Commerce. *See* International commerce and trade

Communist Party of China. *See* Chinese Communist Party

Computers, Chinese commercial innovation in, 99, 100, 110. *See also* Information communication technology

Confucius Institutes, 389–416; achievement statistics of, 410; budget for, 410–11; Confucius's philosophy and image in, 401; controversy over, 393–95; diplomacy role of, 398; geo-cultural goals of, 390–92, 393, 398–401; geo-cultural impacts of, 17–18, 29–30, 389–92, 393, 395–416; in Kenya, 408; key programs of, 408; local contexts for, 392, 396–97, 401–09, 410, 414; overview of, 29–30, 389–92, 413–15; "propaganda" model of, 390, 392, 393–95, 399, 413–14; representations of Chinese culture via, 392, 409–13; in Singapore, 403–05; soft power enhanced by, 18, 389–90, 391, 399, 401; Taiwan Academy projects *vs.,* 400, 413; in U.S., 392, 394–95, 405–09, 412, 414; in Venice, Italy, 402–03

Constitution: Criminal Procedure Law referencing, 295–96; Four Cardinal Principles in, 292, 296; Party leadership under, 292, 294, 302; reverse migration policies supported by, 339

Construction equipment, Chinese commercial innovation in, 99, 100

Convention Against Bribery, 84

Convention on Elimination of All Forms of Discrimination Against Women (CEDAW), 299

Convention on Elimination of All Forms of Racial Discrimination (CEAFRD), 299

Convention on the Law of the Sea (UNCLOS), 240–41, 242, 256, 259–65, 266–69, 271

Correa, Rafael, 141
Costa Rica, Taiwan's economic engagement in, 131
Criminal Procedure Law, 295–96, 307
Crouching Tiger, Hidden Dragon, 374
Cuba: Latin American *vs.* Cuban policies, 128, 130, 131, 146; U.S. relations with, 146, 224
Cui Tiankai, 238
Cultural impacts. *See* Geo-cultural impacts
Cyberspace. *See* Information communication technology; Internet
Cyprus, financial support for, 44

Dai Bingguo, 165–66, 238
Dai Xianglong, 41
Dalai Lama, 191
da Silva, Lula, 144
Democratic People's Republic of Korea. *See* North Korea
Deng Xiaoping: Asia-Pacific security influenced by policies of, 165, 166; Cold War era relations under, 5; Four Cardinal Principles of, 292; Party leadership under, 293; post–Cold War reforms under, 6; reverse migration policies under, 331, 332, 333, 337–38; South and East China Seas disputes under, 273
Denmark, sustainable energy technology development by, 94, 111
Descendants of the Sun (Taiyang de houyi), 373
Detective Dee, 376
Deutsche Bank, 53–54
Developing economies: BRICS as, 11, 39, 47; Latin American (*see* Latin American economic engagement); loans to, 85–86;

reverse migration to, 16–17, 28, 325–58; SOEs's foreign direct investment in, 68, 83, 84–85
Diaoyu/Senkaku islands, disputes over, 239–40, 242–43, 244, 245, 246, 247, 248–49, 252–53, 255, 256–57, 273
Dow Corning, 114
DPRK. *See* North Korea
Dupont, 108–09, 114
Duterte, Rodrigo, 172, 258

East China Sea disputes. *See* South and East China Seas disputes
Economic engagement: Asia-Pacific security protecting, 155–78; Cold War era, 5–6; developing economies and (*see* BRICS; Developing economies); employment and (*see* Employment); Exclusive Economic Zone and, 256, 259, 262, 267, 268–69; in global monetary system, 22, 35–66; human rights policies subordination to, 297–98, 304–05, 306; international trade as (*see* International commerce and trade); interventions impacting, 191; in Latin American economies, 24, 123–54; materialism in Chinese dream ties to, 365–66; naval power funding reflecting, 207–08, 210, 212, 213–14, 221, 222, 224; post–Cold War reforms of, 6–8; twenty-first century expansion of, 8–11
Ecuador: Andean Common Market with, 132; China's economic engagement in, 135, 141, 149
Education: Confucius Institutes for, 17–18, 29–30, 389–416; international, 15–18, 326, 328–30, 331–52, 371; soft power enhanced by, 18; twenty-first century reforms to, 15–18

El Salvador, Taiwan's economic engagement in, 131, 138

Employment: BITs and FTAs on, 83, 84; international education and, 16–17; Latin American economic engagement issues of, 124, 137, 143; reverse migration for, 16–17, 28, 325–58; sustainable energy technology development impacting, 114–15; working conditions in, 83, 84

Energy and mineral resources: Latin American, 124, 126, 132, 134, 135, 139, 140, 141–44, 148; South and East China Seas disputes over, 220, 236, 238, 239, 240, 253–54, 257, 259, 273; sustainable energy technology development, 23–24, 91–121

Equity Joint Venture Implementing Regulations, 76

Equity Joint Venture Law, 76

European Central Bank (ECB), 44, 45, 54

European Union: Confucius Institute concerns of, 393, 395; duties imposed by, 93; euro of, in global monetary system, 35, 36, 37, 43–45, 47, 55; European Financial Stability Facility in, 44; European Stability Mechanism in, 44; FTAs with, 128; global monetary system reform stance in, 51–55, 56, 58; humanitarian crises in, 161; investment trade regulation in, 76; Latin American economic engagement with, 130, 149; sovereign debt crisis in, 35, 44–45; sustainable energy technology development by, 92–94, 110, 114

Eurozone, 37, 42, 44–45

Exclusive Economic Zone (EEZ), 256, 259, 262, 267, 268–69

Facebook, 110, 371

Fast and Furious 7, 360, 382–83

Feng Xiaogang, 374, 376

The Ferryman (Bai du ren), 382

Film and television industry, 359–88; actors in, 366, 373, 374, 375, 381, 382; censorship in, 19, 20, 366, 371–72, 373, 381; Chinese *vs.* American dream competition in, 361–66, 379–81; consumers in, 19–20, 359–62, 365–73; demographics of market for, 371; domestic market for, 19–20, 359–61, 365–73; import restrictions in, 19, 360, 366, 367–68, 370; language considerations in, 371, 374, 376, 381, 411–12; overseas market for, 19, 360–61, 367, 373–79, 381–82; overview of, 29, 359–62, 379–83; partnerships and coproductions in, 360–61, 376–78, 381–83; piracy in, 368, 372; positive Chinese image projected via, 362, 367, 374, 381; producers in, 19, 360–61, 365–79, 381–83; socialist values featured in, 362, 365, 366, 379; streaming impacting, 371–72; twenty-first century opening of, 19–20

Financial crisis. *See* Global financial crisis (2007–09); Sovereign debt crisis

Finding Mr. Right, 373

Finland, China's human rights policy stance of, 302

Fishing, disputes over, 220, 236, 238, 253, 256–57, 259, 273

"Flying geese" model, 97, 109

Food and agriculture, Latin American, 124, 126, 135, 139, 140, 143, 148

Foreign direct investment (FDI): definition of, 69; investment trade regulation of, 22–23,

67–90; by MNCs in China, 67–68, 69, 71, 73–82, 83–85, 86–87; by SOEs, 68, 69, 72, 82–85; WTO exclusion of, 68, 69–71, 80, 82, 83, 87

Foreign policy of global engagement. *See* China's global engagement

Four Cardinal Principles, 292, 295–96

Foxconn, 100, 101, 110

Fox Quesada, Vicente, 133

Framatome, 106

France: Confucius Institutes in, 407; global monetary system reform stance of, 51; naval power of, 210, 211, 223; South and East China Seas disputes involving, 246–47; sustainable energy technology development by, 106, 110

Free Trade Agreements (FTAs): ASEAN-China, 239; Asia-Pacific security impacted by, 163; investment trade regulation with, 83–84; Latin American, 128; NAFTA as, 128, 131

Friedman, Thomas, 363

The Fugitive, 366

Gao Zhisheng, 308

General Agreement in Tariffs and Trade (GATT), 70

General Agreement on Trade in Services (GATS), 70

Generation of International Floaters, 371

Geo-cultural impacts, 389–416; art opening as, 19–20 (*see also* Film and television industry); China's changing role in global society as, 15–22; Communication Power theory of, 396; Confucius Institutes creating, 17–18, 29–30, 389–92, 393, 395–416; cosmopolitan communication

model of, 397; definition and description of, 391; historical regional influences on, 3; human rights considerations as, 20–22, 291–324; international education as, 15–18, 326, 328–30, 331–52, 371; media influence on, 18; of naval power, 210; overview of, 29–30; of reverse migration policies, 327, 328–29, 341, 350; soft power as, 18–19, 239, 350, 389–90, 391, 399, 401

Germany: China's human rights policy stance of, 302; Confucius Institutes in, 407; global monetary system reform stance of, 51, 53–55; immigration policies in, 326; naval power of, 210, 211, 220, 223; sovereign debt crisis stabilization by, 44; sustainable energy technology development by, 92, 94, 110, 112, 113, 114

GlaxoSmithKline, 71, 81–82

Glencore/Xstrata acquisition, 77–78

Global financial crisis (2007–09): China's position in response to, 9, 35, 165; global monetary system impacting, 35, 39, 40, 42–43; interest rates and, 9; Latin American impacts of, 143–44, 147; reverse migration policies impacted by, 331

Global monetary system, 35–66; domestic policies impacting, 49–50, 57; euro in, 35, 36, 37, 43–45, 47, 55; exchange rates in, 40; international reserve currency in, 40, 41, 46; key partners in reform goals for, 37, 50–55; multipolarity and reform goals for, 36–42, 46–55, 58–59; overview of China's interaction with, 22, 35–38, 55–59; RMB internationalization in, 35–36,

Global monetary system (cont.)
37, 40, 46–59; SDRs in, 35, 36, 39,
40, 41, 46, 48, 55–56; stabilization
of, 35, 36, 37, 40, 42–45, 55;
Triffin Dilemma in, 40, 44; true
revisionism approach to, 36–37,
55; U.S. dollar in, 35, 36, 37, 39,
42–43, 47, 48–49, 55, 58
Goldwind, 100
Google, 110
The Grandmaster (Yidai zongshi), 375
Greece, financial support for, 44
Greenfield investments, 76
Group of Seven or Eight (G-7/8),
11, 41, 46
Group of Twenty (G-20), 11, 38–39
Guam, U.S. naval power in, 219
Guatemala, Taiwan's economic
engagement in, 131

He Dongchang, 333
HKND, 136
Hollywood Adventures, 382
Honduras, Taiwan's economic
engagement in, 131, 138
Hong Kong: British sovereignty
over, 245; film and TV industry
in, 366, 377; reverse migration to,
17; RMB in, 48, 51
HSBC, 52
Huang Xiaopeng, 41
Huangyan Island/Scarborough
Shoal, disputes over, 238, 242,
251–52, 256
Huawei, 100
Huayi Brothers, 371
Hu Jintao: Asia-Pacific security
under, 165–66, 167; global
monetary system reform goals of,
38–39; Latin American economic
engagement under, 123, 132,
133–34, 147; Party leadership
under, 293
Humanitarian crises: Asia-Pacific
security distracted by, 161;

intervention in response to,
25–26, 145, 183–205, 300
Human rights policies, 291–324;
conditionality of rights in,
295–96; Criminal Procedure
Law enacting, 295–96, 307;
economic development imperative
superseding, 297–98, 304–05, 306;
local and legal activist resistance
to, 305–08; National Human
Rights Action Plan on, 303–04;
orthodoxy of subordinating rights
to state priorities, 291, 292–98,
302, 303, 304; overview of, 27–28,
291–92, 309; Party leadership
over, 291, 292–96, 302, 303, 304;
regime legitimacy and, 305–08;
repression of dissent under, 298,
302–03, 307–08; resistance to
international legal regimes on,
20–21, 291, 299–305; sovereignty
considerations in, 300, 301;
treaties on, 299–300, 301, 303–05;
twenty-first century reshaping
of, 21–22
Humiliation, century of national, 4
Hundred Talents Plan, 331, 339
Hutchinson Whampoa, 136
Hu Yaobang, 332–33

IBM, 109, 116
IMF. *See* International Monetary
Fund
India: China's security on borders
with, 212, 213; naval power of,
208; reverse migration to, 342.
See also BRICS
Indonesia, global monetary system
reform stance of, 51
Information communication
technology: Chinese commercial
innovation in, 99, 100, 101, 110–12;
intervention analysis via, 192; IT
revolution in, 109–10; military
uses of, 216–17; sustainable

energy technology using, 110–12, 116–17. *See also* Internet

Innovalight, 107–09, 114

Intellectual property: film and TV industry, 372; international trade in, 70; licensing fees for, 78, 79; MNC transfer of, 73–74; sustainable energy technology development via theft of, 93–95, 106, 108; TRIPS on, 70

Inter-America Development Bank, 135

Interdigital, 78

International commerce and trade: Asia-Pacific security protecting, 155–78; FTAs in, 83–84, 128, 131, 163, 239; GATS on, 70; GATT on, 70; in goods, 69, 70; historical resistance to, 3; investment trade regulation, 6–7, 22–23, 53, 67–90; Latin American, 123, 124, 127–29, 131–50; naval power protecting, 208; post–Cold War reforms of, 6–7; RMB Trade Settlement program for, 46–50, 55; in services, 70; Silk Road Economic Belt and Maritime Silk Road initiative for, 9–10, 11, 47, 163, 167–68; South and East China Seas disputes impacting, 236; in sustainable energy technologies, 92–93, 95–96, 98–117; in technology or intellectual property, 70; TPP impacting, 163–64; TRIPS on, 70; twenty-first century expansion of, 8–11; U.S.-China future uncertainty in, 58, 163; Venetian, 402–03

International Commission on Intervention and State Sovereignty, 197

International Convention on Civil and Political Rights (ICCPR), 299, 301

International Covenant on Economic, Social, and Cultural Rights (ICESCR), 299

International Labor Organization, Declaration on Fundamental Principles and Rights, 83

International law: assertions of sovereignty under, 241–45; exercises of sovereignty relevance to, 246–47, 250–58, 266, 272–73; expansive maritime claims relative to land mass under, 258–65; formal dispute resolution mechanisms under, 263–64, 273–74; history and practice of, 240–72; history of sovereignty relevance to, 245–50, 261, 267–68; human rights policies and, 291, 299–309; investment trade regulations not violating, 68; occupancy relevance to, 246; prospective developments in, 272–75; revisionist approaches to, 265–72; South and East China Seas disputes role of, 235, 237, 238–39, 240–75; sovereignty stance under, 237, 240–75. *See also* Treaties

International Monetary Fund (IMF): AIIB *vs.*, 10, 85–86; global monetary system role of, 35, 40, 47–48, 56; Special Drawing Rights issued by, 35

Internet: international standards for regulation of, 21–22; intervention analysis via, 192; streaming of TV shows via, 371–72. *See also* Information communication technology

Interventions, 183–205; accession and support for, 185, 194–97, 199, 201–02; China's maritime claims challenged by, 191–93; divided analysis of China's position on, 184, 187–99;

Interventions (cont.)
economic impacts of, 191; human
rights regimes as, 300; Latin
American economic engagement
and, 145; non-endorsement of,
185; nonintervention principle
vs., 184, 185, 187, 195, 196, 197,
198–99; non-obstruction of other
countries's, 185, 188; opportunity
offered by, 193–97, 201–02;
opposition to and dangers of,
185, 187–93, 200–01, 202;
overview of, 25–26, 183–85;
post–Cold War approach to,
185–87; prospective positions
toward, 200–02; research on
analyses of, 186–87; responsibility
to protect concept in, 187, 194,
197–99; sovereignty considerations
in, 195, 196, 197–98, 200, 300
Investment trade regulation, 67–90;
AIIB development and, 85–86;
analysis of, 69–71; Anti-Monopoly
Law as, 67, 71, 75, 76–80; Anti-
Unfair Competition Law as, 67;
bilateral investment treaties with,
71, 83–84, 163; bribery under, 68,
69, 71, 75, 80–82, 84–85, 87;
context for, 68–69; Equity Joint
Venture Implementing
Regulations as, 76; Equity Joint
Venture Law as, 76; fines under,
79, 80, 82; foreign direct
investment by SOEs under, 68,
69, 72, 82–85; with Free Trade
Agreements, 83–84; global
monetary system reforms
impacting, 53; Greenfield
investments under, 76; Industrial
Policy goals reflected in, 69, 72,
77–78, 80, 87; joint ventures
under, 76; mergers and
acquisitions under, 69, 76–79;
MNCs impacted by, 67–68, 69, 71,
73–82, 83–85, 86–87; nationalistic

policies via, 67, 68, 69, 77, 80;
overview of, 22–23, 67–68, 86–87;
post–Cold War reforms of, 6–7;
recent developments in, 85–86;
registered capital requirements
in, 73; SOEs promoted by, 67–68,
69, 71–73, 74, 77–78, 82–85, 87;
technology licensing fees under,
78, 79; technology transfer
requirements in, 73–75, 77;
WFOEs under, 76; Wholly
Foreign-Owned Enterprise Law
as, 76; WTO exclusion of, 68,
69–71, 80, 82, 83, 87
iQiyi, 372
Iran: China's human rights policy
stance of, 302; interventions via
sanctions in, 190
Iraq, U.S. military in, 12, 13
Ireland, financial support for, 44
Italy: China's investment in, 45;
Confucius Institutes in, 402–03

James Shoal/Zengmu Ansha,
disputes over, 262
Japan: Asia-Pacific security
influence of, 159, 164, 171, 175;
China's maritime reach to, 3; film
and TV industry in, 374; global
monetary system reform stance
of, 46, 51; Latin America lagging
behind, 129; lean production in,
102, 115–16; naval power of, 210,
211, 223–24, 226, 253; reverse
migration to, 342; South and East
China Seas disputes involving,
13, 192, 220, 236, 239–40,
242–43, 244, 246–49, 252–53,
256–57, 269, 273; sustainable
energy technology development
by, 110, 114; Taiwan ceded to,
245, 246; U.S. investment by, 43;
yen of, in global monetary
system, 47, 48, 50, 51, 56–57
JA Solar, 107–09

Jiang Xiaoran, 191
Jiang Zemin: Latin American visit by, 133; Party leadership under, 293; reverse migration policies under, 331, 338–41
Joint ventures: film and television industry, 360–61, 376–78, 381–83; investment trade regulation on, 76; in sustainable energy technology development, 96–97, 103–09

Karate Kid, 377, 378
Kawai Masahiro, 51, 56
Kazakhstan, China's security on borders with, 212
Kenya, Confucius Institutes in, 408
Kirchner, Nestor and Cristina Fernández de, 139, 140–41, 148
Kirgizstan, China's security on borders with, 212
Kung Fu Panda 3, 370, 377, 382

Laos, China's security on borders with, 213
Latin American economic engagement, 123–54; anticommunist policies impacting, 130–31; China's involvement in, 24, 123–54; colonialism concerns for, 123; debt-related, 123, 129, 131, 134–35, 140, 142, 148–49; distance impacting, 126, 130, 144; in energy and mineral industries, 124, 126, 132, 134, 135, 139, 140, 141–44, 148; export dependence impacting, 128–29; in food and agriculture, 124, 126, 135, 139, 140, 143, 148; future prospects for, 144–46; history of, 126–28; import substitution industrialization impacting, 127,

129; in infrastructure supporting trade, 123, 124, 127, 135–38, 141, 142, 147, 148; intervention and, 145; "lost decade" in, 129, 131; nationalist policies impacting, 127, 141, 149; overview of, 123–26, 147–50; in Panama Canal replacement, 135–38; Taiwan's involvement in, 130–31, 136–37, 138; transparency concerns with, 140–41, 144–45; U.S. involvement in, 125, 127, 128, 130, 131, 132–33, 134, 136, 139–40, 141, 144, 145–46, 149. *See also specific countries*
Latin American Free Trade Association, 131–32
Leaders: Party leadership, 291, 292–96, 302, 303, 304, 364; reverse migration policy role of, 325–26, 327–51. *See also specific leaders by name*
Leadership Small Group on Talent, 330, 341
Lee, Ang, 381
Lei Feng, 379
Leung, Tony, 375, 382
Libya: Chinese nationals's evacuation from, 12; interventions in, 13, 188–90, 191, 200, 202
Li Changchun, 390, 399, 413
Li Daokui, 41–42
Li Jingzhi, 191
Li Ka-hsing, 339
Li Keqiang, 123
Lin, Justin, 382
Li Na, 381
Li Peng, 333, 337–38
Liu Xiaobo, 298, 379
Liu Yandong, 390, 399–400, 413
Li Xiangyang, 170
Li Yuanchao, 331, 342–44
Luxembourg, global monetary system reform stance of, 51

Ma, Jack, 382
Machine tools, Chinese commercial innovation in, 99
Macri, Mauricio, 141, 148–49
Maduro, Nicolás, 142, 147–48
"Malacca Dilemma," 146
Malaysia: global monetary system reform stance of, 51; South and East China Seas disputes involving, 260; U.S. naval power in, 219
Mao Zedong, international relations under, 4–5, 15
Maritime power: Asia-Pacific security in relation to, 159, 161–63, 166, 169, 171–72; historical reach of, 2–3; interventions challenging, 191–93; naval power as (*see* Naval power); South and East China Seas disputes, 13–14, 26–27, 171–72, 191–93, 220, 235–89
McKinley, William, 210
Media: on bribery and investment trade regulation, 81–82; CCTV network as, 18, 141; Chinese dream discussed in, 363–65; *Chinese Securities Journal* as, 43; human rights policy coverage by, 302; Latin American economic engagement coverage by, 134, 141; MNC depiction by, 75, 82; *Reference News* as, 363; *Securities Times* as, 41; *Shanghai Daily* as, 365; soft power enhanced via, 18; Xinhua News Agency as, 18, 81, 363
Menem, Carlos Saúl, 139–40
Mergers and acquisitions, regulation on, 69, 76–79
Merkel, Angela, 55, 326
The Mermaid (Meiren yu), 360, 370
Mexico: China's economic engagement in, 124, 131, 138, 146; debt of, 131; economic nationalism in, 127; Fox

Guerrero presidency in, 133; NAFTA with, 128, 131; reverse migration to, 342
Meyer, 100
Microsoft/Nokia acquisition, 78
Military powers: Air Defense Identification Zone for, 238, 239, 243, 252–53, 269; Asia-Pacific security in relation to, 156, 159–60, 161–62, 164–65, 169, 173–74, 175–76, 177; Cold War era, 4–5; historical defeats of, 3, 4; intervention by, 25–26, 145, 183–205, 300; naval power as, 2–3, 12, 26, 207–34, 238–39, 250, 251–53, 256, 257–58, 268–71, 275; post–Cold War approach to, 7–8; South and East China Seas disputes engaging, 13–14, 220, 237–39, 249–50, 251–54, 256, 257–58, 268–71, 275; twenty-first century modernization of, 11–14, 161–62, 207–08, 215–19, 221–26
Mineral resources. *See* Energy and mineral resources
Ministry of Commerce (MOFCOM) regulation, 76, 78–79
Ministry of Education (MOE): Confucius Institutes supported by, 17, 393; reverse migration ties to policies of, 331, 332, 333–34, 339. *See also* State Education Commission
Mischief Reef, 238, 252
Mongolia, China's security on borders with, 212
Morales, Evo, 141
Motorcycles, Chinese commercial innovation in, 99
Movie industry. *See* Film and television industry
Mo Yan, 380
Multinational companies (MNCs): bribery by, 69, 71, 75, 80–82, 84–85, 87; investment trade

regulation impacting, 67–68, 69, 71, 73–82, 83–85, 86–87; joint ventures with, 76; mergers and acquisitions by, 69, 76–79; organizational culture impeding, 102–03; registered capital requirements for, 73; sustainable energy technology development by, 93–95, 102–03, 105–06; technology transfers by, 73–75, 77, 95, 105–06; WFOEs of, 76

Mummy 3, 377, 378

Muyl, Philippe, 377

Myanmar: China's human rights policy stance of, 302; China's security on borders with, 213

My Love from the Star (Laizi xingxing de ni), 372–73

NAFTA (North American Free Trade Agreement), 128, 131

Nagel, Joachim, 54

National Development and Reform Commission (NDRC), 79, 80

Nationalism: Asia-Pacific security impacted by, 172; Chinese dream focus on, 364–65, 380–81; investment trade regulation reflecting, 67, 68, 69, 77, 80; Latin American policies supporting, 127, 141, 149; South and East China Seas disputes reflecting, 240, 259. *See also* Sovereignty

National Science Foundation for China (NSFC), 333, 339

National Security Law, 169

Natural resources. *See* Energy and mineral resources

Naval power, 207–34; antipiracy efforts via, 12, 221; Chinese security protected by, 208, 219–21; continental security balance with, 211, 212–15, 224; "Copenhagen" or preventive attack against rising,

220–21; East Asian balance of, 219–21; economy and funding for, 207–08, 210, 212, 213–14, 221, 222, 224; geopolitical context for, 212–15; geopolitical prerequisites for, 209–11; global expansion of, 208, 221–26; historical regional extent of, 2–3; implications of rise of, 226–27; open seas protection goal of, 208; overview of, 26, 207–09; South and East China Seas disputes impacted by, 220, 238–39, 250, 251–53, 256, 257–58, 268–71, 275; technology developments for, 210, 212, 215–17, 221–22; twenty-first century modernization of, 12, 207–08, 215–19, 221–26; U.S.-China balance of, 207–08, 215–27, 239

Nepal, China's security on borders with, 213

New Development Bank (NDB), 47

New interventionism. *See* Interventions

News media. *See* Media

Nicaragua: China's economic engagement in, 136–37; Panama Canal replacement in, 136–37; Taiwan's economic engagement in, 131, 136–37, 138

Nigeria, global monetary system reform stance of, 51

The Nightingale, 377

9/11 terrorist attacks, 133, 140, 159, 160–61

985 Program, 331, 339, 340

North American Free Trade Agreement (NAFTA), 128, 131

North Korea (DPRK): China's alliance with, 173, 175, 176; China's security on borders with, 212

Norway, textile industry in, 104

Nuclear technology: as energy technology, 92, 93–94, 105–07, 110–11, 112, 114; as weapons technology, 4, 212

Obama, Barack/Obama administration: Asia-Pacific security under, 160–61, 163–64, 168; Cuban relations under, 146; global monetary system under, 58; naval power under, 218, 224; TPP under, 163–64

Oceania, China's maritime reach to, 3. *See also* Australia

Okinawa Reversion Agreement, 249

"One Belt, One Road" (OBOR) initiative, 9–10, 11, 47, 163, 167–68

Optical sorters, Chinese commercial innovation in, 100, 101

Osborne, George, 52–53

Pak Chung Hee, 326

Pakistan: China's alliance with, 164; China's security on borders with, 212, 213

Panama: China's economic engagement in, 135–36; Panama Canal/replacement canal, 135–38; Taiwan's economic engagement in, 131, 136, 138

Paracel/Xisha Islands, disputes over, 237–38, 242, 244, 248, 249, 253–54, 255, 268, 273

Paraguay, Taiwan's economic engagement in, 131, 138

Park Geun-hye, 175, 176

People's Bank of China (PBOC), 39–40, 41–42, 53, 54

People's Liberation Army Navy. *See* Naval power

People's Republic of China. *See* China, People's Republic of

Perón, Juan Domingo, 127, 139

Peru, Andean Common Market with, 132

Philippines: Asia-Pacific security influence of, 171, 172, 175; South and East China Seas disputes

involving, 13, 220, 235, 238, 242, 243, 248, 249, 251–52, 256, 257, 258, 260, 261, 262, 264, 273–74; U.S. naval power in, 219, 224

Popular culture. *See* Art and popular culture; Film and television industry

Portugal: China's human rights policy stance of, 302; China's investment in, 45; financial support for, 44

PRC. *See* China, People's Republic of

Procter & Gamble, 79

Putin, Vladimir, 175

Pu Zhiqiang, 308

Qian Wenrong, 188, 189–90

Qin Yaqing, 167

Qualcomm, 78, 79

Red Cliff (Chi bi) and *Red Cliff 2*, 374–75, 377

Reference News, 363

Regional Comprehensive Economic Partnership (RCEP), 163

Reilly, Mark, 81

Religious beliefs and practices, 2, 130

Renminbi (RMB): in global monetary system, 35–36, 37, 40, 46–58; RMB Center Initiative Group, 54; RMB Trade Settlement program with, 46–50, 55

Ren Zhonglun, 361

Republic of China. *See* Taiwan

Republic of Korea. *See* South Korea

Reverse migration policies, 325–58; administrative resistance to, 326, 330–31, 343–47; bureaucratic responsibilities for, 330–31; change affected by, 328; Changjiang Scholars Program in, 339, 352; current status of, 349–51; Deng Xiaoping's, 331, 332, 333, 337–38; dual citizenship, visa, and green card issues with,

327, 328, 331, 334, 335, 336; economic implications of, 327, 328, 331, 334, 339, 340, 343–44; geo-cultural impacts of, 327, 328–29, 341, 350; Hundred Talents Plan in, 331, 339; Hu Yaobang's, 332–33; international education and, 16–17, 326, 328–30, 331–52; Jiang Zemin's, 331, 338–41; leadership importance in, 325–26, 327–51; Leadership Small Group on Talent driving, 330, 341; Li Peng's, 333, 337–38; Li Yuanchao's, 331, 342–44; locally-trained workers impacted by, 327, 329–30, 343–49; market view of global talent influencing, 338–41; 985 Program in, 331, 339, 340; overview of, 28, 325–26, 349–51; recruitment bias for overseas experience, 347–49; restrictions imposed by, 333–37; science and technology investments supporting, 327, 328, 330, 333, 339; Serving the Nation program in, 339–41; spouses and relatives in, 333, 334, 337; Thousand Talents Program in, 331, 342–47, 352; Xi Jinping's, 349–51; Zeng Qinghong's, 341–42; Zhao Ziyang's, 332–33, 334–35; Zhu Rongji's, 338–39
RMB. *See* Renminbi
ROK. *See* South Korea
Roosevelt, Theodore, 210, 211
Rousseff, Dilma, 144
Ruan Zongze, 170–71
Russia: arms sales by, 11; China's security on borders with, 212, 213–15; Confucius Institutes in, 407; global monetary system reform stance of, 46; human rights policies in, 21; interventions in, 191; military strength and naval power of, 211, 213–15, 223; Ukraine intervention by, 191, 214. *See also* BRICS; Soviet Union

Sahlins, Marshall, 394
Sany, 100
Schauble, Wolfgang, 54–55
SDRs (Special Drawing Rights), 35, 36, 39, 40, 41, 46, 48, 55–56
Securities Times, 41
September 11 terrorist attacks. *See* 9/11 terrorist attacks
Serving the Nation program, 339–41
Shanghai Daily, 365
Shanghai Film Group, 361
Shanghai Nuclear Engineering Research and Design Institute (SNERDI), 106
Shen Dingli, 188–89
Shi Yuzhi, 364
Siemens, 53, 116
Silk Road: historic, 2, 403; Silk Road Economic Belt and Maritime Silk Road initiative, 9–10, 11, 47, 163, 167–68
Singapore: Confucius Institutes in, 403–05; global monetary system reform stance of, 51; Latin America lagging behind, 129; U.S. naval power in, 219
Skilled labor reverse migration. *See* Reverse migration policies
Smart grid technologies, 111, 116
Smart phones, 99, 100, 101, 110. *See also* Information communication technology
Smith, Christopher, 394–95
Society for Worldwide Interbank Financial Telecommunications (SWIFT), 37, 46–47, 48, 51, 56
Soft power: Confucius Institutes enhancing, 18, 389–90, 391, 399, 401; definition and description

Soft power (cont.)
of, 391; South and East China
Seas disputes addressed with,
239; twenty-first century
initiatives enhancing, 18–19, 350
Sohu, 372
Solar photovoltaic cells and
modules, 92, 93, 99, 100, 104–05,
107–09, 112, 113
SolarWorld, 93, 113
Somalia: China's naval antipiracy
presence in, 12; U.S. military in, 13
South Africa, global monetary
system reform stance of, 51.
See also BRICS
South and East China Seas
disputes, 235–89; Air Defense
Identification Zone impacting,
238, 239, 243, 253, 269; ASEAN
agreements on, 239; Asia-Pacific
security in relation to, 171–72;
assertions of sovereignty
impacting, 241–45; Code of
Conduct goals for, 239, 244, 273;
context and background for,
237–40; Declaration on the
Territorial Sea on, 242, 273;
Diaoyu/Senkaku islands dispute
as, 239–40, 242–43, 244, 245,
246, 247, 248–49, 252–53, 255,
256–57, 273; EEZ establishment
and, 256, 259, 262, 267, 268–69;
energy and mineral disputes as,
220, 236, 238, 239, 240, 253–54,
257, 259, 273; exercises of
sovereignty relevance to, 246–47,
250–58, 266, 272–73; expansive
maritime claims relative to land
mass in, 259–65; fishing disputes
as, 220, 236, 238, 253, 256–57,
259, 273; formal mechanisms to
resolve, 263–64, 273–74; history
of sovereignty relevance to,
245–50, 261, 267–68; Huangyan
Island/Scarborough Shoal

dispute as, 238, 242, 251–52, 256;
international commerce and
trade impacted by, 236;
international law role in, 235,
237, 238–39, 240–75;
interventions impacting, 191–93;
island-building and land
reclamation disputes as, 238, 243,
254–55, 262, 268; Law of the Sea
applications to, 240–41, 242, 256,
259–72; Law on the Territorial
Sea and the Contiguous Zone on,
242, 268; military/naval power
impacting, 13–14, 220, 237–39,
249–50, 251–54, 256, 257–58,
268–71, 275; Mischief Reef
dispute as, 238, 252; occupancy
relevance to, 246; overview of,
26–27, 235–37; Paracel/Xisha
Islands dispute as, 237–38, 242,
244, 248, 249, 253–54, 255, 268,
273; prospective developments
in, 272–75; retaliatory escalation
of, 255; revisionist approaches to,
265–72; sovereignty issues
underlying, 237, 240–75; Spratly/
Nansha Islands dispute as, 242,
246, 254, 262, 268; stability and
cooperative efforts toward,
239–40, 256–57, 260, 272, 273;
treaties impacting, 240–41, 242,
245, 246, 247, 248–49, 256,
259–65, 266–69, 273–74
South Korea: Asia-Pacific security
influence of, 175–76; BITs and
FTAs with, 83, 163; Confucius
Institutes in, 407; film and TV
industry in, 360, 372–73, 375;
global monetary system reform
stance of, 51; Latin America
lagging behind, 129; reverse
migration to, 326, 342; South
and East China Seas disputes
involving, 236; sustainable energy
technology development by, 110;

Terminal High Altitude Air Defense system in, 175–76; U.S. naval power in, 219

Sovereign debt crisis, 35, 44–45

Sovereignty: assertions of, 241–45; exercises of, 246–47, 250–58, 266, 272–73; history of, 245–50, 261, 267–68; human rights policies consideration of, 300, 301; International Commission on Intervention and State Sovereignty on, 197; international law on, 237, 240–75; intervention consideration of, 195, 196, 197–98, 200, 300; South and East China Seas disputes related to, 237, 240–75. *See also* Nationalism

Soviet Union: Cold War era relations with, 4–5; demise of, 7, 158; naval power of, 210, 211; South and East China Seas disputes stance of, 248–49

Spain: China's investment in, 45; financial support for, 44; sustainable energy technology development by, 92

Special Drawing Rights (SDRs), 35, 36, 39, 40, 41, 46, 48, 55–56

Spratly/Nansha Islands, disputes over, 242, 246, 254, 262, 268

Standard & Chartered, 52

State Education Commission (SEDC), 333–34, 336–37. *See also* Ministry of Education

State Nuclear Power Technology Corporation, 106

State-owned enterprises (SOEs): bribery by, 68, 82, 84–85, 87; definition of, 72; foreign-direct investment by, 68, 69, 72, 82–85; investment trade regulation promoting, 67–68, 69, 71–73, 74, 77–78, 82–85, 87; joint ventures with, 76; reverse migration policies involving, 331; strengthening of, 72–73, 74, 77–78, 83, 87; sustainable energy technology development by, 94

State Science and Technology Commission (SSTC), 333, 334–35, 339

Sustainable energy technology development, 91–121; capital equipment suppliers in, 103–05, 113, 116; Chinese commercial innovation in, 96, 98–103, 108–09, 110–12; climate change addressed via, 91–92, 95; complementary industrial upgrading with, 97, 109–12; customer accommodation and service considered in, 100–01, 110, 112; delivery speed in, 101; employment considerations with, 114–15; "fight for the middle" in, 98–99; "flying geese" model applied to, 97, 109; information technology in, 110–12, 116–17; innovation in, 92–93, 94, 96–97, 98–117; intellectual property theft in, 93–95, 106, 108; international trade and, 92–93, 95–96, 98–117; low- or middle-cost variant redesign in, 98–103; nuclear technology in, 92, 93–94, 105–07, 110–11, 112, 114; overview of, 23–24, 91–98, 112–17; rivalry in, 91–98, 112–17; scale economies in, 92–93, 98, 100, 107–08; Sino-foreign joint innovation in, 96–97, 103–09; smart grid technologies in, 111, 116; solar photovoltaic cells and modules in, 92, 93, 99, 100, 104–05, 107–09, 112, 113; subsidies for, 92, 93, 94–95, 96; technology transfers in, 95, 105–06; third-party overseas deals for, 106–07; "tragedy of the commons" in, 95, 97; wind turbines in, 92, 99, 100, 101, 111, 112

SWIFT (Society for Worldwide
Interbank Financial
Telecommunications), 37, 46–47,
48, 51, 56
Switzerland: global monetary
system reform stance of, 51;
investment trade regulation of
MNCs from, 77–78
Syria, interventions in, 13, 191, 200,
202

Taiping Island/Itu Aba, disputes
over, 254, 262
Taiwan: China's maritime reach to,
3; Confucius Institutes impact
on, 400, 411, 412–13; film and TV
industry in, 377; Japanese
sovereignty over, 245, 246; Latin
America lagging behind, 129;
Latin American economic
engagement with, 130–31,
136–37, 138; reverse migration
to, 342; South and East China
Seas disputes involving, 245, 246,
247, 249–50, 255, 256–57, 262;
Taiwan Academy projects of, 400,
413; U.S.-China naval power
balance over, 217–18, 225; U.S.
support for independence of, 191
Tajikistan, China's security on
borders with, 212
Takagi Shinji, 50, 56–57
Tang Jiaxuan, 44
Tang Shiping, 170
Teamsun, 109
Technology: Asia-Pacific security
impacted by, 170; information
(*see* Information communication
technology); international trade
in, 70; Internet (*see* Internet);
licensing fees and agreements
for, 78, 79, 108, 109; MNC
transfer of, 73–75, 77, 95, 105–06;
naval, 210, 212, 215–17, 221–22;
reverse migration policy and

investment in, 327, 328;
sustainable energy, 23–24, 91–121
Telecommunications equipment,
Chinese commercial innovation
in, 100
Terminal High Altitude Air
Defense (THAAD) system,
175–76
Terrorism: 9/11 terrorist attacks,
133, 140, 159, 160–61;
intervention ties to, 191
Thailand, global monetary system
reform stance of, 51
Thousand Talents Program, 331,
342–47, 352
Tiananmen Square protests, 7, 11,
16, 293, 307
Tibet, U.S. support for, 191
Tiny Times, 373
Tohti, Ilham, 298
Toshiba, 93–94
Trade. *See* International commerce
and trade
Transformers 4: Age of Extinction, 360,
366
Trans-Pacific Partnership (TPP),
163–64
Treaties: Anglo-Japanese Treaty,
223; bilateral investment treaties,
71, 83–84, 163; Cairo and
Potsdam Declarations, 247, 249;
China-DPRK, 173; international
human rights, 299–300, 301,
303–05; San Francisco Peace
Treaty, 242, 247, 248; Sino-
French, 246; Sino-Soviet, 5;
South and East China Seas
disputes impacted by, 240–41,
242, 245, 246, 247, 248–49, 256,
259–65, 266–69, 273–74; Treaty
of Shimonoseki, 247; Treaty of
Westphalia, 2; unequal, 245, 247;
U.S.-Japan Security Treaty, 192,
249. *See also United Nations
conventions*

Triffin Dilemma, 40, 44
TRIPS (Agreement on Trade Related Intellectual Property Rights), 70
Trump, Donald/Trump administration: Asia-Pacific security under, 156, 163, 164, 177; global monetary system uncertainty under, 58; international commerce and trade uncertainty under, 58, 163; investment trade regulation under, 68; Latin American economic engagement under, 150; "make America great again" slogan of, 116; naval power under, 222, 239; South and East China Seas disputes under, 14, 239, 249–50, 258; sustainable energy technology development under, 92, 115; TPP under, 163, 164
Twitter, 371

Ukraine, interventions in and on behalf of, 191, 214
Unilever, 79
United Kingdom: China's investment in, 45; Confucius Institutes in, 407, 408; global monetary system reform stance of, 37, 46, 51–53, 56, 59; Hong Kong ceded to, 245; immigration policies in, 325–26; investment trade in China by, 53; naval power of, 209–11, 218, 220, 223–24, 225–26; pound of, in global monetary system, 47, 48; sustainable energy technology in, 106; textile industry in, 104; UK Independence Party in, 325–26
United Nations: China's membership in, 130, 162, 185, 198, 301–02; Commission on the Limits of the Continental Shelf, 243, 260; Committee against Torture, 303; Convention Against

Bribery, 84; Convention on Elimination of All Forms of Discrimination Against Women (CEDAW), 299; Convention on Elimination of All Forms of Racial Discrimination (CEAFRD), 299; Convention on the Law of the Sea (UNCLOS), 240–41, 242, 256, 259–65, 266–69, 271; human rights policies of, 299, 300–05; International Convention on Civil and Political Rights, 299, 301; International Covenant on Economic, Social, and Cultural Rights, 299; interventions sanctioned by, 185, 188–89, 198; Universal Declaration of Human Rights, 299, 303, 304–05; Universal Period Review process of, 302, 303
United States: AIIB opposition from, 10, 85–86; American dream in, 361–65; Asia-Pacific security role of, 12–13, 155–78; BITs and FTAs with, 83–84, 128, 131; China's investment in, 9, 35, 42–43, 44; Cold War era relations with, 4–5; Commerce Department of, 93; Confucius Institute concerns of, 393–95; Confucius Institutes in, 392, 394–95, 405–09, 412, 414; dollar of, in global monetary system, 35, 36, 37, 39, 42–43, 47, 48–49, 55, 58; Energy Department in, 107; film and TV industry in, 20, 360–83, 411–12; Foreign Corrupt Practices Act in, 84; future U.S.-China international trade uncertainty, 58, 163; human rights policy objections of, 299–300; interventions by, 145, 187, 188–93, 200–01, 300; investment trade regulation for

United States (cont.)
MNCs from, 68, 69, 83–85, 87;
investment trade regulation in,
76, 83–84; Japan's investment in,
43; Justice Department of,
93–94, 106; Latin American
economic engagement with, 125,
127, 128, 130, 131, 132–33, 134,
136, 139–40, 141, 144, 145–46,
149, 150; naval power of, 207–08,
209–11, 215–27, 239, 268–71;
9/11 terrorist attacks in, 133,
140, 159, 160–61; Office of
Foreign Assets Control of, 84;
post–Cold War relations with,
7–8; reverse migration from,
333–34, 335–36, 341–42; South
and East China Seas dispute
stance of, 13–14, 236, 238–39,
248–50, 254, 258, 263, 264,
267–72, 275; sustainable energy
technology development by,
91–96, 107–08, 110, 112, 114–17;
Taiwan Academy projects in,
400; tariffs imposed by, 93; U.S.
National Renewable Energy
Laboratory in, 107. *See also specific
presidents and administrations*
Universal Declaration of Human
Rights, 299, 303, 304–05
Universal Period Review (UPR)
process, 302, 303
Uruguay: China's economic
engagement in, 131; economic
nationalism in, 127

Venezuela: AIIB interest of, 144;
Andean Common Market with,
132; Bolivarian Revolution in,
141; Chavez Frias presidency in,
141–42, 148; China's economic
engagement in, 134, 135, 141–43,
144, 147–48, 149; Maduro
presidency in, 142, 147–48
Vestas, 111, 116

Vienna Declaration and
Programme of Action, 303–04
Vietnam: Asia-Pacific security
influence of, 171, 175; China's
security on borders with, 213;
South and East China Seas
disputes involving, 13, 192, 220,
237–38, 244, 248, 249, 253–54,
256, 257, 260, 264, 273
The Voice of China, 373
Volkswagen, 53

Wang Jing, 136, 137
Wang Jisi, 166
Wang Qishan, 52
Wang Yi, 167–68
Wang Yizhou, 184, 187, 194–96
Wang Zhonglei, 371
Weber, Max, 305–06
Weinstein, Harvey, 375
Western Returned Scholars
Association (WRSA), 350–51
Westinghouse, 93–94, 106, 114,
116
Where Are We Going, Dad?, 372, 373
Wholly Foreign-Owned Enterprise
Law, 76
Wholly foreign-owned enterprises
(WFOEs), 76
Wind turbines, 92, 99, 100, 101, 111,
112
Wong Kar Wai, 375, 382
Woo, John, 375, 381
World Bank: AIIB *vs.*, 10, 85–86,
359; global monetary system role
of, 40; Latin American loans
from, 135
World Trade Organization (WTO):
China joining, 132; dispute
settlement system of, 68, 70;
investment trade not regulated
by, 68, 69–71, 80, 82, 83, 87;
sustainable energy technology
trade norms of, 93
Wu, Bruno, 382

Xiaomi, 100
Xie Xuren, 40
Xi Jinping: Asia-Pacific security under, 157, 162, 163, 167, 168, 171, 172, 175–76; Chinese dream under, 306, 363–64; Confucius Institute geo-cultural influence under, 398–99; global monetary system reform stance of, 41, 55; human rights policies under, 21, 305–06; investment trade and bribery regulation under, 80; Latin American economic engagement under, 123, 141; Party leadership under, 293; reverse migration policies under, 349–51; South and East China Seas disputes under, 240; twenty-first century economic expansion under, 9
Xinhua News Agency, 18, 81, 363
Xu Lin, 392, 395

Yang Jingyu, 292
Yang Zewei, 198–99
Yan Xuetong, 166–67
Yemen, U.S. military in, 13
Youku Tudou, 372
Yuan Juanjuan, 198
Yu Xiaofeng, 184, 187, 194, 196–97
Yu Zhonghua, 41

Zeng Qinghong, 341–42
Zhang Jiajia, 382
Zhang Jingwei, 192–93
Zhang Yimou, 374, 377, 381
Zhang Yuguan, 193, 196
Zhao Ziyang, 293, 332–33, 334–35
Zhen Ni, 199
Zhou Xiaochuan, 39–40, 41, 44
Zhu Rongji, 338–39